航运法律与政策评论

（第二辑）

曾二秀　主　编
徐锦堂　副主编

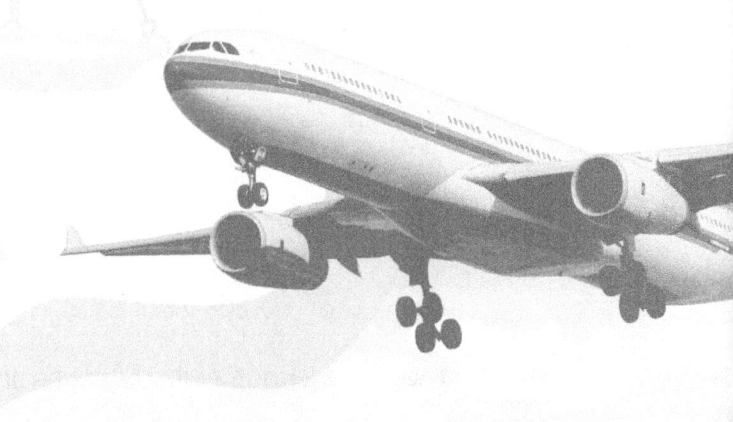

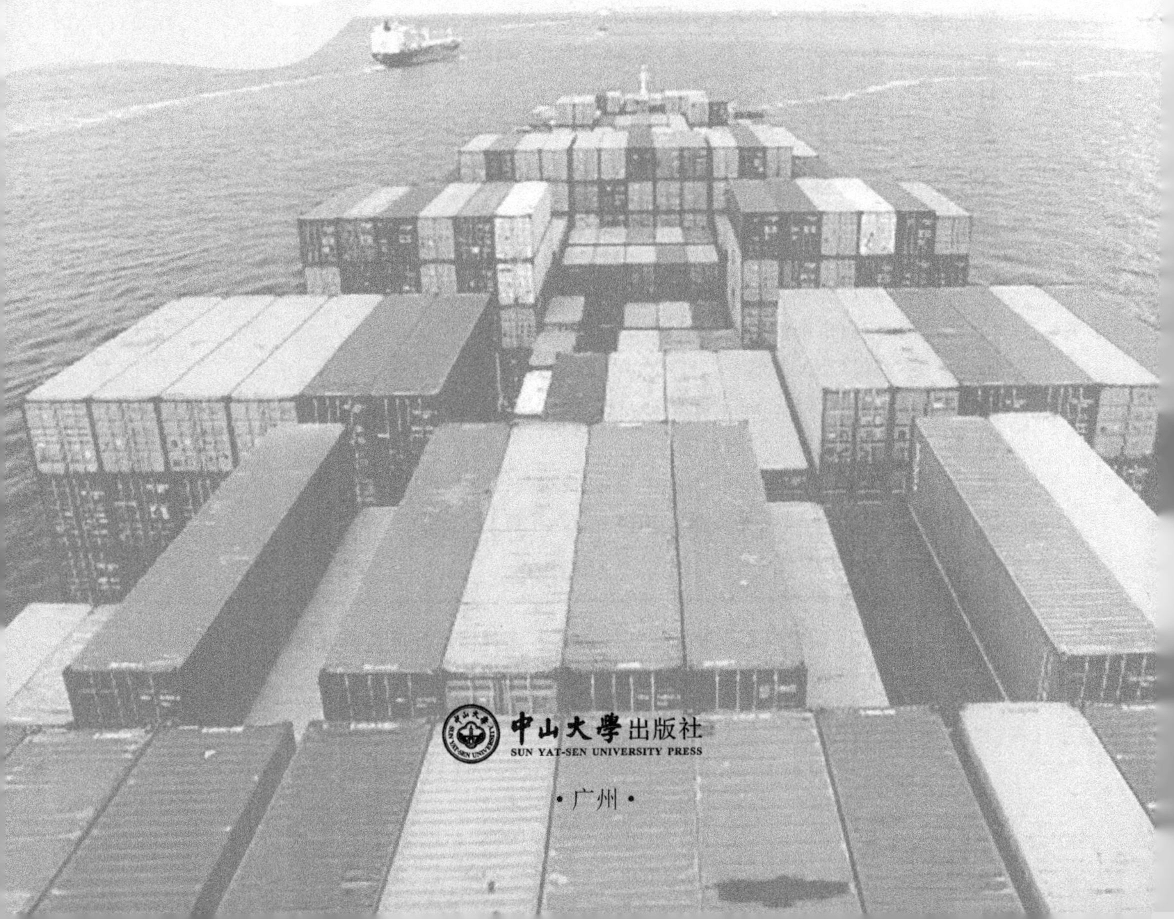

中山大學出版社
SUN YAT-SEN UNIVERSITY PRESS
·广州·

版权所有　翻印必究

图书在版编目（CIP）数据

航运法律与政策评论.第二辑：汉、英/曾二秀主编；徐锦堂副主编.－－广州：中山大学出版社，2024.12.－－ISBN 978－7－306－08311－1

Ⅰ.D993.5

中国国家版本馆CIP数据核字第20241XJ570号

HANGYUN FALÜ YU ZHENGCE PINGLUN（DI-ER JI）

出 版 人：	王天琪
策划编辑：	王旭红
责任编辑：	陈　莹
封面设计：	曾　婷
责任校对：	卢思敏
责任技编：	靳晓虹

出版发行：中山大学出版社
电　　话：编辑部 020－84110283，84113349，84111997，84110779，84110776
　　　　　 发行部 020－84111998，84111981，84111160
地　　址：广州市新港西路135号
邮　　编：510275　　传　真：020－84036565
网　　址：http://www.zsup.com.cn　E-mail：zdcbs@mail.sysu.edu.cn
印 刷 者：广东虎彩云印刷有限公司
规　　格：787mm×1092mm　1/16　21.75印张　388千字
版次印次：2024年12月第1版　2024年12月第1次印刷
定　　价：78.00元

如发现本书因印装质量影响阅读，请与出版社发行部联系调换

本书编委会

主　　任：詹思敏

成　　员：（按姓氏拼音排序）

杜以星　郭　萍　黄　晖　黎晓光　李华文
李天生　林翠珠　倪学伟　孙宏友　王　敬
向明华　许光玉　徐锦堂　张　敏　曾二秀

编辑部：曾二秀　徐锦堂　沈　虹　金　铮　贺　赞
汤　霞　陈喜娜　李少璞　王　皓　姚嘉怡
罗雯清

主　　办：华南师范大学法学院
广东省法学会航运法学研究会
广州市航运法学研究会
广州市法学会交通法学研究会

鸣 谢

广东海建律师事务所
广东恒福律师事务所
广东恒运律师事务所
广东敬海律师事务所

目 录

专题一 海法专论

我国海上旅客运输强制责任保险制度构建研究 ……… 郭 萍 张玮瑜 2

法经济学视角下海事赔偿责任限制制度的"生命力" ……… 刘 美 18

我国水路货物运输承运人管货义务发展新探

——兼评《长江（内河）航运标准合同》中的相关条款

………………………………………………… 刘佳溢 范沣亿 30

船员在船工作关系性质认定 ………………………… 张艺骞 50

北极航道之西北通道的法律地位研究 ……………… 黄 晖 卢秋璇 62

论我国海事强制令制度的完善

——兼论《海事诉讼特别程序法》第四章的修改

………………………………………………… 曾二秀 倪学伟 76

海洋污染公益诉讼若干实务问题探析 ……………………… 许光玉 99

专题二 国际法与比较法专论

英国海盗赎金问题探析及启示 ………………… 孙宏友 丁嫣然 112

An Analysis on Maritime Lien in English Admiralty Jurisdiction

………………………………………………………… Lin Jiannan 126

Party Autonomy in Choice of Court and Its Limitations:
  A Comparative Analysis ……………………… Zeng Erxiu　148
中英两国无单放货法律责任比较分析 …… 魏长庚　曲　霄　吴国生　199

专题三　湾区法评

船舶登记制度改革视野下粤港澳大湾区船舶登记和配套制度
　规则衔接研究 …………………… 徐锦堂　谢雯雯　李少璞　220

专题四　航空法专论

亚轨道飞行多级监管：意大利案例
　………………… 亚历山德罗·卡尔迪　弗朗西斯科·加斯帕里
　　　　　　　　　　　　　王冠丁（译）　张超汉（校）　250

专题五　研究生论坛

后疫情时代保障邮轮复航的法律问题与路径探索 ………… 罗　杰　286
互有过失碰撞非漏油船油污损害赔偿责任问题研究 ……… 李少璞　297

专题一　海法专论

我国海上旅客运输强制责任保险制度构建研究*

郭 萍 张玮瑜**

摘要：随着我国海上旅客运输行业发展，如何通过法律机制防控海上航行风险和保障赔偿责任落实成为亟须解决的问题。海上旅客运输强制责任保险有利于保障受害旅客权利，推进海上客运事业健康发展。目前我国尚未构建该制度，在我国海商法修改的历史契机背景下，有必要对构建我国海上旅客运输强制责任保险制度进行学理研究。文章采用文献分析法和比较研究法，从海上旅客运输强制责任保险制度的特点和价值功能入手，分析当前我国该制度构建的现状和存在的问题，借鉴国外海上旅客运输强制责任保险制度中的相关内容，重点对构建我国海上旅客运输强制责任保险制度中的责任基础和责任限额、保险人资格、直接诉讼等提出具体建议。

关键词：海上旅客运输 海商法修改 海上强制责任保险 直接诉讼

Research on the Construction of China's Compulsory Insurance System for Carriage of Passengers by Sea

Guo Ping, Zhang Weiyu

Abstract: With the development of carriage of passengers by sea in China, how to prevent and control the risks of maritime navigation and deal with the resulting liability through the law has become an urgent problem. Compulsory insurance for carriage of passengers by sea is an important legal system that can promote the development of maritime passenger transportation as well as protect the rights of injured passengers. At present, the specific system of compulsory

---

* 本文系南方海洋科学与工程广东省实验室（珠海）自主科研项目（项目编号：SML2020SP005）阶段性研究成果。

** 郭萍：中山大学法学院（涉外法治研究院）、南方海洋科学与工程广东省实验室（珠海）教授、博士生导师，最高人民法院民事审判第四庭国际海事法律研究基地（中山大学）执行主任。张玮瑜：中山大学2023级硕士研究生。

insurance for carriage of passengers by sea in China is still in the blank, while the revision of the Maritime Law is a historical opportunity for China to build this system. Under this background, it is necessary to study the construction of China's compulsory insurance system for carriage of passengers by sea.

This article based on literature analysis and comparative study, starts with the characteristics and value functions of compulsory insurance system for carriage of passengers by sea, and analyzes the current situation and problems in China's construction of this system. Drawing lessons from relevant content of the compulsory insurance system for carriage of passengers by sea in foreign countries, specific suggestions are proposed for the construction of China's compulsory insurance system for carriage of passengers by sea, focusing on the insurer's qualifications, the basis and limitation of liability and direct action.

Key words: carriage of passengers by sea; amendment of Chinese Maritime Law; marine compulsory insurance; direct action

引 言

在航海技术、造船技术和旅游经济蓬勃发展下，中国海上邮轮旅游业增长迅速，并跃升世界前列。以船舶为载体，以满足海上娱乐、休闲、观光等为主要目的的邮轮旅游成为有别于传统海上旅客运输的新业态。由于海上环境多变、船舶航行状况等不稳定因素存在，海上旅客运输的安全风险问题不容忽视。同时，海上旅客运输具有客运量较大、难以及时救援等特点，一旦发生重大海难事故，往往带来巨大的旅客人身伤亡赔偿责任。例如，菲律宾"群星王子"号沉船、韩国"岁月"号客轮沉没、我国"大舜"号沉船等大型灾难性事故，均造成旅客伤亡及财产损失的严重后果。① 除了发生海上旅客运输重大伤亡的上述典型事件外，2015年6月1日，我国"东方之星"号客船在长江水域发生翻船沉没，造成442人遇难

---

① 2008年6月21日，"群星王子"号渡船遭遇台风沉没，747名乘客和船员中仅有42人获救；2014年4月16日，韩国"岁月"号客轮发生意外进水并最终沉没，造成296人遇难，多人失踪；1999年11月24日，客货滚装船"大舜"号因搁浅倾斜，造成将近300人死亡或失踪，成为20世纪末我国最大的一起海难事故。

的特别重大灾难性后果。因此在巨大的损失与赔偿责任面前，如果出现承运人经济实力不足，甚至濒临破产的情况，不仅使旅客求偿无门，侵害旅客的人身权益，还对海上旅客运输行业的健康发展十分不利。

为解决这一问题，强制责任保险制度被引入国际海上客运立法中。保险是现代社会分散风险的重要制度，有利于增强承运人的履责能力，保障受害旅客在海运事故发生后获得相对足额赔偿的权利，这对于我国海上旅客运输以及快速增长的海上邮轮旅游行业至关重要。因此，有必要探讨在我国构建海上旅客运输强制责任保险制度。

一、海上旅客运输强制责任保险制度国际立法概述

强制责任保险，亦称法定保险，指规定范围内的单位或个人，无论是否自愿均须投保的险种，是由法律规定应当进行的保险。[①] 如果强制责任保险投保的义务主体违反法律规定，则将受到法律制裁。

国际海事组织参考1992年《国际油污损害民事责任公约》，将强制责任保险制度引入海上客运领域。《1974年〈海上旅客及其行李运输雅典公约〉的2002年议定书》（简称2002年《雅典公约》）于2002年通过，将强制责任保险制度首次引入国际海上旅客运输公约。1974年《海上旅客及其行李运输雅典公约》（简称1974年《雅典公约》）仅明确承运人对旅客运输途中因其过失导致的旅客人身伤亡负赔偿责任，并未提及强制责任保险事项。[②] 而2002年《雅典公约》则明确规定，为保证发生旅客人身伤亡的受害人能够得到赔偿，承运人必须提供强制责任保险或其他财务担保。[③]

2002年《雅典公约》规定的强制责任保险制度与承运人的归责原则密切相关，因为公约明确规定承运人实行严格责任原则和过错责任原则并用

---

① 参见邹海林《责任保险论》，法律出版社1999年版，第31页。
② 参见1974年《雅典公约》第三条："对因旅客死亡或人身伤害和行李灭失或损坏造成的损失，如造成此种损失的事故发生在运输期间，而且是因承运人或其在职务范围内行事的雇用人或代理人的过失或疏忽所致，则承运人负有责任。"
③ 参见2002年《雅典公约》第四条："对于旅客人身伤亡案件，根据公约的强制责任保险要求，在缔约国登记的，允许运载多于12位旅客的船舶的承运人，应按照公约规定的责任限额持有保险或其他财务担保（如银行担保或其他类似的担保），以便按公约规定承担对旅客死亡和人身损害的责任。"

的机制，并分别对应双层责任限额机制。即在第一层赔偿责任限额 25 万 SDR①范围内，承运人承担严格责任，不以其对旅客人身伤害存在过失为前提，而且公约规定的强制责任保险或其他财务担保的限额与第一层赔偿责任限额一致，即"不应少于在每一明确事件中每位旅客 25 万 SDR"，目的是确保在责任人承担较高责任限额的前提下能够为旅客提供最基本的保障。公约对第二层赔偿责任的限额是 40 万 SDR，即在第一层赔偿限额 25 万 SDR 以上的部分，如经证明承运人对旅客人身伤害存在过失，则旅客在获得第一层赔偿责任限额的基础上，最多可以获得包括 25 万 SDR 在内的高达 40 万 SDR 的赔偿。从 1974 年《雅典公约》的 1976 年议定书规定的 46666 SDR②到 2002 年《雅典公约》的 25 万 SDR，最高至 40 万 SDR，海上旅客运输责任限额分别提高了 4 倍、7 倍之多。公约之所以做出如此规定，是以航运技术和提升旅客运输安全性为基础的。这一方面体现了对旅客生命权的尊重，另一方面是为了与经济发展水平和船舶技术的提高相适应。③此外，公约对于不同情形下发生的旅客人身伤害的举证责任也做了区别对待。对非航运事故导致的旅客人身伤亡适用过错责任原则，由索赔人证明承运人存在过错。针对航运事故造成的旅客人身伤亡，在 25 万 SDR 范围内承运人承担严格责任，25 万 SDR 限额以上的，承运人承担过错责任，并且通过举证责任倒置，由承运人证明自己或其代理人无过错。④

作为强制责任保险的配套举措，2002 年《雅典公约》同时增设了直接诉讼制度。即在承运人因财务状况发生问题而不能给付其赔偿或怠于行使保险赔偿请求权时，旅客有权直接请求承运人的保险人给付赔偿。⑤

与传统责任保险不同，强制责任保险在一定程度上背离了保险契约的自愿性原则，因此只能基于法律规定实行，强制性是其最基本的特征。由于海上旅客运输可能是跨国运输，又有国际公约的基础，因此海上旅客运输责任保险制度的强制性不仅反映本国政府意志，还具有国际性。

此外，海上旅客运输强制责任保险制度还具有比较明显的公益性。其立法出发点是保障海上旅客损害赔偿权的实现。要实现这一目的，就难以

---

① 特别提款权（SDR）是国际货币基金组织规定的货币计算单位之一。
② 见 1974 年《雅典公约》的 1976 年议定书第七条。
③ 参见张蕴遐《从"东方之星"看海上旅客运输责任限额的"前世今生"》，载《中国保险》2015 年第 6 期。
④ 见 2002 年《雅典公约》第七条。
⑤ 见 2002 年《雅典公约》第四条。

回避保护公众利益而需牺牲商业效率的问题，这体现出国家日益注重人权保护、维护社会公平与正义的价值追求。因此在具体制度设计中，通过与直接诉讼制度的配套，法律赋予受害人享有向保险人索赔的直接请求权，从而突破海上保险合同相对性的束缚。通过优化索赔流程，缩短赔付时间和降低经济成本，提高获得赔付的可能性，也说明该制度致力于维护公众权益，确保旅客权益得到充分保障。

二、我国有关海上旅客运输责任保险制度的现状及其分析

我国是 1974 年《雅典公约》的成员国，但尚未批准参加 2002 年《雅典公约》，并且主要参考 1974 年《雅典公约》规定，通过《中华人民共和国海商法》（简称《海商法》）第五章"海上旅客运输合同"来调整海上旅客运输法律关系。因此《海商法》现有条文内容，没有规定海上旅客运输强制责任保险制度，也没有对直接诉讼制度进行规定。在承运人归责原则方面，我国采用过错和过错推定的归责原则，就承运人责任限制而言，我国对国际海上旅客运输和沿海旅客运输采取不同赔偿责任限额的"双轨制"，前者规定每名旅客人身伤亡不超过 46666 SDR[①]。根据全国银行间同业拆借中心发布的 2023 年 5 月 10 日汇率，1 SDR 相当于 9.546 人民币，因此 46666 SDR 相当于 445473.63 人民币[②]。而根据《海商法》第一百一十七条授权性规定，针对我国港口之间的海上旅客运输，承运人的赔偿责任限额由国务院交通主管部门制定。因此，原交通部（现交通运输部）于 1993 年 12 月 17 日发布《中华人民共和国港口间海上旅客运输赔偿责任限额规定》（简称《沿海旅客赔偿限额规定》），对旅客人身伤亡做出每名旅客不超过 4 万元人民币的限制规定[③]。这使得国际海上旅客运输合同和沿海旅客运输合同之间的承运人赔偿责任限制数额差距十分明显。

海上客运行业涉及的风险因素较多，一旦发生重大海难事故，往往会导致较大的旅客人身伤亡和财产损失。在缺乏海上旅客强制责任保险制度相关规定的情况下，难以确保旅客的合法权益得到保障。

第一，根据《海商法》第二章第三节规定，虽然在船舶营运中发生的

---

① 见《海商法》第一百一十七条第一款。
② 参见中国货币网（www.shibor.org/chinese/bkrmbidx/），2023 年 5 月 10 日访问。
③ 见《沿海旅客赔偿限额规定》第三条。

人身伤亡的赔偿请求具有船舶优先权，较普通债权、船舶留置权、船舶抵押权能够得以优先受偿，但是通常情况下人身伤亡的赔偿请求在船舶优先权请求事项中排在第二顺位，即位于船员工资、其他劳动报酬、遣返费用、社会保险费用的给付请求之后。此外，根据《海商法》第二十三条规定的船舶优先权受偿顺序，如果海难救助报酬发生后于船员工资、人身伤亡赔偿、港口规费等发生，则会逆序排在第一顺位优先受偿，即也会存在优先于旅客人身伤亡赔偿请求受偿的情形。① 所以在航运实践中，如果发生重大海难事故，遭受人身伤亡的旅客恐因顺位排序等原因则难以获得充分赔偿。

第二，存在我国沿海和国际旅客运输承运人单位赔偿责任限额差异过大，以及沿海旅客运输责任限额明显偏低的"同命不同价"的"双轨制"并存现象。除了本文前述的每名旅客人身伤亡可以获赔的责任限额存在区别之外，就某一起海难事故而言，旅客获得人身伤亡损害赔偿，还会涉及一个总责任限额的束缚。《海商法》第一百二十一条规定，海上旅客运输的旅客人身伤亡赔偿责任限制，按照 46666 SDR 乘以船舶证书规定的载客定额计算赔偿限额，但是最高不超过 25 万 SDR。《沿海旅客赔偿限额规定》第四条规定，海上旅客运输的旅客人身伤亡赔偿责任限制，按照 4 万元人民币乘以船舶证书规定的载客定额计算赔偿限额，但是最高不超过 2100 万元人民币。因此就旅客人身伤亡赔偿责任限制的总额规定而言，沿海旅客运输与国际海上旅客运输相差 10 倍之多。基于《海商法》颁布之时的国家贸易及航运经济发展现状、国际运输与国内运输机制的差异化、与国际接轨的限制条件等诸多因素考虑，采取"双轨制"模式具有一定的合理性。《海商法》自 1993 年 7 月 1 日生效实施以来，存在"双轨制"模式的上述基础已经发生了翻天覆地的变化，如果仍然采取"双轨制"模式，就会产生"同命不同价"的明显不公平的后果。结合我国目前的经济发展情况，现行规定的旅客人身伤亡赔偿限额标准未能与我国居民收入发展水平同步，尤其是沿海旅客运输的赔偿责任限额存在明显的滞后性。② 海上强制责任保险制度中的保险人享有海事赔偿责任限制权，责任限额为保险

---

① 见《海商法》第二十二、二十三条。
② 根据最高人民法院《关于审理人身损害赔偿案件适用法律若干问题的解释》和国家统计局发布的《2022 年国民经济和社会发展统计公报》，全国居民人均可支配收入在 2022 年达到 36883 元的水平得出的赔偿金额是 737880 元，而《海商法》规定对涉外海上旅客运输人身伤亡的 46666 SDR 的赔偿责任限额远远低于 737880 元的标准，不符合我国的居民收入水平现状。

人提供了确定风险的手段,合理的限额标准是保障该制度实现的重要一环。责任限额提高则有利于旅客获取足额赔付,是该制度发展和完善的表现。在海上运输领域,提高赔偿责任限额依赖于保险机制,这是全球各国的广泛共识。①

第三,根据我国现行有关责任保险的法律规定,旅客不能对承运人责任保险人提出直接诉讼。《中华人民共和国保险法》(简称《保险法》)第六十五条虽有提及责任保险人向第三人直接赔偿的情形,但无法为责任保险的第三人向保险人提起直接诉讼的制度提供足够支持,② 因为该规定使用的是"可以依照法律的规定或合同约定"的表述,一是由于未能明确《保险法》该条的规定是否属于"法律的规定",故还是需要根据《保险法》以外的其他法律的明确规定,如果根据条文解释的结果是依照《保险法》之外的其他法律规定,则没有该法律规定的,本条仍然无法适用;二是依照"合同的约定"存在不确定性,实践中使用的保险合同条款属于我国民事法律规定的"格式条款",被保险人是否有机会或者能力与保险人约定此事项尚存疑问。如果合同对此未予以约定的,则保险人也就不存在可以直接向责任保险的第三人赔偿的依据。此外,《保险法》第六十五条第二款给第三人行使直接请求权附加了"被保险人怠于行使请求"的条件。但是,对"怠于行使请求"的具体情形缺少明确的规定,在法律实务中难以认定。直接诉讼制度可以有效避免传统的责任保险理赔程序繁杂的现象,以及避免可能会出现由某个环节出现问题而导致索赔人权利实现受阻的情形。直接诉讼制度可以让旅客更直接地获赔,争议解决成本也随之大大降低。③ 因此,应当通过法律明确规定构建海上旅客强制责任保险制度并完善直接诉讼制度。

三、构建我国海上旅客运输强制责任保险制度的必要性

2014年发布的《国务院关于促进海运业健康发展的若干意见》列明了大力发展现代航运服务业,深化海运业改革开放,提升海运业国际竞争力

---

① 参见司玉琢《海商法专题研究》,大连海事大学出版社1999年版,第305页。
② 《保险法》第六十五条:"保险人对责任保险的被保险人给第三者造成的损害,可以依照法律的规定或者合同的约定,直接向该第三者赔偿保险金。被保险人怠于请求的,第三者有权就其应获赔偿部分直接向保险人请求赔偿保险金。"
③ 参见周海涛、李天生《论海上强制保险中的直接诉讼》,载《法学杂志》2011年第1期。

等重点任务，要求加快推动海运业立法。① 在海上旅客运输行业，建立完善的强制责任保险具有紧迫性和必要性。

（一）满足应对重特大海难事故的现实需要

重特大海难事故的发生是对构建我国强制责任保险制度的直接催化剂。1999 年 11 月 24 日，山东烟大汽车轮渡股份有限公司所属的"大舜"号在烟台附近海域发生海难，旅客和船员共 280 余人遇难。尽管根据《海商法》有关沿海旅客运输赔偿责任限额，每名旅客 4 万人民币予以计算，但是由于遇难人数较多，事故发生后，山东烟大汽车轮渡股份有限公司的财产不足以支付赔偿金，故其宣告破产。若有强制责任保险的规定，则不仅可以有效应对船公司破产赔偿支付能力不足的问题，而且受害旅客也能够更方便、充分地获得相应的法定赔偿，并通过直接诉讼制度向保险人索偿。此外，沿海旅客运输赔偿责任限额较低的问题也在该案中充分地暴露出来。据了解，当地政府经过多方筹措，在我国法律规定的赔偿责任限额基础上，又适当向每名受害旅客及其家属多赔付了 2 万余元。为了更好地保护旅客的人身权益，适当提高承运人赔偿责任限额并避免造成运输企业过大的成本压力，强制责任保险是合理的解决路径。正如国务院有关部门在《"11·24"特大海难事故调查处理报告》中明确提出的，通过立法强制实施船舶、船员以及海上旅客运输的人身保险制度，提高遇难者赔偿标准，保障旅客的合法权益。② 因此，构建海上旅客运输强制责任保险制度是保护旅客权益之需要，也是应对和处理重大海难事故的有力措施。

值得注意的是，在 2015 年发生在内河水域的"东方之星"号客轮沉船事故，对外公布的赔偿标准为每位遇难者 82.5 万元，③ 此赔付金额不仅远远高于我国沿海旅客运输赔偿责任限额，而且高于我国《海商法》规定的国际海上旅客运输赔偿责任限额。因此，司法实践的现实做法也反映出我国海上旅客人身损害赔偿责任限额的法律规定存在严重的滞后性，既不符合我国现行经济发展水平，也会限制旅客得到充分赔偿，不利于旅客人身权益保护。

---

① 参见《国务院关于促进海运业健康发展的若干意见》，2014 年 9 月 3 日发布。
② 参见《"11·24"特大海难事故调查处理报告》，见海员之家网（https://www.54seaman.com/index.php?s=/news/index/detail/id/342.html），2023 年 4 月 14 日访问。
③ 参见《"东方之星"客轮翻沉遇难者家属：死亡补偿标准为 82.5 万》，见澎湃新闻网（https://www.thepaper.cn/newsDetail_forward_1367219），2023 年 4 月 14 日访问。

（二）顺应我国海上旅客运输发展新业态的需要

目前我国已成为海运大国、港口大国、船员大国。同时，随着人民生活质量的不断提高，邮轮旅游经济在我国的快速发展，我国有较强的海上旅客运输发展潜力。2023 年 1—11 月，全国水路旅客运输量总计 24491 万人，旅客周转量达到 510389 万人公里。① 尽管海上旅客运输量远远小于内河旅客运输，但与传统海上旅客运输方式不同，海上邮轮旅游发展异军突起，而且邮轮旅客运输中载客数量较大，少至几百人，多至几千人、上万人的体量，一旦发生重大海难事故，不但会给海上旅客运输经营者带来巨大压力，而且后果不堪想象。而保险人凭借其经济实力和基金积聚、风险分散机制通常拥有更为强大的经济补偿能力②，在责任人因财力不足、破产等原因无法承担或者充分承担赔偿责任时，强制责任保险制度将有助于受害旅客及时获得较为充分的赔偿。尽管强制责任保险的实施，尤其是保险费的支出在一定程度上可能提高了运营成本和海上旅客运输业的准入门槛，但是可以倒逼一些经济实力较弱、管理混乱的航运公司或者老龄船撤出市场，客观上能实现优胜劣汰，减少事故发生概率，从而促进海上运输行业的健康发展。③

我国岛屿众多，具备良好的海上旅游观光的自然条件，且东临太平洋，海岸线绵长，与日本、韩国、越南、菲律宾、马来西亚等诸多东北亚、东南亚国家隔海相望，因此以海上旅游为代表的国际海上旅游运输业具有很大的开发潜力。强制责任保险制度的缺失，不利于我国海上客运企业与外国客运企业竞争，因为乘客往往更青睐于保险制度更为健全、运营更加规范的承运人。而强制责任保险作为风险分担机制，是能够同时兼顾被保险人和第三人利益的工具。④ 保障旅客权益、促进航运业发展、不断挖掘海上旅游观光的潜力，都要求对现行制度设计进行修改，平衡承运人

---

① 参见交通部《2023 年 11 月水路旅客运输量》，见 https：//xxgk. mot. gov. cn/2020/jigou/zhghs/202401/t20240102_3979938.html，2024 年 1 月 5 日访问。

② 参见李凤宁《海上强制责任保险的合理性与正当性解析》，载《理论月刊》2008 年第 7 期。

③ 参见初北平《海上强制责任保险研究》，载《中国海商法年刊》2004 年第 15 卷，大连海事大学出版社 2005 年版。

④ See Abraham, Kenneth S. "Liability Insurance and Accident Prevention：The Evolution of an Idea". *Maryland Law Review*, Vol. 64, Issue 1 – 2 (2005), pp. 573 – 612.

与旅客、责任限制主体与索赔人、保险人与被保险人等不同主体的利益，以符合国家整体经济利益和满足国家经济发展需要。① 而构建我国海上旅客运输强制责任保险制度，亦符合《海商法》规定的"维护当事人各方的合法权益、促进海上运输和经济贸易发展"的宗旨。

（三）吻合海上保险法价值转向的趋势

随着科技进步和经济发展，国际海商立法趋向于一改过往过于保护承运人权利的痼疾而呈现加重船方责任的趋势。例如，1978 年《联合国海上货物运输公约》（简称《汉堡规则》）、2008 年《联合国全程或部分海上国际货物运输合同公约》（简称《鹿特丹规则》）改变了以往不完全过失责任制，明确了规定承运人承担完全的过失责任，甚至通过举证责任分配方式加重承运人举证义务，并采取提高承运人单位赔偿责任限制数额等方式，平衡船货方利益。同时，针对人身权益保护、海洋环境与资源保护等意识的不断增强，相关保护性国际立法也在加强，出现向公法化发展的趋势。例如，对于有关油类货物、有毒有害物质的海上运输以及清除残骸等问题，国际海事组织先后制定《1969 年国际油污损害民事责任公约》、《1992 年国际油污损害民事责任公约》（简称 1992 年 CLC 公约）、《1996 年国际海上运输有毒有害物质的损害责任和赔偿公约》（简称 1996 年 HNS 公约）、《2001 年国际燃油污染损害民事责任公约》（简称 2001 年燃油公约）、《2007 年内罗毕国际船舶残骸清除公约》（简称《残骸清除公约》）等国际公约，并明确了责任人的强制保险制度。除 1996 年 HNS 公约尚未生效外，我国已被批准加入上述相关国际公约。很显然，上述国际公约有关强制责任保险制度的规定，也影响到海上旅客运输，因此 2002 年《雅典公约》顺应国际立法的趋势明确规定了承运人强制责任保险制度。

与此同时，海上保险法已从注重保险人利益的保护转向更注重被保险人利益的保护，这表明海上保险法的价值呈现从注重效益转向注重公平的趋势。② 目前世界范围内，旅客人身安全愈发得到重视。采用严格责任的归责原则和提高责任限额虽然能够提高旅客获取较为足额赔偿的可能，但是如果没有配套机制保障，仍不足以全方位保护旅客的合法权益。因为旅

---

① 参见胡正良、孙思琪《我国〈海商法〉修改的基本问题与要点建议》，载《国际法研究》2017 年第 4 期。

② 参见徐仲建《海上保险保证制度论》，法律出版社 2013 年版，第 71 页。

客获取足额赔偿需要建立在承运人有能力赔付或者有足够的能力赔付的基础上，如果因发生重大海难事故，承运人的赔偿能力不足或者濒于破产，即使规定再严格的归责原则和更高的赔偿责任限额，也无法解决受害旅客难以获赔的问题。从本质上看，强制责任保险以民事责任为基础，以国家公权力介入保险政策为手段，将社会中不易解决之难题纳入责任保险运作体系，① 从而保障受害旅客的合法权益。因此，有必要通过发挥强制责任保险的机制解决问题。

（四）顺应海上旅客运输国际立法发展趋势的要求

作为海上保险立法重要问题之一的责任保险，呈现强化并强制化的趋势。② 海上旅客运输强制责任保险正是这一趋势的表现之一。随着2002年《雅典公约》在2013年4月23日生效，海上旅客运输强制责任保险制度得到越来越多国家的重视和认可。截至2023年12月，公约已有34个成员国，这些成员国船舶吨位总和占世界商船总吨位的44.26%。③ 2002年《雅典公约》的主要修改几乎都聚焦于加强承运人的责任和加大对旅客利益的保护方面。这反映出国际社会对海上旅客运输立法制定与修改的发展趋势和意图。除了国际公约，许多国家尤其是发达国家的国内立法也体现出对保护旅客权益的重视程度。对人的生命与健康的日益珍视是形成这一趋势的根本原因。④ 我国虽然尚未批准加入2002年《雅典公约》，但是作为航运大国以及国际海事组织A类理事国，需要直面我国海上旅客运输立法与国际条约发展趋势不协调的现实问题，顺应我国海上旅客运输发展新业态以及推动邮轮旅游经济发展的现实需要，以提升我国承运人从事海上旅客运输业的竞争优势。因此，在我国海商立法历来注重与相关国际海事条约接轨以及当下《海商法》面临修改的背景下，我国应当适当考虑国际立法的发展趋势，不断完善海商立法。

---

① 参见郭锋、胡晓珂《强制责任保险研究》，载《法学杂志》2009年第5期。
② 参见司玉琢《国际海事立法趋势及对策研究》，法律出版社2002年版，第351–352页。
③ 参见国际海事组织官网上公布的"IMO条约现状"文件（STATUS OF IMO TREATIES）。
④ 参见宫倩《国际海上旅客运输法律发展趋势及动因分析——评〈2002年雅典公约〉的修改及对我国的影响》，载《天津市政法管理干部学院学报》2004年第1期。

四、构建我国海上旅客强制责任保险制度的建议

不可否认的是,符合发达国家需求的航运法律未必适合发展中国家。判定法律好坏的一个主要因素在于该法律规定能否与一定的社会现实状况和经济发展水平相协调,只有最适合本国国情的法律才是最好的法律。[①] 构建海上旅客运输强制责任保险制度,应当结合我国经济发展水平和海上旅客运输行业的发展现状,借鉴 2002 年《雅典公约》和其他国家的立法实践中的合理内容,通过修改《海商法》,在第五章"海上旅客运输合同"中增加海上旅客强制责任保险的内容。同时,制定配套的行政法规,对该制度的具体内容予以细化。

(一)明确海上旅客运输强制责任保险的责任基础,适当提高责任限额

承运人责任是责任保险的前提,如果对某一具体损失或损害没有相应责任,则不会有相应的责任保险。[②] 承运人责任归责基础是确定构建海上旅客运输强制责任保险制度的关键。在责任保险中,保险人赔偿的前提条件是被保险人对第三人承担赔偿责任,如果根据责任基础规定不应由承运人承担赔偿责任,第三人就不能向保险人索赔。同时,鉴于保险人承担的责任仅限于被保险人承担的赔偿责任,因此承运人的责任限制亦适用于保险人。[③]

创设海上旅客运输强制责任保险制度的 2002 年《雅典公约》,采取了承运人双层责任制度,欧盟作为 2002 年《雅典公约》的成员组织,也制定了相关法律。欧盟颁布的《海上承运人责任条例》中规定的承运人责任制度框架与 2002 年《雅典公约》基本一致。[④] 因此,对于非航运事故导致的旅客人身伤亡的责任基础,我国应与 2002 年《雅典公约》一致,在沿

---

① 参见郭瑜《海商法的精神——中国的实践和理论》,北京大学出版社 2005 年版,第 52 页。
② See Muhammad Masum Billah. *Effects of Insurance on Maritime Liability Law: A Legal and Economic Analysis*. Springer International Publishing Switzerland, 2014, p. 19.
③ 参见王翼峰《论海上旅客运输的强制责任保险制度》,载《黑龙江省政法管理干部学院学报》2018 年第 4 期。
④ 参见陈琦《邮轮旅游经营者法律定位分歧的破解——以〈旅游法〉〈海商法〉的制度冲突为视角》,载《法学》2020 年第 6 期。

用现有法律规定的前提下，依然采用过错责任原则；但对于船舶碰撞、搁浅、爆炸、火灾、潜在缺陷等航运事故导致的旅客人身伤亡，可以考虑借鉴 2002 年《雅典公约》的规定，采用一定限额以内的严格责任和限额以上的过失责任。① 2002 年《雅典公约》考虑到了承运人在海上旅客运输中的特殊风险性，照顾了承运人的利益，同时保护海上旅客的利益，有利于实现承运人和旅客之间的利益平衡。② 为充分保护海上旅客的利益，这种更为严格的归责原则，有利于促使承运人提高对船舶维护和人员管理的注意水平，从而在根源上预防海难事故。因此，可以考虑借鉴 2002 年《雅典公约》的双层责任体系，修改《海商法》中责任基础的条款。

  责任限额的确定是海上旅客运输强制责任保险的重要问题，在确保受害旅客能够获得充分赔付的同时，也确定保险人所应承担赔偿责任的最高限额。目前，我国法律规定的承运人赔偿限额已经出现与我国经济发展水平不符，难以保障旅客的合法权益的困境，由此基于较低数额的赔偿责任限制所构建的强制责任保险制度也就失去了发挥作用的基础。因此在责任限额的确定方面，应当考虑多方利益之间的平衡和我国的具体国情。因为实事求是，适合中国的现实和国情，既是我国立法工作的出发点，也是检验立法结果是否科学、正确的归宿。③ 一方面，出于保护旅客的角度，有必要利用合理的责任限额来保障旅客获得应得赔付的权利；另一方面，也需要考虑到如采取直接与 2002 年《雅典公约》规定的强制责任保险制度中较高的赔偿责任限额挂钩的方式，会加重我国航运企业的负担，尤其是在"同命同价"的理念下，要求改变国际海上旅客运输与沿海旅客运输责任限额"双轨制"的呼声不断。如果采取国际海上旅客运输与沿海旅客运输责任限额"并轨制"或"单一制"，④ 一旦赔偿责任限额过高，对从事沿海运输的我国航运企业而言，可能面临巨大的赔付和保险压力，最终造成从事国际海上旅客运输的企业不得不撤出国际市场，从事沿海旅客运输

---

① 参见郭萍《〈海商法〉"海上旅客运输合同"章修改：现实困惑与价值选择》，载《地方立法研究》2020 年第 3 期。

② 参见姚爽《论海上旅客运输强制责任保险制度》，载《中国商界（上半月）》2010 年第 12 期。

③ 参见朱力宇、张曙光《立法学》，中国人民大学出版社 2009 年版，第 70 页。

④ 参见郭萍《〈海商法〉"海上旅客运输合同"章修改：现实困惑与价值选择》，载《地方立法研究》2020 年第 3 期。

的企业因不堪重负而不得不退出经营活动的结果。① 所以,应当从我国实际经济背景和航运企业的承受能力出发,在建立强制责任保险制度的同时,科学合理地提高海上强制责任保险的责任限额水平,促使承运人加强管理,降低事故发生的风险。

(二) 确定海上旅客运输强制责任保险的保险人资格

保险人资格的规定是海上旅客运输强制责任保险中的重要问题。在保险人资格的限制上,《保险法》规定,商业保险业务应由依照保险法设立的保险公司经营,其他任何单位和个人不得从事此业务。传统海上旅客人身伤亡的责任风险主要由船东保赔协会承保,但是现在这种格局已经发生变化。实践中,对于保险人资格问题,各国做法不一,主要存在商业保险公司承保与船东保赔协会承保两种模式。日本的立法中,船东保赔协会具有强制责任保险制度中保险人的资格。在航运实践中,船东保赔协会是船东第三方责任险的主要承保人,向其提起直接诉讼是 2002 年《雅典公约》规定的保险义务的显著特点之一。② 西班牙的模式是由独立法人来运营保险机构,该法人直接向政府财政部负责,具体负责风险管理的是西班牙保险赔偿联合会。③

有学者指出,海上责任保险实质上是基于社会保险属性推行的责任保险,其公益性和商业性并存。所以保险人资质问题应留给市场解决,即强制责任保险人应当由实力强的保险人或保赔协会担任。④ 我们认为,正是基于强制责任保险制度具有强制性、公益性的特点,因此不能单纯地将问题留给市场机制。我国在推行海上旅客运输强制责任保险制度时,可以参照油污强制责任保险的实践活动,先指定实力雄厚的保险公司或保赔协会进行试点,制定适用海上强制责任保险的独立条款,之后根据实践发展情况确定是否扩大保险人名单。此外,还应充分发挥保险监管机构的作用,

---

① 参见周洪江《海上旅客运输强制责任保险制度研究》(学位论文),外交学院 2014 年,第 26－27 页。
② See Zhu, Ling. "Probing Compulsory Insurance for Maritime Liability". *Journal of Maritime Law and Commerce*, Vol. 45, Issue 1 (January 2014), pp. 63－76.
③ 参见周海涛《强制保险法律制度国际比较研究》(学位论文),大连海事大学 2010 年,第 89 页。
④ 参见苏如飞《论海上旅客运输强制责任保险制度》,载《河北科技大学学报(社会科学版)》2009 年第 1 期。

结合保障受害旅客利益的立法宗旨,对承保强制责任险的保险公司的经营活动进行监督和引导,以实现社会公共利益的最大化。

(三) 明晰旅客在强制责任保险的直接诉讼权利

直接诉讼是海上旅客强制责任保险制度的重要组成部分,也是其内在要求,是保证其实施和实现其功能的关键要件。鉴于索赔的第三人不是责任保险合同的一方当事人,因此直接诉讼是保险合同规则的例外,是受害人获得赔偿金的保障。① 若缺乏直接诉讼制度,就难以实现保护受害第三人的目的。

英国在 2010 年《第三人对保险人权利法》中明确规定第三人直接起诉保险人时,无须证明相关人的责任,如果第三人因某些特定原因不能起诉投保人,则第三人受害人有权直接对保险人提起赔付诉讼。在海上保险中的人身伤害责任方面,保赔协会不能以"会员先付"(pay to be paid)条款进行抗辩。英国由此确定了第三人在海上旅客运输强制责任保险中的直接请求权。②

美国海商法并未授权或禁止受害第三人直接起诉保险人,因此州法成为受害旅客唯一可以援引的依据。各州对直接请求权的立法态度不一致。其中,纽约州、路易斯安那州、罗德岛州等一些州的法律明确规定了保险人须直接对受害第三人负责。③

根据日本法律规定,日本国内海上旅客有权向事故船的船主或责任人索赔。《韩国商法典》则规定,第三人对因被保险人责任发生的事故造成的损害,在保险金额的限度内可直接请求保险人赔偿。④ 针对保赔协会先付条款的效力,韩国法律规定在强制责任保险下保赔协会不能以先付条款对抗受害第三人。⑤

---

① See Eliseo Sierra. "Direct Action against the Liability Insurer of Carriers of Passengers by Sea". *Marius*, No. 516, 2019, pp. 1 – 13.

② 参见司玉琢、李志文《中国海商法基本理论专题研究》,法律出版社 2013 年版,第 303 – 304 页。

③ 参见[美]小罗伯特·H. 杰瑞、道格拉斯·R. 里士满《美国保险法精解》,李之彦译,北京大学出版社 2009 年版。

④ 参见马炎秋《论第三人对责任保险人的直接诉讼权》,载《中国海洋大学学报(社会科学版)》2005 年第 1 期。

⑤ 参见马炎秋《韩国海上责任保险直接请求权的立法与实践》,载《保险研究》2020 年第 4 期。

从以上四个国家对直接诉讼的规定可以看出，各国立法中立法目的和价值均转向加强对第三人利益的保护，对于海上旅客运输强制责任保险赋予了受害第三人较为充分的直接请求权。大多数国家越来越倾向于给予第三人不附条件的直接请求权，第三人既可以直接向事故船的船东索赔，也可以向责任保险人索赔，我国在立法中也应注意到这一趋势。在具体行使条件上，不应设置过多的限制，不要求承运人丧失偿付能力或怠于行使保险索赔权，受害旅客即有权直接向保险人求偿。

结　语

海上旅客运输强制责任保险制度的根本目的是保护受害人及时得到充分赔偿的权利。相较于一般商业保险，它具有独特的强制性和公益性，而且具有十分重要的社会意义，即除能保护受害人外，还能分散风险，督促承运人改善船舶状况和提高营运质量，促进航运行业健康发展，维护社会公平和稳定社会秩序等。

通过对我国海上旅客运输领域的立法现状和构建海上旅客运输强制责任保险制度的必要性分析，可得出以下结论：海上旅客运输与其他运输方式的旅客运输相比，具有较高的风险性和水上风险的特殊性，且由于载客量大、救援困难等因素，一旦发生事故损害，往往会产生巨大的赔偿责任。如果不能确保责任人赔偿责任的落实，则严重影响受害旅客的人身权益。随着国际社会对海上强制责任保险制度的构建且不断扩大和深化其应用领域，考虑到我国推动海上邮轮旅游经济发展的现实需求以及我国海上运输行业参与国际市场竞争的能力的提升，为了充分保障旅客的权益，有必要在我国构建海上旅客运输强制责任保险制度。而在该制度的具体设计中，应当确定承运人责任基础及责任限额，其与旅客直接诉讼机制如同海上旅客运输强制责任保险的两翼，既密不可分，又不可或缺，因此对于海上旅客运输强制责任保险的具体内容规定，应当以我国经济发展水平和海上客运行业的发展状况为基础，借鉴 2002 年《雅典公约》的合理内容，并参考其他国家的相关规定。在构建我国海上旅客运输强制责任保险时，应当明确承运人的责任基础及归责原则，引入双层责任体系，适当提高承运人赔偿责任限额并采取统一"单轨制"，确定强制责任保险人的资质，同时赋予受害旅客享有直接诉讼强制责任保险人的权利。

法经济学视角下海事赔偿责任限制制度的"生命力"

刘 美*

摘要：作为航运活动中至关重要的一项制度，海事赔偿责任限制制度源起于航运实践，具有经济属性及一定的经济价值。在部分学者质疑该制度的当下，有必要从法经济学的角度重新认识其制度价值。从法经济学下的预防事故成本、过失原则理论、理性人标准以及经济博弈等视角来看，海事赔偿责任限制制度表现出其特有的经济价值。海事赔偿责任限制制度有助于实现社会成本的最小化和社会福利的最大化，其并非"特立独行"，而是具有深刻的经济意涵。在未来相当长一段时期内，该制度将仍然具有蓬勃的"生命力"。

关键词：法经济学 海事赔偿责任限制制度 经济价值

The Vitality of the Limitation of Liability for Maritime Claims from the Perspective of Law and Economics

Liu Mei

Abstract: The limitation of liability for maritime claims originated from shipping practices plays an important role in shipping activities with both economic attributes and value. Some scholars underestimated the system, so it is necessary to rethink its value from the perspective of law and economics. On the view of the cost of accident prevention, the principle of fault, the reasonable standard and economic games, the limitation of liability for maritime claims has its special economic value. The limitation of liability for maritime claims helps to minimize social costs and maximize social benefits. It is not unique but has profound economic implications. The system will still have vigorous vitality for a

---

* 刘美：福建省司法厅干部，华东政法大学法学博士。

long period of time in the future.

Key words: law and economics; limitation of liability for maritime claims; economic value

引　言

近现代以来，随着航海技术的不断进步，人类克服海上风险的能力不断提高，海上活动不再完全是一种"冒险事业"，海事赔偿责任限制制度存在的合理性和必要性开始不断遭到质疑，甚至有人断言，赔偿责任限制制度正逐步走向消亡。正因如此，从法经济学的角度来分析海事赔偿责任限制制度的价值和发展趋势就有了重要的理论与实践意义。"现代法律制度尽管在制度背景上有很大的差别，但它们一般性的融合却可以解释为一种走向效率和公平的运动。"① 而海事赔偿责任限制制度的"生命力"正是取决于这种效率和公平的运动能最终实现无限趋近于"帕累托效率"，即制度下责任主体的利益增加并不导致其他人的利益损失。事实上，经济学与法学的研究各有侧重，但是借助于经济学理论和实践经验可以实现法律制度的完善，从某种程度上说，法律的理性来源于这种开放性。本文基于此，拟通过探究海事赔偿责任限制制度的经济价值一窥其发展前景。

一、海事赔偿责任限制制度的法经济学分析基础

目前，各国立法和国际公约尚未明确定义海事赔偿责任限制制度。有学者认为，海事赔偿责任限制是指责任人根据法律规定，将自己的赔偿责任限制在一定范围内的法律制度。② 亦有学者将其定义为："海商法基于特殊的政策考量，赋予船舶所有人等特定主体将一次海损事故引起的特定海事请求所承担的赔偿责任限定在一定数额的法定权利，规范此项权利的产生、行使与效力的实体和程序规范的总和。"③ 概言之，该制度旨在赋予责任人减免责任的特殊权利。国内立法方面，《中华人民共和国海商法》（简称《海商法》）第十一章详细规定了海事赔偿责任限制制度的实体制度，

---

① [美]乌戈·马太：《比较法律经济学》，沈宗灵译，北京大学出版社2005年版，第20页。
② 参见司玉琢《海商法专论》，中国人民大学出版社2014年版，第314页。
③ 胡正良：《海事法》，北京大学出版社2012年版，第598页。

采用按照船舶吨位计算的金额制,同时辅之以《中华人民共和国海事诉讼特别程序法》(简称《海事诉讼特别程序法》)第九章"设立海事赔偿责任限制基金程序"和第十章"债权登记与受偿程序"的程序规定。值得注意的是,《海商法》第二百零九条规定:"经证明,引起赔偿请求的损失是由于责任人的故意或者明知可能造成损失而轻率地作为或者不作为造成的,责任人无权依照本章规定限制赔偿责任。"按照这一规定,享受海事赔偿责任限制的前提是损害发生的原因是责任人的过失行为。该规定与《1976 年海事赔偿责任限制公约》的规定基本相同。

事实上,海事赔偿责任限制制度最早可以追溯到中世纪远洋运输兴起,由于需要投入大量的资金,而航海技术的落后又使得海上风险难以抵御,因此船舶所有人承担了巨大的经营风险,海上可能突发的各种事件,造成的损失甚至会超过船舶本身的价值。为保护船舶所有人,鼓励海上运输和海外贸易,平衡各方利益,海事赔偿责任限制制度为船舶所有人设定了"安全阀",规定超出限额的部分,不予赔偿。正因如此,英国著名大法官丹宁勋爵曾在 The Bramley Moore 案中直言不讳地指出:"责任限制无关法律公平,而是一项有渊源和理由的公共政策。"[1] 船舶造成的损害作为一种侵权行为,按照传统的民法理论,应当进行全额赔偿。但实际上,遵循此种原则虽然保全了受害人的利益,却很可能使以船舶所有人为代表的加害人因一次事故而血本无归,甚至难以继续维系经营活动。同时,"对物诉讼"通常采用扣船的方式,本身就在很大程度上阻碍了航运业的发展。因此,19 世纪中叶,在老牌航运大国英国的推动下,海事赔偿限制制度应运而生。其制度功能在于保障航运业的稳定发展,鼓励海难救助,促进海上保险业的发展以及符合公平原则的要求。[2]

究其根本,正如经济学家阿瑟·奥肯(Arthur M. Okun)所说,平等和效率是最需要加以慎重权衡的社会经济问题,我们无法按市场效率生产出馅饼之后又完全平等地进行分享。如何在效率和公平二者中找到平衡点,不仅是经济学家关注的问题,还逐步引起法律学者的重视。诚然,经济学属于研究经济"规律"的科学,而法学属于研究社会"规则"的学科,[3] 但是任何法律制度都应服务于经济社会,海事赔偿责任限制制度亦

---

[1] *The Bramley Moore* (1963) 2 Lloyd's Rep. 437.
[2] 参见胡正良《海事法》,北京大学出版社 2012 年版,第 600 – 601 页。
[3] 参见周林军《经济规律与法律规则》,法律出版社 2009 年版,第 3 页。

是如此。概言之，无论是从海事赔偿责任限制制度的源起考证，还是基于其当下的理论及实践来看，海事赔偿责任限制制度的特殊性均显而易见，其一般价值彰显出与生俱来的经济属性，故而对其进行法经济学分析也就具有了必要性与合理性。

二、海事赔偿责任限制制度的法经济学分析维度

（一）预防事故成本与海事赔偿责任限制制度

通常而言，人们为了减少自身损失，实现个体利益最大化，会采取措施避免发生事故，而预期损失的大小将决定人们在多大程度上采取预防措施。以船舶碰撞事故为例，假设事故发生的概率为 P，损失为 L，二者分别为 1% 和 1000 元，则预期损失为 10 元（$P \times L = 1\% \times 1000$ 元 $= 10$ 元）。第一种情况是，若该事故只造成本船损失，毫无疑问，当预防措施的采取者和不采取预防措施可能的受害者是同一个人时，即使没有法律干预也将取得最佳预防，① 该船船东必定会尽最大努力预防损失发生，当然前提是采取预防措施的成本应当少于 10 元，否则预防成本将高于预期收益。第二种情况是该事故仅造成对方船舶的损失，同样假设对方的预期损失是 10 元，在不考虑责任限制的情况下，即该船预期损害赔偿成本是 10 元，所以该船是否采取预防措施取决于预防成本是否低于 10 元，预防成本低于 10 元就足以鼓励该船采取措施将预期损害赔偿降到零。

由于本文论述的海事赔偿责任限制制度涉及的是对他船的赔偿责任，故以上述第二种情况作为参照来进行分析。在海事赔偿领域，首先要否定一个前提，即对方船的预期损失不一定与该船预期损害赔偿成本相等，原因就在于海事赔偿责任限制制度的存在，除非该损失是该船故意或者明知可能的轻率行为导致的。暂且不论赔偿责任限制权利丧失的情况，假设损失由于该船的过失导致，责任人享有责任限制的权利，责任限制为 80%，即本船的预期损害赔偿成本为 8 元（10 元 $\times 80\%$），该船为避免损失发生所采取的措施必然不如没有责任限制的情况，在原先预期损害赔偿成本为 10 元的情况下，该船可以采取成本为 9 元的预防措施，而一旦存在 8 元的

---

① 参见［美］理查·波斯纳《法律经济学》，蒋兆康译，五南图书出版公司 2010 年版，第 175 页。

预期损害赔偿成本，则责任人选择的预防措施成本必然不会超过8元，但对于受害船舶而言，其遭受的损失仍然是10元。根据这一分析，海事赔偿责任限制制度有可能会增加海上航行的人为风险，即由于预防成本投入不够，预防措施不力而增加事故发生的概率。这也是海事赔偿责任限额不断提高的原因之一，以此警示海上活动参与者以最大的谨慎避免事故损害发生。

然而，实际的经济活动毕竟不是理论研究，借助汉德法官在1942年美利坚合众国与卡洛尔拖船公司案中提出的过失公式，我们可以设想另一种情况。假设B为预防损害发生的成本，根据汉德公式，只有当P（事故概率）$\times L$（损失金额）$> B$时，加害人的行为才构成过失。但现实中我们很难量化B、P、L的值，而且存在这种情况：还是以上述第二种情况为例，假设当B为8元时，预期损失降到0元，而当B为2元时，预期损失从10元降到1元，即为了将预期损失从1元降到0元，加害方花费的成本为6元（8元−2元），社会净成本为5元（6元−1元），而此时社会净收益为3元（2元成本和1元预期损失），显而易见，将预期损失从1元降到0元的过程，实际导致了社会收益的负增长。"我们必须对预期损失和事故预防成本进行边际比较，即透过衡量安全的细微增长的成本和收益，并且再花1美元只能得到1美元或更少的安全增长时停止为更安全投资。"[①] 而衡量这一成本变化导致的社会收益变动是极其困难的，实践中几乎不可能将所有数值如此量化，更难以对细微变化导致的变动做出科学判断。但是有一点可以证明，即预防事故发生的成本与预期损失赔偿的减少正相关，但并非与社会收益正相关，实现社会收益的最大化并不等于将预期损害赔偿减少到零，同理也并不意味着海事赔偿责任限额的不断提高所带来的预防事故成本提高必然导致社会收益增长。

除去本文开始讨论的两种事故情况，还有另外一种情况存在，就是采取预防措施的受益者既是潜在的加害者，也是潜在的受害者，简言之，即在海上航行中两船碰撞造成双方各有损失，这也是实践中最常见的情况。基于本文讨论的重点是海事赔偿责任限制制度，在此情况下如果享有赔偿责任限制权利，与上述分析基本一致，则不再赘述。

---

① ［美］理查·波斯纳：《法律经济学》，蒋兆康译，五南图书出版公司2010年版，第176页。

(二) 过失原则与海事赔偿责任限制制度

过失原则，又称为"促成过失""过失相抵"或者"受害人过错"，是指受害人对自己的安全欠缺通常的注意。这是传统的普通法方法在界定加害方和受害方二者过失的关系以及责任分配时采用的概念，这一原则来源于英国贵族院在 1890 年审理的一起上诉案件，上诉人由于骑马速度过快撞到被上诉人占道的支架而受伤，但是该占道的支架并不影响马路的正常通行，艾伦伯鲁勋爵认为，如果一方当事人没有采取通常的谨慎行为，即使对方当事人有过错，其仍然不能主张由对方分摊损失，最终上诉人败诉。在这一案件中，实际上隐含了这样一层意思：有效率的解决方法不是双方注意，而是其中一方注意。法律的目标是鼓励预防损失成本低的一方采取措施避免事故发生，而实际上我们可以发现，双方当事人都为避免事故支付一定成本时效率往往才是最高的。要想达到资源的最优配置，理想的状态是双方当事人在决定各自行动时都考虑负面影响（即妨害）。① 根据过失原则理论，似乎存在一种有违公平的结论，即加害人明明存在过失，却因为受害方的过失而得以豁免。经济学的答案是：几乎所有情况下，当事人双方都会对避免损害发生采取措施并支付一定的成本。一方面，将成本从受害人转向加害人，不利于引导人们为自己的安全尽通常的注意义务；另一方面，由加害人向受害方支付损害赔偿不会增进效率，而且这种行为还会损耗额外的成本（如法律成本）且不会增进社会财富，所以普通法传统是让受害方自担损失。

但是，包括我国在内的大多数国家的立法都采纳了比较过失原则，即双方都有过失的情况下，比较双方的过失比例，按比例承担损害结果。换言之，因为受害人自身的过失，加害人可以相应减少赔偿数额，但是通常不会免除其赔偿责任。这在海事法中体现得尤为明显。例如，根据《海商法》第一百六十九条第一款规定，船舶发生碰撞，碰撞的船舶互有过失的，各船按照过失程度的比例负赔偿责任；过失程度相当或者过失程度的比例无法判定的，平均负赔偿责任。相较于有过失原则，比较过失原则存在明显的优势是既保证了任何一方不面临过高风险，又警示各方对他人及自身安全采取严谨的注意义务，否则将承担必要的损失。

---

① See R. H. Coase. "The Problem of Social Cost". *Journal of Law and Economics*, Vol. 3, 1960, p. 13.

在海事赔偿责任限制制度中，实际上隐含着与比较过失原则同样的精神。首先，海事赔偿责任的确定就是以比较过失为基础的，至于赔偿责任确定后又采取的责任限制制度，无非是在此之上将加害方的责任控制在一定的范围内；其次，海事赔偿责任限制制度也是为了使潜在的任何责任人不至于承担过高的风险，同时又起到足够的警示作用。要保证经济体系的正常运转并实现资源的最佳配置，如何正确处理个体或组织之间的关系即界明产权边界显得至关重要。① 按照法经济学的观点，权利优化配置在很大程度上不过是资源优化配置的代名词而已，如何安排当事人之间的法律权利与义务，实现权利的优化配置乃至资源的优化配置，从而体现出制度的公平和效率，正是海事赔偿责任限制制度存在的价值和意义所在。在某种程度上，请求赔偿权本身就是一种特殊的稀缺资源。

同时，根据波斯纳定理，如果市场交易成本过高而抑制交易，那么权利应该赋予那些最珍视它们的人。该定理的推论是：在法律上，事故责任应该归咎于能以最低成本避免而没有这样做的人。正如前述，避免事故成本低于预期损失（某些情况下的预期损害赔偿成本）并不意味着该行为是最有效率的，理论上存在一个成本值可以使社会净收益达到最高，而需要承担这一成本的既可能是加害人，也可能是受害者，当然也可能需要双方当事人分摊。所以法律设计时必须考虑这方面的因素，引导潜在的双方当事人采取最有利于实现效率的预防措施。最极端的例子是，如果一次事故的预期损失是100元，加害方预防事故发生的成本是50元，受害方预防成本是5元，在不考虑其他因素的情况下，法律应该限制受害方取得赔偿的权利，以此来激励受害方采取必要的预防措施，从而实现社会效益的最大化。海事赔偿责任限制制度也蕴含了这种效率最大化的精神，赔偿受害方全部损失从表面上看似乎是实现了公平，却忽略了海上活动特殊环境下的效率。这种绝对公平在某种程度上蕴含着不公平，最直观的就是限制了海上活动的积极性，带来了难以估量的可怕的预期风险成本，每个受害方同时又是潜在的加害人，其弊害不言而喻。相反，采取限制过失方赔偿责任的做法，一方面使得预期风险可控，另一方面鼓励了每一个海上活动参与者采取必要的预防损害发生措施，分摊预防成本，既实现了潜在当事方之间的平衡，也有利于实现海上活动的效率最大化以及社会经济效益的最大化。事实上，基于人本身的趋利避害性，任何人都会为避免遭受损失而付

---

① 参见高永周《回到科斯：法律经济学理论探源》，法律出版社2016年版，第98页。

出一定的预防成本,只不过法院需要考量的是这种成本支出是否已经达到理性人标准,而经济学研究者则要在此基础上进行社会经济效益的衡量。

(三) 理性人标准与海事赔偿责任限制制度

关于上述的理性人标准,从法经济学的角度我们可以进行如下分析。显然,我们很难在实践中对预防损害发生的成本、事故发生概率、可能的损失金额等做出精确的预计和判断,在决定一场事故是否能由任何一方当事人以低于预期损失的成本避免时,法院没有透过计算个人避免事故的能力而试图衡量当事人双方的实际成本,相反的,他们估计了理性人在各自情势下避免事故的成本。① 理性人标准不要求当事人将预期损失及赔偿降到零,更不要求其投入高于预期损失赔偿的成本来预防损失发生,显然这也是不可能的。在海事赔偿责任限制制度中,判断加害人是否是过失、是否能享受赔偿责任限制,就是以理性人的标准来衡量的。毫无疑问,从经济角度分析,这一规则也节约了司法成本。制度的设计上要考虑行为人对法律规则所可能产生的反应,要通过激励机制来诱导行为人做出法律所期望的行为选择,法律规制要更多地借助于市场自发力量的相互制衡。② 对于海事赔偿责任限制这一制度的考量更应该注意其特殊性,比如一旦发生船舶碰撞事故,其造成的损失与一般车辆碰撞不可同日而语,因此即使是有赔偿责任限制制度的存在,海上活动的参与者仍然会尽最大努力予以避免,这也是理性人标准产生的合理之处,是仅凭数字堆积的理论研究难以得出的结论。当然,理性人的标准是比较模糊的,如何进行评判取决于法院在具体案件中的价值衡量。

(四) 经济博弈与海事赔偿责任限制制度

在海上保险法中存在一项特殊的原则——"近因原则",即只有当导致损失发生的原因是最直接、最有效、起决定作用的"近因"时,保险人才承担赔偿责任。这一原则在很大程度上保证了保险人对风险承担的可预见性。众所周知,只有当风险具有可预见性时,保险公司才能计算费率,进而才能鼓励他们参与经济活动,承保相关风险,否则,即使是当事方也

---

① 参见 [美] 理查·波斯纳《法律经济学》,蒋兆康译,五南图书出版公司2010年版,第179页。
② 参见周林彬《法律经济学:中国的理论与实践》,北京大学出版社2008年版,第365页。

无法确定应该投入多少成本来防止这一事故发生。同样的，在海事赔偿领域，只有当事人基于自身的内部结构和外部环境能合理预计损害赔偿成本时，其才会有充分的勇气和信心投入生产活动中去，海事赔偿数额动辄千万乃至亿计，任何一个企业都难以承受这样的高风险。同时，基于海上环境的复杂性，即使在航海技术高度发展的今天，海上活动安全仍然具有相当大的不确定性，风险的难以预测必然导致了成本的不可预见。这可能导致三种经济现象发生：要么当事人选择退出此类经济活动；要么提高盈利空间，将此项风险成本转嫁给货主；要么通过保险途径将风险转移。但无论如何，这些做法无疑都是"零和博弈"，甚至是"负和博弈"。[①] 众所周知，经济学钟爱于通过"利益激励"途径来诱发或促成对对方有利可图的交易结果，而法学则更倾向于通过"规则控制"途径来规范或保障正常的交易秩序。[②] 而当利益激励无法充分发挥其促进作用时，则需要法律规则来鼓励交易，这也正是海事赔偿责任限制制度的价值所在，直观上其给潜在的赔偿责任主体设定了"安全阀"，保证了其面临风险的可控性，更重要的是为其设定赔偿成本的上限，保障了他们对于潜在经济损失的可预测性。海事赔偿责任限制制度实际上使潜在受害方与加害人之间达成了一种"合作"模式，在不同利益的交汇临界点找到一种平衡状态，最终实现社会收益的最大化或者成本的最小化。

进言之，法律制度产生的经济学初衷就是实现事故发生的社会成本最小化、社会福利最大化，而需要我们考虑的成本变量主要包括事故发生所造成的损害成本、避免事故发生的预防成本、司法规则系统的管理成本。[③] 从这三个变量的角度分析，在海事赔偿案件中，事故发生所造成的损害成本是具体案件中的客观事实，与制度设计无关，而避免事故发生的预防成本和司法规则系统的管理成本则是考虑的重点。基于上述分析可见，海事赔偿责任限制制度实现了资源的优化配置，将避免事故发生的成本合理分摊到每一个潜在的事故当事人身上，使风险事故的潜在受害者和加害方都有适当的激励将他们活动的外部性内化来避免事故发生。这一方面使事故的预防成本效率最大化，另一方面也实现了"预防"优于"补偿"的社会

[①] 参见［美］乔·B. 史蒂文斯《集体选择经济学》，杨晓维等译，上海三联书店、上海人民出版社1999年版，第120页。
[②] 参见周林军《经济规律与法律规则》，法律出版社2009年版，第122页。
[③] 参见周林彬《法律经济学：中国的理论与实践》，北京大学出版社2008年版，第219页。

经济效益。另外，海事赔偿责任限制制度也在一定程度上简化了赔偿的理算，对节省司法成本无疑是有益的。当然，我们不能忽视由这种制度设计的特殊性导致诉讼成本在某种程度上的提高，但是这种个体的成本提高换来的是更广泛而巨大的社会效益的增长，更何况这种制度设计牺牲的是少数人某个时间点的利益。从长远和整体上看，这降低了所有海上活动参与者的潜在风险成本，实现了社会成本的最小化和社会福利的最大化。

三、法经济学视角下海事赔偿责任限制制度的进路

传统法学认为侵权法的目标是消灭所有侵权行为，但这种观点在法经济学的视角下是不恰当的、无效率的。基于效益原则，解决侵权问题的关键在于避免较严重的损害。[①] 基于前述法经济学的分析视角，回归到侵权损害赔偿的制度功能本身来看，海上侵权与其他类型的侵权其实存在一定的差异。众所周知，侵权法的损害赔偿原则之一是全部赔偿原则——侵权行为人承担赔偿责任的大小以行为造成的实际损失为准，予以全部赔偿，其目的在于最大限度地弥补受害人的损失。但其中也存在例外，即如果实际损害远远超出行为人实施侵权行为时的预期，且行为人无法承担损失赔偿责任时，则在可预期损失的范围内适当赔偿。从某种程度上说，海上风险导致的实际损害往往是超出责任人预期且难以承担的，海事赔偿责任限制制度本质上与侵权赔偿的例外具有异曲同工之处。事实上，当今国际海商法领域确实存在一种观点和立法趋势，即原则上人身损害和海洋环境损害应当得到充分的经济补偿。但充分的经济补偿并不意味着必须单纯通过责任者的赔偿实现，而是可以以其他补偿途径作为辅助，毕竟海事赔偿责任限制制度的初衷是对航运投资者进行适当保护，并且使责任者的赔偿责任具有可预见性，进而通过责任保险分散经营风险。[②]

客观而言，法经济学的经济特性决定了其追求效率优先，不过对效率的追求理应服从于公平的价值判断。[③] 进言之，法律不应被视为实现效率、

[①] 参见魏益华、于艾思《法经济学视阈下人工智能产品责任归责原则》，载《吉林大学社会科学学报》2020年第2期。

[②] 参见胡正良《论我国〈海商法〉修改应遵循的从我国实际出发原则》，见上海海事大学海商法研究中心编《海大法律评论（2018—2019）》，上海浦江教育出版社2021年版。

[③] 参见肖崇俊《法经济学的限度——美国公司反收购立法的合宪性论争及其启示》，载《中国政法大学学报》2022年第2期。

创造财富的工具,更不应为了实现"效率最大化"而牺牲法律的公平正义。① 从制度设计的出发点和立足点来看,海事赔偿的首要功能当然是保护受害人的权利,但是,基于这种海上经济活动的重大意义、参与主体的特殊性以及赔偿数额的难以预测且往往巨大,效率是在制度设计中必须更加重视的。给予所有海上经济活动参与者即潜在的加害方赔偿责任限制,既可以防止其投入过度的预防成本而导致社会经济利益的损失,也可以警示其作为潜在受害者应投入必要的预防成本防止事故发生。"当市场过程不能产生被所有参与者接受的结果时,法律必须对竞争主张进行调解。"② 显然,海事赔偿责任限制制度是对这种竞争的调和,避免了责任人因为一次事故而破产,进而减少对社会经济效益造成不利影响。这也恰恰体现了海商法作为一套成本分摊体系的经济价值,其目的就是找到一个对所有参与航运业者都最有利的解决方案。③

无独有偶,我国对核事故等高度危险责任以及交通事故责任、矿山安全事故的赔偿责任也规定了限制赔偿的制度。由此可见,海事赔偿责任限制制度并非"特立独行",而是深植于民法损害赔偿体系中,是民法损害赔偿体系的重要组成部分,其并非对公平原则的背离,而是在当事人双方面临的风险和所获得的利益不对等的前提下,平衡当事人双方利益的有效手段,④ 具有独特而深刻的经济价值考量。根据"科斯定理",侵权行为与契约行为的差异在于无法通过事先的约定来确定和分配各方的责任,在交易成本、信息成本、讨价还价成本过高的情况下,法律的干预和规制在资源的有效分配中显得尤为重要。赔偿责任限制制度并不意味着以权利为基础的侵权法规则系统的崩塌,而是在满足福利经济学分配要求的同时,实现了权利分配的公平和效率之间的平衡。进言之,海事赔偿责任限制制度的设计正是基于实现海上侵权行为下的公平与效率兼顾,从而促成了经济活动的效益最大化。

近年来,国内外学界呼吁提高海事赔偿责任限额的根本原因不是抵制制度本身,而更多的是基于社会经济发展的要求。事实上,从海上货物运

---

① 参见胡睿《法经济学理论功效辨析》,载《中国社会科学报》2022 年 8 月 3 日第 10 版。
② [美] 罗宾·保罗·马洛伊:《法律和市场经济——法律经济学价值的重新诠释》,钱弘道等译,法律出版社 2006 年版,第 10 页。
③ 参见郭瑜《海商法的精神——中国的实践和理论》,北京大学出版社 2005 年版,第 190 页。
④ 参见何丽新、王沛锐《民法公平原则下海事赔偿责任限制正当性之重塑》,载《中山大学学报(社会科学版)》2021 年第 2 期。

输法律制度发展史来看，随着造船、航海等技术的进步，航运生产力水平的提高，人们克服海上风险的能力不断提高，承运人责任的提高呈现不可逆的状态，这是《海商法》发展的一条规律。① 从《海牙规则》到《鹿特丹规则》，赔偿责任限额的上涨并不代表着其相对社会经济总量来说的相对量的提高，人类社会的物质财富已经经历了天翻地覆的变化，相应地提高限额以弥补受害人损失有其必要性及合理性。这不仅不能说明海事赔偿责任限制制度正在走向消亡，反而是其不断发展进步的表现。可以预见，未来航运业的经营主体不仅要面临传统的直接海上风险，还要遭遇新兴的海运问题带来的潜在海上风险，海事赔偿责任限制所具备的分摊海上风险的价值仍将继续发挥作用。② 正如有学者所说，除非海陆差异完全消除，否则海事赔偿责任限制制度仍会继续存在。③ 落脚到经济角度看，法律制度的发展总是试图在公平和效率的运动中找到一个新的平衡点以实现"帕累托最优"，作为维护航运业发展的最后一层保护网，④ 在未来相当长的时期内，海事赔偿责任限制制度仍会处在一个发展上升期，其在海上"冒险"中特有的经济价值决定了其作为法律制度存在的重大意义以及长远的"生命力"。

---

① 参见胡正良《论我国〈海商法〉修改应遵循的从我国实际出发原则》，见上海海事大学海商法研究中心编《海大法律评论（2018—2019）》，上海浦江教育出版社 2021 年版。
② 参见关正义、严凌成《论航次承租人海事赔偿责任限制权利问题——兼谈〈中华人民共和国海商法〉第 204 条的修改》，载《中国海商法研究》2021 年第 4 期。
③ 参见何丽新、王沛锐《民法公平原则下海事赔偿责任限制正当性之重塑》，载《中山大学学报（社会科学版）》2021 年第 2 期。
④ 参见何丽新、王沛锐《论"海事赔偿责任限制"章节修订中的三大问题》，载《中国海商法研究》2019 年第 1 期。

我国水路货物运输承运人管货义务发展新探

——兼评《长江（内河）航运标准合同》中的相关条款

刘佳溢 范沣亿*

摘要：《国内水路货物运输规则》被废止之后，国内水路货物运输承运人管货义务的无法可依给司法实践带来了各类问题，主要体现在管货义务的客观标准无明确规定、管货义务主观标准的证明过于繁杂、管货责任的认定过于严苛三方面。本文以《长江（内河）航运标准合同》文本中承运人管货义务制度的具体条款设计为研究对象，结合对《中华人民共和国海商法（修订征求意见稿）》《中华人民共和国海商法（修改送审稿）》中针对水路货物运输涉及的相关规定的考察，探析《国内水路货物运输规则》被废止后国内水路货物运输承运人管货义务制度的发展趋势，并尝试就前述问题的实践对策及立法方向提出笔者的建议。

关键词：国内水路货物运输 《长江（内河）航运标准合同》 承运人管货义务

A New Probe into the Development of Carrier's Obligation of Care for Cargo by Inland Waterway in China
—Comments on the Related Clauses of the *Yangtze River (Inland Waterway) Standard Form of Shipping Contract*

Liu Jiayi, Fan Fengyi

Abstract: After the *Rules for the Domestic Water Transport of Cargos* was abolished, no specific statutes applied to carrier's obligation of care for cargo by waterway, which has raised a series of problems in the judicial practice, mainly involving the lack of clear objective criteria, the complexity of proving the subjective criteria, and the harshness of the determination of the liability relating

---

* 刘佳溢：大连海事大学法学院海商法系专任讲师，日本早稻田大学法学博士，日本早稻田大学海法研究院特聘研究员。范沣亿：大连海事大学海商法系本科毕业生。

to carrier's obligation of care for cargo. This paper focuses on the specific clauses on carrier's obligation of care for cargo in the *Yangtze River（Inland Waterway） Standard Form of Shipping Contract*, combined with the review of relevant regulations designed for water transport of cargoes in the *Draft for Revision of the Maritime Law of the People's Republic of China* and the *Maritime Law of the People's Republic of China（Revised Draft for Examination）*, analyzes the development trend of the carrier's obligation system of care for cargo by domestic waterway after the repeal of the *Rules for the Domestic Water Transport of Cargos*, and tries to put forward personal suggestions to the practical solution and legislative direction of the above problems.

Key words：inland waterway transportation；*Yangtze River（Inland Waterway）Standard Form of Shipping Contract*；carriers' obligation of care for cargo

引　言

贸易保护主义的抬头和俄乌冲突使我国经济发展的安全性、主动性面临威胁。① 故在"国际国内双循环相互促进"② 的新发展格局下，保障国内水路货物运输稳步发展、充实全运输过程的管货义务规则对建设国内高效顺畅的商品流通体系尤为重要。③ 作为承运人的基本义务，管货义务曾以重要的制度形式规定于《国内水路货物运输规则》（简称《货规》）中。④《货规》被废止后，管货义务制度一时失去了特别法依据，而新出台的《中华人民共和国民法典》（简称《民法典》）仅在第八百三十二条以有限列举的方式对承运人免除管货责任的情形做了一般法意义上的表

---

① 参见易小准、李晓、盛斌等《俄乌冲突对国际经贸格局的影响》，载《国际经济评论》2022 年第 3 期；何志鹏《全球化、逆全球化、再全球化：中国国际法的全球化理论反思与重塑》，载《中国法律评论》2023 年第 2 期。

② 中国共产党中央委员会：《中共中央关于制定国民经济和社会发展第十四个五年规划和二〇三五年远景目标的建议》，人民出版社 2020 年版，第 5 页。

③ 参见习近平《高举中国特色社会主义伟大旗帜　为全面建设社会主义现代化国家而奋斗——在中国共产党第二十次全国代表大会上的报告》，人民出版社 2023 年版，第 7 页。

④ 如无特别说明，本文所述"承运人"均代指"国内水路货物运输承运人"，本文所述"管货义务"均代指"国内水路货物运输承运人的管货义务"。

述，并未对管货义务的主客观标准和责任认定等关键性问题予以规定。故现行国内立法无法满足市场对发展完善管货义务制度的迫切需求，也给国内航运司法实践造成了诸多不便，在一些争议问题的审理上甚至无法可依。

如果说《中华人民共和国海商法（修订征求意见稿）》和《中华人民共和国海商法（修改送审稿）》已经表达了对国内水路货物运输专章规定的立法倾向，那么2020年12月武汉航运交易所发布的我国首个内河航运标准合同——《长江（内河）航运标准合同》（简称《长江合同》）则提供了更为系统的解决方案。① 其制定者在"一带一路"倡议的背景下，充分调研、整合我国航运业各界意见，以中小船东为优先推广对象，以电子化合同为实践方式，力求以标准合同平衡船货双方利益。② 其条款设计为管货义务制度的完善提供了新思路，在一定程度上反映了我国内河航运的实务发展趋势和制度价值取向。但《长江合同》毕竟不是法律本身，其条款的设计也并非面面俱到。本文通过比较分析、案例研习和文献研究，将《长江合同》相关条款与《货规》相关规定进行优劣对比，探究管货义务制度的发展方向，并尝试针对实务中出现的一些问题提出笔者的分析和建议。

一、水路货物运输承运人的管货义务的发展沿革

管货义务，即承运人为将货物安全地运抵目的港所应做出的最低程度的装载、搬运等管理货物的义务，曾经在《货规》中有过不尽完备的规定。《中华人民共和国海商法》（简称《海商法》）的几版修改稿及后来的《长江合同》都试图寻找一条有针对性的策略，从而解决《货规》废止后的"无法（专门立法）可依"状态所滋生的司法实践中的问题。

---

① 《长江合同》按货物种类设计了四类标准合同，本文分别简称为"集装箱合同""液货合同""商品车合同"与"干散货合同"。

② 参见船途《〈长江（内河）航运标准合同〉顺利通过评审》，见 https://mp.weixin.qq.com/s/40tcZ_yV4R9Ik-5eEgzDOg，2021年10月15日访问；蒋跃川《长江航运呼唤标准合同：填补内河航运市场的法律空白》，见 https://mp.weixin.qq.com/s/_IbBLYJSke3cUr6YBVk-rA，2021年10月15日访问；唐松《长江航运呼唤标准合同：彰显航运交易服务价值》，见 https://mp.weixin.qq.com/s/n8u2KiBbu_Of9V9neiKViw，2021年10月15日访问。

（一）承运人管货义务在司法实践中的问题

《货规》在被废止以前，常处于"备而不用的尴尬境地"。《货规》规定因承运人违反管货义务的诉讼纠纷可依照该部门规章的规定来审理，但司法实践中《货规》的适用往往需要以运输合同中的明确约定为前提。以天津海事法院审理的一例运输合同纠纷①为例，当事人在合同中约定适用《货规》，法官基于合同自由原则在判决书的论证部分适用《货规》进行说理，并确定当事人的权利义务，但在判决结果部分仍然适用的是《中华人民共和国合同法》（简称《合同法》）。换言之，不论当事人是否约定适用《货规》，法院更倾向于适用《合同法》（2021年后为《民法典》第三编"合同"）等一般法进行裁判。此时《货规》处于"备而不用"的尴尬境地，这类似于海事司法实践中时有《海商法》劣后于《合同法》适用的情况。导致这类状况的因素具有一定的相似性，有学者认为根本原因是水路货运纠纷类案件中存在"大量基础民事法律关系"②，而且《货规》的行政规章性质在作为法院判案依据的效力方面存在不确定性③。另外，现行水路货物运输法的体系归属又不明确，这一立法空白进一步导致了《货规》的被架空。

《货规》被废止后，承运人管货义务方面的司法实践呈现如下三个方面的问题。

其一，管货义务客观标准的不确定性。④首先，航运技术的进步使水路运输的货物种类日益丰富，管货的客观标准也在逐渐增多，某些货物甚至还存在独立的管货义务客观标准，但我国法律对上述标准尚无规定。对于当事人而言，可通过补充协议或权威检验报告的方式弥补合同约定的不

---

① 南京中金隆达物流有限公司海南分公司与广西新闻航海有限责任公司水路货物运输合同纠纷案，天津海事法院（2015）津海法商初字第284-286号民事判决书。
② 何丽新、梁嘉诚：《〈海商法〉实施25年司法适用研究报告》，载《中国海商法研究》2018年第2期。
③ 《最高人民法院关于适用〈中华人民共和国合同法〉若干问题的解释（一）》第四条规定判断合同效力不得以行政规章作为依据；而《最高人民法院关于裁判文书引用法律、法规等规范性法律文件的规定》第五条又允许审判人员"根据审理需要"适用行政规章。这种模棱两可的规定使得法院在适用法律法规处理管货义务纠纷时主观上不愿适用《货规》的特别规定。
④ 管货义务的客观标准的含义和具体内容详见本文第二部分。

足;① 法院只能以承托双方订立的运输合同为依据同时辅之以《合同法》的一般规则进行延伸来处理纠纷。② 然而，实践中往往存在运输合同约定标准不明的情况，此时针对管货义务客观标准的纠纷的审理便难以找到具体的判断依据。再者，除了新增的管货客观标准和特殊的管货标准外，不同货物因自身性质不同，其各自管货标准也不同。故在水路货运承运人责任相关的司法实践中，承运人对何种货物履行管货义务应达到何种客观标准的问题也就成了审判的主要障碍之一。

其二，管货义务的主观标准证明繁杂。③《货规》废止后，法院对管货义务主观标准的认定只能依靠证据并结合单纯的法理论证进行认定，这使得法官只能通过调取大量证据来提高裁判的公信度，其中最常用到的就是检验报告类的证据。如此，在管货义务证据的调取和质证方面的问题愈加突出——越来越多的当事人通过自行搜集有利货物检验报告意图实现自己的诉求，然而对这些检验报告的证据性质，国内各地法院尚未达成一致意见。例如，在海口海事法院（2019）琼 72 民初 178 号民事判决书④中，托运人的代位人（本案原告）的诉讼请求即因提供的装港商检报告存在诸多重大疑点和前后矛盾而未被法院采信，无法证明货物在船期间发生短少，从而败诉，该案中的商检报告未被认定为证据。在上海市高级人民法院（2009）沪高民四（海）终字第 164 号民事判决书⑤中，因缺少物证支持，法院认为原审原告的公估报告仅系出庭公估人的证人证言。

其三，承运人责任认定过于严苛。《货规》的废止导致法院裁判几乎完全依赖《民法典》和《中华人民共和国民事诉讼法》的规定，忽略了水路货运的自身特性。例如在大连海事法院（2020）辽 72 民初 24 号民事判决书⑥中，由于实际承运人货物系固不牢，存在过错，法院根据《合同

---

① 大连宇阔商贸有限公司与福建省中通海运有限公司、广东仁科海运有限公司海上货物运输合同纠纷案，大连海事法院（2017）辽 72 民初 60 号民事判决书。
② 宋殿磊与中国人民财产保险股份有限公司大连市分公司运输合同纠纷案，湖北省高级人民法院（2021）鄂民终 626 号民事判决书。
③ 管货义务的主观标准的含义和证明相关的内容详见本文第三部分。
④ 中国太平洋财产保险股份有限公司北京分公司与上海中远海运油品运输有限公司保险人代位求偿权纠纷案，海口海事法院（2019）琼 72 民初 178 号民事判决书。
⑤ 中国人民财产保险股份有限公司广东省分公司与威海市鼎鑫海运有限公司运输合同纠纷案，上海市高级人民法院（2009）沪高民四（海）终字第 164 号民事判决书。
⑥ 大连金鼎石油化工机器有限公司与舟山锦弘海运有限公司水路货物运输合同纠纷案，大连海事法院（2020）辽 72 民初 24 号民事判决书。

法》第三百一十一条"承运人对运输过程中货物的毁损、灭失承担损害赔偿责任"①这一规定,认定实际承运人承担货损赔偿责任。但是,若系固不牢非由承运人过错导致,除非符合该条但书列举的三项免责情形②,否则仍有可能对运输中自身无过错的货损承担责任。对水路货物运输承运人适用一般法上的严格责任,与《货规》第四十八条列举的多达十项的具体免责事由的状况相比较而言应当说是过于严苛的,更不用说与《海商法》下海上货物运输承运人的过错责任相比了,关于这一点实务界与学界一直存在着批判的意见。③

（二）《货规》废止后承运人管货义务的立法发展

《货规》被废止后在司法实践中引起的上述问题,使得航运各界对制定水路货运立法的呼声越来越高。故全国人民代表大会常务委员会（简称人大常委会）于2018年9月7日将修改《海商法》正式列入第十三届全国人大常委会立法规划,其中便包括对国内水路货物运输法律制度的立法工作。

2018年11月5日公布的《中华人民共和国海商法（修订征求意见稿）》（简称《海商法（修订意见稿）》）将水路货物运输制度以独立一章（即第5章）的形式全部纳入《海商法》的立法范围,并对国内水路货运承运人的管货义务做出了不同于《货规》的新规定。首先,其主要在第5.7条对水路货运承运人的管货义务内容进行了变革。在管货义务的主观标准方面,新增"谨慎"这一主观标准,更全面地反映出承运人主观上管理货物应当达到的标准。同时将"接收""交付""过驳"写入管货义务的客观标准,并将承运人管货责任期间从《货规》第三十二条规定的"货物装船至货物卸船"延长为"接收货物至交付货物的全过程"。上述这些

---

① 现被《民法典》第八百三十二条所吸收。

② 《民法典》第八百三十七条规定："承运人证明货物的毁损、灭失是因不可抗力、货物本身的自然性质或者合理损耗以及托运人、收货人的过错造成的,不承担赔偿责任。"

③ 学界的批判意见以傅廷中、王利明的观点为代表,他们认为《民法典·合同编》确立的严格责任原则不应适用于我国一切民事交易,可以通过其他归责原则（如完全过错责任制）减轻承运人的沉重负担（参见傅廷中、杨俊杰《国际海运立法中分化与协调的百年变奏——以海上货物运输承运人责任制度为视角》,载《法律科学（西北政法学院学报）》2007年第5期；王利明《〈联合国国际货物销售合同公约〉与我国合同法的制定和完善》,载《环球法律评论》2013年第5期）。

变化反映出管货义务的客观标准逐步扩张的发展趋势。另外，还放宽了部分管货义务主体的资格限制，将装载、搬移、堆放、卸载的义务主体交由承托双方自由约定，以顺应物流市场分工细化的趋势，在一定程度上减轻了承运人的管货负担。其次，《海商法（修订意见稿）》第5.10条在《货规》基础上对违反管货义务的免责条款做出了改动①——在水路货运领域确立完全的过错责任制。最后，《海商法（修订意见稿）》将水路货物运输制度专章立法并不意味着割裂海上货物运输和水路货物运输的管货义务制度的联系，事实上"水路货物运输"章中也准用了一些海上货物运输承运人管货义务制度的规则。例如，其第5.4条在前两项明确指出舱面货、活动物等特殊水路货物管理准用海上货物运输的货物管理规则，以及在第三项强调货损值计算公式和方法也是海上货物运输和水路货物运输所共用。

此后，2019年12月18日发布的《中华人民共和国海商法（修改送审稿）》（简称《海商法（修改送审稿）》）对水路货运承运人管货义务提出了新的修改方案②，这些规定与先前《海商法（修订意见稿）》的内容略有不同。首先，在法律体系上，整个国内水路货运制度被归入"海上货物运输合同"章中，成为该章的一节。这说明《海商法（修改送审稿）》视国内水路货运为海上货物运输之一部分，二者为隶属关系而非《海商法（修订意见稿）》规定的并列关系。其次，《海商法（修改送审稿）》第119条将海运承运人管货义务主客观标准、义务主体、混合原因共同造成货损时承运人仅在其可免责范围内免责等管货义务的核心制度准用于水路货运承运人。而《海商法（修订意见稿）》第5.4条只是对某些特殊货物管理方面准用了海运承运人的相关规定，承运人的大部分管货义务制度仍独立于海运相关规定。可以说，《海商法（修改送审稿）》倾向于通过规则准用突出海上货运与水路货运之间的广泛共性，以促进海上货运承运人和水路货运承运人管货义务制度的统一。

（三）《长江合同》对承运人管货义务制度的探索

前述立法草案的相继出台对《长江合同》许多条款的制定产生了重要影响，该合同的诞生填补了我国国内水路货物运输标准合同的空白，对建

---

① 见《海商法（修订意见稿）》第5.10条第三款第四项。
② 2020年交通运输部《关于提请审议〈中华人民共和国海商法（修改送审稿）〉的请示》，交法发〔2020〕10号。

立完备的国内水路货物运输制度提供了很多新的思路。在承运人管货义务制度的发展完善方面，针对前述水路货物运输实践中出现的问题，《长江合同》进行了许多卓有成效的探索。

第一，受《海商法（修订意见稿）》第5.7条第1款的影响，《长江合同》通过规定承运人具体管货行为进一步完善了管货义务的客观标准，发生争议时便于操作。第二，《长江合同》打破了《货规》的严格责任制，采用完全过错责任制对水路货物承运人给予更为宽松的保护。第三，《长江合同》通过合同附件的形式将管货义务中的附属性义务从合同正文中剥离，简化了合同结构。在区分液货合同、干散货合同与商品车合同各自具体内容以适应长江各流域不同的航道等级、船型标准的同时，[①] 又以相似的合同结构对特殊货物的管理制度进行了专门性规定[②]；既注重地域特色，又尽可能追求各类水路货运市场的统一。第四，在货物的检验、计量方面，《长江合同》在《海商法（修订意见稿）》和《海商法（修改送审稿）》相关修改的基础上进行了初步规定。上述探索既反映了当下长江乃至整个国内水路货物运输实务发展的现状，也在一定程度上揭示了承运人管货义务制度的发展方向。由于《海商法（修订意见稿）》与《海商法（修改送审稿）》中关于水路货物运输承运人义务的规定较少，本文接下来便以《长江合同》中相关的新发展为中心进行细致的考察，分析及探明承运人管货义务制度革新的具体方向。

二、管货义务的客观标准：通过客观标准的新增与调整力求分类适用

管货义务的客观标准是衡量承运人管货义务履行程度的法定要求的总和，依据《货规》第三十二条的规定，水路货物运输承运人履行管货义务的客观标准即为"妥善地装载、搬移、积载、运输、保管、照料和卸载所运货物"。

可以看到，货物的接收和交付并不包含在承运人的管货义务中，原因

---

① 参见刘涛、罗胜平《基于内河航道等级比较的长江航运发展分析》，载《水利水运工程学报》2012年第5期。

② 和通行的集装箱运输合同相比，液货合同、干散货合同、商品车合同的构造具有一定的相似性，均由运输项目、承托双方权利义务、货物交接与验收、货物留置与处分、合同解除、运输费条款、保险条款、违约责任、争议解决等条款构成。

是其作为独立于管货义务的其他义务被单独规定在第五章中。《长江合同》则根据实际情况依货物种类的不同进行了增减：液货合同和干散货合同减少了"七项义务"中的某些标准，集装箱合同完全因袭《货规》的做法，而商品车合同增加了新标准。《长江合同》这一区别货物种类制定不同合同条款的设计理念，体现出实践中管货义务的客观标准逐渐分化的趋势。

（一）新增客观标准——货物交接

货物交接包括货物的接收（即起运地交接验收）和交付（即目的地交接验收），分别构成管货义务的起点和终点。《长江合同》第三章"商品车合同"第三条第二款将货物的交接写入管货义务的基本客观标准，这与《海商法（修订意见稿）》及《海商法（修改送审稿）》相一致。该变化与长江流域货物多式联运的迅速发展有关，[①] 多式联运承运人在运输途中往往会接收新货物，实质上构成了整个多式联运过程中的管货行为的一部分，若依《货规》将货物交接同管货义务分开进行规定实际上不利于综合运输效率的提升。

1. 准备工作标准的细化

货物交接准备工作的新增标准体现在《长江合同》对接收货物准备工作的具体化、细节化方面。

关于普通货物交接准备工作应符合的标准，《货规》第五章并未规定，仅在特殊货物运输中进行了个别规定。第八十一条就集装箱拆装标准这一具体准备工作进行了规定，第八十六条、第八十七条对单元滚装货的检验和接收文件的标准进行了规定。《长江合同》则在几种不同种类的合同条款中都有关于货物交接准备工作标准的规定，[②] 即承运人接收货物前须达验舱、验货、洗舱及承运人在交接文件上签章这些标准，符合前述标准方可进行货物的交接。

关于商品车交接的准备工作，须达到商品车实况同相关交接文件相符这一标准，其目的是保证单位价值较高的商品车运输风险分配明确，保障市场主体的顺利交易。商品车合同第四条通过签发具有证明商品车实时状况的交接文件（如货物运输交接单）来反映商品车交接时的实况。该文件

---

① 参见刘琪、王军丽、周颖等《湖北省道路水路货物运输服务体系建设研究》，载《物流工程与管理》2020年第6期。

② 参见"商品车合同"第四条第一款。

不同于《货规》第六十八条中的货物交付时记录货损状况的货运记录,它涵盖范围较广——不仅包括货运记录的内容,还用于商品车接收;记载的货物状况不限于货损,还包含时间、地点等所有同交接有关的要素。以这种书面货物交接文件为据,承运人或收货人可清楚地了解商品车运输前后的状况,判断商品车是否存在货损。同时,该文件也为法院针对承运人管货行为的调查取证提供了便利。

2. 基本工作标准的丰富

《货规》中货物交接的基本工作标准是基于货物的重量或件数规定的封舱交接和计量交接两种方式,[①]《海商法（修订意见稿）》第 5.17 条也是直接吸收这一标准。《长江合同》基于水路运输实务发展的新需求,对液货与干散货的交接标准做了进一步的丰富。

首先,对接收液货的交接标准的发展分为封舱和计量交接两个方面。在封舱交接方面,《货规》认为承运人的封舱义务只限于封舱行为本身,因而实践中承运人为降低货物交接的时间成本尽可能压缩装卸货时间,往往在货物未完全装入或卸出时即封舱,但托运人无法就这部分未完全装入的货差依《货规》要求承运人赔偿。针对这个问题,《长江合同》第二章液货合同第二条规定封舱前后须达"干舱"标准以保障封舱质量,[②] 更彻底地保障了托运人的合法权益。在计量交接方面,《货规》规定计量交接负责人为托运人和收货人。[③] 但随着我国"薄膜型货舱新技术"[④] 的推广以及液货单船运输量的增多[⑤],船方所运货物多出自不同货方,故实践中常由船方统一负责货物计量以提高交接效率。基于这一实践需求,《长江合同》第二章第二条中的液货合同条款将计量负责人的选任交由当事人约定,并新增了岸罐计量、流量计量和船舱计量这三种交接方式。

其次,对接收干散货基本工作标准的发展方面,《货规》规定散货计

[①] 见《货规》第六十三条、第六十四条。
[②] 《长江合同》第二章"液货合同"第二条第二款强调干舱标准包括形式上要签发"干舱证书"和实质上船舶固定泵系统要达到"无法卸出"的状态。
[③] 见《货规》第六十五条第二款。
[④] 谷林春、何萧:《LNG 船舶液货舱技术市场发展现状》,载《船舶物资与市场》2019 年第 7 期。
[⑤] 中华人民共和国交通运输部:《交通运输部发布〈2020 年上半年国内沿海货运船舶运力分析报告〉》,载《交通财会》2020 年第 10 期。

量交接无法计算货重时可以船舶水尺量数代替,① 该规定因过于片面已不能适应当下多种干散货交接方式相结合的航运实践,故《长江合同》对此进行了更新,② 包括在宏观上新增原船原转、原装原卸、封舱③的交接方式,以及在微观上新增以件数④方式进行计量交接。

此外,《长江合同》规定接收货物还须达到"合理取样和损耗"标准。⑤ 取样是货物装船前承托双方对货物的一小部分所进行的分离和保管工作⑥,目的在于为日后的管货义务纠纷提供物证,保障责任分配公平公正。取样条款是专门针对液货合同设计的,原因是液货化学性质较易改变。损耗是指运输中货物的自然损失,系因货物自身而非承运人过错产生。损耗条款是针对无固定形态的液货和干散货设计的,对这两种合同均可适用。

3. 到货通知义务的细化

到货通知义务,是指水路货运承运人在货物到港后向收货人发出的要求收货人提货的义务。作为承运人交货义务的起点,该义务实质是一种"建立在诚实信用原则基础上的附随义务"⑦,故无论该义务是否有法律规定,承运人一般都要履行。《货规》对到货通知义务标准的规定较全面,而《长江合同》的规定较少。此处主要以《货规》为基础,探究到货通知义务的发展方向。

《货规》第三十八条对到货通知的时间标准和方式标准进行了详细规定,未来立法可予继承。但该规定无法完全涵盖当下及日后到货通知义务出现的新情况、新问题。航海科技的发展使承运人在运输过程中管理货物的方法愈加科学,运输途中因不当管理行为产生的货损日益减少,反而是到货通知迟延产生的货损经常导致承运人管货争议的发生,⑧ 然而《货规》并未将通知迟延规定为货损的原因之一。司法实践中,通知的时间因

---

① 见《货规》第十三条。
② 见《长江合同》第四章"干散货合同"第二条。
③ 《货规》第六十五条虽规定了封舱交接,但这一规定仅适用于液体散货,对液体散货封舱交接的具体规定能否准用于干散货,《货规》未作规定。
④ 该"件数"系散货分割包装后的单位数而非干散货自身数量。
⑤ 见《长江合同》第二章"液货合同"第二条、第四章"干散货合同"第二条。
⑥ 参见陈录《矿石的化学取样与化学分析》,载《化工管理》2014 年第 27 期。
⑦ 刘冰:《水路货物运输合同中承运人的到货通知义务》,载《水运管理》2006 年第 1 期。
⑧ 参见刘冰《水路货物运输合同中承运人的到货通知义务》,载《水运管理》2006 年第 1 期。

通信技术的进步已不再成为取证的难题，故通知迟延与货损之间的因果关系才是取证的关键。我国法院在很多相关案例中普遍认为，除免责事项外，通知延迟导致的货损应由承运人负责，因为通知迟延并不符合管货义务"妥善"这一主观标准。无论通知迟延由何种因素引起，承运人都应在能够克服或避免该因素的情况下"妥善地"履行到货通知义务。①

（二）其他管货义务客观标准的调整

除去上述客观标准的新增外，《长江合同》也根据实务发展针对部分货物的管货义务标准进行了调整甚至降低。如商品车保管与照料义务标准就有所淡化。在《货规》出台前，制约我国商品车水路运输的主因还是承运人对货物的安全监管水平，而这种安全监管需要以一定的科技水平作支撑②。在《货规》施行后，《长江合同》发布前，我国的通信、定位技术不断地相互融合、相互配合、相互促进，③ 故运输途中商品车保管、照料的技术难度逐步降低，承运人管货时达到"保管""照料"的标准不再成为商品车管货义务发展的焦点。《长江合同》在商品车合同的条款设计中顺应了这一趋势，将商品车保管、照料的义务标准从合同正文中抹除，通过另设"商品车物流质量管理规则（附件）"的形式规范承运人对商品车的保管和照料的工作。由此可见，《长江合同》在商品车合同的保管与照料义务制度中注入了更多的意思自治可能性。

另外，在承运人管理液货义务的客观标准方面也有所调整。《货规》第三十二条对管货义务的一般性规定并没有区分货物的种类，但由于液货只能以流动的形式进出货舱，即"搬移"和"积载"这两项管货行为在实际液货运输中并不存在，故《长江合同》的液货合同条款将这两个标准从液货管货义务的客观标准中删除了。

（三）对管货义务客观标准立法的建议

通过上述对《长江合同》中水路承运人管货义务客观标准相关规定的

---

① 参见原告（反诉被告）冼伟东诉被告（反诉原告）深圳市港顺意达物流有限公司通海水域货物运输合同纠纷案，北海海事法院（2014）海商初字第41号民事判决书。
② 参见史克功《滚装货物安全研究》，载《山东航海学会、山东海事局2007年度优秀论文专刊》，2007年11月。
③ 参见王燕青、黄皓、赵艳《无线通讯系统定位技术的研究》，载《计算机产品与流通》2020年第5期。

梳理探讨，结合与过去《货规》规定的对比分析，可以看到前者在细化和完善标准方面所做的努力是值得将来的相关立法借鉴的。在肯定这一发展趋势的基础之上，笔者认为还有如下三点也应在立法中予以考虑。

首先，承运人在交货时应符合催告义务标准。《货规》第四十一条结合了《国家经济委员会关于港口、车站无法交付货物的处理办法》的规定，针对催告义务的主体、催告时间间隔、催告的最多次数、最后一次催告完成后的义务等标准设置了较为完备的承运人催告的客观标准，建议在《海商法》的修改中予以参照。《长江合同》第一章"集装箱合同"第四条第七项虽有类似规定，但相比之下，《货规》更为详细。此外，《货规》第四十一条仍有不足，未规定承运人单次催告的生效方式。故本文建议对催告标准的完善可在《货规》基础上，参照《民法典》第一百三十七条及其立法目的，[1] 增加单次催告的生效方式——承运人的催告到达相对人时生效，以兼顾催告人和相对人的利益。

其次，在承运人到货通知义务中，因承运人到货通知延迟产生的货损应当由承运人负责。如本文前述，《货规》并未将通知迟延规定为货损的原因之一，而通知时间点在通信技术高度发达的今天已不难确定。因此，若承运人的通知晚于法律规定或合同约定的收货时间到达收货人并造成货损，则该部分损失应当由承运人承担。此外，若因承运人自身原因造成通知错误（包括通知对象和通知内容）并产生货损，即使通知的时间毫无延迟，但客观上却给收货人收货增加了困难，为解决该种困难所需的时间仍会造成收货人无法及时提货，实质上亦属"广义"的通知延迟，故本文建议由承运人自身原因所致的到货通知错误而引发的货损也应当由该承运人承担。

最后，承运人可依实际情况灵活确认收货人的提货权。在海上货物运输中，提单是收货人向承运人提货的关键凭证，无单放货被司法实践普遍地认定为违法或侵权行为[2]。而从《货规》第六十七条规定看，水路货运贯彻的提货规则是凭"身份证件"提货，即当收货人出示身份信息表明他是托运人指定的人，那承运人就应当放货。但以身份证件提货并不利于货物运输途中的转卖，因为货物流转往往需要签订一份新的运输合同和制作一份新的运单。过去我国国内水路运输范围有限、运程短，货物在运输过

---

[1] 参见黄薇《中华人民共和国民法典释义》（上卷），法律出版社 2020 年版，第 273 页。
[2] 参见司玉琢《海商法》（第四版），法律出版社 2018 年版，第 106 页。

程中转卖鲜有发生。随着我国内河航道的拓宽和纵深①，水路货运量逐渐增多，运程逐步拉长，这为运输途中的货物周转提供了条件。故笔者认为，未来交付货物义务可以向着凭单提货制度与身份证明制度相结合的方向发展。即如果货物运输途中未发生转卖交易，则收货人可凭身份证件向承运人提货；如果预定货物运输途中将发生转卖交易，则托运人可与承运人约定凭单放货，以提高货物的周转效率。

三、管货义务的主观标准：借助客观的货物检验破除认定困境

承运人管货义务的主观标准通常指"态度和责任心上的要求"②，《长江合同》将其规定为"妥善地、谨慎地"③。与客观标准的单一性和确定性不同，主观标准是基于承运人主观心理状态的标准，在司法实践中往往难以判定。

在我国的司法实践中，法院一般通过货物的检验结果，并结合承运人管理货物的客观行为来证明义务的履行是否符合主观标准。④ 货物检验的结果主要以法院指定或当事人约定的权威检验机构出具的检验证书（如保险公估报告）为主要表现形式。检验证书是法院裁判的重要依据，它的证明力关系到货损事实的存在与否，⑤ 同时它也是判断承运人履行管货义务是否达到主观标准的关键。

（一）检验证书的证明效力问题

在司法实践中，货损的程度往往是承托双方当事人争议的焦点之一。为请求法院支持自己的诉请，双方当事人往往会各自委托合法的检验机构对货物进行检验，从而出现"同货不同检"的冲突局面，对法院判断承运

---

① 参见现代港口物流网《〈中原城市群发展规划〉加大内河港口、航道基建》，见 http://www.xdgkwl.com/cj/info_28.aspx？itemid=3037，2021 年 2 月 13 日访问。
② 杨芳、刘冬花、胡丹：《论承运人管货义务的标准》，载《当代经理人》2006 年第 9 期。
③ 见《长江合同》第一章"集装箱合同"第四条第四款。
④ 江阴市宇联运输有限公司与中国人民财产保险股份有限公司武汉市分公司运输合同纠纷案，湖北省高级人民法院（2022）鄂民终 85 号民事判决书。
⑤ 中国太平洋财产保险股份有限公司北京分公司与上海中远海运油品运输有限公司保险人代位求偿权纠纷案，最高人民法院（2020）最高法民申 5646 号民事裁定书。

人履行管货义务的程度造成了很大困难。《货规》和《长江合同》都没有对证书间效力冲突的问题作出规定,因此法院多通过法律论证的方式进行裁判。虽然法律论证下的裁判结果仍需基于现行有效的法律框架作出,[①]但由于其大量采用法律以外的因素,从而极有可能使得"禁止法官滥用自由裁量权"这一目的落空。所以仍有必要制定明确的、有弹性的合法检验证书的认定规则。

参照(2019)琼72民初178号、(2022)沪民终298号民事判决书[②]的判决理由,可以看出就这些证书的证明效力问题,在法院审理中主要考察的是如下三个方面的因素:一是同一机构多次货物检验的方法相似度。如果用同种方法经多次检验得到的结论相同或高度相似,则该检验报告应当被认定为合法有效,也即具有充分的证明力。二是各证书所必备的内容。在(2022)沪民终298号民事判决书中,法院强调货损发生时间不构成检验报告的必备条款,在(2019)琼72民初178号民事判决书中,法院则依照当事人约定的方式对检验报告的证明效力进行了认定,但上述案件的检验报告均包括货损原因和损失金额。故本文认为,货损原因和损失金额应当是检验报告的必备内容,缺少该内容的检验报告不具有真实性,其他内容则可以根据个案争议的具体事项、依当事人约定确定。三是证书出具人的主观心理状态。如果证书出具人存在故意隐瞒、拖延、篡改检验结果或者其他妨害执业的独立性和公正性的行为,那么该证书就应当被认定为无效证书。

(二)《货规》和《长江合同》的对货物检验的相关规定

《货规》第七十二条仅对承运人向收货人交付货物时所进行的货物检验做了规定,这些规定涉及检验的约定、检验费用和相对人的配合义务。它基本涵盖了除检验证书的问题外管货义务主观标准证明制度的全部内容,但不足之处在于这一规定只适用于承运人向收货人交付货物,并不包括承运人接收托运人货物时所进行的检验。《长江合同》中仅液货合同第二条存在承运人从托运人处接收货物进行运输这一环节的相关规定,但仅

---

① 参见雷磊《法律渊源、法律论证与法治》,载《社会科学战线》2023年第1期。
② 上诉人上海中谷物流股份有限公司与被上诉人中国人民财产保险股份有限公司天津市分公司海上、通海水域货物运输合同纠纷案,上海市高级人民法院(2022)沪民终298号民事判决书。

明确了检验机构的选择以承托双方的合同约定为主,而在检验的时间、地点和其他运输环节的检验方面,《长江合同》并无明确规定。这种空白并非偶然为之,而是目前国内水路货运市场现状使然。由此可见,《货规》和《长江合同》对货物检验制度的规定各有侧重。前者侧重承运人向收货人交货时的检验,后者侧重承运人从托运人接收货物时的检验。

(三) 对管货义务主观标准立法的建议

从上述对比分析可以看到,《货规》和《长江合同》在宏观上均未从承运人的整个管货环节出发来制定货物检验规则,检验规则的适用范围仍十分有限;在微观上两者亦对货物检验证书效力及其相关问题采取了回避态度,但因其所生的纠纷在我国既往判例中已有所体现。为弥补前述阙漏,本文提出以下参考性意见。

首先,对于水路货物承运人接收货物和交付货物两个环节的检验,如前所述《货规》和《长江合同》两者的规定各有侧重,出于优化法律结构和提高法律适用效率的目的,本文认为可以兼取两者之长、将接收和交付两个环节的货物检验进行统一规定。

其次,对于水路运输货物检验证书的证明效力问题,可参考海上货物运输相关制度。在国际海上货物运输领域,业界通过出台《WTO/TBT协定》[①],建立了各国商品检验技术标准化体系使得合法的检验证书具有唯一性。水路货物运输领域亦可参考此商品检验技术标准化体系,将符合该体系要求列为检验证书合法性的形式要件,从而解决水路货物检验证书之间的效力冲突问题。

再次,对于货物检验首先要有明确的、权威的检验机构和具体的检验时间与地点,这是承运人进行货物检验的基本条件,未来立法应予以明确规定。另外,货物检验的费用计算标准、分配主体,托运人对检验的配合程度等因素都会影响检验工作的质量,故也应由法律进行规定;而对检验方法、争议管辖等问题在不违反法律强行性规定的情况下可以允许合同双方自由约定。

最后,货物的实际状况是唯一的,但出自不同检验机构的检验结果可

---

① 《WTO/TBT 协定》即《世界贸易组织/技术性贸易壁垒协定》(*Agreement on Technical Barriers to Trade of the World Trade Organization*),专门协调国际贸易中有关技术法规、标准和合格评定程序方面的有关问题。

能不尽相同,因此在多个不同的"检验结果"并存时,法律还应当明确检验结果有效的要件。

综上所述,笔者认为将《长江合同》中"液货合同"第二条规定同《货规》第七十二条的规定相结合,并在此基础上进一步细化管货义务主观标准的证明问题,是未来管货义务证明制度发展的新方向。

四、违反管货义务的责任:责任减轻制度 与完全过错责任制下的利益再平衡

《货规》废止前,我国承运人管货义务制度长期存在着责任分配不公正、责任减免不到位等问题,这些问题都是制约承运人法律责任制度发展的因素。《货规》废止后,如何让承运人责任的减轻和免除制度朝着公平化的方向发展重新成为课题。

(一)责任减轻的公平化

承运人违反管货义务时,法院一般会根据承运人的主观过错程度和托运人是否有过错来决定是否减轻承运人责任。尽管货损是因承运人违反管货义务直接导致,但若托运人也违反了合理减损义务,① 法院多判定承托双方按各自的过失比例来分担货损。然而,《货规》和《长江合同》并未对承运人违反管货义务后责任减轻的具体制度做出规定。《货规》被废止后,合理确定承运人责任减轻的幅度成为平衡船货双方利益的重点问题。②

影响承托双方过失比例的因素有很多,而它们的占比在每个案件中又不尽相同,因此在发生货损时,无论是法律还是合同都无法准确预测出绝对公平的责任分担方式。换言之,承运人管货义务责任的减轻幅度受承运人的主观过错程度的影响,而承运人的主观过错程度并非一成不变,它会随具体案情的变化发生变化。而影响承运人违反管货义务的各种变量——如违约成本、违约时间、货损价值等,则可以通过对现有案例数据和法律规则进行概括、总结而后加以推理,以多元线性回归法确定责任减轻幅度

---

① 见《中华人民共和国民法典》第五百九十一条第一款。
② 参见李向明、姜淇《〈国内水路货物运输规则〉被废止后的影响和注意事项》,载《科学中国人》2016年第11期。

与上述变量之间的关系。① 随着人工智能科学和法律心理学的发展,② 该方法在未来或可弥补法学作为一种社会科学在探究行为人的主观心理状态、确定行为人的过错程度时所面临的短板。③

(二)责任免除的公平化

《货规》和《长江合同》中的承运人免责条款既有区别,也有联系。《货规》第四十八条采用严格责任制,《长江合同》则是采取完全的过错责任制,即非由于承运人及其受雇人、代理人的过错造成的货损,承运人不承担赔偿责任。

《货规》与《长江合同》对于承运人归责原则的不同规定具有如下的历史原因。长期以来,水路货物运输承运人在履行管货义务的同时还要考虑社会、公益因素,如避免在管货时破坏国内水利工程设施和水域生态环境等,因此《货规》对水路货物运输承运人的责任承担作出了较高的要求。再加上《货规》囿于自身行政规章的位阶,第四十八条只能沿用原《合同法》第三百一十一条确立的严格责任制。这使得本就风险颇高的管货行为又受到法律上更为严格的限制。《货规》废止后,鉴于水路货物运输限于沿海、内河,故风险、成本整体依旧低于国际海上货物运输,为了避免对承运人过度"松绑",《长江合同》没有直接引入《海商法》第五十一条实行不完全的过错责任制,而是在取消因承运人过错引起的免责事项(如航海过失)基础之上实行完全的过错责任制。

《长江合同》的选择在一定程度上反映了水路货物运输承运人管货责任的免除制度逐步趋向公平化。首先,由于目前我国船舶在国内水域的航海技术较《货规》颁行之初已然取得长足进步,进一步降低了承运人运输货物过程中所面临的船舶技术风险,因此目前不宜采用不完全过错责任制,即对承运人的有过错管货行为予以豁免。其次,我国对国内水域水利开发和生态环境的高度重视决定了水路货物运输承运人履行管货义务将在一个较长的历史时期内承担更多的社会责任,即因承运人管货不当(如运

---

① 多元线性回归方法能够科学地揭示单个因变量(责任减轻幅度)与多个自变量之间的复杂联系,在法学领域特别是确定各地海事赔偿责任限额具有很高的实用价值。参见南风艳《我国水路货物运输承运人责任制度的研究》(学位论文),大连海事大学 2003 年,第 69 页以下。

② 参见杜文静、刘海《贝叶斯人工智能的概率证成》,载《科学技术哲学研究》2022 年第 4 期。

③ 参见贾治辉、孔熹《交叉学科范式下"法庭科学"的建设方法与路径》,载《证据科学》2023 年第 1 期。

输过程中泄漏危险品货物）造成水利设施受损或者水域环境污染，承运人也要承担责任。如此承运人在管货时则会尽力避免对水利设施和水域生态造成破坏，从而达到保护生态环境的目的。最后，对承运人管货义务实行完全的过错责任制也是为了反垄断的需要。由于航运具有自身运输规模大、经营成本高、统一开放性强的特点，① 无论是国际航运还是国内航运，各航运企业间都有着紧密合作——如集装箱共享、物流信息共享等，这种联营模式使得承运人的运费议价能力显著提升。如果说国际航运巨头间的合作或许受限于不同法域之间的贸易壁垒，那么单一法域内航运企业间的合作相比较而言则更为简单易行，所以国内水路货物运输市场更易出现垄断集团。反观身处托运人地位的货主，仍旧以中小货主为主，② 其运费议价能力也处于弱势。因此对承运人管货提出更高的标准，也有助于保障广大中小货主的利益，保障国民经济平稳运行。从这一点来看，虽然国内水路货物运输法属于私法，但它依旧具有超越私法范畴的政策工具属性。综上所述，完全过错责任制较不完全的过错责任制更有利于维系承托双方的利益平衡，以及保障货损责任的公平分摊。

结　论

经上述分析，本文认为水路货物运输承运人管货义务制度的发展呈现如下特征。

《海商法（修订意见稿）》和《海商法（修改送审稿）》对水路货物运输承运人管货义务的主观标准、客观标准、免责条款等内容的修改是以广泛征求社会各界意见为基础的，以水路货运市场的需求为方向所进行的局部修改，时效性鲜明而针对性不足。这些修改体现出我国当下水路货运承运人管货义务制度发展具有实践导向性和针对性的特征。为保证自身的法律实用性，《长江合同》在设计条款时将《海商法（修订意见稿）》和《海商法（修改送审稿）》中与管货义务有关的规则作为重要参照文件之一。故两者在管货义务的主要规定上具有一定的沿袭性。

---

① 参见夏旭丽、李天生《航运联盟反垄断规范竞合论：企业联营理论的比较考察》，载《中国海商法研究》2022 年第 4 期。

② 参见夏伊航《海商法中的利益平衡问题——以〈海商法〉第四章为主视角》，载《财富时代》2022 年第 11 期。

《长江合同》在《海商法（修订意见稿）》《海商法（修改送审稿）》的相关规定的基础上，对水路货物运输承运人管货义务条款进行了精心设计，体现在以下四个方面：第一，合同条款相对公平公正，通过结合新旧制度合理分配承托双方的利益、负担——在保留《货规》中管货义务的基本客观标准、免责等实用性制度的同时，对管货的主观标准、调查取证、责任认定问题做出了首创性规定；第二，合同内容比较完备简练，具有宏观的指导性和微观的可操作性；第三，合同条款具有针对性和引导性——针对不同货物种类分别设置，并将表格填制与行文空白相结合，在积极引导合同双方约定方向的同时，允许双方根据实际情况进行意思自治；第四，合同具有鲜明的地方特色——根据货物种类设置不同的标准合同，以应对长江复杂水系不同航道等级对各类货船通航标准的限制。

基于水路货物运输承运人管货义务制度呈现的上述发展状况，本文对于水路货运实践中承托双方的缔约方案及相关立法方向提出如下两方面的建议。

一是在缔约方面，实践中缔结水路货运合同的双方可考虑直接使用《长江合同》管货义务条款或以其条款作为参照。但《长江合同》作为无法可依时期适用范围有限的标准合同文本，其条款尚存不详尽之处，如在货物检验、管货义务标准的证明、货物交付催告、收货人提货权的确认等方面均未涉及。故承托双方使用《长江合同》时应留意其不足并作相应修改，也可以合同附件的形式对某一问题单独约定。此外，若水路货运主体及其主管部门能将标准合同条款与具体实践相结合，助力该合同成为未来建设全国统一大市场的国家级水路货物运输标准合同，则可进一步节约缔约成本，提高缔约效率。

二是在立法方面，本文认为管货义务制度的立法总体上可以《长江合同》作为参考，结合我国海商法的修改草案，逐步建立符合我国水路货运市场和司法实践状况的管货义务制度。具体而言，首先，可依托统一的货物检验标准和完备的检验程序来实现对管货义务主观标准公正、客观的证明；其次，可借助具体的责任归结程序和公平的责任认定方式来平衡承托双方的权利和义务；再次，可区分货物的种类以制定符合货物自身运输特性的管货义务规则；最后，建议制定全国通行性的、针对性较强的国内水路货物运输标准合同文本和运输法规，并纳入新近由国家市场监督管理总局建立的合同示范文本库以供查阅参考。

船员在船工作关系性质认定

张艺骞[*]

摘要：随着我国航运业的不断发展，与船员有关的纠纷日益增多，司法实践中将船员在船工作关系识别为劳动关系的案例寥寥无几，这不仅影响涉外案件中冲突规范的正确适用，而且影响冲突规范的适用与实体法适用的一致性，还影响船员劳动权益的依法保护。因此，船员在船工作关系中的性质认定显得尤为重要。根据劳动与劳务的辨析以及识别劳动关系的三个要件，所有船员在船工作关系应符合劳动关系的主体资格、劳动管理、业务组成，并应落实船员与船东或者船员劳务派遣机构之间的船员劳动关系，以保护船员权益。

关键词：船员在船工作关系　劳动关系　劳务关系

Identification of the Nature of Working Relationship of Seamen on Board

Zhang Yiqian

Abstract: With the continuous development of China's shipping industry, the disputes related to seamen are increasing day by day, and there are few cases that identify the working relationship of seamen on board as labor relationship in judicial practice, which not only affects the correct application of conflict norms in foreign-related cases, but also affects the consistency between the application of conflict norms and the application of substantive law, and affects the legal protection of seamen's labor rights and interests. Therefore, it is particularly important to identify the nature of the working relationship of seamen on board. Based on the discrimination of labor and service and the identification of

---

[*] 张艺骞：浙江工商大学人文与传播学院教学秘书，华南师范大学法学硕士。

the three elements of labor relations, this paper holds that the working relationship of seamen on board conforms to the subject qualification, labor management and business composition of labor relations, and implements the labor relationship between seamen and ship owners or seamen labor dispatch agencies to protect the rights and interests of seamen.

Key words: working relationship of seamen on board; labor relationship; service relations

一、问题的提出

2021年1月10日,索硕与福万通公司(香港)在台州签订船员上船就业协议,约定索硕到福万通公司经营的"中福111"冷藏船上担任实习水手,聘用期限为8个月,后索硕离船,发生了船员在船工作期间船员劳务费争议。因福万通公司系在香港特别行政区注册的法人,所以该案为一起涉外案件。一审宁波海事法院在法律选择过程中没有特别明确的认定这是一份劳动合同还是劳务合同[①],直接适用当事人选择的法律即我国内地法律,但是在实体法部分适用的是《中华人民共和国劳动合同法》(简称《劳动合同法》)。[②] 二审浙江省高级人民法院在法律选择部分认为"各方当事人均同意适用我国内地法律",也就是适用当事人选择的法。根据法院在判决书中适用的《最高人民法院关于审理涉船员纠纷案件若干问题的规定》第十七条,可得知法院将该船员在船工作关系视为"船员与船舶所有人之间的劳务合同",并非"船员与船舶所有人之间的劳动合同",所以才会适用当事人选择的法。但在实体法部分,法院仍然适用了《劳动合同法》,而非劳务合同应当适用的《中华人民共和国民法典》(简称《民法典》)合同编,造成了实体法与冲突法的不一致。因此产生的问题是,船

---

① 《中华人民共和国涉外民事关系法律适用法》对劳动合同的法律适用做了不同于一般合同法律适用的规定,没有赋予当事人合意选法的权利。该法第四十三条规定,"劳动合同,适用劳动者工作地法律;难以确定劳动者工作地的,适用用人单位主营业地法律。劳务派遣,可以适用劳务派出地法律"。

② 索硕与舟山市四通船员服务有限公司等船员劳务合同纠纷,(2022)浙民终414号民事判决书:"参照涉外民事关系法律适用法的规定,当事人可以选择涉外民事关系适用的法律,庭审中各方当事人明确选择适用国内法,故本案适用《中华人民共和国劳动合同法》《中华人民共和国海员外派管理规定》等法律法规。"

员在船工作关系到底属于劳动关系还是劳务关系?

在理论界,船员在船工作关系性质之争未止;在实践中,不乏船东公司以"船员劳务合同"为名,规避应承担的法律责任。2016年最高人民法院首次在司法解释中提出了"船员劳动合同"的概念并将其与"船员劳务合同"一同纳入海事法院的案件受理范围①,但最高人民法院并没有对船员劳动合同与船员劳务合同进行区分,模糊了船员在船工作关系的劳动属性。本文以劳动关系与劳务关系的辨析作为起点,进而提出劳动关系的认定标准,明确船员在船工作关系均具备劳动属性。

二、劳动关系与劳务关系辨析

明确劳动关系及劳务关系的概念,是辨析两者关系的基础。劳动关系是指劳动者与用人单位之间的,为开展工作过程而建立的社会关系,其中一方以供给劳动力来获取报酬,另一方将劳动力同自己的生产资料结合在一起。② 而劳务关系是指两个或者更多的平等主体彼此之间的经济关系,他们围绕劳务有关事项以同等的价值展开互换③。劳务关系有广义和狭义之分,广义的劳务关系包括委托关系、承揽关系等;狭义的劳务关系仅指雇佣关系。本文所指的劳务关系为狭义的劳务关系。

区分劳动关系与劳务关系具有重要的意义。不同于劳务关系,在劳动关系中,用人单位比劳动者具有更多的经济权力和社会权力。在这种的权力结构下,劳动者往往处于更加脆弱的地位。为了平衡用人单位和劳动者之间的力量,必须采取措施保护劳动者权益。因此我国实体法和冲突法都针对劳动合同做出了许多与一般合同(包括劳务合同)不同的特殊规定。在实体法中,劳务合同是一般的民事合同,适用《民法典》合同编;劳动合同属于特殊民事合同,适用《劳动合同法》。在冲突法中也是如此。劳务合同作为一般民事合同,在法律选择上应当根据《中华人民共和国涉外民事关系法律适用法》(简称《法律适用法》)第四十一条冲突规范来确定所适用的法律,如果准据法为我国法律,那么在实体法上应当受到《民

---

① 《最高人民法院关于海事法院受理案件范围的规定》第二项"海商合同纠纷案件"之24"船员劳动合同、劳务合同(含船员劳务派遣协议)项下与船员登船、在船服务、离船遣返相关的报酬给付及人身伤亡赔偿纠纷案件"。
② 参见王全兴《劳动法》,法律出版社2017年版,第53页。
③ 参见杨德敏《论劳动关系与劳务关系》,载《河北法学》2005年第7期,第140页。

法典》中关于一般合同的相关条款约束；而劳动合同作为特殊的民事合同，在法律选择上应当根据《法律适用法》第四十三条专门冲突规范来确定所适用的法律，如果准据法为我国法律，那么在实体法上必须受到《中华人民共和国劳动法》（简称《劳动法》）和《劳动合同法》的相关条款约束。对劳动关系和劳务关系区分的不同理解，在非涉外案件中会直接影响实体判决结果，在涉外案件中还可能会通过准据法的确定间接影响实体判决结果。如何区分劳动关系与劳务关系对于船员在船工作关系的识别及其法律适用至关重要。

劳务关系，与劳动关系类似，也是一种以劳动为标的的法律关系[①]，两者的表现形式十分相似，都是一方提供劳动力，接受劳动力的一方会支付相应的报酬。但是，二者之间仍有许多实质性区别。一般来说，劳动关系和劳务关系区分的标准有以下四个：

第一，主体资格不同。在劳动关系中，双方的主体资格是确定的，提供劳动的一方必定是自然人，接受劳动的一方必定是用人单位即组织，包括《民法典》中规定的法人、非法人组织以及个体工商户。在劳务关系中则不然，双方的主体资格是不确定的：提供劳动的一方既可以是自然人，也可以是法人或者其他组织；接受劳动的一方也不一定非得是组织。换言之，除了组织和自然人之间的关系，劳务关系还可以是自然人之间的关系或者法人之间的关系。

第二，管理方式不同。在劳动关系中，提供劳动的一方必须遵守接受劳动的一方依法制定有关工作的内部规章制度，并且需要从事接受劳动一方组织的有偿工作。也就是说，劳动者受用人单位的劳动管理，比如工作时间和工作地点的规定、绩效考核等；同时，用人单位也要承担相应的义务，合理的保障劳动者权益，比如为劳动者缴纳社会保险、不得违反当地法律关于最低工资的规定等。而在劳务关系中，接受劳动的一方使提供劳动一方得到的是自主管理与职业自由，提供劳动的一方可以根据接受劳动一方的要求自主决定是否工作、工作时间地点或者工作的量，同时接受劳动一方一般不必承担劳动关系中所要承担的义务。

第三，劳动给付不同。在劳动关系中，劳动者被安排在用人单位的经营组织体系之内，出卖的是劳动力，劳动者在工作中供给的劳动力应当归属于用人单位，是用人单位经营业务不可缺少的一部分，而该劳动所组成

[①] 参见王全兴《劳动法》，法律出版社2017年版，第140页。

的业务是用人单位的主要业务还是辅助业务在所不问，只要用人单位需要提供该项业务即可。而在劳务关系中，提供劳动一方的劳动力仍然归属于自己，其所出卖的仅仅是劳动成果。提供劳动一方的劳动与接受劳动一方的业务不一定具有关联性，不是接受劳动一方业务的组成部分，双方的运作体系是相互独立的。

第四，劳动报酬不同。在劳动关系中，用人单位按照国家法律的相关规定以及劳动合同相关条款和工作条件给付报酬，其中包括持续定期支付的工资、社会保险、福利等。而劳务关系中的劳动报酬是在自由的市场经济下，劳动者所提供劳动商品的价格，仅由双方当事人协商同意而确定，国家法律并没有对其进行强制性规定。

三、船员劳动关系构成分析

在船员在船工作关系中，劳动关系和劳务关系是非此即彼的关系。相较于劳务关系，劳动关系更加特殊、重要。劳动和社会保障部《关于确立劳动关系有关事项的通知》（简称《通知》）中的第一条①明确规定构成劳动关系的三个实质要件：主体资格、劳动管理、业务组成。同理，在船员在船工作关系中识别劳动关系也可遵循这三个要件。

（一）船员在船工作关系之主体资格

劳动关系的主体主要包括劳动者和用人单位两方，船员劳动关系也不例外。此外，在船员市场中存在大量的劳务派遣，所以劳务派遣单位也是船员劳动关系中的重要主体。

1. 船员符合劳动关系中的劳动者主体资格

我国的法律并未对劳动者进行过界定，根据《劳动法》《劳动合同法》等法律、行政法规的相关规定，认定劳动者需考虑以下三个因素：一是年

---

① 劳动和社会保障部《关于确立劳动关系有关事项的通知》第一条："用人单位招用劳动者未订立书面劳动合同，但同时具备下列情形的，劳动关系成立。（一）用人单位和劳动者符合法律、法规规定的主体资格；（二）用人单位依法制定的各项劳动规章制度适用于劳动者，劳动者受用人单位的劳动管理，从事用人单位安排的有报酬的劳动；（三）劳动者提供的劳动是用人单位业务的组成部分。"

龄。根据《劳动法》第十五条①，我国对劳动者最低就业年龄规定为十六周岁。根据《中华人民共和国船员条例》（简称《船员条例》）第五条②，年满十八周岁（在船实习、见习人员年满十六周岁）才能申请船员适任证书，而《船员条例》第四条③要求船员必须获得船员适任证书，所以船员最低就业年龄为十八周岁。国际劳工组织的《2006年海事劳工公约》（简称《海事劳工公约》）也对船员就业的最低年龄进行了规定。根据《海事劳工公约》规则和守则中的标题一规则1.1标准A1.1④可得知，《海事劳工公约》规定海员就业的最低年龄为十六周岁。综上所述，无论是国际公约还是国内法，对船员最低就业年龄的要求都符合《劳动法》对劳动者最低就业年龄要求。二是健康状况。劳动者的劳动能力与劳动者的健康状况有关。由于船员在船舶上工作，工作地点较为特殊，故对健康状况要求较高。《船员条例》第五条规定船员取得适任证书需要符合相应的健康要求。《海事劳工公约》规则和守则中的标题一规则1.2⑤对海员的健康状况做出规定，以确保其适合履行海上职责。三是职业资格。不同工作对劳动者的职业资格要求不同。船员也需要有相应的职业资格。虽然《中华人民共和国海商法》（简称《海商法》）没有对船员的职业资格做出具体的规定，但在《船员条例》中有相关规定。《船员条例》第五条规定："船员应当依照本条例的规定取得相应的船员适任证书。"同样，《海事劳工公约》也对船员的职业资格进行了规定。根据《海事劳工公约》规则和守则中的标

---

① 《劳动法》第十五条："禁止用人单位招用未满十六周岁的未成年人。文艺、体育和特种工艺单位招用未满十六周岁的未成年人，必须遵守国家有关规定，并保障其接受义务教育的权利。"
② 《船员条例》第五条："船员应当依照本条例的规定取得相应的船员适任证书。申请船员适任证书，应当具备下列条件：（一）年满18周岁（在船实习、见习人员年满16周岁）且初次申请不超过60周岁；（二）符合船员任职岗位健康要求；（三）经过船员基本安全培训。"
③ 《船员条例》第四条："本条例所称船员，是指依照本条例的规定取得船员适任证书的人员，包括船长、高级船员、普通船员。"
④ 《海事劳工公约》规则和守则标题一规则1.1标准A1.1："应禁止任何16岁以下的人员受雇、受聘或到船上工作。"
⑤ 《海事劳工公约》规则和守则标题一规则1.2："目的：确保所有海员的健康状况适合履行其海上职责。1.除非海员的健康状况经证明适合履行其职责，否则不得上船工作。2.只有在本守则规定的情况下才允许例外。"

题一规则1.3①，海员必须经过严格培训并有在船上履行其职责的资格。综合以上三个条件，船员符合我国法律体系对劳动者的认定。

2. 船东和船员劳务派遣机构符合劳动关系中的用人单位主体资格

"用人单位"这一术语，是指具备用人的身份、安排劳动者参加社会工作且定期给予劳动者相应报酬收入的用工主体。② 依照《劳动法》以及《劳动合同法》的规定，用人单位囊括各种组织，比如企业、民办非企业单位、个体经济组织、政府机关、社会团体等。

船东包括船舶所有人、船舶管理人、船舶经营人、光船承租人等船舶实际使用者。虽然《海事劳工公约》第二条第一款（j）③ 表明船东既可能是组织也可能是个人即自然人，但是船东基本服务于海上商业，商业特点十分明显，它不包括大多数形式的休闲划船。④ 在我国法律体系下，根据《民法典》第五十四条，自然人想要从事工商经营活动就一定要依法登记为个体工商户。⑤ 因此，我国船东应当是指包含船舶所有人、船舶经营人和光船承租人等在内的一切以船舶为载体从事海上运输经营的公司、企业、个体工商户或其他组织。总而言之，无论是何种形式，船东都具备了我国法律下组织的形式，有资格成为《劳动法》以及《劳动合同法》规定的用人单位。

船员劳务派遣机构主要负责劳务派遣下的船员招募与管理，为船东提供更加专业化的船员管理服务，《海事劳工公约》将其称为"海员招募和安置服务机构"。船员劳务派遣机构属于《劳动合同法》中规定的劳务派遣单位，《船员条例》中规定的船员服务机构也可以具有类似职能。《中华人民共和国船员服务管理规定》（简称《船员服务管理规定》）第十八条

---

① 《海事劳工公约》规则和守则标题一规则1.3："目的：确保海员经过培训并具备履行其船上职责的资格。1. 除非海员经过培训或经证明适任或者具备履行其职责的资格，否则不得在船上工作。2. 除非海员成功地完成了船上个人安全培训，否则不得允许其在船上工作。3. 按国际海事组织通过的强制性文件进行的培训和发证应被视为满足本规则第1和2款的要求。"

② 林嘉：《劳动法原理、体系与问题》，法律出版社2016年版，第93页。

③ 《海事劳工公约》第二条第一款（j）："'船东'一词系指船舶所有人或从船舶所有人那里承担了船舶经营责任并在承担这种责任时已同意接受船东根据本公约所承担的职责和责任的任何其他组织或个人，如管理人、代理或光船承租人，无论是否有任何其他组织或个人代表船东履行了某些职责或责任。"

④ See George Rutherglen. "Admiralty, Human Rights, and International Law". *Virginia Journal of International Law*, 2021, Vol. 62, No. 1, p. 181.

⑤ 《民法典》第五十四条："自然人从事工商业经营，经依法登记，为个体工商户。"

也认可了船员劳务派遣机构在船员劳务派遣关系中用人单位的法律地位。[①]毫无疑问,船员劳务派遣机构是《劳动法》以及《劳动合同法》中规定的用人单位,符合用人单位的主体资格。

(二) 船员在船工作关系之劳动管理

劳动管理是指用人单位对劳动者的劳动过程实施管理。其具体表现为:劳动者被用人单位收入其生产组织麾下,管理、指定劳动者的工作具体内容,如工作地点、工作时间、工作量与工作强度、劳动过程等,并支付劳动者的劳动报酬;劳动者成为用人单位生产组织内的一员,且服从用人单位订立的纪律规范和内部规则制度,接受用人单位的日常管理以及为用人单位的工作提供有偿的劳动。在劳动关系中,劳动者的劳动报酬包括工资、福利以及法律要求单位必须为员工缴纳的社会保险。同时,用人单位在对劳动者实施劳动管理的过程中,也必须要符合国家法律规定的劳动者应当享有工作条件与工资报酬的最低标准的要求,比如对工时、休息时间、休假、工资、职业安全与健康、女工与未成年工的特殊保护等。

其实船员只要一上船,船东就对船员进行了劳动管理。根据《海商法》规定,船员必须在船上工作,换言之,船员提供的服务必须在船舶上进行。而船舶由船东提供的,既是劳动的生产资料又是劳动场所。所以,船员在船上工作,不仅是出于职业需要,也是出于船东对于工作地点规定的需要。根据《船员条例》第十六条,船员在船上工作须遵守船舶管理制度和值班制度。[②] 船舶管理制度和值班制度属于船东的劳动规章制度,换言之,船员需要接受船东的劳动规章制度。其中,值班制度还体现了船东对船员在船上工作时间有固定的规定。此外,船员在船上工作的时候,船

---

① 《船员服务管理规定》第十八条:"为与船员服务机构签订劳动合同的船员提供船舶配员服务的,船员服务机构为船员用人单位,船员服务机构应当同时履行船员用人单位的责任和义务。"

② 《船员条例》第十六条:"船员在船上工作期间,应当符合下列要求:(一)携带本条例规定的有效证件;(二)掌握船舶的适航状况和航线的通航保障情况,以及有关航区气象、海况等必要的信息;(三)遵守船舶的管理制度和值班规定,按照海上交通安全和防治船舶污染的操作规则操纵、控制和管理船舶,如实填写有关船舶法定文书,不得隐匿、篡改或者销毁有关船舶法定证书、文书;(四)参加船舶应急训练、演习,按照船舶应急部署的要求,落实各项应急预防措施;(五)遵守船舶报告制度,发现或者发生险情、事故、保安事件或者影响航行安全的情况,应当及时报告;(六)在不严重危及自身安全的情况下,尽力救助遇险人员;(七)不得利用船舶私载旅客、货物,不得携带违禁物品。"

员持续地为船舶提供包括技术、经验、体力、脑力在内的劳动,使船舶能够正常不断地运行,这也是船东对船员工作内容规定的体现。因此,一旦船员上船工作,无论是何种形式,都相当于接受了船东的劳动管理——规定船员劳动固定的工作地点、时间、内容以及规定船员需要遵守的劳动规章制度等。另外,船长的行政隶属性与船东的劳动管理也具有一定的融合性。根据《海商法》和《船员条例》的有关规定,船员在履行劳动职责时必须服从船长的命令。① 船长作为船舶的最高指挥官,有权指挥和管理船员在船舶上的所有工作,这是船东所许可的,代表船东的意志。船员在劳动的过程中听从船长的指令并且服从船长对船舶的管理,其实就相当于接受了船东的劳动管理。综上所述,船员只要上船,就代表接受了船东的劳动管理。

在船员劳务派遣中,船员受雇于劳务派遣机构,劳务派遣机构为船员的用人单位。船员劳务派遣机构将船员派遣至船东的船舶上时,船东是劳动力的直接使用者,是船员的用工单位。但这并不影响船员劳务派遣机构对船员实施劳动管理,船员的劳动过程、劳动地点、劳动时间仍然是在船员劳务派遣机构的授意之下的,只不过船员劳务派遣机构的劳动管理需要船东的辅助。因为《海事劳工公约》和《船员条例》规定许多船员在船工作所需的生活条件和医疗保障,这是船员劳务派遣机构无法直接参与的,必须由船东保障实施。所以,在船员劳务派遣关系中,船东是以船员劳务派遣机构的"债务辅助人"身份对船员实施劳动管理,也就是说,船员劳务派遣机构和船东共同对船员进行劳动管理。

(三) 船员在船工作关系之业务组成

业务组成是指劳动者从事的劳动工作,是用人单位业务的一个组成部分。换言之,劳动者提供的劳动一般与用人单位的业务相关,而这种相关性就是劳动者提供的劳动和用人单位经营业务之间的彼此匹配。劳动者提供的劳动和用人单位的生产资料共同构成用人单位所经营的业务活动。该业务活动既可以是主要业务也可以是辅助业务,只要是用人单位经营所需

---

① 《海商法》第三十五条:"船长负责船舶的管理和驾驶。船长在其职权范围内发布的命令,船员、旅客和其他在船人员都必须执行。船长应当采取必要的措施,保护船舶和在船人员、文件、邮件、货物以及其他财产。"《船员条例》第十七条:"船长在其职权范围内发布的命令,船舶上所有人员必须执行。高级船员应当组织下属船员执行船长命令,督促下属船员履行职责。"

要的业务即可。劳动者劳动成果的收益对外由用人单位享有,劳动者的劳动成果风险对外也由用人单位承担。

我国的船员,按照级别,可分为船长、高级船员、普通船员。按照船上任职的部门和岗位,船员还可以分为甲板部船员、轮机部船员和事务部船员。无论是哪个级别、哪个部门、哪个岗位的船员,其工作岗位的目的都是保证船舶的安全、正常航行与作业。而船东主要依靠船舶进行营业,船舶的用途基本相当于船东的业务范围。根据《海事劳工公约》第二条第四款,公约旨在保护在参与商业贸易行为的船只上工作的船员。[①] 参与商业贸易行为的船只基本用途在于货物水路运输、旅客水路运输、海上开采矿业、海上救援或者打捞作业、拖带船只等。总之,商船的用途不外乎航行运输、海上作业或者海上救助。而船员的工作内容都是与船舶的航行、作业和日常使用等紧密联系的。船员的劳动活动与船东的生产资料——船舶相结合共同构成船东的业务活动。因此,无论是何种类型的船员,他们的劳动都是船东业务的组成部分。

在船员劳务派遣中,船员的劳动既是船东的业务组成部分,又是船员劳务派遣机构的业务组成部分。对船东而言,船员的劳动内容并不会因船员被派遣而有所不同,因此,被派遣船员的劳动当然属于船东需要的业务;无论是对船东来说还是对船员劳务派遣机构来说,船员都存在贡献劳动给付这一事实。也就是说,船员的劳动既提供给船东,也提供给船员劳务派遣机构。船员的劳动满足了船员劳务派遣机构招募和管理船员业务的目的。因此,船员的劳动也属于船员劳务派遣机构管理船员的业务组成部分。

四、船员在船工作关系均为劳动关系

在船员市场中,船员被分为公司船员和自由船员。公司船员与船东或者船员劳务派遣机构签订劳动合同,合同清楚说明劳资双方成立劳动关系,不论船员在船上工作抑或在岸上休假、待岗,都属于船东或者船员劳务派遣机构的成员,直接由船东或者船员劳务派遣机构安排上船工作,接

[①] 《海事劳工公约》第二条第四款:"除非另有明文规定,本公约适用于除从事捕鱼或类似捕捞的船舶和用传统方法制造的船舶,例如独桅三角帆船和舢板以外的通常从事商业活动的所有船舶,无论其为公有或私有。本公约不适用于军舰和军事辅助船。"

受船东或者船员劳务派遣机构的劳动管理,其提供的劳动也是船东或船员劳务派遣机构的组成部分,与其他行业中大部分公司与职工之间的关系并无二致,毫无疑问船员劳动关系应当成立。而自由船员相对于公司船员来说较为自由,他们没有与任何单位签订劳动合同,不是任何单位的成员,通常情况下,根据船员管理公司或船员服务机构所提供的相关信息,到任一船舶上任职,属于"哪里有活就去哪里"的船员。在实践中,公司船员与公司之间的劳动关系是明确的,但自由船员与任职船舶的船东之间的劳动关系往往得不到认定。从船员劳动关系构成的三个要件来看,并不因船员为公司船员抑或是自由船员而有所区别。因此,即使没有签订合同或者合同没有明确是劳动合同,自由船员在船工作关系也应当为劳动关系,更准确地说,应当是事实劳动关系。

事实劳动关系是指劳动者与用人单位之间的劳动关系符合成立劳动关系的实质性要求而缺乏形式性要件的劳动关系。《劳动法》以及《劳动合同法》都要求用人单位必须及时和劳动者订立劳动合同,然而由于社会发展水平各有不同,缺少劳动合同而开展用工的情况仍在一定程度上存在。《劳动合同法》第七条明确,用人单位自用工之日起即与劳动者建立劳动关系,也就是说,我国的劳动关系遵循其他国家普遍认可的"事实优先"原则,将"用工"视为确定劳动关系是否存在的独一要件,即无论双方当事人是否订立书面的劳动合同,也无论签订的合同名称如何,都应重点关注确立劳动关系时当事人的权利义务如何以及用工事实是否存在。[①] 总而言之,即便没有订立劳动合同,符合劳动法规定的劳动关系从劳动者为用人单位供给劳动力之日起就已经成立,即成立事实劳动关系。

事实劳动关系有两个最明显的特点:第一,事实劳动关系缺少符合《劳动法》《劳动合同法》要求的需要签订的书面劳动合同。第二,事实劳动关系应当是一种劳动关系,也就是说,它不同于其他劳务关系,具备劳动关系的实质性要件。如果不符合劳动关系的实质性要件,则不构成劳动关系,更谈不上是否为事实劳动关系。劳动和社会保障部《通知》第一条就是对缺少劳动合同这个形式要件的劳动关系需要符合的实质要件的规定。根据本文上述关于船员在船工作关系性质的论述,无论是公司船员还是自由船员,其船员在船工作关系,都符合《通知》第一条的三个实质要

---

① 参见刘晓雯、侯丽洁《论劳动关系的界定标准》,载《辽宁行政学院学报》2010年第1期,第36页。

件。没有明确规定劳资双方成立劳动关系的船员合同，即为缺少《劳动法》《劳动合同法》要求的书面劳动合同，不具备形式要件。但其具备劳动关系成立所需的实质性要件，成立事实劳动关系。也就是说，对于那些未在合同中明确规定劳资双方成立劳动关系的船员来说，只要一上船，就与船东成立劳动关系。因此，无论是何种形式的船员在船工作关系，均为劳动关系。

五、结　语

随着船员全球化日益发展，我国船员纠纷增加，对于船员在船工作关系的性质界定显得尤为重要。法院常常因船员合同中主体之间复杂的关系以及合同名称，将其识别为劳务关系，这种做法并不合理。本文通过辨析劳动关系与劳务关系，厘清劳动与劳务的关系，再从劳动关系的识别入手，分析船员在船工作关系具备的劳动关系实质性要件，认为所有船员在船工作关系均为劳动关系，希望以此保障船员应享有的劳动者合法权益。

北极航道之西北通道的法律地位研究

黄 晖 卢秋璇*

摘要：北极航道是指穿越北冰洋，连接太平洋和大西洋的海上航线集合。一般而言，北极航道分为中央航道、东北航道与西北通道三条线路。21世纪以来，全球气候变暖加快，北冰洋海冰快速消融，航运和破冰技术持续发展。这些因素为实现北极航道的通航提供了有利条件。如果北极航道投入启用，则很可能发生世界海上贸易重心的转移，进而对地区和国际局势产生深远影响。因此，近年来越来越多国家、地区关注北极航道的开发利用问题，针对北极航道的法律地位及控制权的争议也越发激烈。本文将结合国际海洋法，分析沿岸国对北极航道中西北通道主张的合法性，探讨西北通道的法律地位对我国的影响。

关键词：北极航道 西北通道 国际海峡 历史性水域

Study on the Legal Status of the Northwest Passage

Huang Hui, Lu Qiuxuan

Abstract: The Arctic Waterways are a collection of sea routes through the Arctic Ocean, connecting the Pacific and Atlantic Oceans. In general, the Arctic Waterways are divided into three routes: the Central Passage, the Northeast Passage and the Northwest Passage. This paper studies the legal status of Northwest Passage based on the analysis of the legal claims and disputes over Northwest Passage from a perspective of international laws. In the 21st century, the acceleration of global warming, rapid melting of the sea ice and the development of navigation and ice-breaking technology provide favorable

---

* 黄晖：广东恒运律师事务所主任，大连海事大学法学硕士，"广州十大涉外大律师"，华南师范大学国际航运法律与政策研究中心兼职研究员，广东省法学会航运法学研究会副会长，广州市律协海事海商与航空法律专业委员会主任。卢秋璇：广东恒运律师事务所律师，南安普顿大学法律硕士。

conditions for the utility of the Arctic Waterways. If the Arctic Waterways are put into operation, a shift in the center of gravity of international trade is likely to occur, which will affect the regional and international economy and society profoundly. Therefore, more and more countries and regions show their interests in the usage and development of Northwest Passage, and the controversies over the legal status and control of the Arctic Waterways have become increasingly intense. In this paper, we will analyze the legitimacy of the littoral states' claims to Northwest Passage in the context of international laws and aim to conclude the legal status of Northwest Passage and the impacts of its legal status to China.

Key words: Arctic Waterway; Northwest Passage; international strait; historic waters.

一、引 言

北极，在人类历史上曾代表着人类探索地理的尽头。北极航道常年冰封、气候环境恶劣，数千年来鲜有人类活动痕迹。然而，从大航海时代的韦拉扎诺（Giovanni de Verrazano）、巴芬（William Baffin）等多名探险家到19世纪的"埃里伯斯"号（HMS Erebus）和"惊恐"号（HMS Terror）探险事件，再到20世纪的"佳阿"号（Gjoa）、"SS 曼哈顿"号（SS Manhattan）以及21世纪的中国"雪龙"号等探索队伍，北极航道经历了从未知、探索阶段到开发利用阶段的转变。气候条件的变化和科技水平的提高使得北极航道的研究成为一个不断发展演化的课题。

21世纪以来，由于气候变暖不断加剧，研究预测2030年北极会出现夏季无冰现象，北极航道通航的可能性大大增加。随着北极航道不断开发，北极航道的潜在价值使其逐步成为国际社会争议的话题，也逐渐受到学界关注。加拿大政府通过主张历史性水域、划定直线基线等方式提出对北极航道的西北通道享有主权。美国则对加拿大政府的主张多次明确表示反对，主张西北通道属于国际海峡，应用于国际航行。西北通道法律地位的问题在我国主要是学者之间的学术讨论，政府没有明确表明官方立场。

北极航道的进一步开发或者投入商业通航，可能会改写未来的国际运输航线和国际经济格局。此外，北极航道的开发利用不仅影响国际经济，而且对全球政治、军事均会产生深远影响。北极航道西北通道的法律地位会直接影响沿岸国及非沿岸国利用西北通道。本文通过对比国内外学术研究，致力于厘清错综复杂的西北通道主权争议，为我国参与北极航道治理、选择北极政策提供理论支撑。

国内外学者对于西北通道涉及的国际法问题的讨论，主要集中在加拿大一方提出的历史性水域主张是否成立以及西北通道是否属于用于国际航行的海峡。

通过检索在北极航道法律研究领域相关文献，国内学者对西北通道关注相对较少，西北通道相关法律研究仍待加强。从目前国内研究现状来看，大多国内学者例如王泽林教授认为，加拿大无论依据历史性水域或者直线基线将西北通道划为内水的理论都缺乏合理性；也有少数国内学者认为，北极航道不属于用于国际航行的海峡，构成内水或领海海峡。我国学界对加拿大相关学术主张尚缺乏全面、系统的梳理，加拿大学者在西北通道属于历史性水域的论述中提及关于因纽特人在北极群岛上的历史性权利以及海冰的法律地位等问题尚未得到足够关注。因此，本文将在探究西北通道的国际法律争议以及在分析总结加拿大相关理论的基础上，进一步论述西北通道的法律地位，从而为准确评价西北通道法律地位提供借鉴和参考。

二、西北通道国际化的争议

对于西北通道的法律地位之争，非沿岸国家与沿岸国家主要争议在于：西北通道是国际海峡，抑或是属于加拿大的"内水"。有些国家极力主张西北通道为国际海峡，例如美国在1969年派出"SS 曼哈顿"号实现了穿越西北通道的国际航行，试图印证西北通道实际上是用于国际航行的国际海峡。而加拿大对上述国际海峡的主张持否定态度，并强调北极群岛水域（即西北通道相关水域）为内水。1970年4月16日，加拿大在向美国提交的一份照会表明加拿大一贯认为北极群岛水域是属于加拿大的，加拿大政府不接受任何将该水域国际化的建议。1973年，加拿大的法律事务局针对历史性水域和海湾的问题，提交报告声称："尽管加拿大并没有在任何条约或立法中宣告，但是基于历史，加拿大主张加拿大北极群岛内的水域是加拿大的内水。"

（一）国际海峡的定义

海峡是地处于两块陆地之间、两端连接海洋的狭长的天然水道。①《联合国海洋法公约》第三十七条规定，用于国际航行的海峡是指"在公海或专属经济区的一个部分和公海或专属经济区的另一部分之间的用于国际航行的海峡"②。根据《联合国海洋法公约》的相关规定，在国际海峡中，所有船舶和飞机均享有过境通行的权利，在行使此项权利时应毫不迟延，迅速过境；并不应对海峡沿岸国主权、领土完整或政治独立，有任何武力威胁或动武行为。对于海峡沿岸国而言，其有权制定关于过境通行的法律和规章管理海峡。又依据《联合国海洋法公约》第四十五条，如果国际海峡是由一国岛屿和该国大陆组成，在该岛屿向海一侧有在航行和水文特征方面同样便利的一条航道，过境通行就不应适用，转而适用无害通过制度。

（二）国际海峡的认定标准

上述《联合国海洋法公约》对国际海峡的定义有两项标准：其一是地理标准，即"公海或专属经济区的一个部分和公海或专属经济区的另一部分之间"；其二是功能标准，即"用于国际航行"。根据《联合国海洋法公约》关于"公海"和"专属经济区"的规定，"国际海峡"的地理标准比较容易确定，但《联合国海洋法公约》并没有进一步对"用于国际航行"的含义进行明确。在"科孚海峡案"中，国际法院对国际海峡阐述如下："决定性的标准是其位于连接公海两部分的地理位置和它被用作国际航行的事实。"③ 国际法院进一步指出，相比地理标准更重要的是，国际海峡是"一个用于国际海上交通的航线"④。

从上述内容可知，《联合国海洋法公约》和"科孚海峡案"虽然都采用"用于国际航行"作为国际海峡的认定标准之一，但均没有进一步解释含义。由此，在实践中，各国对"用于国际航行"的解释持有不同的意见。

从字面意义理解，"用于国际航行"的海峡存在两种可能："实际用

---

① 参见屈广清、曲波《海洋法》（第四版），中国人民大学出版社 2017 年版，第 49 页。
② 见《联合国海洋法公约》第三十七条。
③ Corfu Channel case, Judgement of April 9th 1949: I. C. J 1949 Reports, p. 4.
④ Corfu Channel case, Judgement of April 9th 1949: I. C. J 1949 Reports, p. 4.

于"（actual use）和"潜在用于"（potential use）。由于"科孚海峡案"的主要争议在科孚海峡的地理标准，且发生争议时科孚海峡事实上已经用于国际航行，国际法院在"科孚海峡案"中并无特别阐明"用于国际航行"是否包含"过去用于"或"潜在用于"的意思。根据《领海与毗连区公约》第十六条第四款和《联合国海洋法公约》第三十七条的规定，国际海峡是指"straits used for international navigation"，也无指明国际海峡具备"过去用于"或"潜在用于"的因素。

由此可见，国际法院和联合国目前并没有意图将"用于国际航行"的标准扩大适用于未来可能被利用作为国际航行的海峡，但似乎也并未有意排除这一可能性。因此，有学者提出，尽管一个海峡可能目前尚未用于国际航行，但如果具有潜在用于国际航行的可能性，则也应当认定为国际海峡。[①]

（三）国际海峡主张的合法性和合理性

从国际海峡的定义和认定标准来看，将西北通道相关水域认定为国际海峡的主张是符合国际法理论并且具有合理性的。虽然现行有效的国际法对国际海峡功能标准认定的时间因素仅解释为"争议发生之时"，但综合"科孚海峡案"和《领海与毗连区公约》《联合国海洋法公约》的规定，国际海峡的认定应当尊重沿岸国家或地区对争议海峡享有的利益和非沿岸国对国际航线的利用。由于科学技术原因，目前尚存在未被开发利用的航道，如果国际海峡的认定局限于"发生争议之时用于国际航道"这个条件，那么只要沿岸国对非沿岸国利用争议海峡中新开发的航道进行阻挠，该新航道很难被认定为国际海峡，这似乎与航行自由原则和精神相违背。

在西北通道利用问题上，得益于破冰技术的发展和气候变暖，西北通道实现国际通航的可能性逐渐增加。如果坚持固有观念、否定西北通道的"国际航行"属性，这将会违背航行自由精神。因此，笔者认为，西北通道基本上符合国际法理论对国际海峡的定义和认定标准，西北通道国际化的主张具有合法和合理性依据。

---

① See Donald Mcare. "Arctic Sovereignty? What Is at Stake?". *Behind the Headlines*, 2007, Vol. 64, No. 1, pp. 1 – 24.

三、加拿大对西北通道的主张

自西北通道相关水域的法律地位产生争议以来,加拿大在国际社会一直主张西北通道的相关水域为"内水",分别从三个理论路径提出:"扇形原则"(sector principle)、"历史性水域"(historic waters)和"直线基线"(straight baseline)。加拿大在1907年提出"扇形原则",声称位于两条国界线(经度线)之间直到北极点的一切土地应属于邻接这些土地的国家。[1] 因该理论缺乏依据而从未被国际社会普遍接受,加拿大后来也鲜有提及"扇形原则"。为此,本文接下来将围绕加拿大的"历史性水域"和"直线基线"理论进行介绍与分析。

(一)"历史性水域"

1. "历史性水域"的定义

加拿大和俄罗斯分别对西北通道和东北通道均提出"历史性水域"的主张。"历史性水域"这个概念在国际成文法中并没有一个准确的定义。1962年,联合国秘书处在全面梳理和总结国际社会对于历史性权利的研究成果,并广泛征求国际社会意见和建议后,发布了《包括历史性海湾在内的历史性水域法律制度》("Juridical Regime of Historic Water, Including Historic Bays")的报告。该报告认为,"历史性水域"的起源根植于以下历史事实,即国家经过多个世纪,对认为是对本国至关重要的海域主张和维护主权,却没有注意领海划界在一般国际法中不同和不断变化的意见。[2] 国际法院在"英挪渔业案"裁决中认为历史性水域一般被理解为"视为内水,但是如果没有一项历史性权利存在,也不能具有历史性水域的特征"。[3]

学者布歇认为:"历史性水域是指沿岸国在与一般适用的国际法规则相反的情况下,经过一段实质性的时间,明确、有效和持续地行使主权权

---

[1] 参见吴慧《〈北极争夺战〉的国际法分析》,载《国际关系学院学报》2007年第5期。
[2] See United Nations. "Juridical Regime of Historic Waters, Including Historic Bays". *Yearbook of the International Law Commission*, 1962, Vol. II, pp. 1–26.
[3] Anglo-Norwegian Fisheries case, Order of October 4th, 1950; I. C. J. Reports 1950, p. 263.

利,且得到了国际社会默认的水域"①。我国著名学者傅崐成教授认为,一般所谓的"历史性水域"有三种类型:一是一国主张享有主权的海湾;二是一国主张享有主权的沿岸水域;三是一国对于原本属于公海的海域,基于"历史利益"的因素,主张应将之例外地划归其主权之下,成为其"历史性水域"。②

联合国秘书处报告《包括历史性海湾在内的历史性水域法律制度》指出:"原则上应该取决于主张国在特定情况下,在特定区域内是否行使了主权而形成主张的一个基础,以及该主权是在内水中的主权还是在领海中的主权。"依照这个总结,虽然主张国可能是在内水或领海中行使主权,但是会产生不同的法律结果,即主张历史性权利的海域可能是内水,也可能是领海。所以,"历史性水域"的法律地位取决于主张国所主张和行使历史性权利的程度。③ 这一报告总结归纳了国际法理论,即历史性水域的基本构成要件,分别是正式主张、持续有效地行使相关的管辖权和国际社会的默认,这得到国际实践以及学者的认可。加拿大政府正是依据"历史性水域"的国际法理论主张西北通道相关水域为"历史性内水"。

2. 加拿大主张"历史性内水"的权利来源

1969 年 10 月,时任加拿大总理皮埃尔·特鲁多(Pierre Trudeau)向加拿大众议院的议员们发表演讲时表示,关于西北通道的部分,加拿大对西北通道拥有"历史性权利"。④ 在该次讲话中,他表示"爱斯基摩人在冰水之上寻找食物,进行活动,而不注意这些冰是陆上之冰还是水上之冰。所有的这些活动,以及其他活动,包括从勘查到家庭津贴支票的分配意味着,经过 450 年,北美的北极已经逐渐成为加拿大的北极"⑤。

上述内容不仅包含了陆上之冰上的"历史性权利"内容,即很早生活在这里的爱斯基摩人(即因纽特人)就在陆地、冰上活动和寻找食物,还隐含着对水上之冰区的主权主张。加拿大学者认为,加拿大政府对北极群

---

① L. J. Bouchez. *The Regime of Bays in International Law*. Leyden: Sythoff Press, 1964, p. 281.
② 参见傅崐成《海洋法专题研究》,厦门大学出版社 2004 年版,第 324 – 325 页。
③ See Pharand Donat. "Historic Waters in International Law with Special Reference to the Arctic". *University of Toronto Law Journal*, 1971, Vol. 21, pp. 5 – 6.
④ See Nicholas Howson. "Breaking the Ice: The Canadian-American Dispute over the Arctic's Northwest Passage". *Columbia Journal of International Law*, 1988, Vol. 26, p. 363.
⑤ See Nicholas Howson. "Breaking the Ice: The Canadian-American Dispute over the Arctic's Northwest Passage". *Columbia Journal of International Law*, 1988, Vol. 26, p. 363.

岛享有的权利是通过与因纽特人签订条约受让因纽特人对北极群岛及附近水域享有的历史性权利；而因纽特人对北极群岛的历史性权利早在欧洲殖民活动前已经获得，且包含实施主权的权利。①

3. "历史性内水"的合法性审视

我国著名学者王泽林认为，加拿大政府正式对西北通道提出"历史性内水"的主张在1973年才明确提出，其后还受到美国等国家的挑战，不符合"历史性水域"的构成要件。② 笔者认为，该观点似乎简化了加拿大主张北极群岛水域的理论依据，忽略了因纽特人在北极群岛上的历史性权利的因素。

因此，单单从"历史性水域"的构成要件而言，因纽特人对北极群岛以及附近水域享有历史性权利、加拿大政府基于因纽特人的让渡行为对北极群岛水域主张"历史性权利"是成立的。但是，笔者认为，加拿大政府主张北极群岛水域是具有排他性主权的"历史性内水"是缺乏依据的。

首先，依据"西撒哈拉案"③ 以及《联合国土著人民权利宣言》④，因纽特人对北极群岛及附近水域拥有、占有或以其他方式使用或获得土地、领土和资源的权利，应当仅限于因纽特人传统上实施权利的范围。依据国际法，因纽特人长期在北极群岛土地上生活、居住并将其视为他们的领土的历史能够赋予因纽特人对北极群岛的主权权利。但因纽特人历史上只是在北极群岛附近水域进行捕鱼，并无对水域实施排他性的控制行为，或将附近水域视为他们领地的一部分。因此，因纽特人对北极群岛水域享有的历史性权利并不包含主权权利。

其次，由于北极群岛部分水域存在长年冰层，因纽特人在冰面上居住活动，有学者提出北极群岛的海冰（sea ice）与领土法律性质相同，因纽特人能对其主张主权权利。⑤ 但笔者认为，一方面，即使是数十年不融化的冰层，但与土地对比，仍具有易受气候影响、面积易发生变化、不适合

---

① See Byers M, Baker J. *International Law and the Arctic*. Cambridge: Cambridge University Press, 2013, p.132.
② 参见王泽林《北极航道法律地位研究》，上海交通大学出版社2014年版，第175—176页。
③ *Western Sahara Advisory Opinion*, I. C. J Reports 1975, p.12.
④ 见《联合国土著人民权利宣言》第二十六条。
⑤ Susan B. Boyd. "The Legal Status of the Arctic Sea Ice: A Comparative Study and a Proposal". *The Canadian Yearbook of International Law*, Vol. 22. VANCOUVER: University of British Columbia Press, 1984, pp.131—140.

世代繁衍生活的特性；另一方面，如果赋予海冰与领土相同的法律地位，那么很可能对北冰洋中的冰山、浮冰产生很多法律争议。因此，海冰与领土的性质显然不能相提并论，加拿大提出的因纽特人对水上之冰享有主权权利的主张是经不起推敲的。

再次，如果加拿大政府主张"历史性内水"的依据是来源于英国让渡北极岛屿主权行为，但正如王泽林教授的观点，加拿大政府对北极群岛水域的权利直至1973年才完整、明确地提出，且没有得到国际社会的普遍认可，那么加拿大政府不能据此获得对北极群岛水域享有"历史性内水"的权利。

综上所述，从继承因纽特人权利的角度看，因纽特人在历史上仅对北极群岛行使主权权利，对北极群岛水域并无行使主权权利。相应地，加拿大继承因纽特人的历史性权利后，仅对北极群岛享有主权权利，该主权权利并不能及于北极群岛水域。从继承英国让渡北极群岛主权的角度看，加拿大对西北通道提出的"历史性内水"主张并不符合"有效、持续行使管辖""国际社会默认"的要件，无权以此主张西北通道为"历史性内水"。因此，加拿大并没有取得西北通道相关水域主权的合法来源，其对西北通道相关水域提出的"历史性内水"主张是缺乏国际法依据的。

（二）直线基线制度的主张

1. 国际法上的直线基线制度

依据现代海洋法，基线的种类有两种，即正常基线也称为低潮线和直线基线。相对于正常基线而言，直线基线在一国最大化主张可管辖海洋水域中具有更明显的优势，因而在实践中更受青睐。① 为确立对北极群岛水域的主权，1985年9月10日，时任加拿大外长克拉克在国会发表关于北极主权的声明，特别强调："这些基线确定了加拿大历史性内水的外部界限，加拿大的领水从基线向外延伸12海里。"②

在1951年的"英挪渔业案"中，根据国际法院的裁决，紧临沿海国大陆的群岛适用直线基线制度需要满足如下条件：其一，在地理特征上，

---

① See Qureshi Waseem Ahmad. "State Practices of Straight Baselines Institute Excessive Maritime Claims". *Southern Illinois University Law Journal*, 2018, Vol. 42, Issue 3, pp. 421–450.

② *The Canadian Yearbook of International Law*, Vol. 24. VANCOUVER: University of British Columbia Press, 1986, p. 418.

海岸极为曲折或者海岸邻接一个群岛;① 其二,在确定如上地理特征标准时要对直线基线做如下限制:① 基线的划定不得在任何程度上偏离海岸的一般方向。② 基线内的海域应充分接近陆地领土,使其受到内水制度的支配。③ 一个地区特有的经济利益的真实性与重要性已被长期管理证明。② 而加拿大政府正是采用直线基线制度划分北极群岛水域。

其后,1958年的《领海与毗连区公约》和1986年的《联合国海洋法公约》吸收了国际法院在"英挪渔业案"中关于直线基线确定的裁决内容,以成文法方式确定了直线基线制度。概括来说,《领海与毗连区公约》和《联合国海洋法公约》对直线基线制度提出了进一步要求及限制条件,即"除在低潮高地上筑有永久高于海平面的灯塔或类似设施,或以这种高地作为划定基线的起讫点已获得国际一般承认者外,直线基线的划定不应以低潮高地为起讫点"③ 以及"一国不得采用直线基线制度,致使另一国的领海同公海或专属经济区隔断"④。

2. 北极群岛适用直线基线制度的合法性审视

加拿大政府划定北极群岛直线基线时,加拿大并没有加入《领海与毗连区公约》,而《联合国海洋法公约》也未正式生效。因此,加拿大政府主张对北极群岛直线基线制度的依据是国际习惯法,也即沿用"英挪渔业案"的裁决标准。

首先,对于适用直线基线制度的地理特征而言,北极群岛由数量众多的近岸岛屿、暗礁、岩礁组成,与加拿大本土大陆相邻接。并且一年中除夏季融冰期外,多数时间这些岛屿与水道被冰层覆盖使整个北极群岛成为整体。因此,北极群岛符合适用直线基线制度的地理特征标准。⑤

其次,基线的划定须大致符合其海岸的一般方向。关于如何界定"海岸一般方向",却是一个宽松、难以量化的概念。⑥ 在如何判断基线是否偏离海岸的一般方向的问题上,"英挪渔业案"的法官认为:"在划定基线时,基线不能过分地偏离海岸的大致走向,在一定范围内沿岸国可以根据

---

① See *Anglo-Norwegian Fisheries case*, Order of October 4th, 1950: I. C. J. Reports, 1950, p.263.
② 参见王泽林《北极航道法律地位研究》,上海交通大学出版社2014年版,第199页。
③ 见《联合国海洋法公约》第七条第四款。
④ 见《领海与毗连区公约》第四条第五款和《联合国海洋法公约》第七条第六款。
⑤ See McKinnon J. Bruce. "Arctic Baselines: A Litore Usque Ad Litus". *Canadian Bar Review*, 1987, Vol. 66, Issue 4, pp.790 – 817.
⑥ See *Anglo-Norwegian Fisheries case*, Order of October 4th, 1950: I. C. J. Reports, 1950, p.263.

实际需要做出调整。"通过解读国际法院的判决知道，某一基线在一定程度可以存在偏离，只要偏离的程度尚未达到严重扭曲即可以被认为是可接受的。① 加拿大北极群岛位处高纬度地区，呈三角形形态。在按照罗宾逊投影制作的地图中，北极群岛显示为东西走势，② 加拿大北极群岛海岸可以视作符合一般方向。

最后，对于长期的惯例所形成的特别经济利益因素。历史上加拿大北部的因纽特人长期在其北极群岛区域从事捕鱼、狩猎活动，因此加拿大政府对北极群岛水域主张拥有重要经济利益是可以证实的。

因此，笔者认为，加拿大政府依据"英挪渔业案"裁决划定北极群岛的直线基线制度的主张是成立的。加拿大对直线基线的划定，实际上将西北通道海峡水域纳入其本国的内水范围。

3. 直线基线制度适用后的法律效果

尽管直线基线制度适用加拿大对北极群岛的划定，但这也不能改变西北通道用于国际航行之海峡的法律地位。仅仅通过直线基线制度，加拿大不能当然地取得对西北通道的排他性主权。

《领海与毗连区公约》第五条第二款规定："依第四条划定直线基线致使原先认为领海或公海一部分之水面划属内水时，在此水域内应有第十四条至第二十三条所规定之无害通过权。"《联合国海洋法公约》第八条第二款规定："如果按照第七条所规定的方法确定直线基线的效果使原来并未认为是内水的区域被包围在内成为内水，则在此种水域内应有本公约所规定的无害通过权。"因此，在加拿大政府于1985年对北极群岛划定直线基线制度之前，西北通道处于何种法律地位以及是否存在无害通过权将会影响外国船舶在西北通道的航行权。③

如前所述，北极群岛水域不构成"历史性内水"，根据《领海与毗连区公约》和《联合国海洋法公约》，外国船舶应当享有无害通过权。如果西北通道被认定是国际海峡，那么依据《联合国海洋法公约》的规定，西

---

① 参见李靓《直线基线的划法及其对加拿大西北航道的历史性权利主张的影响》，载《知识经济》2015年第7期。
② 参见李靓《直线基线的划法及其对加拿大西北航道的历史性权利主张的影响》，载《知识经济》2015年第7期。
③ See Donald R. Rothwell. "The Canadian-U. S. Northwest Passage Dispute A Reassessment". *Cornell International Law Journal*, 1993, Vol. 26, No. 2, pp. 359 – 360.

北通道应该适用过境通行制度。① 然而无论是无害通过制度还是过境通行制度，都是加拿大政府不能接受的。因此，加拿大政府一直主张北极群岛的直线基线制度是依据国际习惯法划定，不能适用《领海与毗连区公约》和《联合国海洋法公约》的规定，从而适用"英挪渔业案"的裁决，即对于基线所确定的水域，外国船舶不享有无害通过权。

笔者认为，加拿大政府对北极群岛水域提出"历史性内水"的主张难以成立，在北极群岛确立了直线基线制度以后，外国船舶应该在北极群岛水域中的西北通道至少享有无害通过权。此外，西北通道还存在国际化的可能性。如果西北通道成为国际海峡，则应当适用更自由的过境通行制度。

四、西北通道的现状以及我国应对建议

（一）加拿大对西北通道的管辖现状

尽管西北通道的法律地位存在较大争议，但加拿大政府多年来试图通过对西北通道实施一系列的管控政策以巩固其对西北通道的实际控制权，从而为其确立主权铺平道路。

在船舶通行方面，加拿大对西北通道通行制度的管控从自愿申报制转变为强制申报制。在2009年之前，加拿大政府对取道西北通道的船舶实行自愿申报制，鼓励所有船舶在过境其北极水域时自愿提前申报。② 2010年《加拿大北方船舶交通服务规章》生效后，加拿大政府规定进入航行安全控制区的船舶须进行强制性的报告。

在船舶环保标准限制方面，加拿大政府颁布了《北极船舶污染防治法规》与《北极海域污染防治条例》等立法文件，详细规定进入其北极水域船舶的限制条件，并要求船舶航行前必须申请获得"北极污染防治证书"。③ 此外，加拿大政府还依据《联合国海洋法公约》第二百三十四条有关北极环境保护的规定，在北极群岛水域执行一系列的法律和规章，包

---

① See Donald R. Rothwell. "The Canadian-U. S. Northwest Passage Dispute A Reassessment". *Cornell International Law Journal*, 1993, Vol. 26, No. 2, p.232.
② 参见郑雷《北极西北航道：沿海国利益与航行自由》，载《国际论坛》2017年第3期。
③ See *Arctic Waters Pollution Prevention Act*, R.S.C, 1985, c.A – 12, s.12.

括对航行于船舶交通服务区的船舶规定了更加严格的排放义务、报告义务等。

建立这些规章制度的目的一是客观上防止、减少和控制船舶对海洋的污染,二是加强加拿大政府对西北通道相关水域的有效管辖权。加拿大政府对西北通道持续进行有效的管辖行为,长久发展下去有可能会演变成国际社会默认的事实,从而在未来影响西北通道法律地位的确定。

(二) 我国的应对建议

1. 我国应审慎对待加拿大对西北通道的过度主张

我国政府对北极航道的法律地位定性并未有明确的表态。但是,我国发布的《北极政策白皮书》提及以"尊重、合作、共赢、可持续"的基本原则参与北极事务,并特别指出我国会尊重北极国家在北极享有的主权、主权权利和管辖权。在实践中,我国的商船或极地科考船舶在通行西北通道时都遵守了加拿大制定的有关法律、规章,事先向各自的航道管理机构提出申请,在获得批准前提下才顺利通过这些航道。

虽然我国船舶在一定程度上接受加拿大在西北通道实施的管理和规制,但我国并未承认加拿大对西北通道的主权主张。如前所述,加拿大提出的"历史性水域"和"直线基线"并不能充分支撑加拿大对西北通道享有排他性主权的主张。即使西北通道相关水域被认定为"历史性水域"或适用"直线基线",他国船舶根据国际法在西北通道应当至少享有无害通过权。如果默认加拿大对西北通道的主权主张、放任加拿大对西北通道实施排他性的主权管辖,这既违背了国际法,也不利于我国船舶有效利用西北通道。因此,面对加拿大的过度主张,我国应该对此明确表示保留态度。

2. 我国在尊重加拿大正当主张的基础上,应加强与加拿大在低政治领域的合作,积极参与北极治理机制建设

即使西北通道实现了国际化,无论是实行过境通行制度还是无害通过制度,加拿大作为沿岸国根据国际法有权制定关于过境通行的法律和规章管理经过海峡的外国船舶。由于极地的生态环境具有特殊性和脆弱性,环境污染事故对北极生态系统的影响巨大且难以恢复。从保护极地生态环境、当地居住人群乃至全人类共同利益角度考虑,加拿大对西北通道实施管制具有一定的必要性,客观上也有利于生态环境保护。因此,对于加拿大提出的符合国际法以及全人类共同利益的主张,我国应当尊重和支持。

2009年加拿大发布《加拿大北方战略：我们的北方、我们的遗产、我们的未来》①，从中可以看出，加拿大在环境保护、科学研究等低政治领域持开发、合作的态度。② 因此，我国可以进一步加大和加拿大在北极科研、极地环境保护方面合作的谈判力度，深化中加合作，实现共同利益。

此外，由于我国并非环北极国家，虽然我国在北极地区具有重要利益，但我国目前在北极治理事务中并无太大的话语权。为此，我国可以借助北极理事会等北极治理机制参与北极治理事务，积极参与北极治理机制的建设，谋求建立稳定互惠、符合全人类共同利益的国际新秩序。

---

① See Government of Canada. *Canadas Northern Strategy*: *Our North*, *Our Heritage*, *Our Future*. Ottawa-Ontario: Indian and Northern Affairs, 2009.

② 参见朱宝林《解读加拿大的北极战略——基于中等国家视角》，载《世界经济与政治论坛》2016年第4期。

论我国海事强制令制度的完善

——兼论《海事诉讼特别程序法》第四章的修改

曾二秀　倪学伟*

摘要：海事强制令与海事请求保全和海事证据保全一样，都属于海事法院作出的强制措施。但海事强制令具有自身的特殊性，并非单纯的保全强制措施。海事强制令在司法实务中存在使用率不高、效果不优良等现实问题，与制度设计的初衷不吻合。本文通过对各海事法院15年间共119份海事强制令裁判文书的收集分析，总结了相关案件的基本特点与存在的不足。对现有海事强制令制度的改造或完善，应明确该制度的独特性质，明确其与诉讼救济的区别，细化其适用条件，实现海事请求人的权责统一，以节省司法资源、保障海事强制令得到公平公正合理运用、避免对海事被请求人合法利益的损害，在快速解决纠纷的同时，促进或使关联纠纷得到真正的化解。

关键词：海事强制令　《海事诉讼特别程序法》　保全措施　紧急救济

On the Improvement of Maritime Enforcement Order in China
—With Discussion on the Revision of Chapter Four of the *Special Maritime Procedural Law*

Zeng Erxiu, Ni Xuewei

Abstract: Maritime enforcement order, the preservation of maritime claim and preservation of maritime evidence are all enforcement measures decreed by maritime court. However, maritime enforcement order has its own special characteristics; it is not purely a preservative enforcement measure. The relatively rare application of this order and the unsatisfied result of its

---

* 曾二秀：华南师范大学法学院教授，广东省法学会航运法学研究会会长。倪学伟：广州海事法院法官、研究室主任。

application, has not met its original purpose. This paper analyzed 119 rulings of maritime courts relating to maritime enforcement order in 15 years, exposed the main features of those cases and their shortcomings. To revise or perfect the present maritime enforcement order, we shall clarify its unique nature and its differences with litigation remedies, refine the conditions for its application, realize the unification of rights and duties of the maritime claimant, to save judicial resources and ensure its justified and reasonable application, and to prevent any detriment to the maritime respondent and rapidly settle disputes and enhance or make relating disputes be really settled.

Key words: maritime enforcement order; *Special Maritime Procedural Law*; preservative measure; emergent remedy

2000年7月1日,《中华人民共和国海事诉讼特别程序法》(简称《海诉法》)正式生效。该法作为我国海事诉讼领域的专门法,对海事诉讼中的特别程序和制度进行了规定,对于我国《海商法》的实施和海事司法实践的开展起到了积极的作用。但是,《海诉法》实行二十多年来,也暴露出部分不符合现实的问题,难以满足海事司法实践的需要,不利于海事法院实现效率和公平的平衡。为此,亟须对《海诉法》进行修改,其中,《海诉法》第四章海事强制令规定的修改完善尤为值得探讨。

探讨海事强制令制度的完善,必然需要探讨实践中的创新做法及其与该制度本身的相容性,也需要重新检讨该制度的设计。本文先从理论层面分析海事强制令制度的基本问题,分析其制度设计的目的;然后结合案例分析其在司法实践中的运用现状及其创新做法,并在此基础上探讨该制度的完善路径与完善措施。

一、我国海事强制令制度的基本内容分析

要发现海事强制令制度存在的问题并提出解决措施,首先要研究我国《海诉法》关于海事强制令制度的主要内容,明确海事强制令制度的性质及其在司法实践中的实施程序。

《海诉法》设专章(第四章)对海事强制令作出规定,与"海事请求保全"(第三章)及"海事证据保全"(第五章)两章并列,但置于两章之间。海事强制令一章的内容包括:海事强制令的定义,海事强制令案件

的管辖，申请的形式与担保，海事强制令作出的条件、时间与执行，以及对海事强制令裁定的复议与异议期间，拒不执行海事强制令的处罚，错误申请海事强制令的损害赔偿，海事强制令执行后相关案件的管辖。形式上看，这样的规定很全面，既体现了对申请人利益的保护，也反映了对被申请人和其他利害关系人的利益保护，然而，仔细分析其内容，会发现海事强制令制度的设计在对被请求人利益的保护上是失衡的，该制度的定位是模糊的。

（一）海事强制令的性质

探讨海事强制令的性质，要解决的是海事强制令到底是什么的问题。《海诉法》第五十一条将海事强制令定义为"海事法院根据海事请求人的申请，为使其合法权益免受侵害，责令被请求人作为或者不作为的强制措施"。由此可见，海事强制令无疑与海事请求保全和海事证据保全一样，都属于海事法院作出的强制措施。但海事强制令是与海事请求保全和海事证据保全性质相同的强制措施吗？

在民事诉讼法理论中，"保全"是一个很重要的概念，也是财产保全、行为保全、证据保全等相关制度赖以存在的基础。在英文中，"保全"一词通常用"preservation"来表达。根据《布莱克法律词典》，"保全"（preservation）一词是指"保护其安全，防止被损害；避免其被伤害、损害、损坏或腐败；维持。这种措施并不是一种创造行为，而是保全那些已经存在的并且保全那些先前已存在者的连续性"[①]。如此看来，"保全"一词的含义是保持事物的现有状态。

海事请求保全和海事证据保全都有"保全"字样，是典型的保全措施：前者为保障海事请求人"海事请求的实现"，对被请求人的财产采取保全措施；后者是对"有关海事请求的证据"采取保全措施，是为固定证据，也是为保障海事请求人海事请求的顺利进行。两种保全措施都是程序性的保障措施，保障纠纷解决程序的顺利进行，不直接解决当事人之间的实体权利义务纠纷，具有附属性（附属于特定的海事请求）、辅助性（不直接解决争议而是辅助争议的解决）和临时性或中间性（是在诉讼或仲裁前采取或在诉讼或仲裁过程中采取的措施）。这两种保全措施本身不能解

---

① Joseph R. Nolan, M. J. Connolly. *Black's Law Dictionary*, 5th ed., West Publishing Co. 1979, p. 1066.

决当事人之间的争议，只是能促进争议的解决。

与之不同的是，海事强制令虽为强制措施，却很难被界定为一种保全措施。首先，就算可以将"责令被请求人……不作为"视为一种行为保全，那么"责令被请求人作为"又保全了什么呢？其次，海事强制令措施是为使海事请求人"合法权益免受侵害"（第五十一条），针对的是"被请求人违反法律规定或者合同约定的行为"（第五十六条），保障的是海事请求人的实体权利，是实体权利的保护措施，是直接解决特定争议的措施。通过海事强制令，海事请求人的利益保护得到实现，如果海事请求人、被请求人、利害关系人没有向法院提起诉讼，那么只凭海事强制令就可以在一定程度上解决实体争议。海事强制令并不必然导致诉讼，这与财产保全和证据保全这两种保全措施相比，具有截然不同的性质。因此，有些观点认为海事强制令完全等同于海事行为保全，海事强制令是海事行为保全的立法语言，其性质上是一种保全措施，这是不准确的。

那么，海事强制令到底是什么性质的强制措施？其制度设计的目的又是什么？从《海诉法》对海事强制令的定义及进行条件分析，可以得出以下结论：海事请求人和被请求人之间发生了侵权或违约纠纷，即被请求人存在"违反法律规定或者合同约定的行为"，虽然海事请求人通常可以提起侵权之诉或违约之诉来维护自身的合法权益；但是"情况紧急"，不立即采取措施"将造成损害或者使损害扩大"，也就是说，虽然被请求人有违法或违约行为，但损害可能还没发生，纠正被请求人的行为可以阻止损害的发生，或者损害在持续扩大，纠正被请求人的行为，可以阻止损害的扩大；因此，应采取强制措施"责令被请求人作为或者不作为"。

可见，海事强制令事实上是对海事请求人的一种紧急救济措施。其制度价值在于，通过迅速纠正被请求人的行为避免损害的发生或者扩大，使请求人的利益得到维护。

（二）申请海事强制令的程序

作为快速维护请求人利益的紧急救济措施，海事强制令制度在程序设计上体现了从管辖到执行整个案件处理过程中不同于正常案件处理程序的特点。

第一，在管辖上，《海诉法》特别规定了诉前申请（其实也是独立申请）海事强制令的管辖法院是"海事纠纷发生地海事法院"①（第五十二条）。而且，还特别规定了"不受当事人之间关于该海事请求的诉讼管辖协议或者仲裁协议的约束"（第五十三条）。排除当事人之间关于海事请求的诉讼管辖协议或者仲裁协议的约束，而允许海事纠纷地的海事法院享有对案件的管辖权是考虑到事态紧急的情况下，如不立刻制止被请求人的行为恐怕会对请求人造成更大的损失。这样极大地便利了海事请求人向海事法院申请海事强制令，对海事请求人一方极为有利，若申请得到支持，其可以成功规避诉讼管辖协议或者仲裁协议的约束。若被请求人要提起错误申请海事强制令的损害赔偿之诉，也只能在该法院提起。此外，海事请求人还可以利用海事强制令对抗被请求人在境外的诉讼或仲裁。《最高人民法院关于适用〈中华人民共和国海事诉讼特别程序法〉若干问题的解释》（简称《〈海诉法〉司法解释》）第四十一条第二款明确指出"外国法院已受理相关海事案件或者有关纠纷已经提交仲裁的，当事人向中华人民共和国的海事法院提出海事强制令申请，并向法院提供可以执行海事强制令的相关证据的，海事法院应当受理"。

第二，在涉及是否作出海事强制令的审查程序上，《海诉法》并无规定。《海诉法》第五十四条规定了海事请求人应当提交书面申请，申请书应当载明申请理由并附有关证据；第五十六条规定海事请求人申请海事强制令应当具备的条件。至于海事强制令申请的处理，是由一位法官独任还是组成合议庭处理，是书面审查还是要当面听取请求人的意见，是只审查请求人一面之词的单方程序，还是要通知被申请人并给予被申请人书面或口头陈述机会的双方程序？《海诉法》一概无规定。鉴于海事强制令是在实体判决之前作出的裁定，海事法院对海事强制令申请的审查，应当是一种程序上的审查，而不是实体上的审查。这就要求海事法院在对海事强制令的申请进行审查时，应保持一定的尺度，既不能太过宽松以免作出错误的海事强制令裁定，也不能过于严格以至于不合理地限制海事强制令的作出而不利于对海事请求人利益的保护。

第三，在处理时限上，鉴于海事强制令是紧急救助措施，《海诉法》

---

① 海事纠纷发生地是确定海事强制令管辖权的重要概念。但是，海上运输在时间和空间上往往具有很大的延续性，由于事实上可能存在多个纠纷发生地，因此对海事纠纷发生地的理解就容易产生争议。因为，海事强制令的目的是责令被请求人为或者不为一定的行为来减少请求人的损失，所以将海事纠纷地理解为被请求人的不法行为（包括作为和不作为）的发生地。

规定了极短的处理时限，即从接受请求人申请时起，海事法院"应当在48小时内作出裁定"（第五十七条），而且"裁定作出海事强制令的，应当立即执行"（第五十七条）。可见，从受理申请到开始执行一个完整的案件处理程序只需48小时，这充分体现了对请求人利益高效保护这一价值取向。

第四，在执行方面，根据《海诉法》第五十七条规定，海事法院"裁定作出海事强制令的，应当立即执行"，最高院在《〈海诉法〉司法解释》第四十二条进一步明确，"准予申请人海事强制令申请的，应当制作民事裁定书并发布海事强制令"。这些规定表明了关于海事强制令申请的裁定是立即生效的终局裁定，据此发布的海事强制令其实就是执行令，体现了海事强制令制度的裁执一体化特色。《〈海诉法〉司法解释》第四十三条明确指出："海事强制令由海事法院执行。被申请人、其他相关单位或者个人不履行海事强制令的，海事法院应当依据《民事诉讼法》的有关规定强制执行。"由此可见，海事强制令的执行与海事请求保全及海事证据保全的执行不同，后两者可以由海事法院直接执行，前者事实上是被请求人执行/履行。海事强制令的实施需要强制被请求人作为或不作为，对被请求人的配合程度要求高，因此执行难度较大。海事法院若要强制执行海事强制令，得依照《民事诉讼法》的有关规定采取强制执行措施。对被请求人采取强制执行海事强制令的措施，在被请求人是个人的情况下，将直接影响到被请求人的人身权，其影响与对财产的执行相比要大得多。

尽管有强制执行的规定，但《海诉法》对拒不执行海事强制令的被请求人还特别规定了处罚措施。《海诉法》第五十九条细化了《民事诉讼法》第一百一十四条①的规定，明确了罚款的金额以及拘留的期限②。而在海事纠纷中，案件标的额一般比较巨大，是否会因此出现被请求人拒绝配合法院执行海事强制令的情况呢？《海诉法》对于拒不执行海事强制令的规定是否合理呢？这也需要通过对近年来的海事司法实践进行研究得出结论。

由此可见，海事强制令虽为一种强制措施，但对海事强制令的执行与

---

① 《民事诉讼法》第一百一十四条："诉讼参与人或者其他人有下列行为之一的，人民法院可以根据情节轻重予以罚款、拘留；构成犯罪的，依法追究刑事责任：……（六）拒不履行人民法院已经发生法律效力的判决、裁定的。"

② 《海诉法》第五十九条第二款"对个人的罚款金额，为一千元以上三万元以下。对单位的罚款金额，为三万元以上十万元以下"；第三款"拘留的期限，为十五日以下"。

对同为强制措施的海事请求保全措施和海事证据保全措施的执行,除裁执一体化方面相同外,其他方面截然不同,反而在强制执行与拒不执行的处罚方面与经过正常审理程序的民事判决的执行一般无二。

综上所述,海事强制令制度名为强制措施,实质上是对海事请求人的一种紧急救济措施。《海诉法》对海事强制令基于强制措施的定位而做出的规定,与海事请求保全和海事证据保全的规定基本一样,基于海事强制令具有强制性等特点,该强制措施与海事请求保全和海事证据保全的性质不同,必须严格执行海事强制令的申请条件避免海事请求人对海事强制令制度的滥用,以实现对海事请求人、被请求人和利害关系人的利益保护的平衡。而这些规定对于不改变当事人之间实体权利义务关系的海事请求保全和海事证据保全这类程序性保全措施而言是合适的,但作为海事强制令制度的内容,则会导致对被请求人利益保护的严重失衡。

二、司法实践中海事强制令制度运行现状及问题

为分析海事强制令制度在司法实践中的运用现状,一方面在裁判文书网为主的网站收集裁判文书,另一方面到海事法院进行实地调研、与海事法院法官交流访谈。我们从裁判文书网共下载了 119 份涉及海事强制令的裁判文书,裁决时间从 2005 年 4 月到 2019 年 4 月,除北海海事法院外,其他 9 家海事法院均有相关的裁判文书。在实地调研过程中发现,鉴于裁判文书并未全面上网,实际案例要比公布的案例多,案件类型也更加多样化。此外,在与海事法院法官的交流和访谈中,研究团队还了解到了更多的案例和案件的处理细节以及法官处理案件时的考虑因素。

(一)上网裁判文书分析

1. 上网裁判文书统计数据

通过对下载的 119 份涉及海事强制令的裁判文书进行分析,本文整理出了各地海事法院处理海事强制令案件 118 宗,相关信息及案件处理情况见表1。

表1 海事强制令上网裁判文书情况一览

单位：宗

海事法院	案件数	准予	驳回（不受理）	撤回	诉前	诉中	后续损害赔偿诉讼	案件类型
武汉	39	27	3（2）	9	38	1	0	交货19，交单2，交船13，交船舶文件1，停止阻扰卸货1，责令离船1，停止非法留置船舶1
上海	35	18	0	17	35	0	0	交货5，交单24，履行义务6
宁波	12	7	2	3	11	1	0	交货1，交单9，还船1
广州	11	1	0	10	11	0	0	交货1，交单2，交船4
厦门	10	9	0	1	10	0	0	交货（集装箱）7，交单2
海口	4	4	0	0	4	0	0	交货1，交船2，清污1
大连	3	3	0	0	3	0	0	交货1，放船2
青岛	3	3	0	0	3	0	1	交货3
天津	1	1	0	0	1	0	1	交货1
合计	118	73	5	40	116	2	2	—

注：部分撤回案件无具体案件信息。

从表1可见，海事强制令案件总体数量不大，2005—2019年合计118宗，每年平均约8宗，其中得到支持的总计73宗，占比61.9%；驳回（包括不受理）的有5宗，占比4.2%；撤回或按撤回处理的有40宗，占比

33.9%。118 宗案件中，诉中提起的仅有 2 宗①，诉前提起的有 116 宗，占比超过 98%。在准予海事强制令的 73 宗诉前案件中，没有请求人后续提起诉讼的信息，有被请求人提起错误申请海事强制令的案件 2 宗②。案件类型包括：①强制交货；②强制交提单或提货单；③强制交船或放船（停止非法留置船舶）；④强制交付船舶文件；⑤停止阻扰卸货；⑥责令离船；⑦强制履行转运货物义务；⑧强制交还集装箱；⑨强制清污。从表 1 可以看出，案件类型以强制交货占绝大部分，其次是交单和交船。从受案数量上看，武汉海事法院最多，占总数的 33.1%。从撤回案件数据看，广州海事法院的撤回率最高，占受案数的 90.9%；其次是上海海事法院，撤回案件数占受案数的 48.6%。从案件类型上看，基本都是强制被请求人作为，结果都将改变当事人之间的实体权利义务关系。后续损害赔偿诉讼 2 宗，均以败诉结局③。

2. 裁判文书中体现出的特点和不足

从上网案件裁判文书统计信息分析，海事强制令制度在实际运用中出现了五个鲜明的特点。

（1）诉前申请占比高，海事请求人获支持后并无后续诉讼。这说明了实际案件中虽然有被请求人的违约或违法行为，但是海事请求人向海事法院申请海事强制令，责令被请求人进行一定的作为或者不作为，起到了阻止损失发生的作用，避免给请求人造成损失或者损失的扩大。比如，在南通开发区迅诺贸易有限公司、宁波伟仕信达供应链管理有限公司申请海事强制令一案④ 中，因被请求人擅自扣押其所托运货物的全套正本海运提单，请求人向宁波海事法院提出海事强制令申请，要求责令被请求人立即交付该批货物的全套正本海运提单。宁波海事法院经审查认为，请求人的海事强制令申请符合法律规定，所以准许请求人南通开发区迅诺贸易有限公司的海事强制令申请，并责令被请求人立即交付全套正本海运提单。通过海事强制令的申请和实施，海事请求人实现了保护自己利益的目的。海

---

① 参见武汉海事法院（2016）鄂 72 民初 164 号民事判决书、宁波海事法院（2014）甬海法商初字第 436 号民事判决书。
② 参见青岛海事法院（2016）鲁 72 民初 629 号民事判决书、天津市高级人民法院（2012）津高民四终字第 4 号民事判决书。
③ 参见青岛海事法院（2016）鲁 72 民初 629 号民事判决书、天津市高级人民法院（2012）津高民四终字第 4 号民事判决书。
④ 参见宁波海事法院（2019）浙 72 行保 3 号民事裁定书。

事请求人和被请求人后续并未提起诉讼，这也说明了海事强制令制度具有独立性和终局性，即不需要依附诉讼程序或在诉讼程序中得到最终确认，实际上直接解决了当事人之间的侵权或违约的实体权利义务纠纷。

（2）诉中海事强制令案中，海事强制令为原告（请求人）快速先行提供了一部分救济，该救济是独立的和终局的。例如，在武汉海事法院审理的黄金水岸游艇俱乐部有限公司与重庆华中船舶有限公司船舶管理合同纠纷案（简称黄金公司案）① 中，法院先通过海事强制令责成被告（被请求人）交还船舶，然后再审理双方之间的损失赔偿与被告反诉部分。同样，在宁波海事法院审理的宁波市镇海明鼎金属材料有限公司与逢原船务有限公司、大连瑞海船舶管理有限公司非法留置船载货物损害责任纠纷案（简称明鼎公司案）② 中，法院通过海事强制令责成被告（被请求人）交付涉案货物，然后才审理被告留置货物是否合法及原告主张损失是否合理。此外，值得注意的是，在黄金公司案中，经海事强制令处理的部分纠纷，后续不再进行实体审理，法院在判决书中明确表示"本案在审理中，经本院强制执行，华中公司将'长航江山5'号客船交付给黄金公司，因此，黄金公司请求华中公司交付'长航江山5'号客船的请求已履行完毕，本院不再进行实体处理"③。事实上，在后续损失赔偿审理中，法院也是直接依海事强制令认定被告有"拒绝交付船舶的行为"。在明鼎公司案中，法院虽然对被告"留置涉案货物是否合法"作了评析，但也只对损失赔偿问题作出判决。因此，诉中的海事强制令，其本身也是独立的和终局的，法院对其中涉及的实体问题不再进行实体审理和判决，被告（被请求人）即使对海事强制令的裁决不服，也无法通过上诉解决。

（3）被请求人以错误申请海事强制令请求损害赔偿的成功率低。目前仅有2宗案件④ 且均以败诉告终。对于海事强制令的裁定不服的，被请求人只有一次复议的机会：若复议成功时，后续提起损害赔偿诉讼获支持机会大；但是，若不申请复议或复议失败，在同一法院试图通过错误申请海事强制令损害赔偿诉讼来推翻海事强制令裁定并获赔偿几乎没有可能。在

---

① 参见武汉海事法院（2016）鄂72民初164号民事判决书、（2016）鄂72行保7号民事裁定书。
② 参见宁波海事法院（2014）甬海法商初字第436号民事判决书。
③ 武汉海事法院（2016）鄂72民初164号民事判决书。
④ 参见天津市高级人民法院（2012）津高民四终字第4号民事判决书、青岛海事法院（2016）鲁72民初629号民事判决书。

赛奥尔航运有限公司（简称赛奥尔公司）与唐山港陆钢铁有限公司错误申请海事强制令损害赔偿纠纷案（简称赛奥尔公司案）① 中，天津海事法院依港陆公司申请作出海事强制令，责令赛奥尔公司交付涉案货物；赛奥尔公司以港陆公司侵犯其留置权为由起诉，要求港陆公司赔偿经济损失。天津海事法院以赛奥尔公司主张留置权不成立、港陆公司申请海事强制令不具有客观违法性和主观过错性为由，判决驳回赛奥尔公司的诉讼请求。赛奥尔公司向天津市高级人民法院上诉被驳回。②

（4）裁定准予申请案件中的审理程序不一。由于《海诉法》对海事强制令的审查程序并未作出规定，实践中，海事法院的做法并不统一。从裁定准予申请的裁定书观察，8 家海事法院均有组成合议庭审查案件③，其中有 3 家海事法院同时采用独任审判员审查案件④。裁定书中明确其采用了听证程序审理案件的法院有上海海事法院⑤和大连海事法院⑥。

（5）关于《海诉法》第五十六条规定的运用，实践中并不统一。第五十六条规定了作出海事强制令应当具备的三个条件：①被请求人有具体的海事请求；②需要纠正被请求人违反法律规定或合同约定的行为；③情况紧急，不立即作出海事强制令将造成损害或使损害扩大。

《海诉法》第五十六条规定的三个条件应当要同时具备，特别是其中第三个条件是海事强制令作为紧急救济措施的重要特色和特点，也是其区别于一般审理案件程序的重要特点。但是，在实际案件中，真正得到认真审查的通常只有第二个条件。对各海事法院准予海事强制令裁定书的观察发现，绝大多数海事法院只审查被请求人有无违反法律规定或合同约定的

---

① 参见天津市高级人民法院（2012）津高民四终字第 4 号民事判决书。
② 赛奥尔公司向最高人民法院申请再审获准，最高人民法院指令天津市高级人民法院再审赛奥尔公司案（参见最高人民法院（2013）民申字第 413 号民事裁定书），但没有查阅到天津市高级人民法院的再审裁判文书。
③ 参见武汉海事法院（2016）鄂 72 行保 9 号民事裁定书、上海海事法院（2019）沪 72 行保 1 号民事裁定书、宁波海事法院（2019）浙 72 行保 3 号民事裁定书、广州海事法院（2015）广海法强字第 6-3 号民事裁定书、厦门海事法院（2015）厦海法强字第 6 号民事裁定书、海口海事法院（2017）琼 72 行保 2 号民事裁定书、大连海事法院（2017）辽 72 行保 5 号民事裁定书、青岛海事法院（2014）青海法海初字第 3 号民事裁定书。
④ 参见青岛海事法院（2014）青海法强字第 5-1 号民事裁定书、武汉海事法院（2016）鄂 72 行保 7 号民事裁定书、上海海事法院（2010）沪海法强字第 12 号民事裁定书。
⑤ 参见上海海事法院（2005）沪海法强字第 14 号、（2010）沪海法强字第 12 号、（2017）沪 72 行保 4 号、（2019）沪 72 号行保 1 号民事裁定书。
⑥ 参见大连海事法院（2017）辽 72 行保 5 号民事裁定书。

行为①；少数有提及损失将发生或扩大这个条件②；极少数同时提及三个条件③；也有不做分析只简单认定请求人的"申请符合法律规定"的④；只有大连海事法院的一份裁定书分点详细分析了第五十六条规定的条件，但也只分析了第二个和第三个条件。在锦州港城粮食工贸有限公司与中国外运辽宁有限公司锦州分公司海事强制令案⑤中，大连海事法院认为"对于海事强制令案件，本院只做程序性审查，即被申请人是否有违反法律规定或者合同约定行为，是否情况紧急，不立即作出海事强制令将造成损害或者使损害扩大的初步审查"。在分别对这两点做出审查后，大连海事法院得出结论："本院经审查认为，申请人港城公司的海事强制令申请理由属于被申请人违反法律规定的行为，该行为需要立即纠正，符合法律规定的海事强制令成立条件。"

（6）关于请求人提供担保情况，裁定书记载粗略。《海诉法》第五十五条⑥规定，海事法院可以责令准予海事强制令申请的裁定书，海事法院受理海事强制令申请，可以责令海事请求人提供担保。这也说明，海事申请人提供担保不是必需的，海事法院需要在具体的司法实践中自主确定是否需要海事请求人提供担保。一般认为，被请求人的行为明显违反法律规定或者合同约定而给海事请求人带来损害、海事请求人的请求确实有依据时，考虑到实际情况，如海事请求人生活困难、经济情况差，无力提供巨额担保的，海事法院可以不要求海事请求人提供担保。

对于准予海事强制令的申请裁定书，海事法院大多责令海事请求人提供了担保，并且准予海事强制令的裁定书中对请求人提供担保情况多有记

---

① 参见武汉海事法院（2016）鄂72行保9号民事裁定书、上海海事法院（2019）沪72行保1号民事裁定书等。

② 参见上海海事法院（2017）沪72行保4号民事裁定书、广州海事法院（2015）广海法强字第6-3号民事裁定书；青岛海事法院（2014）青海法强字第5-1号民事裁定书。

③ 参见武汉海事法院（2016）鄂72行保3号民事裁定书，该裁定书认为"请求人扬子江公司的请求明确、具体，恒盛公司拒绝交付货物、明阳公司阻挠交付货物的行为违反了法律的规定。请求人扬子江公司要求被请求人恒盛公司、明阳公司立即交付货物，以避免损害扩大，符合法律规定"。

④ 参见宁波海事法院（2019）浙72行保3号民事裁定书、厦门海事法院（2015）厦海法强字第6号民事裁定书、海口海事法院（2017）琼72行保2号民事裁定书等。

⑤ 参见大连海事法院（2017）辽72行保5号民事裁定书。

⑥《海诉法》第五十五条："海事法院受理海事强制令申请，可以责令请求人提供担保。海事求人不提供的，驳回其申请。"

载,但对担保方式、担保数额的记载并不统一。有的只记载了请求人"已(向本院)提供了担保"①或"已(向本院)提供相应的担保"②,未载明担保的方式;有的只记载"请求人已向本院提供现金担保"③,明确了现金担保方式,但没明确担保数额;有的载明了现金担保数额,如请求人"为其强制令申请向本院提交了 54 万元作为担保"④;有的明确了担保函担保并记载了担保人及担保数额或担保责任限额,如请求人"已向本院提供宁波市洪泰担保有限公司 431691.67 元的担保函作为担保"⑤ 或"已向本院提供了由中国人民财产保险股份有限公司海南省分公司为本案及(2017)琼 72 行保 1 号案件共同出具的《诉讼财产保全责任保险保单保函》(单证流水号为 46001600033686),责任限额为 200 万元人民币"⑥。

(二) 调研访谈资料分析

1. 调研访谈资料统计数据

为了更全面地了解海事强制令制度的运用情况,研究团队在广州海事法院、武汉海事法院进行了实地调研,与部分一线法官开展了较为深入的交流,了解了广州海事法院海事强制令案件的更接近实际的案件数据、听证机制的运用、担保的要求以及撤销案件的情况,也了解了武汉海事法院将海事强制令制度创新运用的情况以及北海海事法院将请求人的担保纳入裁定的特色案例。

据广州海事法院林依伊法官统计,从 2000 年至 2018 年广州海事法院共受理了 257 宗诉前海事强制令案件,其中 2000 年 1 宗、2001 年 3 宗、2002 年 6 宗、2003 年 3 宗、2004 年 7 宗、2005 年 7 宗、2006 年 13 宗、2007 年 11 宗、2008 年 49 宗、2009 年 19 宗、2010 年 15 宗、2011 年 20 宗、2012 年 78 宗、2013 年 3 宗、2014 年 5 宗、2015 年 6 宗、2016 年 4

---

① 参见武汉海事法院(2016)鄂 72 行保 3 号民事裁定书、厦门海事法院(2015)厦海法强字第 6 号民事裁定书、青岛海事法院(2014)青海法强字第 5-1 号民事裁定书。
② 参见武汉海事法院(2016)鄂 72 行保 9 号民事裁定书、大连海事法院(2017)辽 72 行保 5 号民事裁定书。
③ 参见上海海事法院(2010)沪海法强字第 12 号民事裁定书。
④ 参见武汉海事法院(2016)鄂 72 行保 7 号民事裁定书。同样记载了担保数额的还有上海海事法院(2019)沪 72 行保 1 号民事裁定书、广州海事法院(2015)广海法强字第 6-3 号民事裁定书。
⑤ 参见宁波海事法院(2019)浙 72 行保 3 号民事裁定书。
⑥ 参见海口海事法院(2017)琼 72 行保 2 号民事裁定书。

宗、2017 年 4 宗、2018 年 3 宗。这一数据表明了海事强制令制度在海事司法实践中实际上得到了较广泛应用，说明了海事请求人清楚该制度对其权利保护的意义和价值，为研究海事强制令制度的实施提供了翔实的资料。

2. 实践操作中海事强制令制度应用情况

（1）听证机制的实际运用。海事强制令虽然没有明确为一种保全措施，但在制度设计上是将其作为保全措施处理的，是为请求人的利益设计的，本来只是一种快速的单方程序，虽然《海诉法》中并未规定听证程序，但在运用过程中，双方听证程序的引入却突破了原来的制度设计。

实践中，有的案件情况可能比较复杂，仅从被请求人一方提供的证据很难做出正确的裁判，而案件牵涉的问题可能比较严重、性质比较敏感，一旦做出错误的裁定不仅很可能给当事一方带来难以弥补的损害，而且可能损害法院司法裁判的公信力和权威性。因此，虽然《海诉法》及其相关解释并没有规定听证制度，但法院在做海事强制令裁定时会保持慎重，甚至会同时传唤请求人和被请求人组成临时听证会，给被请求人一个答辩的机会，从而对整个案情有比较全面的把握，并在此基础上做出海事强制令裁定。

在访谈中我们了解到，在广州海事法院审理的 257 宗案件中，据统计，有 111 宗采用了听证程序，其中 2011 年以后的有 98 宗，包括裁定作出前的听证和复议阶段的听证；在这 111 宗听证案件中，听证后请求人撤回请求的有 96 宗。由双方听证程序的引入而导致的高比例的撤回，在某种程度上可以说明请求人的申请经不起质证，存在滥用海事强制令制度的可能性。因此，基于请求人单方申请材料作出海事强制令出现错误的可能性较大，而由于海事强制令的执行事实上处理了当事人之间的实体权利义务，错误作出的海事强制令将直接损害被请求人的利益，不仅是实体利益，还包括正常诉讼程序中的程序权利。海事强制令制度设计的不足，使海事法院不得不引入双方听证程序以查明案情并确保该制度公正运行。

听证程序作为我国海事法院在海事强制令制度实施中的创新做法，其对于减少纷争和避免错误裁判起到了积极的作用。但是《海诉法》及其司法解释对于听证程序并没有规定，该做法没有法律依据，所以在《海诉法》的修改中引进听证程序，允许海事法院依据案件的具体情况决定是否进行听证值得考虑。

（2）海事强制令案撤销情形中复议机制的应用。据统计，在广州海事法院的实践中，有 5 宗案件的海事强制令被撤销，这在一定程度上说明了单方程序作出裁定存在的漏洞。第 1 宗是船舶承租人请求出租人履行租约不得在租期内收回船舶，海事法院作出了海事强制令①，被请求人提出异议认为请求人未履行支付租金的义务，法院查明属实后撤销了海事强制令。第 2 宗是光船出租人请求光船承租人按租约规定的 2005 年某一日前交还船舶，海事法院作出海事强制令②后，被请求人提出异议并提交了一份期限到 2006 年某一日的租约，因无法查明两份租约的真假，故撤销海事强制令。第 3 宗是请求人以被请求人侵犯了自己对集装箱的所有权为由申请海事强制令，要求被请求人交还涉案集装箱，海事法院作出海事强制令③后，被请求人提出异议，经查明被请求人拒绝交还涉案集装箱并不违反法律规定，故撤销海事强制令。第 4 宗是关于强制交付提单的海事强制令④，被请求人提出异议后，查明被请求人并不持有涉案提单，故撤销海事强制令。第 5 宗是请求人依副本提单交货后要求被请求人交回正本提单或返还该提单项下货物而申请海事强制令⑤，后查明被请求人并不持有涉案正本提单，货物也已不在其控制之下了，故撤销海事强制令。后 2 宗属于无法执行的海事强制令。

  这些撤销案件虽然说明了复议机制对被请求人利益保护的重要意义，但前提条件是海事强制令尚未强制执行。在复议与异议方面，海事请求人、被请求人以及其他利害关系人可能对海事法院作出的准予海事强制令与否的裁定不服。《海诉法》规定，可以在收到裁定书之日起五日内申请复议一次，但复议期间不停止裁定的执行。《海诉法》第五十八条⑥规定当事人提出异议，只能申请复议，而不能上诉。这主要考虑到虽然海事强制令是保护当事人实体权利的措施，但仍是一种程序上的制度，而不是解决实体争议的制度。对于案件实体有争议的，最终也可以通过实体诉讼进行纠正。但是，既然不允许对海事强制令提起上诉，那么对于《海诉法》中规定的一级复议机制，这种机制虽为被请求人提供了抗辩的机会，但只

---

  ① 参见广州海事法院（2002）广海法强字第 3 号民事裁定书。
  ② 参见广州海事法院（2005）广海法强字第 6 号民事裁定书。
  ③ 参见广州海事法院（2008）广海法强字第 32 号民事裁定书。
  ④ 参见广州海事法院（2008）广海法强字第 47 号民事裁定书。
  ⑤ 参见广州海事法院（2009）广海法强字第 18 号民事裁定书。
  ⑥ 《海诉法》第五十八条："当事人对裁定不服的，可以在收到裁定书之日起五日内申请复议一次。海事法院应当在收到复议申请之日起五日内作出复议决定。复议期间不停止裁定的执行。"

是事后的抗辩，阻止不了裁定的执行，改变不了其与请求人之间实体权利义务关系被改变的结果。通常情况下，事后的抗辩是很难改变先入为主的决定的，被请求人往往处于一种极为不利的境况；即使复议成功，准予海事强制令的裁定被撤销，如何以及能否回转海事强制令的执行也还是个问题。那么，是否可以规定二级复议以体现对被请求人的保护，实现救济功能呢？实践中仍存在争议。由此可见，由于只有一次复议机会，若复议被驳回，则被请求人再无救济。因此，可以说，《海诉法》规定的复议机制对海事强制令的被请求人而言，所提供的保护价值并不大。

（3）"海事担保"的实际应用。《海诉法》第五十五条对海事请求人提供担保的规定是非强制性的，即海事法院"可以"责令海事请求人提供担保。上网公开的海事强制令裁定书对请求人提供担保情况多有记载，形式主要为现金担保和保函担保。[①] 在广州海事法院的调研中，我们进一步了解到，广州海事法院在受理前述257宗案件后，一律责令海事请求人提供担保。责成请求人提供担保在一定程度上可以防止其滥用海事强制令制度，还可以在申请错误造成被请求人损失时为其提供赔偿保障。一律提供担保的实践，体现了广州海事法院对被请求人利益的重视与关怀。

关于海事担保的方式，《海诉法》在第六章"海事担保"部分明确规定为"提供现金或者保证、设置抵押或者质押"[②]，但在实践中出现了"活扣船"担保这样的特色担保方式。在北海海事法院处理的张礼添与梁德坤申请海事强制令案[③]中，梁德坤的船舶"柳城612"号与张礼添的船舶"海通6889"号发生碰撞导致"柳城612"号船沉货损人亡事故[④]，梁德坤扣押了"海通6889"号船，张礼添因此向北海海事法院申请海事强制令，请求责令梁德坤立即返还"海通6889号"船，北海海事法院在裁定准予申请并责令被请求人返还被扣船舶的同时，还裁定"自即日起扣押请求人张礼添所有的'海通6889'号；在裁定扣押期间，允许该船舶继续运营，但不得有转让、抵押或其他处分船舶行为"[⑤]。这种以法院裁定扣押涉事船舶的方式作为海事强制令申请的担保，创新了海事强制令的担保方式，直接取代了被请求人对涉事船舶的非法扣押，为被请求人后续提起船舶碰撞

[①] 参见上文对上网海事强制令裁定书分析第（6）小点。
[②] 见《海诉法》第七十三条第二款。
[③] 参见北海海事法院（2008）海法强字第001号民事裁定书。
[④] 参加北海海事法院（2008）海事初字第023号民事判决书。
[⑤] 参见北海海事法院（2008）海法强字第001号民事裁定书。

损害赔偿诉讼提供了财产保全,无疑能使责令被请求人放船的海事强制令得到遵守,并引导案件进入正常的纠纷解决渠道。

三、完善我国海事强制令制度的路径选择与方案

海事强制令制度实施以来,在一定程度上发挥了快速解决纠纷的作用,其存在的价值毋庸置疑。对海事请求人而言,海事强制令是对其提供快速救济的重要措施,很受青睐。然而,对于被请求人而言,这种单方程序快速裁定、一裁终局、裁执一体化的措施却有可能严重影响到其实体利益。错误的海事强制令裁定可能给被请求人造成不可逆转或无法弥补的损失。

为解决实践中出现的这些问题,如何完善海事强制令制度极为重要。海事强制令制度改革必然面临以下两条路径选择。

其一,将海事强制令案件转化为一审终审的简易程序审理的案件。这意味着要接受海事法院目前的创新实践。首先,实践中立案前审查及不予受理的裁定,显然是在 48 小时审查时限之外增加了 7 天的受案时限[1],与一般诉讼案件的受理无异。实践中双方听证程序的引入,保障了被请求人陈述意见的权利,通知被请求人的方式及送达申请书和审查的方式,都符合简易程序的简便方式;[2] 海事强制令案中独任法官审查案件的实践,是简易程序的特点[3];海事强制令案比一般程序审理的案件审结时限更短,也符合简易程序的特点。[4] 此外,海事强制令案件只涉及行为而无标的额,显然符合简易程序的小额诉讼案件"一审终审"的规定。[5] 简易程序中,对于不宜采用简易程序审理的案件可直接转化为普通程序审理[6],这比不受理或驳回海事强制令申请时请求人另行起诉更加简便。

这种方案突出了海事强制令案件解决当事人之间实体权利义务纠纷的实质,在一定程度上确保了被请求人的程序性权利,可以更好地维护被请求人的实体利益。同时,简易程序审理案件比一般程序审理案件快速、简

---

[1] 见《民事诉讼法》第一百二十六条。
[2] 见《民事诉讼法》第一百六十二条。
[3] 见《民事诉讼法》第一百六十三条。
[4] 见《民事诉讼法》第一百六十四条。
[5] 见《民事诉讼法》第一百六十五条。
[6] 见《民事诉讼法》第一百六十九条。

便,也契合海事强制令快速解决纠纷的特色。但是,这种改造的结果使海事强制令只是作为针对被请求人行为(作为或不作为)的一种救济方式而存在,确实极大地弱化了海事强制令制度作为海事诉讼特别程序的独特性和独特地位。

其二,保留其强制措施的特色但将其与保全措施相区分,从限定并细化其适用条件等方面完善现有规定。这种方案保留了海事强制令作为海事诉讼制度的独特性和独特地位,只需在修改《海诉法》时完善相关规定,解决实践中产生的问题,更具可行性。

因此,本文支持第二条路径,即保持海事强制令的制度设计,并完善海事强制令制度的相关规定,如细化该制度的适用条件等,下面将展开详细论述。

(一) 明确海事强制令制度的定位

首先,海事强制令执行的后果,实质上是为特定条件下的海事请求人提供快速救济。由于在制度的设计上《海诉法》并未关注到海事强制令解决实体权益纠纷的实质,只关注其强制措施一面,将其与海事请求保全和海事证据保全这类性质不同的强制措施基本上等同对待,因此实践中为平衡被请求人利益的保护而出现各种创新突破。海事强制令制度在司法实践中的运用状况及海事法院的各种创新突破,充分说明了海事强制令制度不同于保全制度的独特性质,即为请求人实体权利的保护提供快速救济。

其次,《海诉法》只是将海事强制令界定为一种强制措施,并非保全措施。当海事强制令制度出现时,《民事诉讼法》并无对应的制度,《海诉法》专章对其作出规定,置于"海事请求保全"和"海事证据保全"两章之间,但并未明确海事强制令是保全措施,定义上只明确为一种强制措施,各海事法院在案号设置上均体现了该制度的特色。2015年以前,各海事法院对海事强制令案都采用独特的案号,如(2015)武海法强字第00013号、(2015)广海法强字第6-3号、(2015)沪海法强字第6号。然而,自2016年起,各海事法院纷纷将其视为行为保全措施,体现在案号设置上,例如,(2016)鄂72行保1号、(2016)粤72行保1号、(2016)琼72行保2号、(2016)沪72行保3号等。这种形式上的改变,虽然契合了修改后的《民事诉讼法》将责令当事人"作出一定行为或者禁止其作出一定行为"纳入保全措施①（实践中称为"行为保全"）这种认识，但实质上改变不了海事强制令不同于保全措施的性质，反而模糊了海事强制令的独特性，使人们对海事强制令的认识更加混乱。原有的案号设计虽然不能显示海事强制令为被请求人提供快速救济这一性质，但彰显了海事强制令不同于保全措施的独特性，是更准确的选择。

因此，本文建议在《海诉法》修改时应当明确海事强制令制度是为海事请求人提供紧急救济的强制措施这一定位，并在此基础上探讨海事强制令制度的完善，才能保持海事强制令制度的独特地位，发挥其应有的作用。《海诉法》第五十一条应修改为"海事强制令是指海事法院根据海事请求人的申请，为使其合法权益免受侵害，责令被请求人作为或者不作为的紧急救济措施"。

（二）完善海事强制令制度的具体建议

1. 调整海事强制令至《海诉法》第五章

若要彰显海事强制令制度的独特地位，又要体现其不同于保全措施的为请求人提供快速救济的性质，可将《海诉法》海事证据保全调到第四章，而将海事强制令调到第五章，并在保留海事强制令现有制度基本设计的基础上，从细化海事强制令的适用条件、实现海事请求人的权责统一等方面加强对被请求人利益的保护，以保障海事强制令制度得到公平公正的运用。之所以调整海事强制令在《海诉法》中的位置，是为凸显海事强制令之不同于海事请求保全与海事证据保全的性质，后两者都是典型的保全措施，附属于特定海事请求并促进海事请求的实现，而海事强制令更实质的特点是快速救济措施，是实现特定海事请求的手段，是可以独立实施的终局解决纠纷的措施。海事强制令在实际运用中展现的这些特点，立法上的应对就应当是将其与保全措施相区别，将其规定于保全措施之后海事担保之前。这样规定从立法逻辑上看更加合理和顺畅，使立法更具科学性。

2. 细化海事强制令的适用条件

海事强制令是为海事请求人提供的快速救济措施，应当成为正常诉讼程序的有效补充。《海诉法》第五十六条规定的适用条件不足以将海事强制令这种救济与采用审理程序的诉讼救济相区别。那么，在什么情况下提

---

① 见《民事诉讼法》第一百零三条。

供这种快速救济，就是海事强制令的适用范围？针对被请求人的违法或违约行为，请求人依法可以提起侵权诉讼或违约诉讼，要求法院责令被请求人停止侵害、排除妨碍或继续履行合同[①]，诉讼程序中还可以要求损害赔偿救济。海事强制令虽只提供责令被请求人停止侵权或继续履行合同的救济，但不影响请求人后续的损害赔偿诉讼。海事强制令申请被驳回也不构成"一事不再理"的情形，不影响海事请求人提起诉讼。海事强制令能快速简便地提供救济，对请求人百利而无一害，但对被请求人则颇不公平。在诉讼程序中，被告人（被请求人）享有合理时间内提出管辖权异议、答辩、出庭抗辩以及上诉等保障其实体权益的程序权利，但在现行海事强制令的制度设计中，在裁定作出前被请求人不享有任何程序性权利。因此，应当对海事强制令的适用条件加以明确细化。

鉴于其只为请求人提供救济而快速处理纠纷的性质，海事强制令应当限定适用于权利义务关系明确、违法或违约行为事实清楚、争议不大且案情简单的侵权或合同纠纷，对争议大、案情复杂且无法在48小时内查清的申请应予以驳回。例如，在宁波海事法院处理的"万邦公司案"[②]中，法院准确把握了海事强制令与诉讼救济的不同，限定了海事强制令的适用范围，认为被请求人万邦公司虽然依法享有留置权，但留置权是否成立有待查明，被请求人是否违法或违约事实不清，故驳回其海事强制令申请。

所以，本文建议《海诉法》第五十六条可修改为："作出海事强制令，应当具备下列条件：（一）请求人与被请求人之间的权利义务关系明确；（二）被请求人违法或违约行为事实清楚；（三）不立即纠正被请求人的违法或违约行为将造成损害或使损害扩大。"这三个条件，任何一个得不到满足，都不能作出海事强制令。

3. 实现海事请求人的权责统一

现行海事强制令制度是为请求人的单方利益而设立的，但除依法院要求提供担保外，并无其他义务和责任的规定。为实现权利和义务的对等，有必要增加对请求人义务和责任的规定。关于请求人义务和责任的规定，

[①] 《民法典》第一千一百六十七条："侵权行为危及他人人身、财产安全的，被侵权人有权请求侵权人承担停止侵害、排除妨碍、消除危险等侵权责任"；第五百七十七条："当事人一方不履行合同义务或者履行合同义务不符合约定的，应当承担继续履行、采取补救措施或者赔偿损失等违约责任"。

[②] 参见宁波海事法院（2017）浙72行保12号民事裁定书。

可以从保障海事法院准确适用海事强制令，发挥海事强制令快速解决纠纷或促进纠纷解决的作用方面入手。

增加对海事请求人义务和责任的规定，要求提出海事强制令申请时，必须承担如实全面陈述案情和提供证据的义务，使法院对案情有更全面的把握。作为单方程序，海事强制令的准确运用有赖于海事请求人如实全面陈述案情和提供证据。全面真实地反映双方权利义务关系、纠纷产生及协商解决过程的案情材料有助于海事法院审查海事强制令申请是否符合适用条件，如双方之间权利义务关系是否明确，被请求人是否存在违法或违约行为以及采用海事强制令是否还有意义，等等。这样还可以避免或减少在异议阶段因被请求人披露请求人隐瞒的事实导致撤销裁定的情况。例如，在广州海事法院处理的（2002）广海法强字第3号案中，请求人隐瞒了本方违约不支付租金的事实，还假称本方已全面履行了义务，导致法院作出了责令被请求人不得在租期内收回船舶的裁定。若对请求人课以全面披露案情的义务，法院在该案中就极有可能驳回请求人的申请，而不必到异议阶段才全面了解案情全貌并撤销准予海事强制令申请的裁定，从而节省司法资源。

所以，《海诉法》修改时应当增加对海事请求人义务和责任的规定：①海事请求人应当向法庭如实全面陈述案情和提供证据；②海事请求人应使法庭确信被请求人有违反法律规定或者合同约定的行为；③海事请求人应当对"情况紧急"负有充分举证义务。

4. 准予海事强制令申请的裁定书中应详细载明担保的内容

责令海事请求人在提出海事强制令申请时提供担保，主要目的是为可能存在的错误申请海事强制令造成被请求人的损失提供保障，还可以为被请求人的后续诉讼请求提供保全保障，促进海事被请求人对海事强制令的主动履行。实践中，被请求人涉嫌违法或违约行为，很多情况下，可能是为了保障其特定权益的实现，如留置单证或货物可能是为了收取运费、船舶碰撞案件中扣留船舶可能是为了获得赔偿等。若在权利义务关系明确的情况下，被请求人的行为没有任何法定或约定的依据时，海事法院作出海事强制令是合适的，但强制执行海事强制令仍然可能使矛盾激化。此时，请求人提供的合适的担保，若足以为被请求人特定权益的实现提供保障，则有助于被请求人履行海事强制令并转而采用诉讼或仲裁的方式维护自身权益。

鉴于海事强制令案中的担保对于被请求人具有重要的意义，海事强制令裁定书中只写明请求人"提供了担保"或"提供了相应的担保"或"提供了现金担保"这种不能明确担保价值或担保力度的内容是不够的，因为被请求人不能据此判断请求人提供的担保对其是否有保障价值。无论是现金担保还是保函担保，都有必要写明担保的数额，若是采用船舶等实物担保的，裁定书中有必要明确裁定对该实物采取的措施，如查封或扣押等。

5. 完善海事强制令申请错误的责任承担

在申请海事强制令错误的责任承担方面，被请求人或者利害关系人由于海事请求人申请海事强制令错误而遭受损害的，可以向海事法院提起诉讼索赔因此遭受的损失。对申请海事强制令确有错误的，海事法院应当判决海事请求人赔偿被请求人或者利害关系人因此遭受的损失。被请求人依据《海诉法》第六十条的规定要求海事请求人赔偿损失的，由发布海事强制令的海事法院受理。复议成功，准予海事强制令的裁定被撤销的，被请求人可以提出损害赔偿请求。对于被请求人提出的损害赔偿请求，《海诉法》规定的救济措施较为单一，只有损失赔偿。海事强制令是强制被请求人作为或不作为，因此错误海事强制令首要的救济方式应该是行为给付的方式，如恢复原状、返还财产等，而《海诉法》规定的金钱赔偿应当属于次要救济的方式，即当首要救济不能满足被请求人或利害关系人的损失时，才考虑赔偿其损失。

本文建议《海诉法》第六十条修改为："海事请求人申请海事强制令错误的，应当恢复原状、返还财产，并赔偿被请求人或者利害关系人因此所遭受的损失。"

6. 统一和规范各海事法院的实践操作

针对目前各海事法院在海事强制令案件中实践操作不统一的问题，若保留现有海事强制令制度的基本设计，则应当在以下六个方面统一：①将协商解决作为申请海事强制令的前置条件，给予被请求人必要的抗辩机会。②责令海事请求人如实全面陈述案情（包括被请求人的抗辩）并提供全面的证据。这样可以还原海事强制令为单方程序，不必继续采用或引入双方听证程序。③将海事强制令限定适用于处理权利义务关系明确、违法或违约行为事实清楚争议不大的案件，由独任法官审查决定。以上三个方面的操作可以大大节省司法资源，使司法资源得到更加合理地运用。④准予海事强制令申请的裁定书应该详细载明请求人提供担保的方式、担保的数额或实物担保时裁定采取的措施。⑤海事强制令裁定书应加强说理，对准予或不准予的申请都应当结合申请人提供的证据对作出海事强制令的条件是否具备作出认定。⑥鉴于海事强制令一裁终局和裁执一体化的特点,海事强制令裁定书应当写明"本裁定书送达后即发生法律效力,应当立即执行"。

海洋污染公益诉讼若干实务问题探析

许光玉[*]

摘要：海洋污染公益诉讼法律争议大、证据收集困难。在实务中，经常遇到索赔主体争议问题及对公约和国内法的理解与适用问题，而有关调查、评估规范的法律效力问题也是争论不休的话题。同时，在证据收集方面，对漏油量及污染损害的确定、公共证据及监测、评估报告的运用均有着严格的要求。针对以上疑难问题，本文结合法理、实务操作经验及典型案例进行分析并提出相关意见。

关键词：海洋污染公益诉讼　赔偿责任　污染损害　监测评估

Analysis of Practical Legal Issues in Public Interest Litigation for Marine Pollution

Xu Guangyu

Abstract: The legal disputes concerning the public interest litigation for maritime pollution are substantial, and evidence collection poses considerable challenges. In practice, contentious issues often arise regarding disputes over the claimant's legal standing, interpretation and application of conventions and domestic laws. The efficacy of regulations about investigation and assessment standards is a continuously debated topic. Moreover, with regard to evidence collection, stringent criteria govern the determination of oil spill quantities and pollution damage, the utilization of public evidence, monitoring and assessment reports. In addressing these intricate matters, this article combines legal principles, practical operational expertise, and illustrative case studies to conduct

---

[*] 许光玉：全国优秀律师，广东海建律师事务所主任，交通运输部海事局船舶油污损害赔偿基金专家，广东省法学会航运法学研究会副会长，华南师范大学国际航运法律与政策研究中心兼职研究员，高级海事工程师，曾任中华全国律师协会海商海事专业委员会执委、广东省律师协会海事海商法律专业委员会主任、广东海事局（原交通部广州海上安全监督局）法规处处长。

a thorough analysis and propose pertinent recommendations.

Key words: public interest litigation for marine pollution; liability for compensation; pollution damage; monitoring and assessment

20多年来，我国沿海发生的重大海洋污染案件有50多宗，涉及的海洋污染公益诉讼包括海洋自然资源和生态环境公益诉讼。其中，笔者参与的渔业资源公益诉讼案有40多宗，约占80%。但涉及海洋生态环境损害索赔的案件却极少，除笔者参与的2011年美国康菲渤海湾蓬莱19-3钻井平台漏油案（简称蓬莱19-3油污案）及2007年"金玫瑰"轮与"金盛"轮碰撞漏油案生态环境损害索赔案[1]（简称"金玫瑰"轮油污案）外，另外两宗非笔者代理的分别是2002年"塔斯曼海"轮及2005年"阿提哥"轮海洋生态环境损害索赔案[2]。现仅对笔者所参与或了解的海洋污染公益诉讼案件中遇到的问题进行汇总、分析并提出意见，以期抛砖引玉。

一、海洋污染公益诉讼法律问题研究

海洋污染公益诉讼面临诸多法律问题，其中索赔主体问题、对公约和国内法的理解与适用问题以及有关调查、评估规范的法律地位问题几乎在每个案子中都会遇到。

（一）索赔主体问题

在通常情况下，渔业资源损失由渔业主管部门（如海洋与渔业局）负责索赔，海洋生态损失则由海洋部门（如海洋局）负责。但在实务中，索赔主体存在不小争议。比如，在渔业资源索赔案中，由渔民协会、海洋与渔业局属下的渔政支队、渔政渔港监督处等单位索赔的情况亦存在。在上述单位提出索赔时，被告往往抗辩称原告主体不适格。尽管在诉讼中，法院认可上述单位的索赔主体地位，但也耗费大量时间和精力去解决该争议。在国家机构改革时，行政主管机关还可能出现"真空"状况。如"达

---

[1] "金玫瑰"轮油污案，青岛海事法院（2007）青海法确字第45号一审民事判决书、青岛海事法院（2010）青海法海事初字第17号一审民事判决书。

[2] "阿提哥"轮海洋生态环境损害索赔案，最高人民法院（2015）民申字第1637号再审民事裁定书。

飞"轮渔业资源损害索赔案①本由原农业部东海区渔政局代表国家索赔，但诉讼中因国家机构改革该局被撤销。因诉讼仍在进行，当务之急是寻找一个适格主体，而农业农村部渔业渔政管理局在上海地区却未能找到适格的渔业行政主管机关。最终，农业农村部渔业渔政管理局根据《渔业水域污染事故调查处理程序规定》第八条规定，指定下级机构中国水产科学研究院东海水产研究所作为索赔主体。尽管被告提出异议，但法院仍予以支持。

由此可见，为更好地保护海洋公共利益，海洋公益诉讼的主体不应仅限于行政主管机关或社会公益组织，而应采用开放的态度，如科研部门、相关专业协会对海洋渔业、生态资源有比较深入的了解，可通过立法方式来明确其索赔主体地位。

（二）对公约和国内法的理解与适用问题

1. 对公约和国内法的理解问题

每个公约条文的诞生都有特定的背景，公约仅是单行地解决某些特定范围的法律问题。例如，《1969年国际油污损害赔偿责任公约》（简称《CLC公约》）和《2001年国际燃油污染损害民事责任公约》（简称《燃油公约》），该两公约是为了解决船舶装载的持久性油类（前者为货油，后者为燃油）由于搁浅、触礁、碰撞等事故泄漏时应由该船承担的责任问题。上述两公约的第三条均规定，船舶应对由船上或源于船上的油类造成的污染损害负责，许多法学专家、学者、法官由此推导出非漏油船方无需承担赔偿责任的结论。

笔者认为，从《CLC公约》《燃油公约》的条文及其产生背景看，上述法律并不解决两船碰撞时非漏油船的责任问题，非漏油船的责任承担问题应适用《统一船舶碰撞某些法律规定的国际公约》和国内法。而《最高人民法院关于审理船舶油污损害赔偿纠纷案件若干问题的规定》（简称《油污司法解释》）第四条亦沿用《CLC公约》《燃油公约》的表述，规定污染受害方可以请求泄漏油船舶所有人承担全部赔偿责任。笔者认为该条是选择性条款，意为污染受害方可向漏油船方索赔，不影响其向非漏油船索赔的权利。但仍有部分专家、学者、法官认为该条明确应由漏油船承担

---

① 参见"达飞"轮渔业资源损害索赔案，宁波海事法院（2015）甬海法事初字第36号一审民事判决书，浙江省高级人民法院（2021）浙民再95号再审民事判决书。

全部赔偿责任，体现了"谁漏油，谁先赔"的原则。① 如此争论了20年，仍未形成一致意见。

由于上述法律问题未能得到解决，导致公益诉讼的索赔日益艰难，各地法院甚至根据自行理解作出截然不同的判决。如天津海事法院2002年"塔斯曼海"轮与"顺凯1"号碰撞漏油案及广州海事法院1988年的"VLACHERNABREEZE"轮与"潮河"轮碰撞漏油案均认为两船碰撞造成污染损害应承担连带责任；广东省高级人民法院2000年"闽燃供2"轮与"东海209"轮碰撞污染案②及青岛海事法院2007年"金玫瑰"轮与"金盛"轮碰撞污染案则认为碰撞船应根据其过错比例承担责任；而在"达飞"轮与"舟山"轮碰撞污染案中宁波海事法院、浙江省高级人民法院则持漏油船先赔的观点。

笔者认为，漏油船先赔的观点不仅没有法律依据，还与实务相悖，激化社会矛盾。实务中，漏油船无赔付能力或者保险公司倒闭、保额低等情况都有可能存在。如2000年"德航298"轮与"BOW CECIL"轮碰撞案，"德航298"轮是内河小油船，船毁人亡，没有任何赔偿能力，甚至没有购买保险。按照漏油船先赔的观点，因漏油船"德航298"轮船东破产，无力赔付，也就不存在其赔偿污染受害方后再向"BOW CECIL"轮追偿的问题，这将导致非漏油船作为责任者无需承担责任的情况。又如，在2011年"HAMBURG BRIDGE"轮和"ORIENTAL SUNRISE"轮碰撞案中，"ORIENTAL SUNRISE"轮沉没并严重漏油，"ORIENTAL SUNRISE"是在香港注册的单船公司，保险人破产倒闭，如非漏油船不赔，污染受害方根本无从得以获偿。最终，该案以非漏油船按其责任比例赔偿告终。可见，漏油船先赔的观点不可行。

从现行法律规定看，《中华人民共和国民法典》（简称《民法典》）第一千二百三十三条赋予了被侵权人同时向污染者和第三人索赔的权利，该法条源于《中华人民共和国侵权责任法》（简称《侵权责任法》，已废止）第六十八条，在《侵权责任法》之后，《最高人民法院关于审理环境侵权责任纠纷案件适用法律若干问题的解释》（已废止）第五条进一步明确第

---

① 韩立新、刘红：《油污损害赔偿中非漏油方的责任主体地位探析》，载《河北法学》2008年第9期，第151-155页。

② "闽燃供2"轮与"东海209"轮碰撞污染案，广东省高级人民法院（2000）粤高法经二终字第328号二审民事判决书。

三人应根据其过错比例承担赔偿责任。

鉴于上述情况，笔者认为在目前法律框架下，两船碰撞造成污染损害，可以污染损害额及利息为限，由漏油船承担全部责任，非漏油船根据责任比例承担责任。对此，在前述"达飞"轮与"舟山"轮碰撞污染中，笔者亦持以上观点向最高人民法院申请再审，最高人民法院最终支持了此观点。

2. 对公约中污染损害概念的理解问题

在海洋污染公益诉讼中，判断渔业资源或海洋生态资源遭受的污染损害是属于财产损害还是环境损害性质，是一个至关重要的抉择。如果没有准确的把握和定位，将使损害评估调查的对象和方向偏离轨道，可谓一着不慎，满盘皆输。如认为属于财产损害，就可以对物灭失、减损的实际价值进行索赔，而如是环境损害就仅限于索赔实际采取或将要采取的合理恢复措施费用。

在索赔环境损害时，如仅评估渔业或生态资源损失，却无实际采取或将要采取的恢复措施，将无法得到支持。如"阿提哥"轮海洋生态环境损害索赔案，该案经过大连海事法院、辽宁省高级人民法院、最高人民法院的审理，最终仅象征性地支持了极少的鉴定费，原因便在于此。据了解，该案鉴定人认为，经过20多天，受污染水体已自然恢复到二级标准，无需采取恢复措施。如此这般，让法官支持其索赔，实为巧妇难为无米之炊，最终该案以失败告终亦属预料之中。在上述案件中，鉴定人还犯了一个明显的错误。虽然随着时间的推移，油污会挥发、溶解、沉淀、沉积、沉降于茫茫大海中，最终水体化检结果无明显油污亦不足为奇。但油污泄漏不但会造成渔业资源损害，更为严重的是其将严重破坏食物链，这体现在油污对非经济性鱼类、海藻、浮游生物、微生物等的破坏。尽管水体恢复到二级标准，但上述海底生物恢复了吗？显然没有。在"闽燃供2"轮油污案中，中国科学院南海海洋研究所的监测结果表明，尽管水体随时间而逐渐恢复，但水体中的浮游生物、微生物等均成几何级数地锐减。因此，应对环境损害进行完整评估并做出科学、合理、可行的修复方案，方能得到法院的支持。正是基于对公约的正确理解，笔者代理的蓬莱19-3油污案最终获赔16.83亿元、"金玫瑰"轮案亦得到青岛海事法院的支持。

3. 关于公约的适用问题

公约能否直接适用于没有涉外因素的海洋污染公益诉讼案是一个具有争议性的问题。油污事故发生后，诉讼当事人都不可避免地选择适用更能保护其利益的法律。如公约和国内法对索赔主体和责任限额的规定大不相同，导致法律适用问题争议不休。《燃油公约》《CLC 公约》认为"预防措施"系指事故发生后任何人采取的防止和尽量减少污染损害的任何合理措施，即索赔主体可以是"任何人"，但国内法却将预防措施费用的索赔权交由行政主管机关。而《CLC 公约》海事赔偿责任限额小于《海商法》，尽管"闽燃供 2"轮油污案没有任何涉外因素，但漏油船"闽燃供 2"轮仍主张适用《CLC 公约》享受责任限制，其主张得到广州海事法院和广东省高级人民法院的支持。但是，根据《最高人民法院关于非航行国际航线的我国船舶在我国海域造成油污损害的民事赔偿责任适用法律问题的请示的答复》，不具有涉外因素的案件，不适用公约，应适用国内法。由此可见，各法院对公约适用问题的理解不一，导致诉讼中适用法律混乱。

（三）有关调查、评估规范的法律地位问题

海洋污染公益诉讼成功的先决条件是解决好如何进行调查、评估才能满足民事诉讼证据要求的问题。在海洋监测方面，我国国家质量监督检验检疫总局和国家标准化管理委员会发布了《海洋监测规范》（GB 17378—2007）。该规范主要解决海洋常规监测问题，并非专门解决海洋公益诉讼污染监测问题。在实务中，海洋公益诉讼的监测程序和范围可能与《海洋监测规范》不一致，需专门处理。如根据《海洋监测规范》第三部分第 4.5.3 条采样层次的要求，水深小于 10 米要求监测表层水域（海面以下 $0.1\sim1$ m），水深 $10\sim25$ m 要求监测表层和底层水域，而水深 100 m 以上则要求表层、10 m、50 m、以下水层酌情加层、底层……可见，《海洋监测规范》的采样层次烦琐。在海洋公益诉讼索赔案中，如果要求监测多层水域，工作量巨大，往往仅监测表层水域即可。例如，在渔业资源损害索赔案中，索赔方主张遭受渔业资源损害，只需证明事故海域遭受污染并且海水的石油烃类浓度超过了《渔业水质标准》（GB 11607—89）。限定值 0.05 mg/L 便完成举证要求，无须再对事故海域中层和底层海水进行监测。由此可见，针对海洋公益诉讼，有必要制定专门的监测规范，尤其是监测点的密度、数量、监测面积和范围以及水样的萃取、检验时间都应作出特别的规定，以满足海洋公益诉讼案件的监测要求。

在海洋生态损害索赔方面，国家海洋局颁布了《海洋溢油生态损害评估技术导则》（HY/T 095—2007）（简称《导则》），该导则属于行业标准，

在诉讼中如何适用该导则亦产生了不少问题。尽管《导则》是一个技术规范，但其科学性、合理性和可行性仍需要考究。比如，《导则》第 8.2.2 条环境容量损失采取影子工程法进行计算，该办法采用建设污水处理厂的费用加上污水处理费用计算而成。那么，是否可以理解为每发生一起污染损害事故就需建立一个污水处理厂？这显然是不科学、不合理的。所以，在海洋生态公益诉讼中不能机械地适用《导则》，如处理不当，败诉的可能性极大。如"阿提哥"轮、"塔斯曼海"轮生态污染损害索赔案只得到基本的监测、评估成本费用，就是惨痛的教训。因《导则》部分条款不科学、不合理，且其缺乏权威性，所以国家有必要组织专业部门和法律专家对《导则》进行完善并在法律中认可《导则》，提升《导则》的法律认可度和权威性，使海洋生态损害评估有法可依。

  关于渔业资源损害索赔方面，如何确定渔业资源损失恢复费用是一个难题。2008 年，国家质量监督检验检疫总局、国家标准化管理委员会发布《渔业污染事故经济损失计算办法》（GB/T 21678—2018）（简称《办法》），该办法大大提高了渔业资源损害赔偿计算方法的权威，但《办法》第 5.3 条却成为争议焦点。《办法》第 5.3 条规定，天然渔业资源的恢复费用原则上不低于直接经济损失额的 3 倍。对此条款，通常有两种理解：①直接经济损失乘以 3 倍即为天然渔业资源的恢复费用；②通过增殖放流同种鱼类使渔业资源恢复到未污染前状态所产生的费用。如受损鱼类不能直接通过增殖放流方式进行恢复，可通过增殖放流另一种与其经济价值相当的鱼类进行恢复。笔者倾向于第二种方法。在笔者处理"阿提哥"轮和蓬莱 19-3 渔业资源案时，采用第二种方法计算得到的天然渔业资源的恢复费用达到直接经济损失额的 6～7 倍，但基本得到认可。该事实证明，第二种方法相较第一种方法更具科学性和说服力。所以，我们不能机械地使用《办法》，应充分考虑其科学性、合理性和可行性。

二、海洋污染公益诉讼的证据收集问题

(一) 关于漏油量的确定问题

在海洋污染公益诉讼中,无论是渔业资源或海洋生态环境损害赔偿案都涉及污染面积、污染程度的确定问题。其中,漏油量的确定问题至关重要。

船舶泄漏的油污大多是从货舱或油舱泄漏的货油或燃油。对运载数万吨货油的大型油轮而言,一旦遭遇事故导致货舱破损,漏油量之大根本难以查明。有人提出以船舶吃水的变化计算漏油量,因事故前吃水难以查清,且船舶吃水相差千分之二均属合理范围,故该方法根本无从准确判断漏油量。在实务中,肇事船方通常提出漏油量应以装载时提单所载的货油量与事故后卸载的数量差为准。如2002年"塔斯曼海"轮油污案,船东就提出上述抗辩,拟证明漏油只有几吨。但提单通常是船方签发,完全由船方自行制作,真实性存疑,不能作为定案证据。根据《MARPOL 73/78防污公约》的规定,《油类记录簿》是记载船舶装载、使用、装卸油类的法定证据,相较船方签发的提单而言更能体现船舶油类的真实情况,从而可证明船舶真实的漏油量。在笔者办理的"海成"轮案中,法院就是以《油类记录簿》作为确定漏油量的重要证据。

前述船舶漏油量的确定有《油类记录簿》可依,而钻井平台油类泄漏量的确定问题则更为复杂。钻井平台的油类泄漏主要源于以下两种情况:①油井管柱爆炸或故障;②地表承受不了油井的压力而破裂。可见,钻井平台油类泄漏量不可能按照船舶漏油的计算思路进行,应根据石油的原理和特点进行评估。在2011年蓬莱19-3油污案中,我们综合采用卫星、飞机和船舶监控、数据模拟、现场水体监测相结合的办法进行评估,取得了良好的效果。通过卫星监测可以知道每一个时间段石油泄漏的位置和污染的大概范围,但由于距离、气象、云等原因,卫星的监测效果有限,因此用现场船舶和飞机监测为补充。通过对监测数据进行模拟后可得到油污的泄漏、扩散、漂流及扫海面积。要计算漏油量还需进行现场水体监测,根据海面油污的颜色评估油膜的厚度,对污染面积范围内混合在水体中的石油,可对其表层、中层、底层的水样进行检测,得出每一升水的含油量。通过运用以上科学、周密的计算办法,可以求得污染水体中大约的含油

量。该方法在蓬莱 19-3 油污案中取得成功，最终该案达成 16.83 亿元巨额赔款。

（二）关于公共证据的运用问题

"谁主张、谁举证"是民事诉讼的一项基本举证规则，但因海洋污染诉讼系列案涉及众多原告，且各原告对事故漏油量、污染面积和程度的举证能力不尽相同，如任一原告对此进行举证，其他系列案原告能否直接引用，这也是争论不休的问题。污染责任方通常以"谁主张、谁举证"原则为由提出反对意见，以证据规则的角度看，该观点似有一定道理。但毫无疑问，如所有受害方都需委托鉴定，势必耗费巨大，且没有必要。何况大部分受害者为渔民，不具备足够的经济能力。鉴于此，笔者在处理"塔斯曼海"轮油污案时使用了公共证据的做法。法院对公共证据持支持态度，即有关漏油量、污染面积和程度的公共证据，如果有任一原告进行举证，其他系列案件原告就可以直接引用。同理，在蓬莱 19-3 油污案中，原国家海洋局花费大量人力、物力、财力对漏油量及污染情况进行监测，上述监测数据由原农业部黄渤海区渔政局直接引用于渔业资源索赔案，又快又好地完成举证，节省了大量时间和费用，为该案的和解奠定了基础。在海洋污染诉讼案中，因涉及共性问题，可通过立法形式确定公共证据的互用问题，以便更好地保护公共利益。

（三）关于污染损害的举证问题

正确理解污染损害举证责任倒置原则，对原告的索赔非常重要。海洋污染诉讼案中，所谓举证责任倒置，仅在被告以原告的污染损害与其污染行为无因果关系为由作出抗辩的情形下适用，并不免除原告对被告存在污染行为、污染物已经到达索赔海域并造成损害的举证义务。

在海洋污染诉讼案中，证明船舶发生碰撞、触礁等漏油事故并不难，如该油类泄漏造成事故附近海域污染可以理解为油类向四周自然扩散，这是基本常识，无需举证证明油类来源。但如果污染区域远离事故地点，污染受害方则应举证证明被污染海域油类源于事故船舶，否则存在被驳回的可能性。如 2013 年"夏长"轮沉没漏油案[①]，珠海炳君水产品公司的养殖

---

① "夏长"轮沉没漏油案（珠海炳君水产品公司），广州海事法院（2015）广海法初字第 950 号一审民事判决书、广东省高级人民法院（2017）粤民终 520 号二审民事判决书。

海域距离事故地点非常遥远，且其诉称的受污染范围与广东海事局在事故调查报告的认定范围不一，故其养殖损害并未得到广州海事法院和广东高院的支持。再如，2011年蓬莱19-3油污案，山东长岛、烟台等黄渤海地区渔民的索赔均未能得到支持，原因也是不能证明油污来源。所以，应吸取上述案件的经验教训，如果污染受损地与事故地点有一定的距离，则应及时提取油类并进行油指纹鉴定、分析，确认污染源。

解决了污染源问题，还应对污染损害量进行举证。大海茫茫，作为污染受害者如何将其损失量化，是一个难题。例如，为估算渔业资源损失量，以往的做法是根据农业部于1996年10月8日发布的《水域污染事故渔业损失计算方法规定》（已废止），直接以水产品（成品鱼）损失额乘以3倍计算。但该办法过于简单，没有充分的依据和说服力。其实，渔业资源损害不仅包括成品鱼，还包括未投入市场的鱼卵、仔稚鱼。且相比之下，鱼卵、仔稚鱼的生命力更为脆弱，其承受污染的能力远低于成品鱼。因此，有必要监测污染海域在事故前后鱼卵、仔稚鱼的减少量，根据鱼卵、仔稚鱼的生成规律以及污染海域面积与相邻的非污染面积的密度差求得渔业资源的损失量。以这种方法计算得到的渔业资源损失量不单比简单乘以3倍更有说服力，甚至计算结果远大于3倍。

（四）监测、评估报告的证据效力问题

如前所述，在海洋污染公益诉讼中，《海洋监测规范》《导则》等规范得到广泛运用。尽管上述规范对每个监测、调查行为都有严格的要求，但由疏忽大意导致监测数据无效、评估报告不能作为证据使用的情况亦存在。例如，油指纹鉴定对采集油样的要求严格，油样必须以玻璃瓶装载并避免样品受污染，否则将直接影响检验的准确度，难以锁定污染源。在2011年蓬莱19-3油污案中，被告美国康菲石油有限公司因监测样品受到污染而功亏一篑。这警醒我们，细节决定成败，要想取得成功，必须运用科学、周密的调查办法，严格取证。

此外，应运用法律思维进行鉴定和评估，否则将会徒劳无功。在"阿提哥"轮以及"塔斯曼海"轮油污案中，尽管鉴定人员在专门领域具有专业性和权威性，但其出具的鉴定报告晦涩难懂，还对法律问题进行了大篇幅评论。如此一来，反倒使其可信度大打折扣，遭受质疑。在福建闽江三农制药厂排污案以及湛江"春木1号"污染案中，鉴定人员针对鱼类死亡原因进行大量病理性研究，却难以得出结论。实际上，作为原告只需证明污染物到达涉案水域并使渔业资源遭受损害便可，至于鱼类死亡是由于中毒、缺氧还是其他原因所致，根本无须进行举证；相反，如前所述，根据举证责任倒置原则，如被告否认其中的因果关系，应由被告进行举证。

综上所述，海洋污染公益诉讼面临诸多法律和证据问题。只有不断完善、构建海洋污染公益诉讼制度，不断研究、解决难题，我国海洋污染公益诉讼方能走向成熟，进而更好地保护海洋环境，促进海洋可持续发展。

专题二 国际法与比较法专论

英国海盗赎金问题探析及启示

孙宏友　丁嫣然*

摘要：面对海盗劫持船舶事件，行之有效的应对方法之一是由船方交付赎金以安全赎回船舶、船货及船员。鉴于各国对海盗赎金的合法性和性质规定不一，如何对船方损失进行分摊便易陷入瓶颈。本文通过对18世纪以来英国成文法和判例的研究，发现不同时期英国对海盗赎金的态度虽然各有差异，但仍趋向于认定其为共同海损，且并未区分具体赎金种类。此外，作为谈判期间减少赎金的代替费用，船舶营运费用亦可作共同海损分摊。我国虽经历多起海盗劫持事件，却缺乏处理海盗赎金案件的实务经验。合理借鉴英国处理海洋问题的方式，对我国处理类似问题有重要的理论意义与现实意义。

关键词：海盗赎金　共同海损　施救费用　约克－安特卫普规则

An Analysis and Enlightenment of the British Pirates' Ransom Problem

Sun Hongyou, Ding Yanran

Abstract: In the face of hijacking incidents, it has been proved that one effective solution is to deliver the ransom on demand to the pirates in order to redeem the vessel, cargo and crew safely. Because of the great differences between different countries' regulations on the issue of the legality and nature of pirate ransom, disputes exist in determining how to share the ship owner's losses caused by paying the ransom. By analyzing British statutes and precedents emerging since the 18th Century, it is found that British attitudes towards pirate ransom, though varied at different times, tends to identify it as general average

---

* 孙宏友：法学副教授，北京师范大学珠海分校普通法研究中心主任，人和启邦显辉（横琴）律师事务所专家顾问。丁嫣然：香港的近律师事务所驻上海代表处法律助理。

without dividing it into any specific type. In addition, the operating expenses of the vessel, as a kind of alternative costs which are in substitute for the reduced ransom during the negotiation, may also be shared as general average.

Since the founding of the People's Republic of China, our country has experienced a number of ship hijacking events, which has led us to be familiar with piracy, but we still lack experience in dealing with cases relating to the loss apportionment of pirate ransom. Because Britain is an ancient maritime power, its way to deal with marine problems is worth learning from. Drawing lessons from the British ways of dealing with ransom problems is of great theoretical and practical significance for China to deal with similar problems in the future.

Key words: pirate ransom; general average; sue and labour charges; York Antwerp rules

一、引 言

15世纪以来，新航路的开辟便利了各国之间的贸易，直至今日，水上船舶运输依然在促进国际贸易上担任着重要的角色。然而，愈益猖獗的海盗行为却将船舶运输置于危险的境地。根据国际海事局（IMB）海盗报告中心（PRC）的统计数据，2016年世界范围内共有191起记录在案的海盗劫持船舶事件。而在2017年前9个月中，共计有92次海盗强行登船的记录，13次与海盗交火的事件发生，11次海盗登船未遂以及5艘船舶被劫持。① 2020年全球共发生海盗和武装抢劫事件195起，较2019年的162起增加33起，增幅超过20%。② 2022年前9个月共有90多起。③ 这一系列的海盗行为虽然在数量上较上一年度略有缩减，但在部分地区如西非的几内亚湾和亚洲南海仍然十分严重，不容忽视。

由于海盗在通航要域活动频繁，商船运输的危险性不断增加。但船东往往考虑到绕航的高昂成本而选择铤而走险，这种侥幸的心理使得海盗劫持船舶的机会和数量大大增加。除了少数恐怖主义分子，海盗劫持船舶的

---

① ICC-Commercial Crime Services. *4 takeaways from the IMB's latest global piracy report*. ICC Commercial Crime Services organization official website, 2017, pp. 10 – 17.

② 参见袁颀《海盗赎金相关保险比较》，载《集装箱化》2022年第33期。

③ 见 https://www.xindemarinenews.com/topic/haishangbaoan/2022/1101/43038.html，2022年11月访问。

主要目的是获取金钱，故往往会提出以赎金换取船货及船员安全的要求。与此同时，船方亦考虑到船只和人命的高价，而普遍同意支付金额较前者低廉的海盗赎金。例如，2008 年 11 月被索马里海盗劫持的市值 1 亿美元的沙特"天狼星号"油轮支付 300 万美元后成功赎回。

在普通情况下，对船舶的行驶、管理甚至是遭遇海难等不可抗力之后各项支出的分摊均已有较为成熟的规定。但在海盗劫持船舶的情形下，由于海盗赎金的性质和合法与否各国规定不尽相同，因此在案件发生后处理损失之时便难以对赎金进行分摊。① 根据英国 1906 年《海上保险法》（*Marine Insurance Act*）的规定，损失可以分为全损和部分损失，其中全损含实际全损和推定全损两种情况，而部分损失则含单独海损、共同海损和特别费用三种情况。② 所属情况不同，损失的分摊人和具体权重亦不相同。在海盗劫持的案件中，一方面，货主会因船货被劫而试图主张全损，故针对船货常会产生实际全损抑或推定全损的争议；另一方面，船方会为了赎回船货而交纳赎金，由此产生的损失常陷入共同海损抑或施救费用的争议。③ 所谓共同海损，是指在同一航程上船舶、货物及其他财产受到共同的危险，为了保证共同安全，有意合理地采取措施直接导致特殊的牺牲，支付特殊的费用。④ 本文探讨的主要内容则属后者。船方往往会希望将海盗赎金视为共同海损从而可从货方处得到补偿；反观货方，则希望将海盗赎金视为特别费用中的施救费用从而由船方自行承担赎金。因此，为了明确海盗赎金的最终承担人和分摊方式，有两个仍需解决的问题：其一，需要判断该赎金的性质属于前述何种损失；其二，考虑到赎金中可能不仅包含货物的赎回，还包括人质的释放，故在分辨赎金性质的基础上还应当区分船货赎金和船员赎金的性质是否亦有差异。⑤ 本文接下来将主要着眼于英国法对上述问题的解答。

---

① 海盗赎金构成海盗行为造成的损失中最主要的一部分，目前支付赎金给海盗在很多国家是具有合法性的，英国、德国和荷兰等国家的现代立法例对其加以肯定。参见张佳《海盗赎金在共同海损制度下的认定》，载《珠江水运》2021 年第 1 期。
② 见英国 1906 年《海上保险法》第五十五条至六十六条。
③ See Gotthard Gauci. "Total Losses and the Peril of Piracy in English Law of Marine Insurance". *WMU Journal of Maritime Affairs*, 2012, Vol. 11, pp. 115 – 128.
④ 参见张佳《海盗赎金在共同海损制度下的认定》，载《珠江水运》2021 年第 1 期。
⑤ 参见高弘刚《基于新型海盗风险的保险策略研究》，载《管理观察》2013 年第 34 期。

二、英国海盗赎金分摊方式的历史发展

(一) 英国海盗赎金相关制度的历史演进

考察英国关于海盗赎金的历史发展过程，不难发现，无论是英国的国会立法还是法院判例，都存在对海盗赎金合法性认定过程的反复，在其从合法到非法再到合法化的发展变换过程中，存在着诸多争议，充满了不确定性。

英国颁布的关于赎金的最早规定可追溯至1782年的《赎金法案》(*Ransom Act*)，该法案明令禁止了支付赎金以换取被捕船舶或其上货物的行为。然而，在时隔近百年后，英国于1864年6月23日，在《海上捕获行为废除令》(*Naval Prize Acts Repeal Act*)中将《赎金法案》列入行将废止的法规范畴，默示了赎金支付的合法性。此外，同期颁布的《海上捕获法案》(*Naval Prize Act*)第六章"其他规定"中第四十五条也涵盖了关于赎金的规定。虽然相关的具体条文内容已无从可考，但是鉴于该条文已经于1981年被英国颁布的《最高法院法案》(*Senior Court Act*)第一百五十二条第四款明文废止，所以并不影响赎金相关问题的认定。

进入20世纪，除了上述《最高法院法案》，英国尚有若干较为重要的与海盗赎金相关的规定。其中之一为1906年英国《海上保险法》。该法第六十六条第二款言明，"在危险发生时，为保护同一航程处于危困状况的财产而自发且合理作出的额外牺牲，为共同海损行为"。该款虽然仅对共同海损行为下了定义，但不难发现，在海盗劫持船舶的案件中，船方往往是为了解救处于危困情境下的船舶和船货而许诺海盗支付赎金，且此种许诺一则由船方自发作出，二则因其能以较低廉的金额换回更大价值的船舶而具有合理性。因此，海盗赎金也符合该款的规定。不仅如此，1974年《约克·安特卫普规则》(*The York-Antwerp Rules*)中字母规则A也存有如前述近乎一致的表述。虽然该规则属于国际性规则，但因其同为英国所适用，所以同样印证了英国在20世纪后半叶对海盗赎金的态度。

到了21世纪初，英国2000年颁布《反恐法案》(*Terrorism Act*)，其中第十五条第三款a项规定，"提供金钱或其他财产给恐怖主义者即属犯罪"。据此，若将海盗视作恐怖主义者，则海盗赎金的性质为非法。但现实情况是，恐怖主义往往指向通过威胁公共安全、侵犯人身财产而达到其

政治目的的行为,而索取赎金的海盗则往往意在获取金钱之利益,不能与政治目的并论,故本项规定应无法对海盗赎金予以适用。①

无独有偶,2002年的《犯罪收益追缴法案》(Proceeds of Crime Act)第三百二十八条第一款规定,"一个人如果参与了一项其知悉或怀疑有助于他人获取、保留、使用或控制不法财产的安排,即属犯罪"。在船舶遭遇劫持后,船东明知交付赎金有利于海盗获得财产,仍愿意满足对方要求支付款项,倘若将该笔赎金的性质认定为规定中的"不法财产",则支付赎金为非法行为。根据该法案第三百四十条第三款a项的解释,"不法财产系指从犯罪行为中获得的利益"。从文义解释的角度看,海盗劫船固然属于犯罪行为,赎金亦是因劫船而得以向船东方高额索取,符合"不法财产"的定义,因此根据该法案的规定,海盗赎金并不具有合法性。但从体系解释和目的解释的角度看,第三百二十八条置于标题为"洗钱"的第七章之下,其立法目的应当是防止不法财产通过任何途径进行移转而"合法化"。所以,只有进行移转之前该笔财产性质已属"不法",才得以符合第三百二十八条的规定。然而,第三百四十条中的"不法财产"则在不法行为发生前本是合法财产,并非"已然不法",与第三百二十八条的语境不一。本文认为后一种解释方法适用在此更加合理。据此,两者区分立明,虽然根据《犯罪收益追缴法案》第三百四十条该笔赎金在海盗劫船索取成功后成为海盗的"不法财产",但在船东交付前,赎金仍属船东的合法财产,故船东的交付行为并不符合帮助他人获取"非法财产",因此支付赎金并不属于犯罪。

综上所述,通过对18世纪末以来英国相关立法的回顾,可以推论,英国主要着眼于赎金的合法性问题,而对海盗赎金的性质并无明确规定。换言之,在海盗赎金的合法性问题上,英国持有的态度有了质的变化,即从认定非法转变为默示赎金支付为合法。然而在该赎金性质问题上,目前仅能从《海上保险法》和《约克-安特卫普规则》对"共同海损"下的定义中觅得些许相似之处,从而可在个案中予以具体分析适用。据此推断,英国目前从立法层面尚未对海盗赎金的性质作出明确规定,也未对船货和船员赎金的处理方式之差异加以区分。因此,若要明确英国对海盗赎金分摊方式的态度尚需对其历年相关判例进行观察和评析。

---

① 参见蒋圣力《海盗赎金的法律性质问题归谬》,载《经济视角》2013年第1期。

(二) 英国法院海盗赎金相关判例评析

英国判例关于海盗赎金的不同认定，可以概括为三个阶段，即共同海损阶段、施救费用阶段和恢复为共同海损阶段。其中，从18世纪初到20世纪末可以视为第一阶段。当时，英国判例中已展现了对海盗赎金分摊方式的论述。在Lord Salton v. John Ritchie案[①]中，海盗劫持了船舶，在索取了赎金并掠走了部分船货后才将船舶、船员和剩余船货予以释放。法官在推理中表述道，"在海商法中，惯常做法是让存留货物的货主和失去货物的货主一同按比例承担后者的损失，否则便会出现一方承担损失而另一方享有利益的情形。这既违背了法律，又违背了普遍正义"。据此判令，未遭受货损的货主得按比例分摊包括赎金在内的损失。该起海盗劫掠事件包括三方当事人，即货物赎回的货主、货物被掠走的货主以及损失了赎金费用的船东。由未损失的货主介入分摊为本案的推理逻辑。依本案判决理由，赎金的损失不能仅由船方独自承担，而应由受益方（货主）按比例分摊，此举符合共同海损损失的负担形式。此外，考虑到支付赎金是为了使船舶、船货及船员脱离危险而有意且合理支付的特殊费用，该判决并不违背共同海损的适用背景。因此，根据该案的判决依据和结果，海盗赎金被视作共同海损，由船东和货主按比例共同分摊。

第二阶段可以从20世纪末开始。在此阶段，将海盗赎金视为施救费用的探讨最先出现于英国的判例Westminster案[②]中。该案的主审法官LJ Stuart Smith在判决书中指出，"只要赎金的支付合法，因支付赎金而遭受的损失便可依据施救条款（Sue and Labour Clause）予以补救"。而在论及支付赎金合法与否的问题上，Smith法官以海盗赎金为例，指出"支付赎金本身并不属于非法行为，故即使索取赎金行为不合法，也并不影响损失的补救"。该案案情虽与海盗无关，但Smith法官的判决理由显然已将海盗赎金列入可依据施救条款受偿的范畴。海盗索取赎金是非法行为，但船方支付赎金却并不违法，故船方所遭受的损失可依据施救条款向保险人索赔。该案并未谈及该笔损失在船货双方之间如何分摊，仅对承保船舶战争

---

① *Lord Salton v. John Ritchie* [1710] Mor 13421, British and Irish Legal Information Institute, http://www.bailii.org/.

② *Royal Boskalis Westminster N. V. and Others v. Trevor Rex Mountain and Others* [1997] EWCA Civ 1140.

险的被告是否应当承担船方缴付赎金的损失给予肯定性确认。由此可知,该案倾向于认定海盗赎金的性质属施救费用,损失应由船方保险人承担。

步入21世纪,出现了著名的Masefield AG v. Amlin Corporate Member Ltd案①。该案所涉船舶"Bunga Melati Dua"轮于2008年8月19日被索马里海盗劫持,对方要求支付赎金以释放船舶、船货及船员。最终,船东MISC在支付海盗200万美元赎金后,船舶及其上货物和人员获释。本案虽对货方是否须分摊船方的损失并无论及,然而,法官David Steel在提到海盗赎金时,认为"支付赎金并不违法","虽然支付海盗赎金会助长海盗劫船的风气,但保护船员免受伤害的最好手段并非外交手段或军事干预,而只能是支付赎金。考虑到这一点,支付赎金并不违反公共政策"。此外,在该案的上诉审中,主审法官LJ Rix在附带意见中援引了上一案例的观点,直言"支付赎金的损失可作施救费用予以赔偿"。据此,"Bunga Melati Dua"轮案虽然志不在解决海盗赎金性质的问题,但从法官推理中不难做出这样的解读,即赎金的支付既不违反法律法规也不违反公共政策。在公权力无法有效遏制海盗行为的情况下,船方的自救行为显然不应受到诘难;②此外,在赎金的补救上,仍将其视作船方施救费用,由船方保险人承担。

然而,2010年之后,英国法院对海盗赎金的态度又有转变,来到了英国海盗赎金判例发展阶段的第三个时期。2012年,在Metall Market v. Vitorio Shipping Company Ltd案③中,船舶在运输货物途中被海盗劫持,并在船方支付赎金后得以释放,但离开危险海域后,又因船内主要零件发生故障而被拖入港口等待修理,船货双方就船体故障引发的各种问题如何进行共同海损分摊产生争议。事故发生后,仲裁庭裁定:无论支付的海盗赎金还是拖船入港的费用都允许进行共同海损分摊。货方对裁决持有异议并诉至法院。该案的争议焦点也不属于海盗赎金,但从判决意见可推知,法院对仲裁庭裁定"海盗赎金应进行共同海损分摊"并未存有异议。甚至在该案的上诉审理④中,主审法官Bernard Rix直接作出对仲裁裁决上诉无效的结论。因此,通过该案,英国法院间接地认同了"将支付海盗赎金的损

---

① Masefield AG v. Amlin Corporate Member Ltd [2010] EWHC 280 (Comm).
② 参见徐依琳《海盗赎金的共同海损性质》,载《中外企业家》2015年第2期。
③ Metall Market v. Vitorio Shipping Company Ltd [2012] EWHC 844 (Comm).
④ Metall Market v. Vitorio Shipping Company Ltd & Anor [2013] EWCA Civ 650.

失视作共同海损"的观点。不仅如此,在 2013 年的 Venetico Marine SA v. International General Insurance Company Ltd 案①判决中,也能从法官描述的事实情况中推知,在实务中如果发生了海盗索要赎金的事件,船货双方须按照共同海损的原则承担损失。

如果说 Metall Market 案与 Venetico 案仅对海盗赎金的认定走向具有模糊倾向性,那么,2016 年英国高院对"The Long-champ"案②的经典判决似乎使我们对这一倾向性更加肯定。该案所涉"The Long-champ"船舶在航行过程中被 7 名海盗劫持,2009 年 1 月 30 日海盗提出 600 万美元的赎金要求,但经过船方与海盗为期 51 天的交涉谈判后,2009 年 3 月 22 日海盗最终让步将赎金降至 185 万美元,并于赎金交付后的次日释放船舶。该案法官推理中有多处对海盗赎金加以阐明。首先,上诉审法官 Hamblen 在判决书第 25 段指出,"考虑到为使船只、货物和船员从海盗处得以释放而花费了较大数额的金钱,2009 年 2 月 3 日船方申报了共同海损"。此段虽是对事实的描述,却足以可见实务中船方通常将海盗赎金的损失作共同海损处理。其次,Hamblen 法官在"案情介绍"部分第 7 段说明:"本案赎金适用 1974 年《约克-安特卫普规则》字母规则 A,双方对此皆无异议。"最高法院主审法官 Neuberger 在判决书③第 10 段亦有相似的表述。字母规则 A 则规定:"为了保护同一航程的财产免受危险,而有意且合理作出的额外牺牲,属于共同海损行为。"因此,在该案中,船货双方认同支付赎金是船方为了使船、货及人员脱离海盗控制而采取的行动,应认定为共同海损行为。最后,在英国最高法院的审理中,与主流判决意见持有不同观点的法官 Mance 在判决书第 47 段中也写道,"赎金和专家谈判的费用都可直接认定为共同海损损失,受《约克-安特卫普规则》字母规则 A 调整"。

由上述诸案例可见,18 世纪以来英国对海盗赎金的态度已初现雏形。如上所述,可将其概括为三个不同阶段:第一个阶段于 18 世纪初,英国法院将海盗赎金视为共同海损,由船货双方共同分摊;第二个阶段约始于 20 世纪末,海盗赎金被法院认定为施救费用,由船方之保险人承担,与货方无关;第三个阶段始于 21 世纪 10 年代后,英国法院重新恢复了最初对赎

---

① *Venetico Marine SA v. International General Insurance Company Ltd & Ors* [2013] EWHC 3644 (Comm).

② *Mitsui & Co Ltd & Ors v. Beteiligungsgesellschaft LPG & Ors* [2016] EWCA Civ 708.

③ *Mitsui & Co Ltd & Ors v. Beteiligungsgesellschaft LPG Tankerflotte MBH & Co KG & Anor* [2017] UKSC 68.

金性质的认定，仍将之视为共同海损。直至近年，该观点仍处于主流地位。

目前海盗赎金损失处理的案件得以解决主要依靠《约克－安特卫普规则》的字母规则 A，如上所述，该规则将海盗赎金视作共同海损处理。但问题在于该规则并不具有强制性，而是只有在有合同规定时才得以适用。若合同有所规定，如"The Long-champ"案中海运提单上注明了"共同海损事宜适用1974年《约克－安特卫普规则》"，则海盗赎金损失处理方式自不必言。但若合同并无相关规定，考虑到上述相关先例缺乏的困境，知悉英国对海盗赎金的大致态度确有必要。

根据前述结论，首先，在立法层面，英国并未明确海盗赎金的性质，亦未区分船货和船员赎金，但倾向于统一适用《海上保险法》和《约克－安特卫普规则》中"共同海损"相关条文。虽然"共同海损"的定义中损失项仅包含"财产"而不包含人命，但虑及船员不仅是为了船方的需要而配备，而且客观上在航程中也保护了货方的利益，故根据共同海损的原理，将船员赎金视同其他船货赎金一样由所有受益方——船货双方共同负担并无不妥。[①] 其次，在判例层面，英国在历史上仅将海盗赎金视为施救费用和共同海损，但多数案例甚至近期案例都倾向于后者，且这些案例均未对船货赎金和船员赎金有所区分，而是统一将海盗赎金自动视作包含船舶、船货和船员三种类型。综上所述，无论合同是否有对于《约克－安特卫普规则》的适用规定，英国目前的做法仍倾向于将海盗赎金损失统一视作共同海损，由船货双方共同承担，并且对赎金不再继续分类，而是作统一赔偿。

三、英国营运费用之分摊方式——以"The Long-champ"案为例

在海盗劫持案件中，海盗首次提出的赎金金额往往通过谈判可以减少。如此，首次索要的赎金金额就包含两个部分：一是最终确定的赎金金额，二是通过谈判减少的金额。海盗赎金分摊所产生的争议也多体现在这两个部分。本文已经探讨过船方与海盗交涉后最终确定的金额如何分摊，下面将继续探寻作为代替船方通过谈判减少的赎金而产生的船舶营运费用

[①] 参见陈琦《海盗行为所致损失在共同海损制度下的认定——兼评英国最高法院最新判例"The Long-champ"案》，载《大连海事大学学报（社会科学版）》2017年第6期。

应如何进行分摊。

事实上,被海盗索要赎金后,船方为将损失降至最低而经常提出与对方谈判,在谈判过程中一方面减少了赎金金额,但另一方面却也产生了一笔不小的船舶营运费用,得失各半。若无后者,则前者数额不会减少,且最终会被认定作共同海损使船方得到补偿,而在有后者的情况下,前者数额减少,取而代之的是后者数额增加。该笔船舶营运费用倘若不予分摊,则船方虽付出了辛劳却损失更甚,显然不公;倘若予以分摊,当以何种方式进行分摊?换言之,通过本文前述结论已知,最终确定的海盗赎金属于共同海损,通过谈判减少的赎金本应也属于共同海损,那么代替本应认定为共同海损的费用而产生的额外花销(即谈判期间船舶营运费用)是否仍能认定为共同海损以补偿船方的损失呢?2017年英国最高法院审理的"The Long-champ"案所给出的答案值得参考。

该案的基本案情如前所述。除了海盗赎金,船方对谈判期间产生的各项船舶营运费用(包括船员工资、高风险海域航行津贴、船员生活供给和燃油消耗)也申报了共同海损理算,在经理算师成功认定后,却遭到了货方的反对。货方申请"海损理算师协会咨询委员会"重新认定,在得到后者认可的同时又将船方起诉到法院。虽然船货双方各自找到的专业人士给出了不同的结论,但这些意见对法院审理没有约束力,故下面只着重探讨法院的裁定理由。

"The Long-champ"案经历了一审法院、上诉法院直至最高法院,其中两个最主要的焦点问题贯穿着法庭审理的始终:第一,减少的赎金是否被"替代"(in place of);第二,若不经过谈判,船方直接同意海盗的第一次赎金要求,是否"合理"(reasonable)?

(一)减少的赎金是否被"替代"

1974年《约克–安特卫普规则》的字母规则F规定:"代替(in place of)本可认定为共同海损的费用而产生的额外费用,可作为共同海损受偿……其数额不得超过被代替的共同海损费用。"该案中,从字面上看,"本可认定为共同海损的费用"意指减少的赎金,若增加的营运费用"代替"了减少的赎金,则可作共同海损处理。

一审法院支持了船方的观点,认定减少赎金被营运费用所"替代",而上诉法院则推翻了该结论。上诉法院认为,即使是支付海盗第一次要求的600万美元赎金,船方也会就交易地点等问题进行谈判,即无论是否减少了赎金，都会存在谈判期间，继而都会产生船舶营运费用，故营运费用并非使赎金减少的替代手段。

在最高法院的审理中，法院又推翻了上诉法院对该问题的判决，认定"最终支付的185万美元赎金"并非"海盗最初要求的600万美元赎金"的替代措施，此两者之间只有数量上的变化。但"16万美元的船舶营运费用"却是"减少的415万美元赎金"的替代措施，因为此两者方式有异，属于两条不同的救济路径，可相互"替代"。

本文认为，最高法院的观点更具有合理性。反观上诉法院，其观点过于关注两者间的因果关系。实际上，即使支付了海盗首次索要的600万美元赎金，随即又在谈判中产生了营运费用，此种情况下不能适用规则F只是基于营运费用无法找到可替代的费用（如本案中减少的赎金），而并不代表在出现了可替代费用的情况下仍无法适用规则F。

综上所述，为了使谈判顺利进行而产生的营运费用便是代替（减少的）海盗赎金而产生的额外费用，符合字母规则F的适用前提，故该笔营运费用可作共同海损处理。

（二）同意海盗首次赎金要求是否"合理"

如上所述，1974年《约克-安特卫普规则》字母规则A要求共同海损行为需满足作出的牺牲是"合理"的。根据该规则，若牺牲不合理，则不能认定为共同海损，继而因不满足"本可认定为共同海损的费用"这一前提而无法适用规则F，最终无法将营运费用认定为共同海损。

一审法院和上诉法院就该问题持有共同的观点，皆认为即使支付海盗首次提出的600万美元赎金要求也是合理的，因为尽快支付赎金能保障船员尽早脱离危险。以往索马里海盗为了在赎金谈判中获得更为有利的地位，会注重扣押期间船舶的保养和船员健康，但近年来已不再如此。[①] 因此，考虑到人命无价，以及船货极有可能再次遭到海盗的破坏，高价尽早赎回做法也属情理之中。

然而，最高法院法官却认为对首次索要的赎金"合理"与否的讨论全无必要。若600万美元赎金合理，则按照上述推理营运费用可作为共同海损，从而使船方得到补偿；若600万美元不合理，船方事实上却通过自身

[①] Samuel Pyeatt Menefee, Maximo Q. Mejia. "A Rutter for Piracy in 2012". *WMU Journal of Maritime Affairs*, 2012, Vol. 11, pp. 1–13.

的不懈努力使所谓不合理的 600 万美元最终变成了所谓合理的 185 万美元，其付诸的辛劳较前种情况更多，但根据上述推理却不能适用规则 F，船方反而得不到补偿，这种结果是完全不合理的。因此，该法官主张不论最初赎金合理与否，都不影响规则 F 的适用。

本文认为，虽然上诉法院和最高法院对该问题的观点不同，但殊途同归。前者认可 600 万美元赎金的合理性，进而默许了规则 F 的适用；后者则不考虑合理性，统一允许适用规则 F，两者的结论都是支持船方支出的营运费用作共同海损受偿。

至此，"The Long-champ" 案中的两大焦点问题随着诉讼的进行结论已然明晰（如表 1 所示）。最高法院全然支持船方的上诉，赞同在船方与海盗谈判过程中，船舶的营运费用可视作通过谈判减少的赎金的替代费用，继而作共同海损分摊以补偿船方的损失。

表 1 "The Long-champ" 案两大焦点问题在三级审理中的判决结果

审级/性质	可否"替代"	是否"合理"
一审法院	可	合理
上诉法院（货方上诉）	否	合理
最高法院（船方上诉）	可	无意义

资料来源：*Mitsui & Co Ltd & Ors v. Beteiligungsgesellschaft LPG & Ors*［2016］EWCA Civ 708.［2017］UKSC 68。

倘若从此结论出发进行反向推理：已知营运费用按照共同海损的原则补偿船方，说明本案允许适用规则 F，从中可推知，被营运费用所代替的支出即属于共同海损。而在本案中，船方通过营运费用的支出，延长了与海盗的斡旋时间，进而实现了减少赎金金额的目标。换言之，赎金减少是以营运费用增加为代价的，两者有取代关系。因此，减少的赎金本属于共同海损，此亦说明海盗赎金应作共同海损解。

值得思考的是，该案解决了谈判成功减少赎金的情形下营运费用的分摊问题，但若出现船方虽然尽力谈判但仍未成功减少赎金的情形呢？此时又当何如？这一假设情况和本案上诉法院假设的"直接支付海盗首次索要的 600 万美元赎金"的情况略有类似。两者皆产生了营运费用，但却因找不出替代费用无法适用字母规则 F 而不知作何解。对此，本文认为，首先，就现实情况而言，几乎不存在不谈判或通过谈判后不能降低赎金的案件，故对此问题的研究意义较小；其次，即使出现了此种情况，虽不能适用规则 F，但考虑到营运费用是为了安全赎回被海盗掠走的财产而选择与海盗交涉所产生的牺牲，该牺牲是船方有意且合理做出的，本不应有或本不应达此数额的额外花销，符合字母规则 A 中的共同海损定义，仍可作共同海损处理。此情况与"The Long-champ"案唯一的不同点仅在于适用规则不同，但结果无异。

四、对我国的启示

20 世纪 80 年代以后，我国经历过 1998 年"长胜"轮的海盗案，以及 2008 年"德新海"轮遭遇的海盗劫持事件，对海盗行为并不陌生。虽然这些案件皆未对赎金损失如何分摊产生争议，但随着近几年海盗之患的日益猖獗，我国在"一带一路"倡议实施过程中，极有可能面对海盗赎金性质的决断问题，故增强我国海上航运的措施应加速推进。

目前在立法领域，我国《海商法》未明文论及海盗赎金，而在司法领域，我国亦暂未有可供参考的指导案例，故难以借此知悉法院会适用何规则认定赎金性质。因此，在恰逢《海商法》修订讨论之际，为弥补我国在赎金问题上的认识空缺，有必要参考借鉴他国对该问题较成熟的处理方式。英国作为古老的海洋强国，对于海盗赎金问题处理经验丰富，当为参考对象不二选择。

首先，在赎金性质的问题上，英国的成文法缺乏明确规定，但从判例中可见，英国认为海盗赎金符合《海上保险法》和《约克－安特卫普规则》字母规则 A 中对共同海损的定义，故选择将共同海损的规定适用于海盗赎金。而反观我国，其一，《海商法》中同样缺乏对海盗赎金的规定；其二，《海商法》第一百九十三条第一款规定，"共同海损，是指在同一海上航程中，船舶、货物和其他财产遭遇共同危险，为了共同安全，有意地合理地采取措施所直接造成的特殊牺牲、支付的特殊费用"。由于我国《海商法》中的"共同海损"章便是对 1974 年《约克－安特卫普规则》的吸收，故此规定和英国适用的共同海损定义表述全然一致。[①] 但与英国不同的是，由于我国法院从未处理过赎金分摊案件，在实践中法院是否同

---

① 参见张丽英《海商法》，中国政法大学出版社 2021 年版，第 252 页。

样会将共同海损的规定适用于海盗赎金不得而知。因此，本文认为，我国在未来处理赎金案件时，可借鉴英国的做法，将共同海损的规定（《海商法》第一百九十三条）适用于海盗赎金，即将赎金认定作共同海损，由船货双方共同按比例承担。

其次，在谈判期间船舶营运费用性质的问题上，英国在判例中选择适用1974年《约克－安特卫普规则》字母规则F。同样，我国曾在修法时对该字母规则F进行吸收而有了类似的规定——《海商法》第一百九十五条前段规定，"为代替可以列为共同海损的特殊费用而支付的额外费用，可以作为代替费用列入共同海损"。该规定与字母规则F的区别在于后者需要合同选择适用，而前者却无此限制。考虑到我国虽然有对"代替费用"的规定，但无对"营运费用"的规定，且由于我国法院未处理过类似案件，其是否会将"营运费用"适用于"代替费用"的规定亦暂无定论。因此，为了避免争议，本文认为可参考英国的做法，若产生关于营运费用的争议即可直接适用《海商法》第一百九十五条，将之认定为减少赎金的代替费用，同样作共同海损分摊。

最后，鉴于赎金的不可分性，英国并未区分船舶、船货和船员赎金的性质，而是统一视作共同海损。然而在共同海损理算时，船员赎金所占的比例难以确定，易导致船货多方之间产生关于具体分摊费用的争议。[1] 因此，我国在未来遇到赎金案件时，一方面可借鉴英国的做法，在承认赎金合法性的基础上，适用《海商法》第一百九十三条和第一百九十五条，于认定赎金性质阶段，为了使船方损失得到更大程度的弥补而不区分赎金种类，一律认定为共同海损；另一方面可作出更为细致的规定——虽然支付赎金目的也包括船员的赎回，但考虑到生命无价，于分摊阶段可只计赎回的船舶和船货各自占获救总价值的比例，由此计算船货多方分摊金额，以解决更多的潜在纠纷。

---

[1] 参见蒋圣力《我国海上保险条款针对海盗赎金保险理赔的适用情况研究》，载《黑河学刊》2014年第6期。

An Analysis on Maritime Lien in English Admiralty Jurisdiction

Lin Jiannan[*]

Abstract: It is difficult to fully untangle the intricate maze of a maritime lien in English Admiralty Jurisdiction even for British Academics and lawyers, due to the long historical and special cultural background of the lien. This essay tries to give a clarifying analysis of a maritime lien in British Maritime Law based on cross-referencing different sets of academic sources and judicial precedents. Liens, including maritime liens, have vital elements and features in substantive law and procedural law. Wide classes of maritime liens have their unique ranking, and make it more important to discuss the origination, assignment, subrogation and extinction of maritime liens.

Key words: maritime lien; action *in rem*; action *in personam*

浅析英国海事法下的船舶优先权

林剑南

摘要：基于船舶优先权具有悠久的历史和特殊的文化背景，即便是英国本土学者和律师想要完全解构英国海事法域中的船舶优先权也是件不容易的事。本文通过对照学术研究和权威判例对英国海商法中的船舶优先权进行分析，发现优先权（包括船舶优先权）的要素及特征在实体法和程序法中都有重要体现。船舶优先权细分种类众多且具有优先顺位，此种特殊性值得我们对其产生、转移和消灭等内容进行深入的讨论。

关键词：船舶优先权　对物诉讼　对人诉讼

---

[*] Lin Jiannan（林剑南），远海私募基金管理（天津）有限公司法务，上海海事大学、University of Exeter 海商法硕士。

Introduction

Maritime lien forms an important part of English Admiralty Jurisdiction. Generally, when services are provided to a ship or when damages are caused by a ship, a maritime lien will appear and attach to the ship in favour of these service providers and victims of the wrong. However, it has never had a legislative interpretation except for a hint in section 21(3) of *Senior Courts Act 1981*. Actions *in rem* could draw ships, aircraft or other properties into the Queen's Bench Division of the High Court by virtue of a maritime lien or other charge attached to these properties. So a maritime lien holder has a right to arrest the ship before a court hearing and clarification of responsibility. The ship is unable to leave until a fund is tendered to secure the claim *in rem*. A maritime lien is secret and adheres to properties regardless of the change of owners. The legal basis of a maritime lien is to solve the inaccessibility of the shipowner, because the shipowner may be difficult to identify, may live abroad, and may even be caught by insolvency. [1] An action *in rem* can help to implement a maritime lien with a very high priority over other rights. The essay firstly focuses on the related concepts concerning a maritime lien with the purpose of differentiating a claim *in rem* from a claim *in personam* and clarifying the relationships among different liens. Secondly, the nature of a maritime lien and the position of a foreign maritime lien in the UK will be discussed. And then special attention is given to specific contents of maritime liens and the priority-ranking among different classes of maritime liens. And the next part is to analyze assignment and subrogation of a maritime lien. At the end of this essay, ways of extinction of maritime liens will be commented on.

I. Related concepts

Some basic information should be analyzed at first in order to understand better the nature of maritime liens.

---

[1] Mansfield, *Maritime Liens*(1888) 16 LQR 381.

A. Theories and cases mentioned about a maritime lien

Traditionally, there are a number of theories referring to maritime liens. The most important one of them is the personification theory.① According to this theory, a ship is considered a juristic entity, like a person capable of independently performing contracts and committing torts. But this theory has a significant influence in US law rather than UK law. The other is the procedural theory, which is prevalent in the UK. The arrest of a ship allows to force a defendant to attend a court and to obtain security for the claim. With the development of this theory, a maritime lien becomes a legal *nexus* (connection) between the claimant and the arrested ship.②

Except for theories, case law offers more supplementary instructions on its characters. *The Bold Buccleugh*③ established the three main foundations of a maritime lien. The first is to differentiate a maritime lien and a possessory lien in common law, due to the fact that a maritime lien is independent of gaining possession of a property. The second is to confirm that a maritime lien could reach and seize a foreign property. The last is to make it clear that a maritime lien does not disappear just because of the defendant's appearance at the hearing. *The Two Ellens*④ showed when the relevant fact generates a maritime lien, the lien will not disappear but live with a ship until the lien is satisfied or is bared by the laches or is discharged by law. *The Ripon City*⑤ indicates that a maritime lien is like a *jus in re aliena*, which means that a maritime lien seems like having a right over the property of another. *The Tervaete*⑥ expresses that a maritime lien entitles the holder through some authorities' coercive methods to seize the ship and sell the ship under the condition that the ship is not released on bail. This essay will further analyze a maritime lien in detail in the next parts.

---

① Phill P. Wells, "Maritime Liens", in David S. Garland et al. eds. *The American and English Encyclopedia of law* (2nd 1901), p. 1079.
② D. R. Thomas, *Thomas: Maritime Liens* (Stevens & Sons 1980).
③ (1851) 7 Moore, P. C. 267.
④ (1872) L. R. 4 P. C. 161.
⑤ [1897] p. 226.
⑥ [1922] p. 259.

B. The relationship between a claim *in rem* and a claim *in personam*

Actions *in rem* and actions *in personam* have different natures. The former is directed against the properties (in the Admiralty context ship, cargo or freight) with a maritime privilege or lien, making sure of the execution of the judgment; the latter is directed against specific persons in order to compel the defendant to act or cease from acting. Compared to a claim *in personam*, an *in rem* claim has two superiorities, namely gaining security contributing to the claim and establishing jurisdiction. [1] They are not in an absolutely adversarial relationship, although they are sometimes conflicted. According to section 34 of *the Civil Jurisdiction and Judgements Act 1982* ("the 1982 Act"), two proceedings between the same parties with the same matter or the same cause of action are prohibited regardless of these proceedings both *in rem* and *in personam* or both at home and abroad. In *India v. India Steamship Co Ltd* (*the Indian Grace No. 2*)[2] the Indian government brought an action *in personam* in India against shipowners and then continuously filed an action *in rem* in the UK against a sister ship belonging to the shipowners. House of Lords rejected the second legal action on the ground that an *in rem* proceeding against a vessel should be deemed to be against the shipowners, as a consequence of section 34 of *the 1982 Act* should apply in bar of the second action *in rem* to proceed. *The Indian Grace No. 2* case abandoned the assumption that an action *in rem* was not against the owners of a ship but against the ship. However, harmonious coexistence between an *in rem* claim and an *in personam* claim sometimes seems to be feasible. In other words, an action *in rem* could be concurrently or consecutively available with an action *in personam*. For example, they could be submitted together in a claim form. [3] The basic reason for the above-mentioned conflict is that a claim *in rem* has two categories. [4] One

---

[1] David James Demordaunt, "Admiralty in rem and in personam procedures: Are they exempt from common law constitutional standards" (1989) 29 2 Santa Clara L. Rev. 331.

[2] [1998] A. C. 878.

[3] D. C. Jackson, *Enforcement of Maritime Claim* (4th LLP 2005).

[4] Nigel Meeson, John A. Kimbell, *Admiralty Jurisdiction and Practice* (4th ed. Informa 2011).

is a truly *in rem* claim, which directly points to the vessel rather than a person. A maritime claim secured by a maritime lien falls within this scope, which also covers claims for forfeiture, droits of admiralty and a claim concerning the possession or ownership of a ship.① The other is a *quasi in rem* claim, which ties up with a liability *in personam*. *The Indian Grace No. 2* in fact is a *quasi in rem* claim which has an *in personam* characteristic and shares the same cause of action with an *in personam* claim, due to the statement of Steyn L. who underlined that "this case is not concerned with maritime liens".② So a truly *in rem* claim and a claim *in personam* can co-exist. Lord Watson in *the Castlegate*③ said that "a proper maritime lien must have its root in the personal liability of the owner". In addition, if the value of an arrested property is less than the amount awarded by an *in rem* judgment, the gap could be remedied in the next claim *in personam*.④ It is also clear that if the shipowner does not attend the true proceeding *in rem*, the claim is only enforced within the value of the ship.

C. The relationship between a claim *in rem* and a maritime lien

One function of a claim *in rem* is to arrest a ship. Arresting a ship is the advantage to provide security and establish English Jurisdiction.⑤ According to clauses 6.1 and 6.4(3) of the Practice Direction - Admiralty, the arrest is an entitlement to have property immobilized physically or banned from marketing. The concept of arrest related to an action *in rem* for the sake of enforcing maritime claims by means of the judicial sale under section 21 of the *Senior Court Act 1981* is different from the concept of arrest under the Practice Direction.

An action *in rem* may be brought to enforce a maritime lien, to create a statutory lien, or to obtain security.⑥ A lien could be created and operated both by law and by contract, so does a maritime lien. The creation of a maritime lien

---

① Nigel Meeson, John A. Kimbell, *Admiralty Jurisdiction and Practice*(4th ed. Informa 2011).
② *The Indian Grace No.2* [1998] 1 Lloyd's 1, 7.
③ [1893] A. C. 38, 52.
④ *The Dictator* [1892] p. 304.
⑤ *The Anna H* [1995] 1 Lloyd's Rep. 11.
⑥ D. C. Jackson, *Enforcement of Maritime Claim*(4th LLP 2005).

does not depend on a contract, but a contract contributes to identifying the amount of money by way of *quantum meruit*. [1] A statutory lien only appears after an arrest writ is issued. [2] Statutory liens are prescribed by law. Apart from that a harbor authority has a right to arrest and sell a vessel to recover unpaid fees and damages under *the Harbours Dock and Piers Clauses Act 1847*, most of the other statutory liens are stipulated under *the Senior Court Act 1981* (some maritime liens are also stated in *SCA 1981*). A possessory lienee has to take possession of the property for the sake of enforcing his possessory lien. [3] For example, a ship repairer has a possessory lien against a ship to cover all the repair costs. Broadly speaking, protections provided by a maritime lien are more powerful and convenient.

II. The nature of a maritime lien

It is well-known that a maritime lien is a right. What is not certain is whether a maritime lien is a procedural right or a substantive right in nature. In *The Halcyon Isle*[4], the justices holding the minority view used *the Colorado*[5] for reference and held that a maritime lien was a property right because a maritime lien shares and partakes of a proprietary right of a vessel. It explains why a maritime lien is triggered and then adheres to the ship regardless of changes of ownership. On the other hand, Lord Diplock on behalf of the majority drew from the opinion of Lord Justice Atkin in *the Tervaete*[6] and considered that the function of a maritime lien is to act as procedural or remedial only, due to the fact that a maritime lien performs as an anchor point facilitating a procedure of enforcement

---

[1] *The Ever Success* [1999] 1 Lloyd's Rep. 824.

[2] Hill Dickinson, "Maritime Liens" (http: //www. hilldickinson. com/pdf/Maritime% 20liens. pdf) accessed May 26, 2017.

[3] William Tetley, "Maritime Liens in the Conflict of Laws", in Nafziger & symeon C. Symeonides ed. *Law and Justice in a Multistate World: Esseys in Honor of Arthur T. von Mehren* (Ardsley 2002).

[4] *Bankers Trust International Ltd v. Todd Shipyard Corp* [1981] A. C. 221.

[5] [1923] p. 102.

[6] [1922] p. 259, 274. Atkin L. J. states that "[The maritime lien] is confined to a right to take proceedings in a court of law..." and "The right of maritime lien appears...to be essentially different from a right of property, hypothec or pledge created by [a] voluntary act ...".

and securing a claim. But priorities of propriety right (qui prior est tempore potior est jure) that "first in time, first in right"① cannot explain the ranking among maritime liens. A maritime lien in a higher classification could be found later than other maritime liens in a lower classification. In addition, some maritime liens have their own priorities in time-reverse order. Based on this reason, The *Halcyon Isle* establishes the legal authority that the nature of a maritime lien is a procedural right. This reason is not yet noncontroversial, because the ranking of preference of maritime lien indeed belongs to a procedural issue, but the ranking and the nature of a maritime lien are not inseparable. In an Australian case *Pfeiffer v. Goerson*②, a brand new principle was established that if a matter has an impact on the existence, extent or enforceability of the rights and responsibility of the parties, this matter is a substantive issue. And if a matter has an influence on the rule of proceeding, this matter is a procedural issue. In this sense, a maritime lien should be considered substantive. It is also arguable that *the Halcyon Isle* was rendered by the Privy Council rather than the higher hierarchy like the Supreme Court, so this opinion only has a highly persuasive effect on courts at the grass-roots level.③ Furthermore, Jackson holds a view that a maritime lien still possesses some substantive characteristics.④ Some authors say that a maritime lien possesses a dual characteristic. The reason is that a maritime lien provides the lienee with a cause of action. It seems like the lienee is conferred a substantive right.⑤

III. Priorities in *in rem* claims

Priorities hold the key to *in rem* claims when the value of a ship is insufficient to meet the requirement of all valid claims. Generally speaking, the

---

① James W. Simonton, *Austin's Classification of Proprietary Rights* (1926) 11 Cornell L. Rev. 227.
② *John Pfeifer Pty Ltd v. Rogerson* (2000) 203 CLR 503.
③ Paul Myburgh, *Recognition of Foreign Maritime Liens* (1989) 106 S. African L. J. 263.
④ D. C. Jackson, *Enforcement of Maritime Claim* (4th LLP 2005).
⑤ John lane, "Should Australian Court accept or refuse the aid of private international law when considering to enforce foreign maritime liens?" (2009) 16 eLaw J. 32.

ranking rule stated in *the Aline*① is that *ex delicto* liens (arising out of torts) have precedence over *ex contractu* liens (arising out of express or implied terms). This lies in the reason that the *ex contractu* lien on the vessel is created on the lien holder's own accord for profits, but *ex delicto* liens are created under maritime perils or by negligent navigation beyond the control of the lien holder. At first, the expenses of the Admiralty Marshal or his substitute② and harbor authorities' statutory rights③ have precedence of being paid off over all other claims, including maritime liens, possessory liens and other kinds of statutory liens. Maritime liens belong to the second rank over other kinds of liens *in rem*, except for the first rank. But *the Tergeste*④ shows that the possessory lien may surpass maritime liens when the possessory lien appears before maritime liens. Another exception is related to the sister ship arrest situation. Before 1957, an action *in rem* could be brought against nothing but only the offending ship. ⑤ When the *Administration of Justice Act 1956* (*the 1956 Act*) took effect on Jan 1, 1957, an *in rem* action could be litigated for the claimant's satisfaction against the offending ship or other ship under the same beneficial shipowner. In *the Bance*,⑥ three Lord Justices of Appeal held that "...an action in rem against-that ship...; or any other ship..." in section 3(4) of *the 1956 Act* should be interpreted that an action *in rem* could be brought against any ship or ships beneficially owned by the offending ship-owner when the claim arises. So a maritime lien holder is able to arrest the sister ship to enforce his right, in this situation, the priority of a maritime lien is inferior to other liens. In *the Leoborg* (*No. 2*)⑦, the wages lien from the vessel *Havsborg* was ranked the lowest scale among liens on the sister vessel *Leoborg*. Thirdly, the priority of possessory liens ranks lower than the first

---

① (1839) 1 Wm. Rob. 111.

② *The Falcon* [1981] 1 Lloyd's Rep. 13.

③ *The Ousel* [1957] 1 Lloyd's Rep. 151 the harbor authority is entitled to arrest and sell the ship according its statutory right, which should not be affected by maritime liens. All other maritime liens are only able to reach the proceeds. See also *The Freightline One* [1986] 1 Lloyd's Rep. 266.

④ [1903] p. 26.

⑤ *The Beldis* [1936] p. 51.

⑥ [1971] 1 Lloyd's Rep. 49.

⑦ [1964] 1 Lloyd's Rep. 383.

rank and the previous maritime lien,[1] and never yields to other claims.[2] But taking possession of the ship is the necessary prerequisite to assert possessory liens. Finally, the rank of statutory rights of actions *in rem* is at the bottom. But a mortgage as a separate label is at the top over other normal statutory liens. Mortgages are divided into two groups, namely British registered mortgages and other mortgages. This is not a matter of the date of creation, but the former is endowed with preferential right of payment against the latter.

Ⅳ. Non-recognition of foreign maritime liens

A foreign maritime lien may come in two forms in the UK. One is that the claimant directly files a claim *in rem* before the Admiralty court. The other is that the claimant enforces a judgement *in rem* before the English court. In the first case, a procedural nature of a maritime lien requires the Admiralty court to recognize and rank a foreign maritime lien by the *lex fori*.[3] So the judging criteria for whether a right could be seen as a maritime lien relies on English Law. It follows that The United Kingdom never recognizes a foreign maritime lien if it is not within the scope of maritime liens in the UK. Ships could be found all over the world, so conflicts among different legal systems are inevitable. Taking American law for example, a master is regarded as the credit of the shipowner rather than the ship, so a maritime lien for the master's wages could not be established according to American law.[4] But under English law, the master's wages are sacred and are multiply protected by means of authorizing it as a maritime lien and giving it higher priority in rank. Moreover, a ship repairer could claim for the costs of repair and the value of supplies by virtue of maritime liens in American law.[5] On the positive side, there is no a maritime lien for

---

[1] *The Gustaf* (1862) Lush. 506.

[2] *Williams v. Allsup* (1861) 10 CB(NS) 417.

[3] John Lane, "Should Australian Court Accept or Refuse the Aid of Private International Law When Considering to Enforce Foreign Maritime Liens?" (2009) 16 eLaw J. 32.

[4] Edward L. "Willard, Priorities among maritime liens (1930—1931)", 16 Cornell L. Q. 522

[5] Ivon D Almeida Pires Filho, "Priority of Maritime Liens in the Western Hemisphere: How Secure is Your Claim?" (1984) 16 U. Miami Inter-Am. L. Rev. 505.

repairs and supplies in the UK. In *the Halcyon Isie*,[①] American necessaries men gained a valid verdict of the Supreme Court of Canada beforehand where a ship repairer had a right to enforce an *in rem* claim against the vessel without a mention of a maritime lien. The UK did not ratify the International Convention on Maritime Liens and Mortgage 1926 which provides a ship repairer with a maritime lien to enforce necessaries. In the light of the rule that a maritime lien is not a substantive right but a procedural right and the scope of maritime liens in English law, a ship repairer had no maritime lien for necessities. However, it is unfair to some extent that both the foreign parties under a claim arising *ex contractu* clearly understand their legal rights and responsibilities in light of their own *lex causae*, but this clear-cut legal consequence compulsively yields to a foreign jurisdiction. In the second case, if a judgement is made out of a truly *in rem* claim, which has already arrested a ship for security, with no need for enforcement in the UK. On the other hand, if a ship is arrested in the UK, which means that a foreign judgement has a *quasi in rem* jurisdiction. As a result, an admiralty court will not admit the existence of a maritime lien in the judgement. Unfortunately, a *quasi in rem* judgement will prohibit a claim *in personam* against the shipowner or his sister ship in the UK according to *the Indian Grace No. 2* and *the 1982 Act*. All in all, a foreign maritime lien is no way to be recognized by the Admiralty court. The category of maritime liens and their priorities will be mentioned below.

V. Specific contents of maritime liens and their ranking

The assets could be attached to a maritime lien including not only a ship and its associated property but also other properties, such as aircraft and hovercraft and their associated property.[②] Maritime liens are commonly believed not to be expanded to other things besides salvage, wages, master's wages and disbursements, damage and bottomry.[③] The ranking of a maritime lien is important. Except for a maritime lien referring to salvage and bottomry, the

---

① [1980] 1 Lloyd's Rep. 325.
② D. C. Jackson, *Enforcement of maritime claim*(4th LLP 2005).
③ D. R. Thomas, *Maritime Liens*(Stevens & Sons 1980).

holder of the same kind of maritime lien should be treated equally and without preference. In *the Stream Fisher* case①, the vessel *Stream Fisher* separately collides with four vessels in rival. Informed Bateson J. considered that all salvage claims in rem rank *Pari Passu* on the ground that no authorities support the connection between the priorities and time of the collisions or the verdicts. However, it is hard to adhere to a strict rule or principle to establish precedence levels among different categories of maritime liens, because some peculiar circumstances should be taken into consideration. Basically, the theory, which has a significant impact on the hierarchy in the enforcement of maritime liens, is that the court should pay closer attention to equity, public policy and business convenience when deciding the priorization of enforcing various maritime liens in each case. ②

A. Salvage

1. Content

The concept of salvage is unique to the maritime domain. If an individual tries to preserve a ship or save a ship and his property from the perils of the sea, this individual has a right to get a salvage reward. The salvage lien arises and attaches to some property identified in the legal scope of salvage subject matter when a ship in danger receives beneficial services. For example, human life is not involved in this scope, but saving a life could possibly provide a salvor with a maritime lien for other property. ③ And rescue services without any benefits do not generate a maritime lien. ④ The creation of a salvage lien is on the basis of statutes rather than a contract. International convention on salvage 1989 incorporated into the *Merchant Shipping (Salvage and Pollution) Act 1994*; the convention 1989 makes clear that the salvor's maritime lien should not be affected in any event. However, the maritime lien for salvage services does not intend to impose a heavy burden on the owner of the salved vessel, due to article 20(2) of

---

① [1926] 26 Lloyd's Rep. 4.
② D. R. Thomas, *Maritime Liens* (Stevens & Sons 1980).
③ *The Merchant Shipp Act* 1894, S544.
④ The India(1842) 1 W. Rob. 406.

the convention 1989 that if security for a salvage claim is satisfied, a maritime lien could not be enforced. This view is supported by *the Tervaete*. ①

2. Priorities

It is well established that the last salvage lien takes priority over the previous one. The reason is that the effect of the later salvage salvor benefits earlier salvors by preserving the *res* in danger. ② The same rationale generally applies in all cases. Brandon J. held in *the Lyrma* (*No. 2*)③ that a salvor's lien should be enforced in priority over all maritime liens, and there was really no justified excuse not to apply this long-accepted principle in this case merely because of other wages liens happened next to the salvage service. If several salvors together provide aggregative services, maritime liens for salvage should rank *Pari Passu*. ④

B. Seamen's wages, Master's wages and disbursements

1. Content

Merchant Shipping Act and its subsequent Acts specify that the seamen and mariners are allowed to claim for their wages and disbursements in the name of maritime liens before the Admiralty Court. ⑤ In *the Sydney Cove*, the court said that "a seaman's claim for his wages was sacred as long as a single plank of the ship remained" and the wages lien defeated the hypothecation of a vessel. ⑥ The master and other mariners who manage and navigate the ship are the heart of the ship. The admiralty law always attaches importance to protecting mariner's rights. For example, if ambiguities appear in seafarers' employment contracts, the interpretation is to be held in favour of the mariner. ⑦ The wages lien does not

---

① [1922] p. 259.

② *The Veritas* [1901] p. 304.

③ [1978] 2 Lloyd's Rep. 30.

④ *The Russland* [1924] p. 55.

⑤ *Merchant Shipping Act 1995* S41: "The master of a ship shall have the same lien for his remuneration, and all disbursements or liabilities properly made or incurred by him on account of the ship, as a seaman has for his wages."

⑥ (1815) 2 Dods. 11, 13.

⑦ *The Nonparell* (1864) Brown. & Lush. 355.

derive from the contract but from factual services linked with the ship.① This kind of maritime liens expand their field and scope of wages to bonuses,② a victualing allowance,③ national insurance contributions (only under the requirement of the contract),④ and employee benefits, like redundancy pay, paid leave, sick leave⑤ and repatriation costs. ⑥ In addition, wages claim *truly in rem* could be brought against a foreign ship. ⑦ It is likely that seamen in a foreign ship could claim a lien for unpaid wages, due to the fact that a maritime lien is a procedural right. So it is not a matter of whether a foreign country admits to the wages lien or not, it is a matter of that English law admits that unpaid wages constitute a maritime lien.

When the performance of master administrative duties leads to master's costs and liability, these proper and necessary costs and liability are master's disbursements. ⑧ The existence of disbursements lien is unobjectionable, according to section 18 of *the Merchant Shipping Act 1970*⑨.

2. Priorities

The liens for master's disbursements and wages are regarded as the same ranking as seamen's wages. ⑩ However, in situations where the master is personally liable for the seamen's wages, maritime liens for master's disbursements and wages are subject to that for the seamen's wages. ⑪ Generally, the wages lien is likely to be next to the salvage lien in order of precedence. But there is one exception when a seaman claims for wages on account of the service of preserving the *res*, this kind of wages claim will be provided with a higher

---

① *The Ever Success* [1999] 1 Lloyd's Rep. 824.
② *The Elmville* (No. 2) [1904] p. 422.
③ *The Tergeste* [1903] p. 26.
④ *The Gee Whiz* [1951] 1 Lloyd's Rep. 145.
⑤ *The Arose Star* [1959] 2 Lloyd's Rep. 397.
⑥ *Westport, the*(No. 4) [1968] 2 Lloyd's Rep. 559.
⑦ *The Administration of Justice Act 1956* S1(4)(6).
⑧ D. R. Thomas, *Maritime Liens*(Stevens & Sons 1980).
⑨ "The master of a ship shall have the same lien for his remuneration, and all disbursements or liabilities properly made or incurred by him on account of the ship, as a seaman has for his wages."
⑩ Nigel Meeson, John A. Kimbell, *Admiralty jurisdiction and practice*(4th ed., Informa 2011).
⑪ D. C. Jackson, *Enforcement of Maritime Claim*(4th LLP 2005).

priority over a salvage claim. ①

C. The damage or loss

1. Content

The range of claims related to damage is basically stated in section 1(1) (d) – (h) of the Administration of Justice Act 1956. There is a saying for the first time in *the Bold Buccleugh*② that a claim for loss or damage caused by collision should be treated as the same way as suits for salvage and wages. In *Berliner Bank A. G. v. C. Czarnikow Sugar Ltd.* (*the "Rama"*)③, Justice Clarke clarified that a navigating ship as the actual instrument should directly cause physical damage. For example, a collision between ships,④ a crash between shoreside facility and a ship,⑤ stranding of a ship (due to a failed salvation),⑥ dangerous and reckless navigation⑦ will give rise to maritime liens for damages or losses. He further stated that a cause factor of the damage should arise from intentional or unintentional seaman's operations. In addition, the Damage Lien Could Expand to Personal Injury Caused by a Ship⑧ without the requirement of being tied to the collision of ships. Historically, doubts persisted on whether personal injuries fall within the scope of actions *in rem*. *The Maritime Conventions Act 1911* says that damages for loss of life or personal injury could be set forth on both actions *in rem* and *in personam*. A negative view held by Price is that there might be no link between maritime liens and personal injury. ⑨ However,

---

① *The Elin* (1882) LR 8 PD 39; *The Linda Flor* (1857) Swa. 309; *The Chimera* (1852) 11 LT 113.

② (1851) 7 Moore, P. C. 267.

③ [1996] 2 Lloyd's Rep. 281.

④ Not only the ship damage but also the cargo loss in other struck ship are in this scope. The latter could be seen in *Victoria* (1887) 12 P. D. 105. No maritime lien could be created on a ship because of the loss or damage of good in the same ship. See the Pieve Superiore (1874) LR 5 PC 482.

⑤ *The Tolten* [1946] p. 135.

⑥ *The Eschersheim* [1976] 1 W. L. R. 430. The salvage ship suffers a maritime lien due to its negligent salvage in relation to the salved vessel's claim.

⑦ *Dagmara, the and Ama Antxine* [1988] 1 lloyd's Rep. 431.

⑧ *The Vera Cruz* (No. 2) (1884) 9 P. D. 96.

⑨ G. Price, *The Law of Maritime Liens* (London, Sweet & Maxwell, 1940).

positive views become more prevalent and are supported by *the Sylph*① and *the Beta*②, although the supporting reason why an action *in rem* could involve personal injuries is wholly dependent on section 7 of *the Admiralty Court Act 1861*.

2. Priorities

The ranking rationale of maritime lien for damage caused by a vessel is based on the need of keeping a ship safe in navigation. The damage lien possibly tends to be ranked last. However, it is worth noticing that, in *the Veritas*③ when the damage lien is supported by an effective judgment (not involving priorities) and at the same time the salvage lien arising *ex contractu*, the damage lien will be enforced in priority over the salvage lien due to the interest of safe navigation.

D. Bottomry

1. Content

Bottomry in short is an agreement of a loan that is secured by a ship and should be repaid at the time of the ship's safe arrival④. *Stainbank v. Shepard*⑤ classically established that the responsibility of a bottomry bond lies with the ship instead of the owner. According to a relatively new case, *The James W. Elwell*⑥, a maritime lien created by a bottomry bond could exist secretly and chronically. Unlike other maritime liens, it is possible for a bottomry lien to be assigned and transferred to a third party. ⑦

2. Priorities

In the same category of the bottomry lien, the ranking between bottomry bonds is the same as salvage liens, which means that the last one prevails over the previous ones. ⑧ While among bottomry liens and other maritime liens, the

---

① (1867) L. R. 2 A. & E. 24.
② (1869) L. R. 2 P. C. 447.
③ [1901] p. 304.
④ *The Atlas* 2 Hagg. Adm. 48.
⑤ (1853) 13 C. B. 418.
⑥ [1921] p. 351.
⑦ *The Rebecca* (1804) 5 C. Rob. 102. See also the discussion in *the Petone* [1917] p. 198.
⑧ *Cargo ex Galam* (1863) 2 Moo. P. C. N. S. 216.

priority of a bottomry lien is subordinated to a wages lien in the same voyage but prevails over wages liens arising from previous voyages. ①

According to the above analysis with regard to the classes and the priorities of maritime liens, a maritime lien has several functions. The first function is to maintain safe navigation of a ship. The purpose of a higher priority of the salvage lien is to encourage third parties to do their best to rescue a ship in danger. It also shows that human life is to be placed in an important place. The second is that English law pays closer attention to the protection of seafarers' rights. The scope of wage liens extends in all ages, compared with the category of maritime liens has been unchanged for nearly a century. The legal consideration on wages lien is flexible and not rigid for maintaining seamen's interests. Admiralty law prompts seamen to rescue the damaged ship where they are aboard with might and main, because seamen know their own ship fully well and are easier to gain better results. Third, maritime liens have made it easy for investors to pump more capital in order to facilitate the development of shipping industry.

Ⅵ. Assignment and subrogation of a maritime lien

Due to the fact that a maritime lien is a procedural right, the Admiralty court is unlikely to recognize an assignment of a maritime lien, except that these assignments are supported by statutes. ② The maritime lien subrogation, which is supported by a court order, is feasible. In *the Petone*, ③ Justice Hill rejected the view that the principle, "the man who has paid off the privileged claimant stands in the shoes of the privileged claimant", could apply to the assignment of a maritime lien. A third party voluntarily pays off a debt attached to a maritime lien, as a consequence, the underlying claim is satisfied, and the maritime lien vanishes. Nothingness the claimant has could be assigned to the third party. But

---

① *The Mary Ann* (1845) 9 Jur. 94; *the Hope* (1873) 1 Asp. M. L. C. 563.

② William Tetley, "Assignment and Transfer of Maritime Liens: Is There Subrogation of the Privilege" (1984) 15 J. M. L. C. 3 393; For example, *the Bankruptcy Act 1914* S38 (b), *Law Reform (Miscellaneous Provisions) Act* S1(1), *Maritime Convention Act 1911* S3(2), *Supreme Court Act 1981* S21(6).

③ [1917] p. 198, 208.

the Petone did not touch on the effectiveness of the assignment arising out of the contract.① Furthermore, there is an exception that a bottomry lien holder is able to assign his bond to a third party.② However, the subrogation of a maritime lien is feasible under a court order in order to preserve the priority.③ On the other hand, a claim secured by a maritime lien is paid voluntarily by the third party without an order from a court, the third party is unable to be subrogated to the claim.④ Except for the legal subrogation, the effect of the contractual subrogation is also unclear.⑤ According to section 79 of *Marine Insurance Act 1906*, the insurer is entitled to be subrogated to all rights and remedies of the insured after the compensation.⑥

VII. Extinction of maritime liens

A maritime lien powerfully overwhelms other rights. Once it appears, it is almost indestructible. Normally, the continuation of a maritime lien will come to an end when the maritime lien is enforced by an *in rem* action or is extinguished. But some modes acting as a terminator carry maritime liens away.

1. Loss of a ship

A maritime line, which has fastened itself to the vessel like a barnacle, finally perishes together with the vessel. The ship should be completely destroyed, otherwise, a maritime lien may still attach to the wreck or its fragment.⑦ As salvage-operation technologies have developed, a sunken ship in the depths of the sea still is likely to be retrieved in the future.

---

① [1917] p. 198, 208. Hill J. said that "I say nothing about contractual assignments of debts or claims supported by maritime liens".

② *The Catherine* (1847) 3 W Rob. 1.

③ *The Word star* [1987] 1 Lloyd's Rep. 452; see also *the Berostar* [1970] 2 Lloyd's Rep. 403.

④ *The Leoborg* No. 2 [1964] 1 Lloyd's Rep. 380.

⑤ Konrad Zweigert, Ulrich Drobing (eds), *International Encyclopedia of Comparative Law*: *Installment* 12 (Kluwer Academic Publishers, 1981).

⑥ International Convention on Maritime Liens and Mortgages 1993, which is not signed by the United Kingdom, denies this right in its article 10.

⑦ *The Sydney Cove* (1815) 2 Dods. 11.

2. Ship sold by the court executing *in rem* jurisdiction

It is well-known that a judicial sale is able to absolutely destroy all maritime liens and its consequence is effective against the world,① because a judgement sale *in rem* not only has openness, but also authority, stability. Firstly, unlike other court sales without judgment *in rem* only known to the shipowner and a few litigant participants,② an action *in rem* aims at driving everyone who has a connection with the vessel to appear. This ensures that all claimants have access to the ship or the fund via claims *in rem*. Secondly, a judicial sale *in rem* undoubtedly put an end to all litigations. In *Cerro Colorado*③, a loan was secured against the vessel *Cerro Colorado* that would be sold under the jurisdiction of the UK. However, before the sale, the Spanish Embassy informed that the vessel would be rearrested for a Spanish judgement for unpaid wages after the judicial sale. This conflict was disposed of by the court in the UK that the judicial sale *in rem* would provide the buyer with a clear title of the vessel free from all liens and encumbrances. The reason was that the Spanish judgment was not made in proceedings *in rem* due to the fact that the vessel was not actually seized by the Spanish court and it held no *in rem* jurisdiction, and Spain, as a member of the International Convention for the Unification of Certain Rules Relating to the Arrest of Seagoing Ships, should recognize the decrees made by the Admiralty Court in the UK. Therefore, an *in rem* sale is able to remove any proprietorial limitations from the vessel. However, it is worth noticing that the maritime lien holder could make an *in rem* claim against the vessel before or after the judicial sale with the condition that the claim form should be submitted before the court sale. The only difference is that his action *in rem* is made against the proceeds of sale instead of the vessel, which is already sold by the admiralty court.④ Furthermore, in

---

① *The Tremont* (1841) 1 W. Robinson 163.

② *The Charles Amelia* (1867—1869) L. R. 2 A. & E. 330, 335. Sir R. Phillimore said that "The proceedings in the French court were certainly not proceedings 'in rem', but apparently resembled those which would be taken in bankruptcy in this country, which would not extinguish a maritime lien".

③ [1993] 1 Lloyd's Rep. 58.

④ *The Bank of Tokyo-Mitsuibishi UFJ Limited v. The Owners of the MV Sanko Mineral v. Glencore Limited* [2014] EWHC 3927 (Admity).

Castrique v. Imrie,[①] the House of Lords recognized the validity of a foreign judgement in equivalent jurisdiction *in rem*. As a result, the overseas judicial sale *in rem* acts as an estoppel against relevant maritime liens.[②] On the contrary, non-judicial *in rem* sale is an unsuccessful defense against a maritime lien.

There are two types of non-judicial *in rem* sale, one is personal sale. An equitable lien created by law could be vanished when a *bona fide* buyer makes an acquisition of the property by good will without notice of the claim.[③] If a claim *in rem* without a maritime lien arises after a personal sale, there are no charges or rights attached to the ship.[④] A maritime lien still exists and attaches itself to the property which is resold to a *bona fide* buyer, whenever a truly *in rem* claim arises within the time bar.[⑤] The other one is judicial sale *in personam*. Except for a judicial sale acting *in rem*, other forms of judicial sales have no effect of surpassing maritime liens. In *the Goulandris*,[⑥] the steamship in question accepted salvage services from an English company, and a consequent arbitration brought in a verdict that the ship and the cargo owner should separately bear salvage remuneration, but the award was unsatisfied as the shipowner went bankrupt and the ship sold by an Egyptian court. The ship was later arrested in the UK by virtue of the salvage lien. Justice Bateson held that the court sale following an *in personam* judgement could not get rid of the salvor's lien.

3. Finalized claim

The maritime lien only entangles itself with the relevant maritime claim, which means when the basic maritime claim is withdrawn or satisfied by full payment, the related maritime lien disappears. Jeremy Browne[⑦] held that a lien

---

[①] (1870) L. R. 4 H. L. 414.

[②] Lawrence Collins, C G J Morse, David McClean, Adrian Briggs, Jonathan Harris, Campbell McLachlan, *Dicey, Morris & Collins on the Conflict of Laws* (Sweet & Maxwell 2012).

[③] Aleka Mandarake-Sheppard, *Modern Maritime Law and Risk Management* (2nd ed. Routledge-Cavendish 2008).

[④] Nigel Meeson, John A. Kimbell, *Admiralty jurisdiction and practice* (4th ed., Informa 2011).

[⑤] *The Bold Buccleugh* (1851) 7 Moore, P. C. 267.

[⑥] [1927] p. 182.

[⑦] Jeremy Browne, *The Extinction of Maritime Liens* (2003) LMCLQ 361.

holder's consent is able to extinguish the lien. And his view is supported by *the Goulandris*,① in which Bateson J. stated that the maritime lien could be fulfilled by any bargain. However, a lien holder's consent may not work if a lien holder's bargaining power is overwhelmed by the opponent in negotiations.② It may be feasible that a settlement is reached after the start of the trial. But this payment in the settlement only effects the settlement parties rather than other parties. However, it does not mean that the maritime lien completely secures all claims or lawsuits between the claimant and his opponent.

4. Laches and the statutory time bar

The doctrine of laches is that if a legal right or claim is unreasonably delayed to be asserted for a long time, the negligence of the claimant or the right-holder will either lead to the dismissal of a claim or make a right unenforceable.③ It is necessary to put an equitably procedural bar on it. One reason is that a maritime line always makes itself invisible without a need of notice or possession. On the other hand, if the maritime lienee does not enforce his lien in diligent, the innocent parties will suffer unduly prejudice.④ An action *in rem* is still enslaved by the time limitations, yet the doctrine of laches only applies under legal vacancy conditions⑤ so that few cases have the practical application of laches to prevent a maritime lien. For example, in *the Alletta*⑥, the court did not accept the excuse of laches.

Statutory time bars, which do not allow any excuse, are of more importance. English courts are reluctant to recognize a foreign maritime lien, so the *Foreign Limitation Period Act 1984* is useless in this field. The damage lien may be unenforceable after two years from the time of the appearance of damages, according to section 190(3) of the *Merchant Shipping Act 1995*. Actually, the court has a discretionary power to decide whether or not to extend the time

---

① [1927] p. 182.

② *The Juliana*(1822) 165 E. R. 1560.

③ Uisdean R. Vass, Xia Chen, "The Admiralty Doctrine of Laches" 53 La. L. Rev. (1992).

④ Geoge L. Canfield, George W. Dalzell, *The Law of the Sea: A Manual of the Principles of Admiralty Law for Students*, (1921) 15 AJIL 4, 615.

⑤ *Re Paulings Settlement Trusts* [1963] 3 All E. R. 1.

⑥ [1974] 1 Lloyd's Rep. 40.

limitation based on how hard it is for the claimant to arrest the vessel. The salvage lien is subject to a two-years-time bar according to Article 23 of the Salvage Convention. And the court does not have a discretionary power to extend the time bar period. The shipowner and his ship are free from all responsibilities related to transportation unless the suit is filed within one year from the delivery date or the supposed delivery date in the light of section 3(6) of the *Carriage of Good by the Sea Act 1971*. But this period can be prolonged by a mutual agreement. Under the 36(1) of the *Limitation Act 1980*, the rule① that the six-year statutory time bar is not suitable for the claim *in rem* has been removed. The purpose of the time bar requires the claimant to assert their right as soon as possible, since a long delay may cause troubles.

  5. Laws and regulations that offer immunity to an attachment of a maritime lien

  A maritime lien is unable to attach itself to any Crown ship and a foreign state-owned ship at the very beginning. According to section 29(1) of the *Crown Proceedings Act 1947*, a claim *in rem* is forbidden against Her Majesty's ship or aircraft or any other property belonging to the Crown, not to mention the arrest, detention, or sale. In light of the *State Immunity Act 1978*, a sovereign ship performing a public function is prohibited from an *in rem* proceeding. In *The Tervaete*②, the vessel, the tervaete, belonged to the Belgian Government when the collision happened. After its sale to an individual or private company, the vessel was arrested in a claim *in rem*. The court said that firstly, a maritime lien was unable to attach to the vessel at the time of the collision; secondly, if the value of the second-hand vessel would be affected by the lien, as a result, the merits of the *State Immunity Act 1978* would lose, due to the fact that the benefits of a foreign sovereign's property were indirectly affected. The consequence is that the private second-hand ship was still safe from the maritime lien. ③ Actually, this case could be explained by the nature of a maritime lien. A maritime lien is a procedural right rather than a substantive right, so a maritime lien is unable to be resurrected.

---

 ① *The Limitation Act 1939* S2(6).
 ② [1922] 12 Lloyd's Rep. 252.
 ③ *The Tervaete* [1922] p. 259.

Except for the above modes, forfeiture, which has a long tradition in the common law, could extinguish all maritime liens and all ownership interests. ① So several modes with some limitations could extinguish maritime liens, including procedural ways and substantive ways.

VIII. Conclusion

A maritime lien is very awesome and powerful. It is like an invisible Ninja, who safeguards the lien holder immediately upon receiving the task. The emergence and existence of a maritime lien is basically unrestricted and free from notification and registration. Now the nature of a maritime lien is defined and established as a procedural right. But there is a general trend to reconsider it as a substantive right around the world. Usually, a maritime lien gains a higher priority level among all liens. This lies in his unique maritime features. English courts are reluctant to recognize foreign maritime liens. If the nature of a maritime lien would change in the future, a foreign maritime lien might be admitted accordingly in the UK. Maritime liens are limited to specific contents. The priorities of maritime liens mainly result from the considerations of safe navigation of a ship, the protection of seamen's welfare, public interest, and special circumstances in each cases. Normally, if a person gains a maritime lien, he is utmost likely to be reimbursed. Not many ways could extinguish a maritime lien, and these ways also have some limitations.

---

① Jeremy Browne, *The Extinction of Maritime Liens*, (2003) LMCLQ 361.

Party Autonomy in Choice of Court and Its Limitations: A Comparative Analysis

Zeng Erxiu[*]

Abstract: While party autonomy in choice of court in civil and commercial matters is generally recognized, the scope of recognition or limitations varies in different jurisdictions due to a balance of the interests of the parties and the domestic jurisdiction protection. An examination of relevant rules and judicial practices relating to party autonomy in choice of court reveals the diversity in the protection of one party and the strength of protection to the domestic jurisdiction.

Key words: party autonomy; choice of court; protection of jurisdiction; private interest; public policy

当事人合意选择法院及其限制比较分析

曾二秀

摘要：虽然在民商事案件中当事人合意选择法院得到广泛认可，但是这种认可的范围或限制却因对当事人利益平衡的考虑及国内管辖权维护的不同而不同。对当事人合意选择法院及其限制立法与司法实践的研究表明，各国对一方当事人的保护和本国法院管辖权的维护力度方面存在巨大差异。

关键词：当事人合意　选择法院　管辖权保护　私人利益　公共政策

---

[*] Zeng Erxiu (曾二秀), professor in law, South China Normal Universtiy, Chair of Guangdong Provincial Shipping Law Society.

Introduction

Whenever disputes arise out of civil or commercial activities, the parties have to find a way to settle the disputes. There are various choices. The parties may be able to settle the disputes amicably and privately, with or without the help of a third party; otherwise, they have to resort to public legal remedies with an enforcement mechanism. Arbitration and litigation are the two kinds of means to settle disputes with the enforcement mechanism, but only the court has the judicial power to hear the case and enforce its judgment and the arbitral award. This judicial power derives from state sovereignty and is mandatory. Arbitration is based on party autonomy, but litigation is not. The jurisdiction of law court is not created by the parties' choice, but to some extent the parties' mutual choice of court is recognized.

Whether and to what extent the parties are given the right to choose the court to settle their disputes may be different in different jurisdictionss. The parties' mutual choice of court may not always be given effect, it may be recognized in the court of a state but not in that of another, especially one whose jurisdiction is not chosen. Furthermore, the validity of a choice of court agreement may be decided differently in different jurisdictions. Although conflict of jurisdictions exists even without party autonomy in choice of court, this conflict may become more aggravated with the parties' choice of a court that may not have jurisdiction but for the parties' choice. It is just the case in *Compania Sud Americana v. Hin-Pro International Logistics* (the Hin-Pro)①, where the jurisdiction clause choosing the English High Court of Justice in London was not recognized by Chinese courts, as the English court has no actual connection with the disputes under

---

① The Hin-Pro is a case between parties from Hong Kong SDR and Chile, involving transportation of goods from various ports in China to various ports in Venezuela, the disputes arising from delivery of goods without production of original bill of lading. The disputes resulted in proceedings in six maritime courts in China (Wuhan Maritime Court, Ningbo Maritime Court, Shanghai Maritime Court, Qingdao Maritime Court, Tianjin Maritime Court and Guangzhou Maritime Court) and choice of court clause enforcement proceedings in United Kingdom and Hong Kong SDR. See [2014] EWHC 3632 (Comm); [2015] 1 Lloyd' Rep. 301. [2015] EWCA Civ 401 [2015]; 2 Lloyd' Rep. 1. [2016] HKCFA 79; [2017] 1 Lloyd' Rep. Plus 23.

Chinese *Civil Procedural Law*.①

Therefore, it is of great importance to explore the limitations of party autonomy in choice of court in different jurisdictions and in international conventions relating to party autonomy in choice of court. This article will base its discussion on relevant rules and judicial decisions in China, the United Kingdom, and the rules in certain international conventions and EU regulations. It will explore the various limitations of party autonomy in choice of court in civil and commercial disputes and will end with an assessment of China's rules and the room for improvement.

Ⅰ. Party autonomy in choice of court in China

A. Legislative development

In China, the civil jurisdiction of courts is specified in codified civil procedural law, including *Civil Procedural Law of the People's Republic of China* (hereafter CPL) and *Special Procedural Law of the People's Republic of China for Maritime Proceedings* (hereafter SPLMP), the latter implementing the former in maritime cases. The first CPL was enacted in 1982 (hereafter CPL 1982) in which the plaintiff was given a very limited forum choice② and there was no party autonomy in choice of court existed. It was not until 1991 when the current CPL was enacted that the parties were given the right to choose the court by agreement while the plaintiff was given wider choices③ than before if no agreement was reached. The CPL 1991 was amended in 2007, 2012, 2017, 2021, and 2023, the amendments relating to choice of court appeared in the 2012 and 2023 revision (hereafter respectively CPL 2012 and CPL 2023). The CPL 2023 mainly revised the chapter relating to matters in foreign-related cases, including

---

① The defendant Compania Sud Americana submitted to the jurisdiction of Guangzhou Maritime Court but contested jurisdictions of the other five Chinese maritime courts. The main reason for the five maritime courts to deny their objection was that the chosen English High Court has no connection with the disputes. See, for example, No. 00972 Civil Ruling (2012) by Wuhan Maritime Court (Wuhaifashangzidi00972hao).
② See Art. 20 – 28 of the CPL 1982.
③ See Art. 22 – 33 of the CPL 1991.

jurisdiction relating to cases involving foreign elements.

The CPL 1991 provides for party autonomy in two articles respectively for domestic cases and cases involving foreign elements. Art. 25 of the CPL 1991 provides for party autonomy in choice of court in contract cases only, which also limits the courts being chosen within those located in the place of the defendant's domicile, the place where the contract was performed or made, the place of the plaintiff's domicile and the location of the subject matter. Art. 244 of the CPL 1991 is a special provision for cases involving foreign elements, which provides for party autonomy in choice of court in cases relating to contracts or other property rights. Art. 244 does not specify the scope of the chosen courts but requires that the court chosen shall be located in a place which has actual connection with the disputes. Apparently, the parties to cases involving foreign elements have a wider autonomy in choice of court in terms of case varieties and scope of chosen courts.

In the 2012 amendments to the CPL 1991, Art. 244 was canceled. Instead Art. 25 was revised and renumbered as Art. 34 of the 2012 CPL stating as following.

> The parties to a dispute arising from contracts or other property rights may, by written agreement, choose the people's court located in such a place having actual connection with the disputes as the place of the defendant's domicile, the place where the contract was performed or made, the place of the plaintiff's domicile, or the location of the subject matter etc. to have jurisdiction over the case, as long as this jurisdiction choice does not violate the provisions of this Law regarding the vertical jurisdiction competence and exclusive jurisdiction.

Compared with Art. 25 of the CPL 1991, this article covers not only disputes relating to contracts but also disputes relating to other property rights, and the scope of courts being chosen is no longer limited to those located in specified places, instead those specified places became examples of places "having actual connection with the disputes", court in any place that has actual connection with the dispute can be chosen. Therefore, Art. 34 of the CPL 2012 is actually a combination of Art. 25 and Art. 244 of the CPL 1991, bringing party autonomy in choice of court in domestic cases into line with those in cases with foreign elements. Compared with the plaintiff's choice of jurisdiction which is clearly defined under the CPL 2012 and its predecessors, the scope of choice of court by agreement is broader. Under Art. 34, among the listed connecting factors, the place of the plaintiff's domicile and the place where the contract was made were not available to the plaintiff's unilateral choice in domestic cases, not to say other places which could be admitted as having actual connection with the disputes.

As Art. 34 appears in the second chapter of General Provisions of the CPL 2012, and uses the term "choose the people's court", the Supreme People's Court in her interpretation on the application of the CPL 2012 clarifies the issue of choice of foreign court as following①.

> The parties to a dispute arising from foreign-related contracts or other property rights may, by written agreement, choose the foreign court located in such a place having actual connection with the disputes as the place of the defendant's domicile, the place where the contract was performed or made, the place of the plaintiff's domicile, the location of the subject matter or the place of tort etc. to have jurisdiction over the case.
>
> The parties are not permitted to choose the jurisdiction of foreign court for those cases under the exclusive jurisdiction of the court of the People's Republic of China under Art. 33 and Art. 266 of Civil Procedural Law, this is not applicable to the choice of arbitration by agreement.

The above interpretation has a minor difference from Art. 34 of the CPL 2012 in that it adds one more place— "the place of tort"—for the location of the foreign court capable of being chosen and clarifies the exclusive jurisdiction provisions as including that under the General Provisions and Provisions specially provided for civil procedural issues for foreign-related cases.

---

① Art. 531 of the *Supreme People's Court Interpretation on the Application of the Civil Procedural Law of the People's Republic of China* (Fashi [2015] 5), specifically provided for the parties' right to choose the jurisdiction of a foreign court. This Article is renumbered 529 in the 2022 revision of this Interpretation.

There are no changes in later amendments to the CPL 1991 relating to party autonomy in choice of court other than that Art. 34 was renumbered Art. 35 in 2021. The CPL 2023 added two provisions respectively providing for the choice of China's court and the choice of foreign court in foreign-related cases.

The CPL 2023 provides in Art. 277 that "the parties to foreign-related civil disputes choose the jurisdiction of the people's court by written agreement, the people court may exercise jurisdiction." Then, in Art. 280, the CPL 2023 in dealing with parallel proceedings provides that "The parties choose the jurisdiction of a foreign court in an exclusive jurisdiction agreement which does not violate the provisions of exclusive jurisdiction under this Law and not concern the sovereign right, security or social public interest of the People's Republic of China, the people's court may order not to accept the case; if the case has been accepted, then order to dismiss the case." Those two new articles by themselves seemingly provide the parties to civil disputes a much more broad autonomy or loosen the limitations on the parties' choice of the jurisdiction of a court.

B. General limitations for choice of court

The revisions in the CPL 2023 come into force on 1 Jan. 2024, there are now 3 articles governing choice of court. It is anticipated that the Supreme People's Court will accordingly revise its interpretation of the Civil Procedural Law relating to choice of foreign court. An examination of Art. 35, Art. 277 and Art. 280 of the CPL 2023 and relevant articles will reveal general limitations for choice of court by the parties, including the scope of disputes, the requirement of actual connection and the written form of the agreement.

1. Scope of disputes subject to jurisdiction of the court chosen by the parties

Under Art. 35, not all disputes could be heard by the court chosen by the parties. It permits the parties to choose the court to settle their disputes only those relating to contracts or other property rights. This scope is quite broad, including all contractual disputes, civil contracts as well as commercial contracts, thus consumer contracts, employment contracts and insurance contracts are all included. Non-contractual disputes should involve property rights, which obviously exclude non-property matters such as status, legal capacity, matrimonial and family matters. Property disputes arising from cohabitation or after the dissolution of marriage or adoption will be included. ①

Art. 277 permits the parties to "foreign-related civil disputes" to choose the jurisdiction of the people's court. We could see that under Art. 277 there are no restrictions to the scope of civil disputes where the parties could choose the jurisdiction of the people's court. Therefore, disputes relating to such non-property matters as status, legal capacity, matrimonial and family matters could also be heard by a people's court chosen by the parties.

Art. 280 recognizes the parties' choice of foreign court by directing the people's court to give up jurisdiction, without any mention of the kinds of disputes. It follows that, in any kinds of civil disputes, the parties are permitted to choose the jurisdiction of foreign court.

Therefore, under Art. 277 and Art. 280, there are no restrictions or limitations in the scope of disputes capable of being heard by the parties' chosen court as long as they are foreign-related disputes.

2. Scope of disputes under exclusive jurisdiction of the people's court

Exclusive jurisdiction of the people's court is mandatory, parties to the dispute are not permitted to choose court other than those prescribed. Among the three articles relating to choice of courts, Art. 35 and Art. 280 mention the exclusive jurisdiction to restrict the parties' choice of court. Art. 35 makes clear that the jurisdiction choice agreement should not violate the exclusive jurisdiction provisions, and Art. 280 only recognizes the parties' exclusive choice of foreign court which are not in violation of the exclusive jurisdiction provisions. The relevant provisions providing for exclusive jurisdiction are Art. 34 and Art. 279 of the CPL 2023 and Art. 7 of the SPLMP.

Art. 34 of the CPL 2023 is not a new provision, the first CPL 1982 has such provision in its Art. 30 which includes four kinds of disputes under exclusive jurisdiction, three kinds of disputes remain under exclusive jurisdiction in Art. 34 of the CPL 1991 with some changes in wording. Throughout the five amendments, this provision remains intact other than being renumbered Art. 33 in 2012 and

---

① Art. 34 of the *Supreme People's Court's Interpretation on the Application of the Civil Procedural Law of the People's Republic of China* (Fashi [2015] 5). This Interpretation has been modified in 2020 and 2022, Art. 34 stays intact.

renumbered Art. 34 again in 2021.

Art. 34 put three kinds of disputes under the exclusive jurisdiction of certain people's courts which have close territorial connection with the disputes, namely, (1) disputes relating to immovable property shall be under the exclusive jurisdiction of the court at the place where the property located; (2) disputes arising from harbor operations shall be under the exclusive jurisdiction of the maritime court at the place where the harbor located; (3) disputes relating to succession shall be under the exclusive jurisdiction of the court at the place where the decedent's domicile upon his death or where the principal portion of his estate located. As Art. 34 provides for courts in two different locations to exercise jurisdiction over disputes relating to succession, the parties' choice of court located in either place will not be denied.

It is worth noting that Art. 7 of the SPLMP added two more kinds of disputes to the exclusive jurisdiction of the maritime court, that is, (1) marine pollution caused by discharging, leaking or dumping oil or other hazardous substances from the ships, by offshore production or operation or by ship breaking or repairing, shall be under the exclusive jurisdiction of the maritime court at the place where the pollution took place or caused damages, or the place where the pollution prevention measures are taken; (2) disputes arising out of an offshore exploration and exploitation contract performed within Chinese territory and sea areas within Chinese jurisdiction, shall be under the exclusive jurisdiction of the maritime court at the place where the contract was performed. The first dispute is also subject to the jurisdiction of courts in several specified locations. Parties therefore are permitted to choose one of them.

Unlike Art. 7 of the SPLMP and Art. 34 of the CPL 2023 which provides for the exclusive jurisdiction of the people's court in the specified location, Art. 279 of the CPL 2023 only provides for the exclusive jurisdiction of the people's court. Parties to the specified foreign-related cases are permitted to choose the people's court in any location. This is a provision refraining the parties from choosing foreign court. Under Art. 279, litigation relating to the following disputes shall be under the exclusive jurisdiction of the people's court: 1) such disputes of legal persons or other organizations incorporated in China as relating to their establishment, dissolution, liquidation or validity of their resolution etc; 2) disputes relating to the validity of the intellectual properties reviewed and granted in China;

3) disputes arising from three kinds of contracts performed in China, namely contract of Chinese-foreign equity joint ventures, contract of Chinese-foreign contractual joint ventures, and contract of Chinese-foreign cooperative exploration and development of the natural resources. The first two kinds of litigation are newly added, the third one could be found in Art. 246 of the CPL 1991.

Art. 279 of the CPL 2023 does not limit the location of the people's court, the parties to the prescribed disputes could choose any one of the people's court. This provision only prohibits the relevant parties from choosing foreign court. Where Art. 7 of the SPLMP and Art. 34 of the CPL 2023 provide for specified court or courts to have exclusive jurisdiction over disputes covered by these two provisions, such provisions should prohibit the relevant parties from choosing foreign court as well as the people's court other than that in the prescribed location. However, Art. 277 which provides for the parties' choice of the people's court in foreign-related cases does not subject the parties' choice to any restriction. It is not clear whether Art. 7 of the SPLMP and Art. 34 of the CPL 2023 will render the parties' choice of the people's court in violation of such provisions in foreign-related cases void.

3. Scope of courts being chosen: actual connection?

Since the enactment of the CPL 1991, the scope of courts being chosen has been confined to those having actual connection with the disputes and has been discussed in many cases, especially when the chosen court is a foreign court. Although two new articles Art. 277 and Art. 280 have been added to the CPL 2023, Art. 35 which contained the requirement of actual connection was not altered. The two new articles applied only to choice of court in foreign related cases have no mention of actual connection.

What does actual connection mean under Art. 35? There is no definition in the CPL, nor judicial interpretation given by the Supreme People's Court. The list of five places[1] in Art. 35 is not an exhaustive one. A restrictive construction[2] of Art. 35 is neither in conformity with the meaning of Art. 35 nor with the judicial

---

[1] The place of the defendant's domicile, the place of the plaintiff's domicile, the place where the contract was performed or made, or the place where the subject matter located.

[2] See Zheng Sophia Tang, "Effectiveness of Exclusive Jurisdiction Clauses in the Chinese Courts – A Pragmatic Study", I. C. L. Q (2012), p. 466.

practices of Chinese Courts.

Firstly, the courts having actual connection with the dispute are not restricted to the five listed places. Art. 35 is a combination of Art. 25 and Art. 244 of the 1991 CPL, which enlarged the scope of party autonomy in domestic cases both in the matters and chosen courts under Art. 25 of the 1991 CPL. If the Legislature intended to restrict the scope of courts being chosen to the five listed places, it could have done so by the same wording in Art. 25 of 1991 CPL without the words of "actual connection".

Secondly, there are decided cases illustrating that a place having "actual connection" with the dispute is not necessarily the listed five places, it could be any place having territorial connection with the dispute. In *Swiss Marine Services SA v. Zhuhai YYF Steel Co. Ltd*,① the plaintiff made a contract of affreightment with YYF International Ltd BVI to transport iron ore from Chile to China, the defendant as guarantor of the YYF International Ltd BVI for her performance of the contract provided a letter of guarantee to the plaintiff, which designated for the exclusive jurisdiction of court in England. As a result of the breach of contract by the YYF International Ltd BVI and her failure to honor London Arbitral Award, the plaintiff sued the defendant in Guangzhou Maritime Court, the defendant contested the court's jurisdiction on the ground of the jurisdiction clause in the letter of guarantee. The court held the jurisdiction clause valid and dismissed the case, as "the parties expressly agreed on the exclusive jurisdiction of court in England, and the guarantee-debtor the YYF International Ltd BVI domiciled in the British Virgin Islands, within the English jurisdiction, thus the agreed-upon court has connection with the disputes". It is obvious in this case that the place having actual connection with the chosen court is none of the five places listed in Art. 35.

As to the question of whether the choice of law and jurisdiction constitutes "actual connection", a construction of Art. 35 and judicial practice all gave a negative answer.

The requirement of actual connection is a limitation to the parties' choice of jurisdiction, if the parties' choice of law and jurisdiction itself constitutes actual

---

① No. 147 Civil Ruling (2015) by Guangzhou Maritime Court (guanghaifachuzidi147hao).

connection, then the limitation by "actual connection" will be rendered meaningless. It is obvious that the five places listed in Art. 35 exemplify places of territorial connection. And in judicial practice, if the chosen foreign court did not have any territorial connection with the dispute, Chinese courts would not dismiss the case under their proper jurisdiction. For example, in *Hin-Pro International Logistics v. Compania Sud American*, the law and jurisdiction clause in the bills of lading provided for the jurisdiction of the English High Court of Justice in London, the Chinese maritime courts held the jurisdiction clause not valid, as the dispute did not have any territorial connection with the United Kingdom. [①]

As to the closeness of the connection, there is no such requirement in Art. 35 or any judicial interpretation. Therefore, the choice of foreign court agreement will not be denied because of the closer connection of a Chinese court with the dispute. For example, in *Zhongshan Olym Home Appliance Co. v. American International Cargo Services (Shenzhen) Limited Guangzhou Branch et al.* [②], a clause in the bill of lading provided that "The contract evidenced by this Bill of Lading is governed by the laws of the Hong Kong Special Administrative Region. Any claim or dispute must be determined exclusively by the courts in the Hong Kong Special Administrative Region and no other court." The plaintiff cargo-owner took proceedings in Guangzhou Maritime Court holding the defendant carrier liable for delivery without production of original bill of lading. The shipper named in the bill of lading is Olym Group Home Appliance (Hong Kong) Co. Limited, the cargo was transshipped in Hong Kong. The Guangzhou Maritime Court held the choice of court agreement valid, as it met the requirements of the previous Art. 34 of CPL 2012 and was not void under Art. 40 of the Contract Law. In this case, in giving effect to the choice of court jurisdiction, Guangzhou Maritime Court did not compare the comparative closeness of connection of the chosen court and the seized court with the dispute, although Guangzhou Maritime Court may be a court of closer connection with the dispute, as the plaintiff and defendants all domiciled within its jurisdiction, the port of shipment of the cargo

---

① See, for example, No. 00972 Civil Ruling (2012) by Wuhan Maritime Court (Wuhaifashangzidi 00972 hao).
② No. 285 Civil Ruling (2014) by Guangzhou Maritime Court (Guanghaifachuzidi285hao).

was also within its jurisdiction.

With the addition of the two new articles specifically providing for the choice of the people's court and the choice of foreign court in foreign-related cases, Art. 35 should only be applied to domestic cases. The requirement of actual connection will no longer constitute a limitation to the choice of court by the parties in foreign-related cases, especially the choice of foreign court.

4. Written form of the agreement

Art. 35 requires the choice of court agreement to be in written form, the newly added Art. 277 also has such a requirement, but Art. 280 does not mention the form of the jurisdiction agreement. There is no definition of "written form" in the CPL; the Supreme People's Court indicates that "written agreements include choice of jurisdiction clause in a written contract or a choice of jurisdiction agreement in written form entered into before the taking of the proceedings". ① A broad definition of "written form" is given in Art. 469 of Chinese Civil Code. Paragraph 2 of Art. 469 provides that "written form means such form as contractual document, letter, telegram, telex, fax etc., which could tangibly express the contents contained therein". Paragraph 3 of Art. 469 further provides for digital data in such form as electronic data exchange and e-mail etc., which could tangibly express the contents contained therein and could be obtained and used at any time, to be regarded as written form. Therefore, this written form requirement is actually not difficult to meet.

C. Substantive validity of jurisdiction clause

Mutual assent is the most important element for a contract to be valid. Bearing in mind that it is the plaintiff who will enjoy the right to forum shopping, the choice of court agreement will inevitably deprive the plaintiff's choice, therefore the assent of the plaintiff to a choice of court agreement is of vital importance, especially when the agreement is in the form of a jurisdiction clause in a standard form contract.

---

① Art. 29 of the *Supreme People's Court's Interpretation on the Application of the Civil Procedural Law of the People's Republic of China* (Fashi [2015] 5). This Interpretation has been modified in 2020 and 2022, Art. 29 stays intact.

Chinese Contract Law enacted in 1999 has two provisions relating to standard form clause. Art. 39 requires the party who drafts the standard form contract to take reasonable measures to draw the other party's attention to the clauses which will exempt or limit his liabilities and shall give an explanation of such clauses in response to the other party's request. Art. 39 defines "standard form clauses" to be clauses pre-made by one party for repeating use and without discussion with the other party at the time of contracting. Art. 40 renders a clause in a standard form contract null and void under certain circumstances, including when the drafter exempts his liability, aggravates the other party's liability and excludes the other party's main rights. These two articles are modified and specified in more details in Art. 496 and Art. 497 of the Chinese Civil Code. By far, most disputes arose from jurisdiction clauses in a consumer contract or in a bill of lading. Hereafter is a survey of judicial practices relating to the validity of such jurisdiction clauses, illustrating limitations to party autonomy in choice of court by the application of substantive law.

1. Validity of jurisdiction clause in a consumer contract

Compared with the provider of goods or services, a consumer is often in a less advantageous position, he/she has less or no bargaining powers in the making of a consumer contract which may include a jurisdiction clause. Consumer contract is almost always a standard form contract. The Consumer Protection Law of the People's Republic of China① provides substantive law protection to consumers against providers of goods or services, but there are no special rules in the CPL 2023 and any of its previous versions in favor of consumers.

To provide the consumer some protection in choice of court, the Supreme People's Court in its interpretation of the CPL 2012 clarifies that "if the business dealer who made a jurisdiction agreement in standard form with the consumer has not taken reasonable measure to notify the consumer of such agreement, the court

---

① First adopted in 1993, the first revision was made in 2009, the second revision was in 2013 and is the current version.

should support the consumer's argument to invalidate such jurisdiction agreement"①. This provision does not make the jurisdiction clause in standard form consumer contract null and void but provides the consumer a choice whether to quash such a jurisdiction clause. If the business dealer could establish that he has taken reasonable measures to notify the consumer of such a jurisdiction clause, the court would accordingly hold the clause valid and enforceable. ②

The Supreme People's Court's construction relating to the jurisdiction clause in consumer contract is in line with its interpretation of Art. 39 of the Contract Law, which provides that

> where the party who provides the standard clause violated the provision of Art. 39 of the Contract Law concerning his duty of drawing attention to and explanation of provisions exempting or limiting his liabilities and resulted in the failure of the other party to notice such provisions, if the other party moves to invalidate such a standard clause, the People's Court shall support such a motion. ③

The above provision was incorporated with some modification into the second paragraph of Art. 496 of Chinese Civil Code where the affected party can argue against the inclusion of such a standard clause into the relevant contract. Furthermore, Art. 497 of Chinese Civil Code provides for the void and null of standard form clause in certain circumstances, including where the provider of the standard clause unreasonably exempts or alleviates his own liabilities, aggravates the other party's liabilities or restricts the other party's main rights or excludes the other party's main rights.

The Supreme People's Court recognizes the application of Art. 496 and Art.

---

① Art. 31 of the Supreme People's Court's Interpretation on the Application of the Civil Procedural Law of the People's Republic of China (Fashi [2015] 5). This Interpretation has been modified in 2020 and 2022, Art. 31 stays intact.

② See, e. g. *Fu Xiaoyan v. Jiangsu Suning Yigou Ecommerce Co. Ltd*, No. 10249 Civil Ruling (2015) by the Beijing Second Intermediate People's Court (erminzhongzidi10249hao).

③ Art. 9 of the *Supreme People's Court's Interpretation on Several Issues Relating to the Application of the Contract Law of the People's Republic of China* (Ⅱ) (Fashi [2009] 5).

497 of the Civil Code to jurisdiction clause in cross-border consumer online contract in its publication of a meeting memo of the nationwide people's courts relating to foreign-related commercial and maritime judicial work in January 2022 (hereafter the 2022 meeting memo), where in part one point 3 it clarifies that the people's court shall support the consumer's argument against the inclusion of a jurisdiction clause in a standard form contract if the online e-commercial platform failed to take reasonable measures to notify the consumer of such clause, and the people's court shall support the consumer's argument to void such a clause if the clause chooses a court in a state other than the state where the consumer has his domicile which unreasonably increases the consumer's costs to seek reliefs even if the online e-commercial platform has complied with the obligation of notification.

The 2022 meeting memo in part one point 2 denies the argument on the basis of obvious unfairness to void an asymmetric jurisdiction agreement but makes such agreement relating to the interest of consumers and employees as an exception. It seemingly implies that consumers and employees may be able to challenge the validity of asymmetric jurisdiction agreements based on obvious unfairness.

Therefore, a conclusion may be drawn that jurisdiction clause is taken by the Supreme People's Court as clause capable of exempting or limiting the liabilities of the drawer of such clause, although it is hard to say what kind of liability of the drawer has been exempted or limited by such clause without an examination of the substantive law applicable in the chosen court. Anyway, as the jurisdiction clause in a standard form consumer contract is in fact limiting the choice of court by the consumer as a plaintiff and may highly probably result in exempting or limiting the liabilities of the drawer, or at least may cause the increase of costs in seeking relief, the Supreme People's Court tried to provide some protection to the consumer in that the consumer shall not be bound by an unfavorable jurisdiction clause in certain circumstances.

2. Validity of jurisdiction clause in a bill of lading

Bill of lading itself is not a contract for carriage of goods by sea between the shipper and carrier, but it functions to evidence the contract, and when endorsed to a third party, it will become the contract between the carrier and the third party. The bill of lading is usually provided by the carrier in a standard form and may insert a law and jurisdiction clause. Is such a jurisdiction clause binding on the shipper and holder of the bill of lading? The Supreme People's Court has not yet given any opinions, the answers given by the rulings of the local maritime courts and the provincial high court are not quite in line with each other.

In *Hin-Pro International Logistics v. Compania Sud American*, there were six maritime courts hearing the disputes arising from 75 bills of lading, except for Guangzhou Maritime Court where the defendant didn't contest the jurisdiction, the other five maritime courts① and their respective provincial high courts all refused to give effect to the jurisdiction clause in the bill of lading because the chosen court (English High Court) did not have actual connection with the disputes. In addition, the Zhejiang Provincial High Court, in hearing appeals from the decisions of Ningbo Maritime Court, interpreted the clause as a non-exclusive jurisdiction clause. ② And the Wuhan Maritime Court held the clause no binding effect on the plaintiff, since "bill of lading is the evidence of the contract of carriage of goods by sea, the clauses are made by the carrier only, and therefore are standard form clauses. ... the present plaintiff, as the shipper named on the bill of lading, at the time of accepting the bill, didn't express his acceptance of the jurisdiction clause in a written form, therefore the jurisdiction clause has no binding effect on him. "③

The Fujian Provincial High Court in hearing an appealing case from Xiamen Maritime Court took similar attitudes towards jurisdiction clause in bill of lading. In *Rich Shipping Company Limited v. Xiamen Zhong Hai Unite Trade Co. Ltd*④, a clause in the bill of lading provided that the parties agreed to take the case, if any, to the court in Hong Kong where the carrier has his principal place of business. Fujian Provincial High Court held the clause no binding force. The Court held that "Rich Shipping Company and the carrier failed to draw the other party's attention to the clause; Zhong Hai got the bill of lading after he delivered

---

① Wuhan Maritime Court, Ningbo Maritime Court, Shanghai Maritime Court, Qingdao Maritime Court, Tianjin Maritime Court.

② See No. 128 Civil Ruling (2013) by Zhejiang Provincial High Court (Zhexiazhongzidi128hao).

③ No. 00972 Civil Ruling (2012) by Wuhan Maritime Court (wuhaifashangzidi00972hao). The Hubei Provincial High Court upheld this ruling: No. 00104 Final Civil Ruling by Hubei Provincial High Court (eminsizhongzidi00104hao).

④ No. 450 Final Civil Ruling (2010) by Fujian Provincial High Court (minminzhongzidi450hao).

the goods on board, by then, it was not possible to change the clause, thus was deprived of any option for the means of settling the disputes, the clause in fact became the unilateral intent of the carrier; Zhong Hai disagreed with the clause by taking the case before Xiamen Maritime Court. As there is no evidence proving the bill-holder's consent or the parties' consensus, this jurisdiction clause shall not have binding force on Zhong Hai"①.

Shanghai Maritime Court and Shanghai High Court also held that jurisdiction clause in bill of lading has no binding force. In *CMA CGM S. A. v. Shaoxin Haoyi Trading Company*②, a jurisdiction clause in a bill of lading provided

> All claims and actions arising between the Carrier and Merchant in relation with the contract of Carriage evidenced by this Bill of Lading shall exclusively be brought before the Tribunal de Marseille and no other Court shall have jurisdiction with regards to any such claim or action. Notwithstanding the above, the Carrier is also entitled to bring the claim or action before the Court of the place where the defendant has its registered office.

Shanghai Maritime Court held this clause as "non-exclusive jurisdiction clause, as the carrier CMA CGM S. A. has option under this clause. There is no evidence proving to the effect that the carrier CMA CGM S. A. has ever discussed with shipper-plaintiff about this carrier-favorable jurisdiction clause and reached an agreement, that is, no proof of mutual assent towards this jurisdiction clause, therefore it shall not have binding force on the plaintiff"③. Shanghai High Court upheld this ruling, emphasizing that the present bill of lading is a standard form clause, "as this standard form clause improperly limits the shipper Haoyi's litigation right, CMA CGM S. A. should prove that he has discussed such

---

① No. 450 Final Civil Ruling (2010) by Fujian Provincial High Court (minminzhongzidi450hao). Fujian Provincial High Court reaffirmed its holding in a 2016 ruling in *Shenzhen Pengchenghai Logistic Company v. Xiamen Yo-Rain Co. Ltd*: No. 178 Final Civil Ruling (2016) (minminxiazhongzidi178hao).
② No. 2542 Civil Ruling (2016) by Shanghai Maritime Court (hu72minchu2542hao).
③ No. 2542 Civil Ruling (2016) by Shanghai Maritime Court (hu72minchu2542hao).

jurisdiction clause with Hao yi and has reached an agreement"[1].

Ningbo Maritime Court and Zhejiang Provincial High Court have held jurisdiction clause in bill of lading no binding force and null and void according to Art. 40 of Chinese Contract Law. In Yiwu New Rainbow Craft Carpet Co. Ltd. v. Shenzhen RS Logistics Limited,[2] the Ningbo Maritime Court held a jurisdiction clause in the bill of lading void according to Art. 40 of the Chinese Contract Law, as the clause is "pre-printed standard form clause, exclude the other party's right to choose the court when the disputes arise. At the time the shipper got the bill of lading, he had no choice to decide the court for settling disputes, lacking consensus of both parties and is clearly unjust"[3]. Zhejiang Provincial High Court upheld this ruling clarifying that the jurisdiction clause "exclude the shipper's right to choose the court for settling disputes when the disputes arise, to some extent limit the carrier's liability and aggravate the shipper's duties to take part in the litigation"[4]. In *CMA CGM S. A. v. Shaoxin Haoyi Trading Company*[5], the two courts also applied Art. 39 and Art. 40 of the Chinese Contract Law to hold the jurisdiction clause in a bill of lading no binding force and null and void.

Contrary to the aforesaid courts' holding, Guangzhou Maritime Court held a jurisdiction clause in a bill of lading valid in *Zhongshan Olym Home Appliance Co. v. American International Cargo Services (Shenzhen) Limited Guangzhou Branch et al*[6]. In the ruling, the Court first quoted the provision of Art. 34 of the CPL 2012 and then stated that "the rights in a bill of lading are property rights subject to be heard in a court chosen by the parties, the jurisdiction clause in the present bill of lading agreed in writing to subject the case to the jurisdiction of the court where the transshipping port is located—the court of Hong Kong SAR". Obviously, the requirements of Art. 34 were met. The Court went further to hold that "not all standard form clause is null and void, as the plaintiff failed to put

---

[1] No. 291 Final Civil Ruling (2016) by Shanghai High Court (huminxiazhongzi291hao).
[2] No. 2 Final Civil Ruling (2014) by Zhejiang Provincial High Court (zhexiazhongzidi2hao).
[3] No. 2 Final Civil Ruling (2014) by Zhejiang Provincial High Court (zhexiazhongzidi2hao).
[4] No. 2 Final Civil Ruling (2014) by Zhejiang Provincial High Court (zhexiazhongzidi2hao).
[5] No. 294 Final Civil Ruling (2016) by Zhejiang Provincial High Court (zheminxiazhongzidi294hao).
[6] No. 285 Civil Ruling (2014) by Guangzhou Maritime Court (Guanghaifachuzidi285hao).

forward effective evidence to prove that there were any circumstances proscribed by Art. 40 of Chinese *Contract Law*, the jurisdiction clause should therefore be deemed valid". Although the jurisdiction clause in a bill of lading actually deprives the plaintiff of his forum shopping, the Court was not ready to accept that it exempts the carrier's liability, aggravates the other party's liability and excludes the other party's main rights under Art. 40 of the *Contract Law*.

The relevant issues reflected in the above cases in difference provincial jurisdictions could be reframed into questions and answers in Table 1:

Table 1

Does accepting bill of lading mean accepting the jurisdiction clause in the bill?		Effectiveness	Jurisdictions
No,	(1) jurisdiction clause need to be negotiated separately and be accepted in a written form	otherwise no binding force on the shipper	Hubei
	(2) jurisdiction clause need to be negotiated separately and be accepted by the shipper	otherwise no binding force on the shipper	Fujian Zhejiang Shanghai
Probably yes, but	(1) jurisdiction clause is a standard form clause exempting or limiting the carrier's liability	(1) voidable if the carrier didn't take reasonable measures to draw the other party's attention to the clause under Art. 39 of the *Contract Law*	Zhejiang
	(2) jurisdiction clause is a standard form clause exempting the carrier's liability, aggravating the shipper's liability and excluding his main rights	(2) void under Art. 40 of the *Contract Law*	
Yes, unless	—	valid unless proved void under Art. 40 of the *Contract Law*	Guangdong

The first "No" approach, adopted by at least four provincial jurisdictions, paid great attention to the protection of the shipper by strictly applying the general principle of contract law relating to mutual assent in the formation of contract. From the viewpoint of contract law, this approach shall not be regarded as wrong. However, it is not in conformity with commercial practice. Firstly, it is a common commercial practice to include a jurisdiction clause in a carriage of goods contract as well as in other kinds of contract. Secondly, it is not practical for the carrier to negotiate a carriage of goods contract with each shipper, bill of lading is thus generally accepted as evidence of carriage of goods contract between the shipper and carrier. Thirdly, for a negotiable bill of lading, once it is endorsed to a third party, it is the only document governing legal relationships between the carrier and holder of the bill of lading, as the carrier does not have any part in the endorsement and delivery of the bill of lading. It is practically not possible for the carrier to negotiate any clauses whatever in the bill of lading with the endorsee of the bill. Furthermore, requiring for specific negotiation for a jurisdiction clause and expressing consent from the shipper is actually denying the existence of any jurisdiction clause in a bill of lading. Therefore, it is not commercially justified and not really in the interest of the parties to deny the binding effect of the jurisdiction clause in a bill of lading on the shipper or holder of bill of lading for lack of negotiation and express consent.

The second "yes but" approach, while ready to give the same treatment to the jurisdiction clause as other clauses in the bill of lading, subject the jurisdiction clause to the restrictions imposed on standard form contract under Chinese *Contract Law*. Given that Chinese *Maritime Law* will make clauses in a bill of lading null and void if they violate its mandatory provisions which are designed for the protection of shippers or holders of bill of ladings against carriers,[①] as there is not any provision relating to jurisdiction clause in a bill of lading in *Maritime Law*, it is reasonable to examine the validity of such jurisdiction clause under Chinese *Contract Law*. The question is whether it is proper to hold the jurisdiction clause in a bill of lading voidable or void respectively under Art. 39 and Art. 40 of Chinese *Contract Law*. It is true that the

---

① Art. 44 of *Maritime Law of the People's Republic of China*.

jurisdiction clause limits the plaintiff's choice of court after the disputes arise, but it is the inherent nature of any jurisdiction clause or agreement, holding jurisdiction clause in a bill of lading void under Art. 40 because of its inherent nature will invalid all jurisdiction clauses in all standard form contract, making incorporation of a jurisdiction clause in standard form contract meaningless. Such an arbitrary denial of jurisdiction clause in bill of lading is not in line either with the intent of the Legislature in admitting party autonomy in choice of court or with the Supreme People's Court's interpretation of jurisdiction clause in standard form consumer contract. Given that carriage of goods contract by sea is heavily regulated by domestic law as well as international law, and carriers are prohibited from taking too much advantage of their dominating position to exempt or limit their liabilities, it is necessary and justified to provide some protection to the shipper and holder of bill of lading against unfair jurisdiction clause. Thus, it is fair to impose on the carrier the duty to take reasonable measures to draw attention of any other party to a bill of lading to the jurisdiction clause in such bill in accordance with Art. 39 of Chinese *Contract Law*. Anyway, this is a formal requirement and not a difficult task for the carrier to implement. However, frankly speaking, the protection to the shipper or holder of bill of lading is quite limit, unless he has chance and bargaining power to say no to the jurisdiction clause.

As to the third "yes unless" approach, it does not regard the jurisdiction clause in a bill of lading as of right exempting or limiting the liability of the carrier under Art. 39 of Chinese *Contract Law*, nor hold it null and void under Art. 40, instead it invites the shipper and holder of bill of lading to invalidate the jurisdiction clause from other aspects, presumably from the substantive law aspect, if any. For example, if the disputes relate to the limitation of the carrier's liability, a jurisdiction clause which choose a foreign court where Hague Rules would be applied as governing law, such a jurisdiction clause will probably be taking as limiting the carriers' liability as Chinese *Maritime Law* provides higher per package or per unit limitation than that of Hague Rules. [1] This approach will

---

[1] See Art. 56 of *Maritime Law of the People's Republic of China*, which adopts the same limit of liability as the Hague-Visby Rules.

therefore provide substantial protection to the shipper and holder of bill of lading.

In conclusion, due to the nature of the jurisdiction clause in a bill of lading, it is not proper to deny its binding effect for lack of negotiation and express assent, it is more reasonable to impose on the carrier a duty to draw relevant parties' attention to the jurisdiction clause. That is to say, a non-negotiated jurisdiction clause shall be given the same effect as standard clause, therefore be subject to the same test. Art. 39 and Art. 40 of Chinese *Contract Law* has been replaced respectively by Art. 496 and Art. 497 of Chinese Civil Code, which differentiate the adverse effects of standard clause on the non-drafting party in deciding whether to set aside or invalidate such clause. Accordingly, if the jurisdiction clause leads to the application of a substantive law which will unreasonably exempt or mitigate the carrier's liability, aggravate the other party's liability and deprive them of their main rights, the jurisdiction clause may quite probably be deemed null and void under Art. 497 of the Civil Code. The 2022 meeting memo does not deal with jurisdiction clause in a bill of lading, the effectiveness of which will be left to the relevant maritime court to decide.

D. Special limitations for choice of foreign court

The newly added Art. 280 in the CPL 2023 provides three conditions for the people's court to admit the parties' choice of foreign court. Firstly, the jurisdiction agreement should be exclusive; secondly, the agreement should not violate the provisions of exclusive jurisdiction of the people's court; and thirdly, the agreement should not concern the sovereign right, security or social public interest of China. Among these three conditions, two are special limitations for choice of foreign court, which worth further discussion.

1. Exclusiveness of jurisdiction clause

The jurisdiction clause which choose a foreign court shall vest such court with exclusive jurisdiction to preclude the jurisdiction of a people's court. If it is not clear from the jurisdiction agreement whether it is exclusive or non-exclusive, it has been held by the Zhejiang Provincial High Court as non-exclusive in the case *Hin-Pro International Logistics v. Compania Sud American*.[1] Even if a

---

[1] See No. 128 Civil Ruling (2013) by Zhejiang Provincial High Court (Zhexiazhongzidi128hao).

jurisdiction clause clearly vested the chosen court with exclusive jurisdiction, where one party still has choice as in an asymmetric jurisdiction clause, the people's court may still hold such jurisdiction as non-exclusive as in the case *CMA CGM S. A. v. Shaoxin Haoyi Trading Company.* [1] The 2022 meeting memo in its part one point 1 provides for a presumption of exclusive jurisdiction as following.

> The jurisdiction agreement concluded by the parties to a dispute arising from a foreign-related contract or other property rights expressly agreed on the jurisdiction of the court of a state, but did not make clear that it is an exclusive jurisdiction agreement, such agreement shall be presumed as exclusive jurisdiction agreement.

Such presumption of exclusive jurisdiction will preclude the people's court from arbitrarily holding a jurisdiction agreement as non-exclusive but still leave room for a party to prove otherwise. This presumption is in line with the Hague Convention of 30 June 2005 on Choice of Court Agreements[2]. Notably, this presumption has not been seen in the Supreme People's Court's amendment to its interpretation of the CPL made two months later in the same year, there is no provision relating to such presumption in the CPL 2023. It is worth waiting to see whether this presumption will become a formal interpretation of the Supreme People's Court.

2. Public interest exception

Art. 280 in the CPL 2023 gives broad autonomy to the parties to choose foreign court, giving up the restrictions relating to the scope of courts and the scope of disputes, but adds a new exception. If a foreign-related case concerns sovereign rights, security or social public interest of China, the parties' choice of foreign court will not be accepted. This exception, though a new one in the CPL, is actually one of the five reasons under the Hague Convention on Choice of Court

---

[1] No. 2542 Civil Ruling (2016) by Shanghai Maritime Court (hu 72 minchu 2542 hao).

[2] Art. 3 b) provides that "a choice of court agreement which designates the courts of one Contracting State or one or more specific courts of one Contracting State shall be deemed to be exclusive unless the parties have expressly provided otherwise".

Agreements for the court not chosen to exercise her jurisdiction irrespective of the exclusive choice of court agreement①.

II. Party autonomy in choice of court in UK

There are no statutory rules relating to choice of court in the United Kingdom except those under European Regulations and relevant international conventions which have been incorporated into English Law. Under English common law, English courts will generally uphold the validity of the jurisdiction agreement, but it does not mean they will give effect to such jurisdiction agreement. Party autonomy in choice of English court has always been welcomed, but party autonomy in choice of foreign court has been subject to greater restrictions to protect the jurisdiction of English court. Such restrictions are actually limitations on party autonomy in choice of court. This part will examine the common law rules relating to limitations on choice of foreign court.

A. Different attitudes towards party autonomy in choice of foreign court

The court in the United Kingdom prides itself as the place of forum shopping,② going to great strength to guard the jurisdiction of its courts by enforcing English jurisdiction agreements through such measures as anti-suit injunction, contempt of court, damages for breach of contract, as exemplified in the case of Hin-Pro③: "The English courts will override foreign public policy by anti-suit injunctions in order to enforce English forum clauses, but will override

---

① Art. 6 provides that "A court of a Contracting State other than that of the chosen court shall suspend or dismiss proceedings to which an exclusive choice of court agreement applies unless; c) giving effect to the agreement would lead to a manifest injustice or would be manifestly contrary to the public policy of the State of the court seised".

② Lord Denning has once said that the plaintiff "can seek the aid of our Courts if he desires to do so. You may call this 'forum shopping' if you please, but if the forum is England, it is a good place to shop in, both for the quality of the goods and the speed of service": *The Atlantic Star* [1972] 2 Lloyd's Rep. 446, 451.

③ See [2014] EWHC 3632 (Comm); [2015] 1 Lloyd' Rep. 301. [2015] EWCA Civ 401 [2015]; 2 Lloyd' Rep. 1.

comparable foreign forum clauses by anti-suit injunction to enforce English public policy"①. Even, under the Brussels-Lugano regimes, when the English courts could not make anti-suit injunction against a proceeding in the court of an EU member state, they still allow damages for breach of jurisdiction agreement.②

In contrast, a valid choice of foreign court is not absolutely binding on the English court and was regarded as ouster of English Jurisdiction, as Lord Denning once held in The Fehmarn③ that

> The English Courts are in charge of their own proceedings, and one of the rules which they apply is that a stipulation that all disputes should be judged by the tribunals of a particular country is not absolutely binding. It is a matter to which the Courts of this country will pay much regard and to which they will normally give effect, but it is subject to the overriding principle that no one, by his private stipulation, can oust these Courts of their jurisdiction in a matter that properly belongs to them.

It is quite clear that the English courts are not willing and ready to give the same effect to a valid choice of foreign court agreement as that they give to choice of English jurisdiction. Dicey, Morris and Collins on the Conflict of Laws therefore categories the rule on jurisdiction agreement into different clauses:

> Rule 39④ — (1) Where a contract provides that all disputes between the parties are to be referred to the jurisdiction of the English courts, the court normally has jurisdiction to hear and determine proceedings in respect thereof.

---

① Thomas Raphael, "Do as You Would be Done by? System-Transcendent Justification and Anti-Suit Injuctions", (2016) *LMCLQ*, p. 256.

② See Yvonne Baatz and Ainhoa Campas Velasco et al. (eds), *Maritime Law* (Informa Law from Routledge 2018), 51, and *Barclays Bank plc v. Ente Nazionale Di Previdenza Ed Assistenza Der Medici e Degli Odeontoiatri*, [2015] EWHC 2857; [2015] 2 Lloyd's Rep. 527. [2016] EWCA Civ 1261.

③ [1957] 2 Lloyd's Rep. 551.

④ Lord Collins of Mapesbury (Gen. Ed.), *Dicey, Morris and Collins on the Conflict of Laws* v. 1 (London: Sweet and Maxwell, 2012), p. 599.

(2) Subject to clause (3) of this Rule, where a contract provides that all disputes between the parties are to be referred to the exclusive jurisdiction of a foreign tribunal, the English court will stay proceedings instituted in England in breach of such agreement (or, as the case may be, refuse to give permission to serve process out of the jurisdiction) unless the claimant satisfies the court that strong cause exists to allow them to continue.

Accordingly, the English court will give effect only to exclusive jurisdiction of a foreign court, but the party are permitted to breach such an exclusive jurisdiction with "strong cause" in support of an English jurisdiction. Such "strong cause", even if applying to an English jurisdiction agreement, would inevitably be constructed differently by the judges in exercising their discretion.

B. Limitations

As party autonomy in choice of foreign court is more restrict in the UK, an examination of the relevant rules relating to enforcement of valid choice of foreign court agreement could better reveal the limitations of party autonomy in choice of court in the United Kingdom.

1. General principles relating to enforcement of choice of foreign court agreement

a) Close connection approach: The Fehmarn

In the Fehmarn[1], a Russian company loaded cargoes on a German ship Fehmarn and presented to the master a bill of lading for signature. There were clauses in the bill of lading providing for the application of Russian law and the jurisdiction of Russian court which says "all claims and disputes arising under and in connection with this bill of lading shall be judged in the USSR". The Fehmarn made her journey to London, and the Russian shippers sold the goods to English buyers, who became holders of the bill of lading. Upon receipt of the cargoes, the English buyer as the cargo owner made complaint of short delivery and contamination, and eventually brought an action against the German owners of the ship in the Admiralty Division of the High Court, claiming damages. The

---

[1] [1957] 2 Lloyd's Rep. 551.

German owners moved to set aside the writ on the ground that the English Courts had no jurisdiction, or, alternatively, that, by the agreement, the parties had agreed that all the disputes should be adjudged in the Courts of Russia and not in this country.

In the judgement of the Court of Appeal, the validity of the jurisdiction clause was not questioned, instead, Lord Denning set out to ask, "Is this dispute a matter which properly belongs to the Courts of this country?" Following an affirmative answer is the second question: "Ought these Courts, in their discretion, to stay this action?" Although the parties also chose the Russian law as governing law, Lord Denning did not "regard the choice of law in the contract as decisive", he preferred to "look to see with what country is the dispute most closely concerned". After an examination of the comparative connection of the dispute with Russia and England, Lord Denning concluded that "the dispute is more closely connected with England than Russia", thus dismissed the appeal and refused to give effect to the Russian jurisdiction clause.

Apparently, in the Fehmarn the valid jurisdiction clause itself did not play any role in conferring jurisdiction on a foreign court, connection with the dispute was the only element to be considered. It seems that freedom of choice was not to be respected if it was in conflict with the jurisdiction interest of English courts.

b) General principles and their application: the Eleftheria and other cases

In the Eleftheria[①], Mr. Justice Brandon summarized the principles of law on which an application to stay an action on the ground of a foreign jurisdiction clause should be decided as follows:

(1) Where plaintiffs sue in England in breach of an agreement to refer disputes to a foreign Court, and the defendants apply for a stay, the English Court, assuming the claim to be otherwise within its jurisdiction, is not bound to grant a stay but has a discretion whether to do so or not.

(2) The discretion should be exercised by granting a stay unless strong cause for not doing so is shown.

(3) The burden of proving such strong cause is on the plaintiffs.

---

① [1969] 1 Lloyd's Rep. 237.

(4) In exercising its discretion the Court should take into account all the circumstances of the particular case.

(5) In particular, but without prejudice to (4), the following matters, where they arise, may properly be regarded:

(a) In what country the evidence on the issues of fact is situated, or more readily available, and the effect of that on the relative convenience and expense of trial as between the English and foreign Courts.

(b) Whether the law of the foreign Court applies and, if so, whether it differs from English law in any material respects.

(c) With what country either party is connected, and how closely.

(d) Whether the defendants genuinely desire trial in the foreign country, or are only seeking procedural advantages.

(e) Whether the plaintiffs would be prejudiced by having to sue in the foreign Court because they would:

(i) be deprived of security for their claim;

(ii) be unable to enforce any judgment obtained;

(iii) be faced with a time-bar not applicable in England; or

(iv) for political, racial, religious or other reasons be unlikely to get a fair trial.

Principle (1) is a restatement of Lord Denning's views towards foreign jurisdiction clauses expressed in the Fehmarn, which reaffirmed the English court's discretion to decide whether to give effect to a valid foreign jurisdiction clause. Principles (2) and (3) put forward a "strong reasons" standard and its burden of proof, for purpose of exercising such discretion. Principle (4) gives the court a very broad circumstances— "all the circumstances of the particular case" to be taken into account in exercising its discretion. Principle (5) set out particular matters to be considered, which worth a detailed discussion.

Under principle (5), point (a) is about the location of the evidence on the issues of facts respectively in the territory of England and the state of the chosen court; point (c) is about the closeness of connection of the parties with England and the state of the chosen court. These two points depend on the facts of the case, while the party's connection with a particular state is foreseeable, the location of the evidence on issues of fact largely depends on the dispute which is not foreseeable at the time of the conclusion of the contract. These two points will deprive the parties of their right to choose a foreign court which has less or no connection with the dispute either on points of evidence or with the parties. It is also unreasonable to deny the enforcement of a foreign jurisdiction agreement by the unforeseeable allocation of evidences.

Point (d) seeks to redefine the intention of the party who wants to enforce the foreign jurisdiction agreement, especially the intention of seeking procedural advantages. Given the differences of procedural laws in different states, it is possible that some rules in foreign procedural law be more advantageous to one party than those in English procedural law, and there is no reason why the party shouldn't seek and enjoy such advantages by jurisdiction agreement. To take this point into account in deciding whether to give effect to a foreign jurisdiction clause is not justified.

Point (b) refers to the governing foreign law and point (e) refers to foreign procedural law. These two points actually set out to compare the substantive law and procedural law of a foreign state with the English law for the protection of the plaintiff, thus combine the plaintiff's interest with the interest of English jurisdiction. Unless the foreign jurisdiction applies the same substantive law and procedural law as the English Court does, proceeding in the foreign chosen court may probably result differently in the favor of either party, therefore the disfavored party may seek to breach the jurisdiction agreement by bringing a proceeding in English court. A review of foreign law in the interest of the plaintiff will encourage him to breach the foreign jurisdiction agreement whenever the English jurisdiction is more favorable to his interest. At the time of contracting, the plaintiff ought to have known the substantive law and procedural law of the chosen court, whether it is different from the English law or not, then why not hold the plaintiff to his own bargain? Due to different legal cultures and different stages of development, a balance between private interests or between public interest and private interest will result in different legislations, either in the field of substantive law or in the field of procedural law, which is always foreseeable but not capable of being changed by the parties. To support the plaintiff's breach of foreign jurisdiction agreement based on these reasons is not only unfair to the other party but also not in line with the international comity which requires respect to and equal treatment of foreign law.

Applying principle (5) in the Eleftheria, the Greek jurisdiction clause was given effect as "there are considerations of substantial weight on either side, which more or less balance each other out, leaving the *prima facie* case for a stay largely, if or entirely, intact"[1], and accordingly, plaintiffs had not established good cause why they should not be held to their bargain. Again, the valid foreign jurisdiction clause was not given much weight, it is only a starting point to balance the various considerations.

What principle (5) mentioned are not the only circumstances to be taken into account by the English court, principle (4) allowed all circumstances to be taken into consideration. Whatever is in favor of English jurisdiction and the benefit of the plaintiff will be considered to a great extent.

In *Evans Marshall & Co. v. Bertola SA*[2], where there is a jurisdiction clause conferring exclusive jurisdiction on the court in Barcelona between the plaintiffs and the first defendants, the jurisdiction clause was not given effect and an interlocutory injunction was granted, as (a) the substance of the case, i.e. the proper marketing of sherry, was exclusively concerned with the UK; (b) all the essential witnesses were in the UK; (c) the first defendants were a proper and necessary party to the plaintiffs' proceedings against the second defendants, and the plaintiffs did not need to fight one battle in the UK and the other in Spain; (d) proceedings in Spain would be "extremely slow", the Spanish Court would grant no interlocutory relief and no procedure for a speedy trial. In this case, apart from some matters mentioned in principle (5), the existence of co-defendants not bound by the foreign jurisdiction clause was regarded as an important matter in supporting the plaintiffs' breach of foreign jurisdiction clause, although this was a situation created and chosen by the plaintiff—the plaintiff could have fought only one battle against the co-defendants in the court of Barcelona as well.

---

[1] [1969] 1 Lloyd's Rep. 237, 246.
[2] [1973] 1 Lloyd's Rep. 453.

In the El Amria①, there was no co-defendant in the English proceeding, but a separate related proceeding in English court was considered to override a valid foreign jurisdiction clause. In this case, the cargo-owners loaded cargo on the vessel EL Amria to be carried from Egypt to England, the bills of lading providing for any disputes arising under the bills be decided in the country where the carrier has his principal place of business and apply the law of such country. The cargo was alleged to be damaged on unloading. The cargo-owners commenced action in the English court for damage to cargo. The Egyptian shipowner applied for an order to stay the proceedings on the grounds that the parties had agreed that the dispute was to be decided by an Egyptian Court. In refusing a stay of English proceedings, Lord Brandon restated his principles in the Eleftheria and balanced the factors, then decided it was more convenient to hear the case in England despite the fact that the parties had a closer connection with Egypt, as there was a separate but related proceeding taken by the plaintiff against a third party for the slow discharge of the relevant cargoes.

In *Citi-March v. Neptune*②, the jurisdiction clause in the bills of lading conferring exclusive jurisdiction on the Courts of Singapore was also not given effect. Although the claim against the first defendants was contractually time barred in the contractual forum, i. e. Singapore, due to the plaintiffs "own self-induced prejudice", Mr. Justice Colman thought it would not "be just to deprive the plaintiff of the benefit of having started proceedings within the limitation period applicable in this country"③. Furthermore, as the evidence were in Hong Kong and England, a trial in Singapore was held to "involve more movement of witnesses and documents and therefore probably greater administrative costs than a trial in London"④ ; giving effect to the jurisdiction clause was held to be inconvenient and unjust for it would leave the plaintiff "in the position where they could not advance their alternative claims against the four defendants all in the same forum"⑤, and "would preclude the plaintiffs from having the benefit of

---

① [1981] 1 Lloyd's Rep. 119.
② [1997] 1 Lloyd's Rep. 72.
③ [1997] 1 Lloyd's Rep. 76.
④ [1997] 1 Lloyd's Rep. 77.
⑤ [1997] 1 Lloyd's Rep. 77.

getting the evidence of all four defendants before the same Court"① ; and there was risk of "inconsistent decision if proceedings were to be split between Singapore and London"②. It is obvious in this case, if the jurisdiction clause was given effect, the proceedings against the first defendants in Singapore was time barred, there would not be any case in Singapore, not to say any inconvenience or inconsistent decisions. To deny the effect of the jurisdiction clause is only for the purpose of subjecting the first defendants to English jurisdiction and for the benefit of the plaintiffs to escape the time bar in his contractual forum.

Similarly, in the M C Pearl③, a jurisdiction clause in a bill of lading conferring exclusive jurisdiction on the Courts of Seoul was not enforced, where the claims of two of the plaintiffs against the 15th defendant Cho Yang (a South Korean company) were time barred in the contractual forum, South Korea. In this case, the casualty which is the subject matter of the relevant proceedings had nothing to do with England, the two plaintiffs concerned with the claims against Cho Yang were not involved in any other claims. Nevertheless, Mr. Justice Rix held that there was strong cause not to stay the English proceeding as this is "a paradigm case, for concentrating all claims arising out of a single casualty in a single jurisdiction, which in the circumstances can only be in England."④

The general principles summarized by Mr. Justice Brandon was approved by Lord Bingham in *Donohue v. Armco*⑤. In this case, Lord Bingham laid down a general rule equally applied to foreign jurisdiction clause and English jurisdiction clause:

> If contracting parties agree to give a particular Court exclusive jurisdiction to rule on claims between those parties, and a claim falling within the scope of the agreement is made in proceedings in a forum other than that which the parties have agreed, the English Court will ordinarily

---

① [1997] 1 Lloyd's Rep. 77.
② [1997] 1 Lloyd's Rep. 78.
③ [1997] 1 Lloyd's Rep. 566.
④ [1997] 1 Lloyd's Rep. 575.
⑤ [2002] 1 Lloyd's Rep. 425, 433.

exercise its discretion (whether by granting a stay of proceedings in England, or by restraining the prosecution of proceedings in the non-contractual forum abroad, or by such other procedural order as is appropriate in the circumstances) to secure compliance with the contractual bargain, unless the party suing in the non-contractual forum (the burden being on him) can show strong reasons for suing in that forum. [1]

However, reading into the cases relating to jurisdiction clauses demonstrates that the English courts could always exercise its discretion not to give effect to a foreign jurisdiction clause while enforcing an English jurisdiction clause by considering different circumstances or the same circumstances differently to decide whether there are strong reasons. Therefore, while in the case of foreign jurisdiction clause, e. g. in the Fehmarn, the Russian jurisdiction clause was not given effect as "the dispute is more closely connected with England than Russia"; but in the case of English jurisdiction clause, even an non-exclusive jurisdiction clause will be enforced against proceedings in a foreign jurisdiction which has much closer connection with the case and more convenient to try the case, e. g. in *JPMSA v. MNI* [2] where an non-exclusive English jurisdiction clause in a underwriting agreement between the parties was enforced although the dispute did not have any links or connections with UK. Similarly, while there is a risk of parallel proceedings and inconsistent decisions, the English Courts would not give effect to foreign jurisdiction clause as discussed supra in *Evans Marshall & Co. v. Bertola SA*[3], in the El Amria[4], in *Citi-March v. Neptune*[5] and in the M C Pearl[6]; but if it is an English jurisdiction clause, it could nevertheless be enforced. For example, in *Akai Pty Limited v. People's Insurance Co. Limited*[7], the English courts refused to stay English proceedings although the effect of

---

[1] [2002] 1 Lloyd's Rep. 432 – 433.
[2] [2001] 2 Lloyd's Rep. 41.
[3] [1973] 1 Lloyd's Rep. 453.
[4] [1981] 1 Lloyd's Rep. 119.
[5] [1997] 1 Lloyd's Rep. 72.
[6] [1997] 1 Lloyd's Rep. 566.
[7] [1998] 1 Lloyd's Rep. 90.

refusing to a stay would result simultaneous litigations in England and in New South Wales, Mr. Justice Thomas held that "it is the consequences of Akai not abiding by a freely negotiated jurisdiction clause; it would not be just that they should be entitled to take advantage of their own breach of contract to achieve this result"①.

2. Mandatory rules and the validity of foreign jurisdiction clause

a) Validity of jurisdiction clause in a bill of lading: the Morviken

In 1982, the House of Lords in the Morviken② rendered a jurisdiction clause "null and void and of no effect" as it violated the provisions of Hague-Visby Rules. In Morviken, the bill of lading contained a law of application and jurisdiction clause providing for the application of the law of Netherlands in which the Hague Rules are incorporated and the exclusive jurisdiction of Court of Amsterdam. The House of Lords held that the Hague-Visby Rules were to have the force of law in the United Kingdom and the bill of lading was one to which the Hague-Visby Rules were expressly made applicable, the choice of Netherlands law as applicable law "purports to lessen, as it expressly does, the liability of the carriers for which art. Ⅳ, r. 5 of the Hague-Visby Rules provides, it unquestionably contravenes art. Ⅲ, r. 8 and by that rules is deprived of any effect in English or Scots law"③. The Hague-Visby Rules rendered "null and void and of no effect" not only choice of foreign law provision but also choice of foreign court provision. Lord Diplock held that "the only sensible meaning to be given to the description of provisions in contracts of carriage which are rendered 'null and void and of no effect' by this rule is one which would embrace every provision in a contract of carriage which, if it were applied, would have the effect of lessening the carrier's liability otherwise than as provided in the rules", otherwise "would leave it open to any shipowner to evade the provisions of art. Ⅲ, r. 8 by the simple device of inserting in his bill of lading issued in, or for carriage from a port in, any contracting state a clause in standard form providing as the exclusive forum for

---

① [1998] 1 Lloyd's Rep. 107. See also David Joseph, *Jurisdiction and arbitration agreements and their enforcement*, (2005) London: Sweet & Maxwell, p. 248.
② [1983] 1 Lloyd's Rep. 1.
③ [1983] 1 Lloyd's Rep. 6.

resolution of disputes what might aptly be described as a Court of convenience, viz. one situated in a country which did not apply the Hague-Visby Rules or, for that matter, a country whose law recognized an unfettered right in a shipowner by the terms of the bill of lading to relieve himself from all liability for loss or damage to the goods caused by his own negligence, fault or breach of contract."① Although the Hague-Visby Rules do not have any provisions relating to jurisdiction, it was constructed to render a jurisdiction clause "null and void and of no effect" under English common law.

b) Validity of jurisdiction clause in an employment contract: The Samango-Turner

In 2007, the Court of Appeal in *Samango-Turner and Ors v. J&H Marsh & McLennan (Services) Limited and Ors (the Samango-Turner)*② applied Section 5 of the Council Regulation 44/2001 on Jurisdiction in Civil and Commercial Matters (the Brussels Regulation) to invalidate an agreement for the exclusive New York jurisdiction in a bonus agreement between US employer and UK employee, because the jurisdiction clause "was agreed before the dispute arose"③. The Brussels Regulation made clear that "there must be a link between proceedings to which this Regulation applies and the territory of the Member States bound by this Regulation. Accordingly, common rules on jurisdiction should, in principle, apply when the defendant is domiciled in one of those Member States"④. In *the Samango-Turner*, the second and third defendants (who were the plaintiffs in the New York proceedings) were domiciled in the United States, the Brussels Regulation should not be applicable to them. Nevertheless, Lord Justice Tuckey held that "if section 5 is engaged the fact that the employer is not domiciled in a Member State is irrelevant"⑤. To deny the New York jurisdiction clause and justify English jurisdiction, Lord Justice Tuckey held that it is for the purpose of certainty and avoiding multiplicity of proceedings to require the two American-domiciled defendants to sue in

---

① [1983] 1 Lloyd's Rep. 6 – 7.
② [2007] EWCA Civ 723.
③ [2007] EWCA Civ 723, paragraph 37.
④ Preamble (8) of the Brussels Regulation.
⑤ [2007] EWCA Civ 723, paragraph 25.

England and English Courts had the closest connection with the disputes:

> It achieves certainty and avoids multiplicity of proceedings by ensuring that all those companies in the MM group who wish to sue on the terms of the bonus agreement are required to sue in the courts of the employees' domicile. Otherwise, MMC and any other company in the MM group could sue in New York and MSL would have to sue in England. The English courts have the closest connection with the dispute, concerning as it does the claimants' activities during their employment and receipt of the award in England. The fact that the plan is administered and regulated in New York is of no relevance to the present proceedings. [1]

In conclusion, if the jurisdiction of a case is allocated by the Brussels Regulation to English courts, even if the Brussels Regulation is not applicable to the defendants and the jurisdiction allocated is not exclusive, the English courts will exercise their discretion to justify English jurisdiction and disregard a foreign jurisdiction clause.

III. Party autonomy in choice of court under international conventions and EU regulations

A. Hague convention on choice of court agreements

The Convention of 25 November 1965 on the Choice of Court[2] by the Hague Conference on Private International Law was the first effort in international level trying to give effect to choice of court agreement. It failed with only one signatory state.[3] 40 years later, the Hague Conference adopted a new convention: Convention of 30 June 2005 on Choice of Court Agreements (the 2005 Hague Convention) which came into force in 2015 with 33 contracting states by April

---

[1] [2007] EWCA Civ 723.
[2] https://www.hcch.net/en/instruments/conventions/full-text/?cid=77.
[3] https://www.hcch.net/en/instruments/conventions/status-table/?cid=77.

28, 2023①.

The 2005 Hague Convention applies in international cases to exclusive choice of court agreements concluded in civil and commercial matters,② it excludes from its scope of application the choice of court agreements relating to consumer contract and contract of employment and some civil or commercial matters relating to certain subject matters, e. g. carriage of passengers and goods.③ It deems a choice of court agreement which designates the courts of one Contracting States or one of more specific courts of one Contracting States to be exclusive unless the parties have expressly provided otherwise.④ It provides for the formal requirement of an exclusive choice of court agreement, the agreement must be concluded or documented in "writing, or by any other means of communication which renders information accessible so as to be usable for subsequent reference"⑤.

Under the 2005 Hague Convention, the court not chosen has to give effect to a choice of court agreement unless:

(a) the agreement is null and void under the law of the State of the chosen court;

(b) a party to the agreement lacked the capacity to contract under the law of the State of the court seised;

(c) giving effect to the agreement would lead to a manifest injustice or would be manifestly contrary to the public policy of the State of the court seised;

(d) for exceptional reasons beyond the control of the parties, the agreement cannot reasonably be performed; or

(e) the chosen court has decided not to hear the case.⑥

---

① https: //www. hcch. net/en/instruments/conventions/status-table/? cid = 98.
② See Art. 1 (1) of Convention of the 30 June 2005 on Choice of Court Agreements.
③ See Art. 2 of Convention of the 30 June 2005 on Choice of Court Agreements.
④ See Art. 3 b) of Convention of the 30 June 2005 on Choice of Court Agreements.
⑤ Art. 3 c) of Convention of the 30 June 2005 on Choice of Court Agreements.
⑥ Art. 6 of Convention of the 30 June 2005 on Choice of Court Agreements.

The first two points (a) and (b) relate to the validity of the choice of court agreement, but it only provides for the law applicable. Accordingly, only the law of the State of the chosen court be applied to determine the validity of the choice of court agreement, the court seised shall not apply its own law to decide the validity of foreign jurisdiction agreement. However, the court seised could apply its law to decide the contracting capacity of the parties to a choice of court agreement. In addition, the court seised still has relatively great discretion not to give effect to a valid choice of foreign court agreement due to the "manifest injustice" or "public policy" exceptions.

B. Choice of court under Hamburg Rules and the Athens Convention

1. Choice of court under Hamburg Rules

The United Nations Convention on the Carriage of Goods by Sea (Hamburg Rules)[1] was the only international convention in force specifying the plaintiff's choice of court and party autonomy in matters relating to carriage of goods by sea. Under Hamburg Rules, "an agreement made by the parties, after a claim under the contract of carriage by sea has arisen, which designates the place where the claimant may institute an action, is effective"[2]. Accordingly, the parties to a dispute relating to the carriage of goods by sea can choose the court to settle their dispute, but such a choice is heavily restricted.

The first limitation is the time when the parties can make the choice. Only a choice of court agreement made "after a claim under the contract of carriage by sea has arisen" may be effective, therefore, a jurisdiction clause in a bill of lading is definitely not effective, a jurisdiction clause in a contract for carriage of goods by sea is also not effective. Such a limitation is without doubt providing full protection for the shipper and the holder of bill of lading, as it makes the jurisdiction clause unilaterally inserted in a bill of lading or contract for the carriage of goods by sea by the carrier ineffective.

The second limitation is the scope of the courts the parties can choose. The

---

[1] The Hamburg Rules entered into force in Nov. 11, 1992, it has 34 contracting parties: http://www.uncitral.org/uncitral/en/uncitral_texts/transport_goods/Hamburg_status.html.

[2] Art. 21 (5) of Hamburg Rules.

scope of the courts the parties can agree on are only those competent courts the plaintiff may institute an action. Art. 21 (1) of Hamburg Rules providesfor the location of such courts as:

(a) the principal place of business or, in the absence thereof, the habitual residence of the defendant; or

(b) the place where the contract was made, provided that the defendant has there a place of business, branch or agency through which the contract was made; or

(c) the port of loading or the port of discharge; or

(d) any additional place designated for that purpose in the contract of carriage by sea.

Art. 21 (2) further clarifies the jurisdiction of "any port or place in a Contracting State at which the carrying vessel or any other vessel of the same ownership may have been arrested". The lists of the places show that the scope of choice by the parties is quite limited, the court chosen will always have close territorial connection with the disputes.

2. Choice of court under the Athens Convention

The Athens Convention relating to the Carriage of Passengers and their Luggage by Sea 1974 (the Athens Convention 1974) adopted by the International Maritime Organization in 1974 is an important convention governing international carriage of passengers and their luggage. Art. 17 provides for competent jurisdiction and party autonomy. The courts having competent jurisdiction are (a) the court of the place of permanent residence or principal place of business of the defendant, (b) the court of the place of departure or that of the destination according to the contract of carriage, (c) a court of the State of the domicile or permanent residence of the claimant if the defendant has a place of business and is subject to jurisdiction in that State, (d) a court of the State where the contract of carriage was made if the defendant has a place of business and is subject to jurisdiction in that State. [1] All listed courts have quite a close connection with the defendant.

---

[1] Art. 17 (1) of the Athens Convention 1974.

Nevertheless, the parties may choose any jurisdiction to submit the claim for damages, the only limitation is the time of the choice, they can only make the choice "after the occurrence of the incident which has caused the damage"[①]. This limitation will render ineffective any jurisdiction clause in a passenger contract or passenger ticket, and will therefore protect the passenger from agreement unilaterally made by the carrier.

C. Choice of court under EU Regulations

The 1968 Brussels Convention on jurisdiction and the enforcement of judgments in civil and commercial matters (the Brussels Convention), concluded between the then Member States of the European Communities, was the first convention in force recognizing the party autonomy in choice of court. This Convention was replaced by the Council Regulation (EC) No. 44/2001 on jurisdiction and the recognition and enforcement of judgments in civil and commercial matters (the Brussels Regulation), which was then recast in 2012 as Regulation (EU) No. 1215/2012 of the European Parliament and of the Council of 12 December 2012 on jurisdiction and the recognition and enforcement of judgments in civil and commercial matters [the Brussels Regulation (recast)]. These three documents all give effect to party autonomy in choice of courts in civil and commercial matters (except those being excluded) with limitations for the protection of the weaker party and subject to exclusive jurisdiction. In addition, there is a more specific regulation which gives effect to party autonomy in choice of court with limitation—Council Regulation (EC) No. 4/2009 of 18 December 2008 on jurisdiction, applicable law, recognition and enforcement of decisions and cooperation in matters relating to maintenance obligations (the Maintenance Regulation).

1. Choice of court under Brussels Regulation (recast)

a) General rules

Section 7 (Prorogation of Jurisdiction) of the Brussels Regulation (recast) has two articles, Art. 25 relates to jurisdiction agreement while Art. 26 is about

---

[①] Art. 17 (2) of the Athens Convention 1974 or Art. 17 (3) of the 2002 Protocol to the Athens Convention.

submission to jurisdiction. Art. 25 permits the parties to make an agreement to choose a court or courts of a Member State to settle disputes which have arisen or which may arise in connection with a particular legal relationship, it provides that the chosen court "shall have jurisdiction, unless the agreement is null and void as to its substantive validity under the law of that Member State", and the jurisdiction shall be exclusive unless the parties have agreed otherwise.[①] It further provides for the formal requirement of a jurisdiction agreement.

Under Art. 25, a formally and substantively valid jurisdiction agreement should be enforced, the court not chosen is not allowed to exercise any discretion to disregard such a valid jurisdiction agreement, neither could the court apply its own law or any laws other than that of the chosen court to determine the substantive validity of the jurisdiction agreement.

b) Limitations

While Art. 25 provides for the formal requirement and governing law of the substantive validity of a jurisdiction agreement, articles in other sections of the Brussels Regulation (recast) contain limitations of party autonomy in choice of court. Parties to certain civil and commercial matters may enjoy limited autonomy or no autonomy in choice of court.

1) Matters not covered by the Brussels Regulation (recast)

The scope of the Brussels Regulation (recast) covers the main civil and commercial matters with certain exception[②]: (a) the status or legal capacity of natural persons; (b) rights in property arising out of a matrimonial relationship or out of a relationship deemed by the law applicable to such relationship to have comparable effects to marriage; (c) wills and succession; (d) bankruptcy, proceedings relating to the winding-up of insolvent companies or other legal persons, judicial arrangements, compositions and analogous proceedings. The parties in dispute relating to these matters do not enjoy party autonomy in choice of court.

2) Matters under exclusive jurisdiction

Where the matters are under the exclusive jurisdiction of the courts of a

---

① Art. 25 (1) of the Brussels Regulation (recast).
② Art. 1 (2) of the Brussels Regulation (recast).

Member States, party autonomy has no room of existence. Relevant matters include: a) rights in rem in immovable property or tenancies of immovable property; b) the validity of the constitution, the nullity or the dissolution of companies or other legal persons or associations of natural or legal persons or the validity of the decisions of their organs; c) the validity of entries in public; d) the registration or validity of patents, trade marks, designs, or other similar rights required to be deposited or registered. ①

3) Matters relating to weaker party protection

For the protection of weaker party, the Brussels Regulations provide for specific jurisdiction rules which give more choices to the weaker party and permit limited party autonomy. ②

There are three relevant sections under the Brussels Regulation (recast), respectively, section 3 jurisdiction in matters relating to insurance, section 4 jurisdiction over consumer contracts and section 5 jurisdiction over individual contracts of employment. In these matters, the party in a relatively stronger position, i.e. the insurer, the employer or goods/service provider in a consumer contract, may take proceedings only in the court where the defendant has his domicile;③ while the weaker party, i.e. the policy holder, the insured and the beneficiary in insurance, the employee or the consumer has at least two choices, he may choose to bring proceeding in the court where the defendant has his domicile④ or with matters relating to insurance and consumer contract in the court where he himself has domiciles⑤ or in matters relating to contract of employment in the court where he habitually carries out his work⑥.

This policy of weaker party protection is also carried out in the case of jurisdiction agreement. Thus, in matters relating to insurance, consumer contract or individual contract of employment, an effective jurisdiction agreement shall be: (a) made after the dispute has arisen; or (b) allow the weaker party to

---

① Art. 24 of the Brussels Regulation (recast).
② See preamble (18) and (19) of the Brussels Regulation (recast).
③ See Art. 14 (1), Art. 18 (2) and Art. 22 (1) of the Brussels Regulation (recast).
④ See Art. 11 (1) (a), Art. 18 (1) and Art. 21 (1) (a) of the Brussels Regulation (recast).
⑤ See Art. 11 (1) (b), Art. 18 (1) of the Brussels Regulation (recast).
⑥ See Art. 21 (1) (b) of the Brussels Regulation (recast).

bring proceedings in courts other than those provided by the relevant sections. ①
In the case of insurance contract and consumer contract, an agreement conferring
jurisdiction to the court of the common domicile or common habitual residence of
the parties is also effective. ② Accordingly, a jurisdiction clause inserted in
insurance contract, consumer contract or individual employment contract will not
be given effect if it deprives the weaker party of their choice of jurisdiction to
bring suit. ③

2. Choice of court under the Maintenance Regulation

"In order to increase legal certainty, predictability and the autonomy of the
parties"④, the Maintenance Regulation allowed the parties to choose the
competent court by agreement "on the basis of specific connecting factors"⑤.
The scope of the courts is not broad, the court chosen shall be in the Member
State in which one of the parties is habitually resident or of which one of the
parties has nationality. ⑥ In the case of maintenance obligations between spouses
or former spouses, the chosen court could be one which has jurisdiction to settle
their dispute in matrimonial matters or that court located in the last common
habitual residence of the spouses for a period of at least one year. ⑦

The Maintenance Regulation also provides for the formal requirement of a
choice of court agreement. It requires the agreement to be in writing and also
provides for communication by electronic means which provides a durable record
of the agreement to be equivalent to writing. ⑧

The Maintenance Regulation excludes its application to a maintenance
obligation towards a child under the age of 18. ⑨ Child under age 18 is regarded
as a weaker party, so "to protect the weaker party, such a choice of court should

---

① Art. 15 (1) (2), Art. 19 (1) (2) and Art. 23 of the Brussels Regulation (recast).
② Art. 15 (3) and Art. 19 (3) of the Brussels Regulation (recast).
③ Except those situations under Art. 15 (5) and Art. 16 of the Brussels Regulation (recast) which give effect to jurisdiction clause in contract of insurance covering certain prescribed risks.
④ Preamble (19) of the Maintenance Regulation.
⑤ Preamble (19) of the Maintenance Regulation.
⑥ Art. 4 (1) of the Maintenance Regulation.
⑦ Art. 4 (1) of the Maintenance Regulation.
⑧ Art. 4 (2) of the Maintenance Regulaiton.
⑨ Art. 4 (3) of the Maintenance Regulation.

not be allowed in the case of maintenance obligations towards a child under the age of 18"①.

Ⅳ. Comparative analysis

Limitations on party autonomy in choice of court could be roughly classified into two kinds, one relating to the validity of the jurisdiction agreement, the other relating to the effectiveness of the jurisdiction agreement. Jurisdiction agreement, as a kind of contract, is subject to the validity requirements of a contract, formally and substantively. However, as it is not just a contract, it is also a means to determine the jurisdiction of the court, it affects not only the interests of the parties but also the interests of the courts, and is therefore subject to public interest limitations, a valid jurisdiction agreement may not always be given effect. A balance between private interests or between private interest and public interest results in different scope of protection and different degree of protection for a certain party or jurisdiction.

A. Balance of private interests and protection of weaker party

1. Plaintiff's forum shopping and party autonomy in choice of court

Different jurisdiction rules may result in plaintiff's forum shopping. In every state, with the development of a court system is the allocation of jurisdictions among the courts horizontally and vertically. If there is only one clearly identified court, the plaintiff has no chance in choosing the court to take proceedings. When there is more than one court capable of hearing a case, the plaintiff may choose that one more favorable to him/her, e. g. a claimant in a shipping matter will seek out the forum where it may easily and cheaply arrest a vessel as security for its claim②. Thus, the parties to the disputes may sue each other in different

---

① Preamble (19) of the Maintenance Regulation.
② Hohn Hare, "Shopping for the Best Admiralty Bargain" in Martin Davies (ed), *Jurisdiction and Forum Selection in International Maritime Law: Essays in Honor of Robert Force* (Kluwer Law International 2005), p. 163.

courts. In domestic case, the domestic Civil Procedural Law could more easily settle this conflict of jurisdictions, but in an international case, without common arrangement, plaintiff's forum shopping may result in parallel proceedings in different states and the difficulties for the recognition and enforcement of foreign judgment.

Plaintiff's forum shopping may be detrimental to the defendant, especially in an international case. In domestic case, under the same legal system, the plaintiff's choice of court may only involve the convenience and costs of litigation, while in international case the applicable law may be a more important consideration. ① Unless the relevant courts apply the same international substantive law, e. g. the Athens Convention 1974, or apply the same choice of law rules leading to the application of the same substantive law, the choice of courts in different states will lead to application of different laws ending in different results. The plaintiff will logically and reasonably seek the best result for his interest.

Therefore, among other arrangements unilaterally or internationally by the state or states, ② party autonomy in the form of jurisdiction agreement provides a solution by the parties themselves to the problem of conflict of jurisdictions and detrimental effect to the defendant by limiting the plaintiff's forum shopping, and to ensure certainty and the reasonable expectation of the parties, more significantly, of the would-be defendant.

2. Party autonomy in choice of court and the protection of weaker party

While party autonomy in choice of court is beneficial for avoiding conflict of jurisdictions and ensuring reasonable expectation of the parties, it shall not impose exotic burden on the plaintiff and cause injustice and unfairness on a party. A jurisdiction agreement, different from a contract expressly setting out the

---

① Hohn Hare, "Shopping for the Best Admiralty Bargain" in Martin Davies (ed), *Jurisdiction and Forum Selection in International Maritime Law*: *Essays in Honor of Robert Force* (Kluwer Law International 2005), pp. 164 – 165.

② Unilateral arrangement against plaintiff's forum shopping may be anti-suit injunction or forum non conveniens, the former trying to solve the conflict of jurisdictions by restraining a party from taking proceedings in a foreign court, the latter by staying its own jurisdiction. International arrangements include adopting unified substantive laws, unified choice of law rules, or unified jurisdiction laws.

rights and obligations of the parties, only directs a dispute-settling court. It seemingly affects only the choice of court by the plaintiffs, but enforcing the jurisdiction agreement will affect not only their procedural rights but also their substantive rights, as emphatical survey shows, "enforcement of a forum selection clause adversely affects the rights of the plaintiff, either by diminishing the value of its claim or, in some cases, by depriving it of the claim altogether"[1]. The justification of party autonomy or freedom of choice by the parties largely depends on their equal bargaining powers. In making a jurisdiction agreement, the parties ought to have known its legal consequences, thus, a willingly and knowingly made jurisdiction agreement between parties with equal bargaining power, whether before or after the dispute has arisen, will generally be regarded as valid between the parties. Issues often arise from jurisdiction clause in a standard form contract which is adopted by one party and the other party has no choice but to accept. Similar to the plaintiff's forum shopping, the party who has the advantage of inserting the jurisdiction clause into a standard form contract or document evidencing a contract will naturally choose the jurisdiction most convenient and favorable to him under the guise of party autonomy, e.g. the carrier may insert a jurisdiction clause in his bill of lading subjecting the shipper and holder of bill of lading to the jurisdiction where he has his principal place of business, either because he or his advisor is familiar with the language, the procedural law as well as the substantive law of that jurisdiction or because the governing law will provide the best protection to his interest. What is more, the party in advantageous position may draft a so-called asymmetric jurisdiction clause[2] which only subject the other party to a certain jurisdiction while leaving himself wide choice of jurisdiction. Giving effect to such a jurisdiction clause is actually giving choice of court to the dominating party and may constitute injustice or unfairness to the other party. Thus, in giving force to a jurisdiction clause, a balance of the interests of the parties is necessary and the protection of the weaker party shall be

---

[1] Robert Force and Martin Davies, "Forum Selection Clauses in International Maritime Contracts", in Martin Davies (ed), *Jurisdiction and Forum Selection in International Maritime Law: Essays in Honor of Robert Force* (Kluwer Law International 2005), p. 8.

[2] For a further discussion of asymmetric jurisdiction agreement, see Louise Merrett, "The Future Enforcement of Asymmetric Jurisdiction Agreements", I. C. L. Q (2018).

taken into consideration.

Who is the weaker party necessary for protection in deciding the validity of a jurisdiction clause? The Brussels Regulations make it clear that the policy holder, the insured and the beneficiary in insurance matters, the employee in individual contract of employment and the consumer in consumer contract are the weaker parties in the relevant legal relationships. The Maintenance Regulation also regards a child under the age of 18 as a weaker party. Passenger could be protected as a consumer under the Brussels Regulations, and the Athens Convention also provides protection to passenger in international carriage of passengers by sea. Shippers and holders of bill of lading may not be regarded as weaker parties but are actually given protection in various ways under Hamburg Rules, English common law and in Chinese courts. There are no rules providing for weaker party protection under Chinese *Civil Procedural Law*, however, consumers are actually given somewhat more protection by the Supreme People's Court when it directs the People's courts to support the consumer's argument to invalidate a jurisdiction clause in certain circumstances.

The approaches adopted to protect the weaker party could be summarized as followings:

(a) excluding certain party from party autonomy, as exemplified by the Maintenance Obligation Regulation for the protection of child under 18 years old;

(b) permitting choice of court only after the dispute has arisen, and the chosen court shall be one of the courts capable of being chosen by the plaintiff, as provided by the Hamburg Rules;

(c) permitting choice of any court only after the dispute has arisen, as the relevant rules under the Brussels Regulation (recast), and the Athens Convention 1974;

(d) permitting only choice of court agreement giving more choice to the weaker party, as the relevant rules under the Brussels Regulation (recast);

(e) invalidating choice of foreign court agreement where the governing law will deprive the plaintiff of mandatory substantive law protection, as showed by the Morviken.

Approach (a) is the simplest one denying party autonomy in choice of court in any event. Approach (b) and (c) deny the validity of any jurisdiction clause in any contract or document evidencing a contract, and a separate jurisdiction agreement made before the dispute has arisen. These two approaches ensure the right of choice by the weaker party after the dispute has arisen, then they could choose to or not to make a jurisdiction agreement with the other party. Approach (d) ensures the right of choice by the weaker party not to be diminished by jurisdiction clause or agreement. Approach (e) ensures the application of mandatory substantive law for the protection of the interest of the weaker party. Approaches (a) — (d) all aim to protect only the right to choice of court by the weaker party from being deprived of or being diminished, what they provided are still procedural law protection other than substantive law protection, as they are not concerned with the application of law which shall be determined by the competent court; approach (e) provides substantive law protection, it protects the substantive right of the weaker party, but would mix jurisdiction with application of law resulting in failure to give equal treatment to forum law and foreign law.

B. Party autonomy and jurisdiction protection

Party autonomy in choice of court may also be forum shopping, but it is not the plaintiff's forum shopping, instead it is the mutual forum shopping of both parties to the dispute. Party autonomy in choice of court may or may not alter the allocation of jurisdictions among the courts depending on whether the chosen courts are among those the plaintiff could choose. A choice of court in domestic case, whether altering the allocation of jurisdictions of the domestic courts or not, won't have any effect on judicial sovereignty. However, it is not the case for the choice of court in international case, which, at the same time of designating jurisdiction to the court of a state, will normally exclude the jurisdiction of courts in other states, thus affecting the judicial sovereignty of the states whose courts are not chosen. Therefore, a choice of court agreement may not always be given effect even if it is formally and substantively valid.

Firstly, for matters under exclusive jurisdiction, the plaintiff does not have any choice, the parties will consequently have no choice. Rules relating to general jurisdiction will always provide for exclusive jurisdiction of a court over certain matters, but the scope of matters may be different with different considerations. Besides, civil matters relating to issues which could not be negotiated or traded off, e. g. status of civil persons, matrimonial relationship, shall only be subject to designated jurisdiction. In comparison with the Brussels Regulation (recast) and the 2005 Hague Convention, the scope of matters excluded from party autonomy in choice of court under Chinese Civil Procedural Law are narrow. What is more, in foreign-related cases the limitation on the scope of matters disappeared in the CPL 2023.

Secondly, considerations relating to the connection and appropriateness of the chosen court to the disputes would constitute barrier to giving effect to a valid jurisdiction agreement. In comparison, the English common law imposes the most limitations on the choice of foreign court and therefore provides the best protection to the jurisdiction of domestic court; the *Hamburg Rules* limits the chosen court within those courts the plaintiff has option to choose①, this ensures the jurisdiction of the competent courts and keeps to a minimum degree the impact of jurisdiction agreement on the plaintiff as well; the Maintenance Regulation also limits the chosen court within the designated courts, but the scope are a little broader than that the plaintiff has option to choose, since the parties could also agree to submit their disputes to a court where one of the parties has nationality② while the courts the plaintiff could choose are only those one of the parties is habitually resident③ ; the scope of chosen courts are much broader under Chinese Civil Procedural Law, the only limitation is "actual connection" to the disputes which is understood as minimum territorial connection to the disputes, such a limitation on the scope of the chosen court is eliminated in the CPL 2023 for foreign-related cases; the Athens Convention 1974, the 2005 Hague Convention and the Brussels Regulation do not have limitation on the scope of the chosen court. China is Contracting Party to the Athens Convention 1974 and its

---

① See Art. 21 (5) of the Hamburg Rules.
② See Art. 4 (1) (b) of the Maintenance Regulation.
③ See Art. 3 of the Maintenance Regulation.

1976 Protocol and will hopefully ratify the 2005 Hague Convention, the elimination of any limitation on the scope of chosen court is actually in line with these conventions.

V. Conclusion

Limitations of party autonomy in choice of court center on two parts: one is related to validity of the jurisdiction agreement, the other is for the purpose of competent jurisdiction protection.

The Brussels Regulation (recast) and the 2005 Hague Convention both provide for the law of the chosen court to be applicable law of the substantive validity of the jurisdiction agreement, but the Brussels Regulation (recast) also clearly laid down limitations on choice of court for the protection of the weaker party. The Hamburg Rules equals shipper and holder of bill of lading to weaker party, thus confine choice of court to the time after the dispute has arisen and among the courts the plaintiff could choose, therefore also protect the jurisdiction of the competent court. The Maintenance Regulation confines the range of the chosen courts, but the scope of chosen courts by the parties is somewhat broader than what the plaintiff could choose.

The English courts could apply rules of the Brussels Regulation to protect the consumer, the employee, the insured etc., and apply the Moviken to protect the shipper and holders of bill of lading, the scope of the weaker parties is comparatively the broadest. In addition, under common law the English courts have not yet been able to treat foreign jurisdiction clause the same as English jurisdiction clause, the protection for domestic jurisdiction is still very strong.

Rules relating to jurisdiction agreement under Chinese *Civil Procedural Law* are relatively straight and simple, there is no room for the protection of the weaker party and thus no such limitation on party autonomy. The interpretation of the Supreme People's Court shows some protection for consumer but is still quite limited. The "actual connection" requirement is a doubt-edged sword affecting not only the choice of foreign court but also the choice of domestic court, is not actually for the protection of the competent court or for domestic court, the elimination of such requirement in foreign-related cases will make parties easier to choose foreign court. China's rules on choice of court manifest equal treatment of parties to a dispute, whether it is the plaintiff or the defendant, but failed to take into consideration of the special protection for the weaker party; domestic law and foreign law, whether it is procedural law or substantive law, are equally treated, demonstrating respect for judicial sovereignty of other states, in other words, lacking special protection for her own judicial sovereignty. Rules relating to choice of court agreement under Chinese *Civil Procedural Law* still need to be in more detail to provide protection for certain weaker parties and special protection of her own jurisdiction in matters of public interest.

中英两国无单放货法律责任比较分析

魏长庚 曲霄 吴国生[*]

摘要：有些国家为了提高货物清关效率，要求承运人向当地海关或者港口当局先行交付货物，并存放在港口当地进行保管。承运人往往主观认为将货物交给海关或港口当局指定的保税区仓库就完成交货任务，导致收货人不用凭借正本提单而是通过其他便利渠道将货物取走，保留提单的托运人在没有收到货款的情况下不得不向承运人索赔无单放货导致的损失。本文在对温州佰利兰德橡胶轮胎有限公司与地中海航运有限公司无单放货一案进行讨论后，拟对近年来我国实行《海商法》下的承运人责任的案例进行梳理和分析，分别就承运人面对不同的提单合同方所承担的责任，贸易习惯、港口规定是否能改变承运人凭单放货责任等问题进行中国法和英国法下的比较研究，试图避免在承运人责任概念上的误区，为货物提单的相关方明确自己的法律地位提供一个清晰的认识。

关键词：无单放货 放货责任 提单索赔

Comparative Analysis of Legal Liability Between China and UK for Cargo Release Without Original Bills of Lading

Wei Changgeng, Qu Xiao, Wu Guosheng

Abstract: In some countries, in order to improve the efficiency of customs clearance of goods, the carrier is always required to deliver the goods to the local customs or port authorities firstly and store them in the port for safe keeping. The carrier often subjectively believes that the delivery will be completed by delivering the goods to the customs or port authority designated bonded warehouse, which possibly results in the goods taken delivery by the consignee without surrendering

---

[*] 魏长庚：高级船长，英国斯旺西大学海商法硕士。曲霄：高级船长，华洋海事中心希腊办事处工作。吴国生：高级船长，北京华航天虹天气科技有限公司工作。

the original bill of lading but through other convenient channels, and the unpaid shipper who retains the original bill of lading has to sue the carrier for the damages caused by the release of the goods without the original bill of lading. This article, after discussing the case named Wenzhou Briland Rubber Tire Co. Ltd. v. Mediterranean Shipping Co. Ltd., intends to sort out and analyse the cases of carrier's liability under China's Maritime Law in recent years, and to make a comparative study of carrier's liability against the different parties of the bill of lading contract, and to probe into the issues such as whether the trade customs and port regulations can change the carrier's liability for releasing goods without a bill of lading under Chinese law and English law, attempts to avoid the reader's misunderstanding of the concept of carrier's liability and to provide a clear understanding and clarify their legal position for the parties concerned with the bill of lading.

Key words: release without original bill of lading; responsibility of delivery; claim for bill of lading

引　言

承运人在海上货物运输合同下交货责任是严格的。然而，这一严格责任往往会受到卸货港口当地的习惯、规定或者不正规航运操作的影响，导致出现不正常的无单放货现象。本文在中国裁判文书网以"无单放货"为索引进行查询，共查询到1137件相关案例，经分类、筛选和整理，仅保留最高人民法院审理的35件具有典型意义的案例（见本文附表）。在这些案例中，有7件涉及巴西无单放货问题，7件涉及货损举证责任问题，5件涉及仓储合同（保管协议）无单放货问题，5件涉及确认提单合同当事方问题，3件涉及无单放货是否属于贸易惯例问题，1件涉及提单融资担保问题，1件涉及提单管辖权问题，1件涉及提单索赔时效问题，1件涉及托运人懈怠问题，1件涉及无单放货纠纷下的借贷合同的欠款担保问题，1件涉及未核实提单连续背书正确性问题，1件涉及无船承运人提单合同的有效性问题，1件涉及无单放货的损失计算问题。从最高人民法院关于无单放货的案例中，我们可以厘清我国对承运人责任的法律观点，而从最新的判例中，则可以看出对这方面问题的进一步澄清，法院对提单神圣的严格责任再次确认，可为将来在遇到相似或相同的问题时提供法律遵循，有利于商业争议快速解决，避免不必要的诉讼浪费。在温州佰利兰德橡胶轮胎有限公司与地中海航运有限公司等海上、通海水域货物运输合同纠纷案（简称佰利兰德公司案）[①]中，法院重申了船东试图免除无单放货责任必须承担严格的举证责任。本文基于佰利兰德公司案的论述，尝试将英国法律中运输合同下"无单放货"的判例与中国的案例进行对比，使读者能够了解两国有关的法律规定，增强对提单索赔中无单放货知识的了解。

一、佰利兰德公司案

2015年10月，温州佰利兰德橡胶轮胎有限公司（简称佰利兰德公司）委托地中海航运有限公司（简称地中海公司，MSC）运输一个40尺集装箱高柜的汽车轮胎，运输条件为CY – CY，运费预付。该票货物于同年10月2日装船出运，温州中外运公司代理地中海公司向佰利兰德公司签发了一套正本记名提单，载明托运人为佰利兰德公司，收货人为 Turbo Auto Pecas Eaccessrios LTD，启运港是宁波，目的港是巴西。涉案货物出运后，因国外买方未曾付款买单，全套正本提单仍保留在佰利兰德公司。2015年12月9日，涉案集装箱在目的港被卸至巴西港口 Portonave 码头，并在巴西外贸综合系统（Siscomex）办理了相关登记，随后该集装箱于2015年12月11日被当地海关转移至 Poly 港口保税码头。Poly 港口保税码头在接受货物后，于2016年6月30日将涉案集装箱货物交付给收货人。Poly 码头股份有限公司出具的巴西外贸综合系统中的系统信息显示，涉案集装箱在清关前在 Poly 港口保税码头保管。

（一）争议焦点

该案承运人是地中海公司，其注册地在瑞士，因此该案属于涉外民事纠纷的海上货物运输合同履行的争议。当事方均表示接受中国法院管辖，适用中国法作为合同准据法。案件双方当事人对佰利兰德公司与地中海公司之间成立海上货物运输关系、地中海公司作为承运人、佰利兰德公司持有提单和涉案货物已在目的港被放行的事实均表示没有异议。

该案争议的焦点是地中海公司作为承运人是否应当承担无单放货的责任。对于这一争议焦点，双方当事人也表示没有异议。同时双方也都认为

[①] 参见最高人民法院（2020）最高法民再171号民事判决书。

按照卸货港法律规定，必须将到港货物交付给当地海关或港口当局，以及在货物抵港后确实交付给当地海关或港口当局的事实。

但是，地中海公司主张依据《最高人民法院关于审理无正本提单交付货物案件适用法律若干问题的规定》（简称《无单放货司法解释》）第七条免责，[①] 并提供货物转移至 Poly 港口保税码头的证据。而佰利兰德公司声称，地中海公司提供的巴西法律证据并不能证明其是被强制将进口到港的货物交付目的港的海关，巴西海关相关法规的目的是提高货物清关效率、简化进口程序，并不影响正常国际贸易的物权交割，不能否定提单的物权效力和剥夺承运人对货物的控制权利，因此，承运人所提供的证据是不能证明其被强制要求必须将进口到港的货物交付给目的港的港口当局而免除其无单放货的责任。

（二）裁判要旨

该案在宁波海事法院、浙江省高级人民法院经两次审理，均认为应适用《无单放货司法解释》第七条的规定。但该案在再审时，最高人民法院并没有纠结《无单放货司法解释》，而是直接依据《海商法》第七十一条进行判决："《中华人民共和国海商法》第七十一条规定：'提单，是指用以证明海上货物运输合同和货物已经由承运人接收或者装船，以及承运人保证据以交付货物的单证。提单中载明的向记名人交付货物，或者按照指示人的指示交付货物，或者向提单持有人交付货物的条款，构成承运人据以交付货物的保证。'根据该条规定，承运人负有在卸货港凭正本提单交付货物的义务。地中海公司在卸货港未收回其签发的正本记名提单即将货物交给收货人构成无单放货，应当承担因其无单放货造成的托运人的货款和运费损失。地中海公司主张免责，但其提供的证据不足以证明依照提单载明的卸货港所在地法律规定，必须将承运到港的货物交付给当地海关或者港口当局，本院对其抗辩主张不予支持。"因此，最高人民法院推翻了一审、二审的判决，强调了即使承运人在目的港将货物交给海关或港口当局，除非出现政府的强制行为，仍不能免除承运人无单放货的责任。

在后来的德莎国际货运代理（深圳）有限公司（简称德莎公司）与广

[①] 《最高人民法院关于审理无正本提单交付货物案件适用法律若干问题的规定》第七条：承运人依照提单载明的卸货港所在地法律规定，必须将承运到港的货物交付给当地海关或者港口当局的，不承担无正本提单交付货物的民事责任。

东成虹照明科技有限公司海上、通海水域货物运输合同纠纷案（简称德莎案）① 中，争议的焦点问题仍然是承运人是否可以援引《无单放货司法解释》第七条主张免除其无单放货责任。最高人民法院认为，"承运人负有向收货人交付货物的法定义务，承运人援引《无单放货司法解释》第七条主张免除其无单放货责任，除必须证明卸货港所在地国家法律有必须将承运的到港货物交给当地海关或者港口当局的相关规定之外，还需证明其在向当地海关或者港口当局交接货物后丧失对货物的控制权。德莎公司主张根据巴西法律，其在卸货港失去了对货物的控制权，但其提交的巴西法律的内容不足以证明其主张。"因此，德莎案遵循佰利兰德公司案的判决，再次重申了承运人无单放货的严格责任。下面本文将针对提单无单放货索赔中涉及的不同争议以及不同情况下承运人的责任逐一进行分析。

二、承运人面对不同的提单合同方所承担责任的比较

对提单合同的当事方而言，英国法和中国法基本上都是按照《海牙规则》或《海牙维斯比规则》和《海商法》中"承运人""托运人"和"提单持有人"的定义，确立各方的责任和义务，二者在法律概念上的差异不大。只是涉及承租人提单下的实际承运人方面，在我国法律中，提单索赔方可以根据提单合同直接起诉；而在英国法律中，只能以侵权而非根据提单合同提起诉讼。

由于英国普通法坚持一个合同只属于缔约双方之间的事情且与第三人无关的合同相对性原则（privity of contract），除了合同的缔约双方之外，第三人不能获得合同权利（to acquire right under a contract）。因此，提单作为英国法中合同的一种，同样适用合同相对性原则，只有提单的当事方才有权向另一方提起诉讼。如果不是提单上的托运人或后来的合法持有人，则无权向承运人提起诉讼，承运人面对非提单合同的另一方，是不用承担提单责任的。例如，在 East & West Steamship v. Hossain Brothers 案② 中，承运人面对已经背书转让的提单托运人，就可以免除无单放货的责任。尽管后来提单托运人迂回通过条件托管成功起诉，但对于实际未在提单上列明的托运

---

① 参见最高人民法院（2021）最高法民申 7603 号民事裁定书。
② *East & West Steamship v. Hossain Brothers* [1968] 2 Lloyd's Rep. 145.

人、提单中间持有人或未在提单上列明的最终收货人,① 既不存在托管关系,也不存在提单合同关系,承运人就可以免除承担提单方面的责任。

在实际托运人诉讼方面,我国法律与英国法稍微有些差别。特别是面临非提单合同的实际托运人的索赔,在我国法律下仍需要承担提单的相应责任。例如,在深圳市璟翰实业有限公司(简称深圳璟翰公司)与利通物流有限公司海上货物运输合同纠纷案②中,深圳璟翰公司是实际托运人,并不是提单上的托运人,提单上载明的托运人是 FOB 买方,大连海事法院判决是根据《无单放货司法解释》第十二条的规定,③ 虽然在正本提单上没有载明其托运人身份,但持有指示提单的实际托运人有权要求承运人依据海上货物运输合同承担无单放货的责任,以立法形式给予这一类型的托运人法律上的救济,强制要求承运人承担提单方面的责任。

当船东作为实际承运人时,有时其是作为船东自己签发提单,称为"船东提单";有时是船舶的承租人签发提单,称为"租船提单"。如果所签发的不是船东提单,而是承租人的租船提单,则在英国法下,不存在实际承运人和合约承运人区分,作为承运人的船东可以不受承租人提单的约束。例如,在 The Hector 案④中,提单持有人是船舶次级租船合同的承租人,因二船东破产倒闭没有支付给原船东租金,原船东留置船舶租金,法院判决,该提单是二船东签发的运费预付承租人提单,原船东可以不受承租人提单的约束,没有义务将托运人的货物运往目的地。实际承运人在面临没有货物所有权的提单收货人,既不用承担提单合同责任,也无须承担托管责任,这在上议院 The Starsin 案⑤中得到很好的体现。在该案中,其中 17 份提单分为 4 名收货人,只有其中 1 名收货人在货损发生之前取得货物所有权,其他 3 名收货人则没有及时取得货物的所有权。对于这 3 名收货人而言,在承租人提单下,实际承运人可以免于货损的责任。同样,无单放货的责任也适用类似的原则。只要承运人没有重大过失或疏忽,也不

---

① *The David Agmshenebeli* [2003] 1 Lloyd's Rep. 92.
② 参见大连海事法院(2006)大海商初字第 385 号民事判决书。
③ 《最高人民法院关于审理无正本提单交付货物案件适用法律若干问题的规定》第十二条:向承运人实际交付货物并持有指示提单的托运人,虽然在正本提单上没有载明其托运人身份,因承运人无正本提单交付货物,要求承运人依据海上货物运输合同承担无正本提单交付货物民事责任的,人民法院应予支持。
④ *The Hector* [1998] 2 Lloyd's Rep. 287.
⑤ *The Starsin* [2003] 1 Lloyd's Rep. 571.

用承担托管方面的责任。即使作为合同承运人，没有诉权的收货人仍然可以避免承担无单放货的责任。

而在中国法下，实际承运人和合同承运人二者需要承担的责任几乎没有区别。① 我国法律几乎不允许没有提单合同关系的实际承运人逃避提单合同下无单放货的责任。例如，在泛太集运有限公司与咸宁市汇美达工贸有限公司海上、通海水域货物运输合同纠纷案②中，占有提单的卖方（并非 FOB 提单上的托运人）既可以起诉合同承运人，也可以起诉实际承运人，无论哪一种承运人，他们的责任都是连带的、不可分割的。

三、关于贸易习惯是否改变提单责任的比较

鉴于提单在商贸活动中的重要性，任何贸易习惯都很难改变成文法或判例法中已经确立的提单原则。但最近，英国法曾经一度认为当地的贸易习惯可以改变提单的性质。例如，在 2022 年的 The Luna 案③中，法官认为，即使提单格式完整，也不具有物权凭证的功能。当地的贸易习惯改变了提单作为索赔依据的法律观点。但法院还认为，只有大量的贸易习惯做法才能达到这种效果。例如，在 Kum v. Wah Tat Bank Ltd 案④，在马来西亚东半部分沙捞越至新加坡运输橡胶，多达 90%～95% 的货物运输是不签发海运提单，仅凭借一份大副收据进行卸货的。而在回程航次新加坡至沙捞越段，默认这种习惯做法的情况仍多达 75%～80%。上议院判决这种贸易习惯可以使大副收据成为提单，但需要该单证的持有人（融资银行）举证才能成立，且不得和立法或单证中明示条款有矛盾。在 The Sormovskiy 3068 案⑤中，涉案承运人主张在俄罗斯维堡港的一贯做法是船长把货物卸下交给港口当局，导致船东失去对货物的控制而被提单持有人以无单放货为由进行索赔。在该案中，承运人辩称货物卸给 Commercial Sea Port（CSP）是当地港口的习惯做法，但法院认为承运人只是证明了该港有一个

---

① 《海商法》第四章第一节第四十二条：（一）"承运人"，是指本人或者委托他人以本人名义与托运人订立海上货物运输合同的人。（二）"实际承运人"，是指接受承运人委托，从事货物运输或者部分运输的人，包括接受转委托从事此项运输的其他人。
② 参见最高人民法院（2016）最高法民申 2284 号民事裁决书。
③ The Luna［2022］1 Lloyd's Rep. 216.
④ Kum v. Wah Tat Bank Ltd［1971］1 Lloyd's Rep. 439.
⑤ The Sormovskiy 3068［1994］2 Lloyd's Rep. 266.

宽松的做法，而这还不足以构成"贸易习惯"而使承运人免责。在英国法无数的案例中，除非承运人证明自己完全没有过错，否则很难逃避无单放货的赔偿责任。① 试图通过贸易惯例改变无单放货的索赔规则，虽然存在可能性，但举证责任非常繁重。

目前中国法律仍然对贸易惯例采取严格的审慎态度。例如，上海鼎衡船务有限责任公司与江苏舜天国际集团机械进出口有限公司海上、通海水域货物运输合同纠纷案②，上海君正船务有限公司与江苏舜天国际集团机械进出口有限公司海上、通海水域货物运输合同纠纷案③，上海中船重工万邦航运有限公司与江苏舜天国际集团机械进出口有限公司海上、通海水域货物运输合同纠纷案④，这三件案例都是江苏舜天国际集团机械进出口有限公司以无单放货为由起诉承运人，而承运人以江苏舜天国际集团机械进出口有限公司与收货人存在滚动式贸易账款结算为由，没有要求收货人出示正本提单就释放货物。对此，最高人民法院均裁定，在运输中无正本提单放货是行业交易习惯的主张，是没有事实和法律依据的，法院不予支持。由此可见，在英国法下，需要承担繁重的举证责任才能通过贸易惯例改变承运人无单放货的责任；而在中国法下，索赔人几乎不存在改变提单责任的可能。

四、关于港口规定是否改变提单责任的比较

很多国家为了提高货物清关效率、简化进口程序、加快货物流通，强制要求承运人只能向当地海关或者港口当局交付货物，再由收货人持正本提单向海关或者港口当局提取货物，如巴西、俄罗斯等。

2013年6月，我国商务部公平贸易局网站发布《关于巴西无正本提单提货的新规说明》，⑤ 提醒存在无单放货的风险。巴西财政部于2013年5月6日起执行1356号令，清关完毕后凭海关货物放行证明提货，进口商

---

① The Songa Winds（Songa Chemicals AS v. Navig 8 Chemical Pool Inc［2018］EWHC 397）；The Zagora［2017］1 Lloyd's Rep. 194；The Jag Ravi［2012］EWCA Civ 180；The Bremen Max［2009］1 Lloyd's Rep. 81；The Laemthong Glory［2005］1 Lloyd's Rep. 632.

② 参见最高人民法院（2020）最高法民申2549号民事裁定书。

③ 参见最高人民法院（2020）最高法民申2408号民事裁定书。

④ 参见最高人民法院（2020）最高法民申2397号民事裁定书。

⑤ 见http：//shangwutousu. mofcom. gov. cn/article/resume/dzgg/201306/20130600161823. shtml。

无须再出示正本提单就可以在某些未结汇的情况下提走货物。虽然巴西财政部海关管理司解释说所有的规定都是为了方便清关，不影响正常国际贸易的物权交割，但在实施新政过程中银行、出口企业、货代公司以及船代公司都面临政策不确定带来的风险，存在船东与进口商勾结或在货物报关时海关外贸系统被选择为绿色通道通关直接结关提货的可能。鉴于此项政令带来的无单放货危险，巴西海关重新引入过去曾经放弃的收货人需出示正本提单才能提货的要求，再次申明只有使用正本提单才能提货的规定。①

在巴西无单放货相关规定的背景下，我国最高人民法院曾经审理的案例中，3件承运人无法免除责任，2件承运人成功援引《无单放货司法解释》第七条，案件结果完全相反。笔者认为，虽然审议的时间不同，但性质基本相同，最高人民法院多数法官倾向于认为，在没有强制司法命令的情况下，承运人是无法援引《无单放货司法解释》第七条免除无单放货的责任的。由于我国法院判案很少援引早期的判例，主要以法律条文为依据进行判决，因此就个案而言，还是存在不确定性的，主要症结是对《无单放货司法解释》第七条没有一项权威的解读或理解。而在英国法律中，船长可以不用理会复杂的港口规定，只需坚持"见单交货"的基本原则即可，否则会面临无单放货的索赔。②

五、关于其他情况下无单放货法律责任的比较

无论是在中国法下还是在英国法下，在没有绝对有利证据的情况下，船东很难抗辩已取得转让提单的第三方，即使提单是伪造的或者货物交错对象，船东也很难逃避无单放货的赔偿责任。③ 在 The MSC Amsterdam 案④

---

① 参见三家著名的船东互保协会（Steamship Mutual, West of England, North of England & Standard）就此曾发布的巴西当地互保协会的通函，见 https://proinde.com.br/circulars/brazilian-customs-reintroduce-the-obligation-to-produce-the-original-bill-of-lading/。

② The Houda ［1994］2 Lloyd's Rep. 541：Delivery without production of the bill of lading constitutes a breach of contract even when made to the person entitled to possession（即使面临拥有货物占有权的人，无单放货就构成违约）.

③ Motis Exports v. Dampskibsselskabet AF 1912 ［1999］1 Lloyd's Rep. 837；［2000］1 Lloyd's Rep. 211.

④ Trafigura Beheer BV v. Mediterranean Shipping Co. SA（The MSC Amsterdam）［2007］EWHC 944（Comm），［2007］2 All E. R.（Comm）149 at［65］and［2007］EWCA Civ 794；［2007］2 Lloyd's Rep. 622.

中，骗子使用假提单骗取了承运人的提货单，然后将货物提走，法院仍然认为承运人应承担错误交付的赔偿责任。即使是使用电子密钥骗取的提单，承运人也无法免责。①

为了免除提单错误交付的责任。② 为了保护自己免于承担责任，船东不但要检查提单的真实性，还要查验提单背书的连续性。最近，最高人民法院在湖南华升工贸有限公司与长荣海运股份有限公司海上、通海水域货物运输合同纠纷案中作出澄清，承运人不但需要验证提单的真实性，还需要承担查验背书连续性担将来的无单放货责任，在合同没有明确规定的情况下，没有收到提单就可以拒绝交货。③ 因此，万一提单没有及时送达船上，船东最好是选择继续等待，直到提单持有人出示正本提单④或提供银行担保或法院作出命令⑤。

对于托运人而言，帮助收货人劝说承运人无单放货是极其不明智的行为。如果承运人接到托运人这样的指示，托运人就会因"禁止反言"原则而不能再以无单放货作为理由起诉承运人。

对于收货人而言，为了早日卸货，目前最好的办法是自己安排运输（贸易条款是 FOB）并在运输合同内加上可凭保函卸货的要求。如果没有这方面的合同要求，即使是 FOB 条款运输，承运人也可以不去遵守承租人无正本提单要求卸货或放货的指令。⑥

鉴于《海牙规则》或《海牙维斯比规则》以及我国《海商法》的一年索赔时效的紧迫性，货物利益方应尽早确定实际承担责任的承运人。在这一点上，中国法和英国法没有实质的差别。例如，普及国际货运代理（中国）有限公司与槟榔国际公司海上、通海水域货物运输合同纠纷案⑦。如果错过时效，不能在适格的地方向正确的被索赔方提起诉讼或仲裁，则受损失的一方很难再获得损失赔偿。即使事实证明存在明显的无单放货责任，也无法再提起诉讼，承运人也无须承担责任。2023 年 5 月，英国高等

---

① Glencore International AG v. MSC Mediterranean Shipping Co. SA（2015）EWHC 1989（Comm）.
② 参见最高人民法院（2020）最高法民申 6937 号民事裁定书。
③ Sze Hai Tong Bank Ltd v. Rambler Cycle Co. Ltd ［1959］2 Lloyd's Rep. 114.
④ Carlberg v. Wemyss（1915）SC 616：托运人和收货人联合要求船长将货物卸至岸上仓库并等待提单，但被船长拒绝。
⑤ The Houda ［1994］2 Lloyd's Rep. 541.
⑥ The Future Express ［1992］2 Lloyd's Rep. 79.
⑦ 参见最高人民法院（2019）最高法民再 117 号民事判决书。

法院在 FIM Bank PLC v. KCH Shipping Co. Ltd 案中就此问题进一步表明了货物利益方因错过时效而无法成功索赔无单放货的损失,从这一案例充分认识到时效对于无单放货责任索赔的重要性。①

总　　结

综上所述,虽然中、英法律都规定了无单放货的严格责任,但在面对不同的货物利益方以及在不同的贸易背景下,也有可能存在承运人可以免于承担无单放货责任的一些例外情况。本文分析了中国法和英国法下承运人在面临无单放货索赔时于不同合同背景下所承担的责任,有助于读者更深入地了解不同法律制度下承运人承担责任的差异性。

由于我国企业出口贸易大多选择 FOB 贸易条款,一旦面临提单收货人拒货、弃货,或者没有出示提单提货的情况,出口方除及时向收货人索赔外,还需要查核承运人是否有无单放货的过失、是否需要向承运人索赔无单放货的损失。当出现无单放货索赔时,出口方能够及时查明问题的起因,清楚了解自己的立场,迅速采取正确的措施,保护自己的权益。同时,承运人在面对无单放货索赔时,也需要查验对方的法律身份,了解对方的法律地位,确定自己承担的责任。

附表　最高人民法院2013年以来"无单放货"的案例

序号	案例号	案例名称	案例概况	案件结果
1	(2021)最高法民申7603号民事裁定书	德莎国际货运代理(深圳)有限公司与广东成虹照明科技有限公司海上、通海水域货物运输合同纠纷案	在巴西"绿色"清关后,放货给收货人	承运人提交的巴西法律的内容不足以证明其免责的主张

---

① *FIM Bank PLC v. KCH Shipping Co. Ltd*〔2023〕EWCA Civ. 569（24 May 2023）.

续附表

序号	案例号	案例名称	案例概况	案件结果
2	（2021）最高法民申6016号民事裁定书	中国福州外轮代理有限公司与厦门中艺抽纱进出口有限公司等海上、通海水域货物运输合同纠纷案	货物尚在福州海关监管之下，却将提货单交给非提单持有人提货	提单持有人丧失对货物控制权，应承担赔偿责任
3	（2020）最高法民申6937号民事裁定书	湖南华升工贸有限公司与长荣海运股份有限公司海上、通海水域货物运输合同纠纷案	托运人没有持有提单，但货物却在土耳其使用提单被提走，提单没有背书	法院以承运人没有核实提单连续背书为由，判决承运人错误交付货物
4	（2020）最高法民申6609号民事裁定书	宁波天盛海运有限公司与厦门中艺抽纱进出口有限公司等侵权责任纠纷案	卸货后未收回正本提单，货物已被案外人提取	即使承运人将货物卸到提单持有人选定的码头，也不能证明承运人完成了单证方面的交货任务
5	（2020）最高法民申5517号民事裁定书	青岛中孚英华国际贸易有限公司与上海平帆货运代理有限公司海上、通海水域货物运输合同纠纷案	被告无单放货，系因执行巴西法院裁决	司法扣押导致无单放货，承运人不承担赔偿责任
6	（2020）最高法民申2549号民事裁定书	上海鼎衡船务有限责任公司与江苏舜天国际集团机械进出口有限公司海上、通海水域货物运输合同纠纷案	试图以存在无正本提单放货的贸易习惯，否定提单的物权和持有人的货物所有权	有关近洋运输中无正本提单放货已成为行业交易习惯的主张，没有事实和法律依据，承运人须承担赔偿责任

续附表

序号	案例号	案例名称	案例概况	案件结果
7	（2020）最高法民申2546号民事裁定书	重庆太平洋国际物流有限公司与成都海岸进出口贸易有限公司海上、通海水域货运代理合同纠纷案	原告没有保留完整的提单证据	无法证明其在记名提单下货物的权利
8	（2020）最高法民申2408号民事裁定书	上海君正船务有限公司与江苏舜天国际集团机械进出口有限公司海上、通海水域货物运输合同纠纷案	承运人无正本提单放货造成提单持有人权利受损	近洋运输中无正本提单放货已成为行业交易习惯的主张，没有事实和法律依据，承运人须承担赔偿责任
9	（2020）最高法民申2397号民事裁定书	上海中船重工万邦航运有限公司与江苏舜天国际集团机械进出口有限公司海上、通海水域货物运输合同纠纷案	无正本提单放货	近洋运输中无正本提单放货已成为行业交易习惯的主张，没有事实和法律依据，法院不予支持
10	（2020）最高法民申377号民事裁定书	宋泯珈与嘉吉凡锐钢铁贸易（上海）有限公司（简称嘉吉凡锐）等信用证开证纠纷案	宋先生为世嘉公司提供无单放货担保，中行日照分行将提单质押权利转让给嘉吉凡锐	1.中行有权不先行选择申请执行法院抵押而优先选择第三方担保；2.处理国有资产受让质押权利符合规定
11	（2020）最高法民再214号民事判决书	宁波柯泰医疗器械有限公司与上海展宸国际货物运输代理有限公司（简称展宸）海上、通海水域货物运输合同纠纷案	FOB收货人没有支付全部货款，展宸以无船承运人名义签发了货代提单	法院判决以无船承运人名义签发的正本提单合法有效，可以认定存在海上货物通海水域运输合同关系，应当承担无单放货的责任

续附表

序号	案例号	案例名称	案例概况	案件结果
12	（2020）最高法民再172号民事判决书	温州佰利兰德橡胶轮胎有限公司与地中海航运有限公司等海上、通海水域货物运输合同纠纷案	根据巴西新规，进口货物清关完毕后，进口方可不凭正本提单提货	承运人没有完成举证责任，以证明依照卸货港所在地法律规定必须将承运到港的货物交付给当地海关或者港口当局
13	（2019）最高法民申6813号民事裁定书	中国矿产有限责任公司与福州松下码头有限公司（简称松下码头）港口作业纠纷案	松下码头对案涉货物系依约合法占有而非不法占有	松下码头按照仓储合同不承担买卖合同的义务
14	（2019）最高法民申5580号民事裁定书	浙商中拓集团股份有限公司（简称中拓公司）与天津港第四港埠有限公司仓储合同纠纷案	涉案货物因中拓公司拖欠港口费被留置，且已被法院拍卖	买卖合同下的违约与仓储合同无关
15	（2019）最高法民申4943号民事裁定书	深圳市巡洋国际物流有限公司与地中海航运有限公司海上、通海水域货物运输合同纠纷案	货物在巴西清关后被收货人提走	法院裁决适用《无单放货司法解释》第七条。（结果有待商榷）
16	（2019）最高法民申4904号民事裁定书	唐山市秦皇贸易有限公司（简称秦皇贸易公司）与IFL国际货运公司（简称IFL公司）海上、通海水域货物运输合同纠纷案	该提单作为双方存在海上货物运输合同关系的证明，并未明确承运人IFL公司具有整箱交货的合同义务	1. 秦皇贸易公司未成功举证IFL公司拆箱违反常规交货模式，不构成无单放货的初步证据；2. IFL公司证明涉案货物仍仓储在仓库内，无单放货指控不成立

续附表

序号	案例号	案例名称	案例概况	案件结果
17	（2019）最高法民申3189号民事裁定书	深圳柏域斯浩航国际货运代理有限公司与商船三井株式会社海上、通海水域货物运输合同纠纷案	承运人将货物运至巴西码头，未收回正本提单就解开巴西海关系统的电子锁，导致货物灭失	承运人成功援引《无单放货司法解释》第七条。（结果有待商榷）
18	（2019）最高法民申3119号民事裁定书	中铁物总进出口有限公司（简称中铁）与福州松下码头有限公司港口作业纠纷案	松下码头只接收仓储委托的指令进行放货，中铁应基于合同的相对性，不应向存储保管人提出无单放货的索赔	中铁持有提货单之事实，不能赋予其获得优于松下码头基于合同对涉案货物合法占有的权利，当然亦无法消灭松下码头应负有的仓储合同义务
19	（2019）最高法民再117号民事判决书	普及国际货运代理（中国）有限公司（简称普及公司）与槟榔国际公司（简称槟榔公司）海上、通海水域货物运输合同纠纷案	槟榔公司采购一批夹式烤箱，FOB委托普及公司从宁波运往以色列。因普及公司目的港代理破产导致涉案货物下落不明	最高人民法院对宁波海事法院一审中认为"普及宁波分公司是普及公司的分支机构，没有证据显示普及宁波分公司是运输合同当事方，也没有证据证明普及宁波分公司实施了无单放货的行为，所以普及宁波分公司在本案中与槟榔公司无任何法律关系"。该案以超过一年时效而失败

213

续附表

序号	案例号	案例名称	案例概况	案件结果
20	（2018）最高法民申3347号民事裁定书	力高国际企业集团有限公司与中进物流（深圳）有限公司（简称中进深圳）海上、通海水域货物运输合同纠纷案	货物抵达巴西目的港后查询无果	1.中进深圳作为独立法人，其上级公司无需承担连带合同责任；2.货物下落不明或已经灭失的主张举证不足，无法支持无单放货的诉讼请求
21	（2018）最高法民再230号民事判决书	中国铁路物资厦门钢铁有限公司（简称中铁公司）与宁德市港务集团有限公司（简称宁德港务集团）仓储合同纠纷案	中铁公司与宁德港务集团签订仓储保管合同	不能免除宁德港务集团无单放货的违约责任
22	（2017）最高法民终863号民事判决书	上海旭中仓储有限公司（简称旭中公司）与诚通集团南方金属有限公司财产损害赔偿纠纷案	旭中公司没有按照仓储协议凭发货单放货	仓储合同中提货方式的变更需要书面确认，没有充分证明改变了仓储规定的提货方式
23	（2017）最高法民再412号民事判决书	A.P.穆勒－马士基有限公司（简称马士基）与浙江隆达不锈钢有限公司海上、通海水域货物运输合同纠纷案	再次申请退运时，马士基告知涉案货物已被斯里兰卡海关拍卖	在卸货港长达8个月的时间里托运人没有采取措施处理涉案货导致被海关拍卖，不符合无单放货的索赔

续附表

序号	案例号	案例名称	案例概况	案件结果
24	（2016）最高法民申 3238 号民事裁定书	深圳亚航国际货运代理有限公司与上海富家家具有限公司海上、通海水域货物运输合同纠纷案	承运人将货物交给巴西港口海关或场站人员后，收货人没有出示正本提单提走	无证据证明巴西海关新规定可以免除承运人无单放货的赔偿责任
25	（2016）最高法民申 2284 号民事裁定书	泛太集运有限公司与咸宁市汇美达工贸有限公司（简称汇美达公司）海上、通海水域货物运输合同纠纷案	承运人将货物交给收货人，未收回正本提单	汇美达公司作为实际托运人有权向承运人代理人要求交付提单，并有权依据海上货物运输合同向承运人索赔无单放货导致的货款损失
26	（2016）最高法民再 35 号民事判决书	康立信（亚洲）有限公司［Connexions（Asia）Limited］与深圳市翊达运通国际货运代理有限公司（简称翊达公司）、韩进海运株式会社（简称韩进公司）海上、通海水域货物运输合同纠纷案	翊达公司和实际承运人韩进公司在未收回正本提单的情况下将货物放行	承运人赔偿扣除预付款后的 FOB 离岸价。（货代往往把海运提单的托运人改为自己，需特别警惕）
27	（2016）最高法民申 12 号民事裁定书	轩辉国际物流有限公司（简称轩辉公司）与智利南美轮船有限公司（简称南美公司）海上、通海水域货物运输合同纠纷案	轩辉公司没有举证其与收货人之间的贸易合同关系和正常交易	轩辉公司不能举证其因南美公司无单放货遭受相应货款损失，损失赔偿请求失败

续附表

序号	案例号	案例名称	案例概况	案件结果
28	（2015）民申字第3479号民事裁定书	中国人民财产保险股份有限公司上海市分公司（简称上海人保）与自然环保集团（私人）有限公司海上保险合同纠纷案	货物被船东留置，后来船舶被拆解，导致货物灭失	上海人保没有提供证据证明货物灭失是由被保险人自身原因造成的，故败诉
29	（2015）民申字第998号民事裁定书	永辉滨江港建设（南京）有限公司（简称永辉）与青岛建发物资有限公司委托合同纠纷案	本案是欠款担保，主张采购合同实为借贷导致基础合同无效	因永辉在明知欠款，还承诺提供保证，在出具保函时就认为已经认可该欠款关系的真实性，事后提出基础合同无效，法院不予支持
30	（2014）民申字第1226号民事裁定书	旗锋货运（中国）有限公司与宁波际翔进出口有限公司（简称际翔公司）、旗锋国际货运（上海）有限公司宁波分公司海上、通海水域货物运输合同纠纷案	承运人称际翔公司收到的7笔货款，又称金额不足是因为部分货物做了退运处理，但仅提供了1份提单	际翔公司就案外三票货运指示旗锋公司进行电放操作，应对提单持有人际翔公司由此遭受的损失承担赔偿责任，托运人同意电放与是否收到货款并无必然联系
31	（2014）民申字第446号民事裁定书	海捷耐国际货物运输代理有限公司；JIF物流有限公司与无锡新中润国际集团中润有限公司（简称中润）海上货物运输合同纠纷案	中润因信用证拒付仍持有正本提单。后来回运发现短少，JIF物流有限公司愿意就回运费用作出抵扣	货物短少并不能充分证明涉案货物已经被无单交付，无单放货索赔失败

216

续附表

序号	案例号	案例名称	案例概况	案件结果
32	（2013）民申字第2122号民事裁定书	浙江天海纸业有限公司与浙江中外运有限公司海上货物运输合同纠纷案	浙江中外运有限公司是案外人，代理承运人奥柏公司委托签发提单	浙江中外运有限公司仅是货物运输的代理人，不应承担无单放货的责任
33	（2013）民申字第2120号民事裁定书	SCANWELL CONTAINER LINE LIMITED与宁波利登休闲用品有限公司（简称利登公司）、中航狮威国际货运代理有限公司宁波分公司海上货物运输合同纠纷案	承运人对涉案货物的价值和利登公司是否收回涉案货物价款提出质疑	承运人承担利登公司收回涉案货款的举证责任，否则应当承担举证不能的不利后果，承运人举证失败
34	（2013）民提字第243号民事裁定书	吉林新元木业有限公司与欧航（上海）国际货运代理有限公司海上、通海水域货物运输合同纠纷案	欧航从大连港运输木板到鹿特丹港，货物被无单放货	欧航（香港）国际物流有限公司作为承运人，大连是提单签发地、运输合同起运港，大连海事法院拥有管辖权
35	（2006）大海商初字第385号民事判决书	深圳市璟翰实业有限公司与利通物流有限公司海上货物运输合同纠纷案	从国内运输庭院装饰用品到美国，货物在目的港被无单放货	原告作为非提单列明的托运人在证明其合法持有提单的条件下可以享有向承运人索赔的权利

专题三　湾区法评

船舶登记制度改革视野下粤港澳大湾区船舶登记和配套制度规则衔接研究

徐锦堂　谢雯雯　李少璞*

摘要：我国长期以来在全国范围内实行严格的船舶登记制度，对航运企业而言存在运营税费过多、注册手续繁杂、停航损失巨大，在船东条件、船员聘用等方面限制过多，以及船检机构选择单一、融资难、保险贵等问题，这使得大量中资船舶到境外登记。在全面深化改革开放、建设粤港澳大湾区和自由贸易试验区的新时代，我国进行了特案免税登记、保税登记和国际船舶登记制度改革，取得了一定的成效。在广东自由贸易试验区对国际船舶登记及配套制度持续进行系统性制度创新，促进粤港澳大湾区船舶登记和配套制度规则衔接，进一步减税降费，放宽登记限制条件，实现所需材料精减化、标准化、电子化，实现登记不停航，加快放开船舶检验市场，打造优质高效的船旗国监管系统，加大航运服务人才培养培训等举措，可推动粤港澳大湾区国际登记船舶在湾区内从事货物运输及沿海捎带业务，建立并完善一套有全球竞争力的国际船舶登记制度和服务体系。

关键词：粤港澳大湾区　自由贸易试验区　船舶登记　规则衔接

---

* 徐锦堂：华南师范大学法学院副教授，国际航运法律与政策研究中心主任，广东省法学会航运法学研究会副会长兼秘书长。谢雯雯：广东华侨友谊有限公司业务主管，华南师范大学法学硕士。李少璞：华南师范大学2021级海商法硕士，大连海事大学2024级海商法博士研究生。

The Regulatory Alignment of Ship Registration and Supporting System in the Guangdong-Hong Kong-Macao Greater Bay Area from the Perspective of the Reform of China's Ship Registration System

Xu Jintang, Xie Wenwen, Li Shaopu

Abstract: China has long implemented a strict ship registration system nationwide. For shipping enterprises, such a registration system makes many disadvantages, such as excessive operating taxes, complex registration procedures, huge suspension losses, excessive restrictions on ship owner conditions and crew employment, as well as a single choice of ship inspection agencies, difficult financing, and expensive insurance. This has led to a large number of Chinese funded ships registering overseas. In the new era of comprehensively deepening reform and opening up, and building the Guangdong-Hong Kong-Macao Greater Bay Area and the Pilot Free Trade Experimental Zone, China has carried out the reform of special tax exemption registration, bonded registration and international ship registration systems, and has achieved certain results, but not ideal. Continuously innovating the international ship registration and supporting systems in the Greater Bay Area Pilot Free Trade Zone, promoting the connection of ship registration rules and mechanisms in the Greater Bay Area, further reducing taxes and fees, relaxing registration restrictions, achieving the refinement, standardization, and electrification of required materials, achieving non-stop registration, and accelerating the opening up of the ship inspection market, building a flag state regulatory system that balances the rapid development of the industry with maintaining effective regulation, increasing the training of shipping service talents, and other measures to promote the international registration of ships in the Guangdong-Hong Kong-Macao Greater Bay Area to engage in cargo transportation and coastal carrying business within the Guangdong-Hong Kong-Macao Greater Bay Area, and establishing and improving a globally competitive international ship registration system and service system in the Greater Bay Area.

Key words: Guangdong-Hong Kong-Macao Greater Bay Area; Pilot Free

Trade Zone；ship registration；regulatory alignment

任何一艘船舶在建造或者购买之后，船舶所有人，即船东，必须向一个国家的政府主管机关进行登记，取得登记国的国籍，悬挂登记国的国旗，并以登记国的某一个港口作为船籍港。现阶段，我国在全国范围内实行的是船舶严格登记制度，其主要规则与世界上大多数严格登记国家相似，对船舶所有人的国籍、船舶资产中本国资本所占比例、船员聘用、船舶检验以及航运税收等方面都有严格的要求。

一、我国船舶国籍登记制度体系下中资船舶大量注册于境外

全球著名的航运咨询机构克拉克森的调查结果显示，2023年全球航运企业拥有的商船总吨位约15.67亿吨，其中70%以上的船舶注册外国国籍；同年，我国航运企业拥有商船总吨位达2.492亿吨，超过希腊的2.49亿吨，全球市场份额占比为15.9%，成为世界上最大的"船东国"。不过，国籍登记在国内的船舶总吨位约为8000万吨，约占中资船舶总吨位的32%。这意味着2023年中资船舶国籍登记于境外的比例为68%，这一数字高于2015年的62%[①]。

大量中资船舶到境外注册，一方面是船舶在国内登记存在税费过多、手续繁杂、条件过严、可选船检机构单一等问题；另一方面，由于国内"贷款难""贷款贵"，船东，特别是民营船东，大多从境外通过融资租赁、抵押贷款等途径融资造船，而境外资方一般都会要求船舶登记于境外并选择境外船级社检验以降低成本，因此大量中资船舶，特别是大船新船登记于境外。这使得国内船队规模减小、船舶状况下降，不利于航运安全、环境保护和航运管理水平的提高，同时间接导致税收和就业岗位流失，在特殊时期也将不利于船舶作为战略资源进行调动。尽管多年来我国在船舶登记条件和手续、税费、融资、船检等方面已经有所改善，但整体而言船舶国内登记对航运企业仍然缺乏吸引力。

---

① 据交通运输部数据，截至2015年年底，我国航运企业海运控制运力为2.03亿载重吨，其中登记于境外的约占62%。

（一）船运税费名目多、税率高、无封顶

船运税费名目多、标准高是制约中资船舶国内登记的最大因素。在我国登记的船舶需缴纳的直接和间接税费包括关税、增值税、企业所得税、个人所得税、船舶吨税、车船税、城建税、教育附加费、印花税等。我国现行的税收政策实际上加剧了中资国际航行船舶的境外登记形势。①

在关税方面，我国仍然采取"进口征税、出口退税"的鼓励出口的关税政策，船舶进出口也是如此。国内造船企业出口船舶享有17%的退税率，航运企业进口船舶则要分别缴纳9%的进口关税和17%的进口环节增值税，合计占到船舶造价的27.5%。在船舶越来越大、价值越来越高以至通常数以亿元计的情况下，中资航运企业出于利润最大化的考虑大量采取"境内造船、境外登记"的避税做法，而缺乏"境外船舶、境内登记"的内在动力。我国香港地区是自由港，船舶进出口均无须缴纳关税。仅此一项优惠，航运企业即可节约千万计的成本。

在企业税收方面，我国内地航运业企业所得税税率为25%、增值税税率为9%，另有车船税②等多种税费。而我国香港地区没有增值税等流转税，企业所得税的标准税率为16.5%，盈利在200万港币以下的减半征收，而且香港实行属地征税原则，对香港注册船舶从事国际运营所得的利润可豁免利得税。我国澳门地区的公司所得税标准税率为12%。

在船员个人所得税方面，考虑到船员的职业风险性、工作艰苦性，每年有8个多月时间在海上漂泊，③工作生活在狭小封闭颠簸的船舱里，远离陆地和亲人，更加重要的是，船员在船期间不占用公共资源，是唯一一个由国际劳工组织制定强制性国际劳动标准的职业群体，所以多数航海国家对本国船员个人所得税实行减免优惠政策，如新加坡、菲律宾、瑞典等

---

① 参见常富治、王婕丽、俞勤伟《中国洋山港：船舶登记制度的创新》，载《中国海事》2012年第3期，第38页。

② 车船税属于财产税，根据2011年修正的《中华人民共和国车船税法》及其《实施条例》，在我国境内的船舶应当缴纳车船税。机动船舶的税率为：（1）净吨位小于或者等于200吨的，每吨3元；（2）净吨位201～2000吨的，每吨4元；（3）净吨位2001～10000吨的，每吨5元；（4）净吨位10001吨及以上的，每吨6元。按照规定缴纳船舶吨税的机动船舶，自车船税法实施之日起5年内免征车船税。

③ 根据中国海员建设工会此前的一项《船员劳动关系现状》调查结果，中国海员平均在船时间为8.7个月。

国家完全免征船员个人所得税。英国和我国香港地区也规定在国际航行船舶服役超过半年,船员个人所得税予以免征。长期以来,我国对船员工作的特殊性缺乏足够的认识和重视,船员一直按《中华人民共和国个人所得税法》的普通标准计算缴纳个人所得税,唯一的优惠是2006年规定海员个人所得税起征点为每月4800元,高于普通公民的个税起征点每月1600元;此后普通公民个税起征点逐步提至每年60000元(每月5000元),不过海员个税起征点一直没有调整。① 事实上,我国海员收入相对于陆地工作已无性价比,海员"弃海登陆"现象明显。直到2019年国家财政部、税务总局发布《关于远洋船员个人所得税政策的公告》,规定一个纳税年度内在船航行时间累计满183天的远洋船员,其取得的工资薪金收入减按50%缴纳个人所得税。该个税新政有助于提高远洋船员,特别是高级船员的实际收入,激励远洋船员海上工作的积极性。

在船舶吨税②方面,我国实行以净吨分段模式的计算标准收取船舶吨税,税率高且上不封顶,净吨数越大、税率就越高,如表1所示。我国香港地区也按净吨分段模式收取船舶吨位年费,但收费标准低且有封顶价格,船舶净吨位低于或者等于1000吨的,收费标准为1500港元;船舶净吨位在1000吨到15000吨之间的部分,收费标准为每净吨3.5港元;船舶净吨大于15000吨的部分,收费标准为每净吨3港元,且设有77500港元的最高上限。而且香港海事处自2006年2月1日起实施香港注册船舶吨位年费减免计划。根据该计划,香港注册船舶如持续在香港注册两年,并在该两年内从未有在港口国监督(PSC)③制度下的滞留记录,且于过去一年全额缴付吨位年费,即可在随后一年减免吨位年费6个月。这种"奖优"的政策激励机制势必鼓励船东加强船舶安全管理。

---

① 2006年1月1日,普通公民个税起征点为1600元时,船员的起征点调整为4800元。在2008年普通公民个税起征点调整为2000元,2011年普通公民个人所得税起征点提高到3500元,2018年个税起征点提高至每年6万元(每月5000元)。

② 船舶吨税,早期被称为灯塔税,属于公共资源利用税。自中国境外港口进入境内港口的船舶应当缴纳吨税,中国籍的应税船舶,以及船籍国(地区)与中国签订含有相互给予船舶税费最惠国待遇条款的条约或者协定的应税船舶适用优惠税率。2017年全国人民代表大会常务委员会制定的《中华人民共和国船舶吨税法》是对2011年国务院公布的《中华人民共和国船舶吨税暂行条例》主要内容的平移上升,没有对原有规定进行大的调整。

③ 港口国监督(Port State Control)是各国政府依据国际公约对抵达本国港口的外国籍船舶实施安全检查、消除安全隐患、维护水上交通安全的重要措施。

表 1　我国内地船舶吨税科目税率（按年计算）

税目	普通税率（元/净吨）	优惠税率（元/净吨）
不超过 2000 净吨	12.6	9.0
超过 2000 净吨，但不超过 10000 净吨	24.0	17.4
超过 10000 净吨，但不超过 50000 净吨	27.6	19.8
超过 50000 净吨	31.6	22.8

除了税收外，我国在船舶登记费用方面也存在收费项目多、标准高的问题。在船舶所有权登记方面，我国内地船舶以 200 元为基数（未满 50 净吨的，以 100 元为基数），每增加 1 净吨加收 1 元，超过 1 万吨，减半收取。① 我国香港地区则以 500 吨为分界线，不超过 500 吨为 3500 港币，超过 500 吨为 15000 港币。② 据计算，在净吨位小于 13502 吨时，船舶登记为五星红旗费用较少；当净吨位大于 13502 吨时，船舶登记为香港特别行政区区旗费用较少。整体而言，内地对小企小船更加友好，而香港特别行政区对大企大船更加友好，这也是在我国航运企业愿意将大船新船登记于香港地区的重要原因之一。

（二）注册手续繁杂、停航损失大

根据我国 2014 年《中华人民共和国船舶登记条例》（简称《船舶登记条例》）规定，航行国际航线船舶的所有人申请船舶国籍，除应当交验船舶所有权登记证书外，还需要交验多达 10 余项的文件证书，且还有内容并不明确的"其他有关证书"，导致相关文件要求不周全、标准不清晰，缺乏透明度和可预见性。而《中华人民共和国船舶登记办法》（简称《船舶登记办法》）规定的办理时限为 7 个工作日，即在相关资料齐备、一切顺

---

① 为进一步减轻企业特别是小微企业负担，2014 年财政部发布《关于取消、停征和免征一批行政事业性收费的通知》，对 100 总吨以下内河船和 500 总吨以下海船予以免收船舶登记费。

② 参见陈景斌、张婕妹《中国、香港、新加坡船舶登记注册环境比较》，载《水运管理》2013 年第 8 期，第 8 页。

利的情况下,办理时间为 7 个工作日。倘若出现部门之间沟通不畅、证书材料难以提供的情况,船舶登记时间就难以预控。2011 年,经交通运输部批准我国成立了新的船籍港中国洋山港,并规定只要符合条件,就可以申请洋山港保税船舶一站式登记。然而第一艘洋山港籍船舶"冠海朝阳"轮的登记就让这一新的尝试受挫。该轮在 2011 年 6 月 27 日申请保税登记,具体流程花了差不多半个月,且卡在了提供"国际性运输船舶备案证明书"这一"其他有关证书"上,最后"冠海朝阳"轮耗时 5 个多月才完成全部手续。①

此外,船舶为了登记必须提交运营必备的证书供主管机关审核,由于缺乏运营必备的证书,因此船舶在登记期间必然停航,而停航期间又会给航运企业带来巨大的运营损失和港口费用。这使得在"冠海朝阳"轮后的很长时间里,几乎没有船舶选择在洋山港进行保税登记,材料要求非标准化、缺乏可预见性、手续繁杂让很多船东望而却步。

香港特别行政区通过《香港船舶注册用户须知》对船舶注册所需文件和主要流程进行规定。所需证书类文件仅有 4 项,其他文件如申请书、声明和授权表格由船东自己制作,船东和代表人的身份证明也容易提供且仅需提供副本,并不影响相关人士出差办公,更加重要的是没有不可预见的"其他证书"要求,如表 2 所示。此外,为了配合船舶实际运营,提高船舶注册效率,香港海事处注册和注销注册一般进行形式审查,均可以在两个小时以内完成。其人性化之处还体现在香港海事处下设船舶事务科并且安排专员,有需要的人员可以在任意时间拨打紧急技术支持的热线电话,以此方式高效地为船东办理注册手续提供支持,最大限度地减少因时差导致的船舶注册服务空档。

---

① 参见邢丹《中国船舶登记制度之变》,载《中国船检》2013 年第 11 期,第 22 页。

表2　我国内地和香港特别行政区船东登记船舶所需文件对比

序号	我国内地船东登记船舶所需证书	香港特别行政区船东注册船舶所需文件
1	船舶所有权登记证书	所有权文件 （A）建造证明书（新建船适用） （B）卖契（买卖船适用） （C）法院命令（拍卖船适用） （D）所有权证明书（适用于转旗而没有改变所有权的船舶）
2	注销原国籍证明书（转籍时适用）	注销证据（转籍时适用）
3	国际吨位丈量证书	标记证明书或声明书
4	国际船舶载重线证书	验船证明书（COS）
5	货船构造安全证书	船舶注册申请书； 由船东作出之拥有权声明； 授权表格（适用于公司授权公司董事或公司秘书以外的人士签署申请书及声明书用）； 船东的身份证明文件（核实副本）； 代表人的身份证明文件（核实副本）
6	货船设备安全证书	—
7	货船无线电报安全证书	—
8	国际防止油污证书	—
9	船舶航行安全证书	—
10	其他有关技术证书	

（三）船东、船龄、船员方面限制条件过多

在船舶登记条件方面，香港特别行政区在船东、船员和船龄等方面都没有限制性规定和僵化性要求。在船东的条件方面，按照我国2014年修订的《船舶登记条例》第二条规定，主要有下列三类船东拥有或光船租赁的船舶可以在中国登记国籍：一是在境内有住所或者主要经营场所的中国公

民；二是主要经营场所在境内且中方投资额不低于50%的中国企业法人；三是中国政府部门和事业单位。也就是说，外国人、住所位于境外的中国公民、主要经营场所位于境外的中国企业法人，以及主要经营场所位于境内但属于非法人组织或者外方投资高于50%的中国企业法人，其拥有或光船租赁的船舶在中国内地无法登记。这样就自我限制了可在中国登记船舶的范围。2016年底交通运输部《船舶登记办法》稍稍放宽了可登记船舶的范围，包括外商出资额超过50%的中国企业法人仅供本企业内部生产使用，不从事水路运输经营的趸船、浮船坞，以及在自由贸易试验区注册的企业法人所有或者光船租赁的船舶。但这不能从根本上改变我国船舶国籍登记船东条件较为严格、不够开放的局面。

在香港特别行政区完成船舶注册只需两个积极条件，一是该船舶的过半数权益由一名或超过一名"合资格的人"拥有，或者该船舶由一个身为"合资格的人"的法人团体在光船租赁（转管租约）下经营；二是该船舶有船东或光船承租人委任的代表人。① 香港居民、香港法人和非香港公司均可为"合资格的人"，可见香港特别行政区并未限定船舶为本地船东所有，对本地船东的资金来源和股权比例也没有限制。

在船龄要求方面，香港特别行政区在船舶安全的前提下，没有船舶到达相应船龄即强制报废的制度。我国交通运输部《老旧运输船舶管理规定》第六条则明确"国家对已达到强制报废船龄的运输船舶实施强制报废制度"，拥有中国国籍的不同类型的船舶在达到相应的船龄之后必须强制报废。② 这种僵化的规定会造成两种不利的情况：一是没有达到报废船龄

---

① 香港特别行政区《商船（注册）条例》第十一（四）条：合资格的人是（a）持有有效身分证并通常居于香港的个别人士；或（b）在香港成立的法人团体；或（c）根据香港《公司条例》第XI部注册的非香港公司。非香港公司（Non-Hong Kong Company）是指在香港以外地区成立，并在香港设立营业地点的公司。非香港公司可以开户、年检、审计，也可以缴纳社保，但在香港不具备独立的法人资质，其财务和责任由总公司承担。非香港公司实为香港分公司。香港特别行政区《商船（注册）条例》第六十八条：代表人是船东或转管租约承租人委任的船舶注册期间的代表人，该代表人须是（a）合资格的人，并须是该船舶的船东或部分船东；或（b）法人团体，须在香港成立并从事船舶管理业务或作为船舶代理人。

② 交通运输部2021年修改的《老旧运输船舶管理规定》规定了不同海船的强制报废船龄分为：一类船舶，特别定期检验船舶18年以上，强制报废船龄25年以上；二类船舶，特别定期检验船舶24年以上，强制报废船龄30年以上；三类船舶，特别定期检验船舶26年以上，强制报废船龄31年以上；四类船舶，特别定期检验船舶28年以上，强制报废船龄33年以上；五类船舶，特别定期检验船舶29年以上，强制报废船龄34年以上。

的船因为忽视保养维护而存在安全方面的漏洞；二是对于保养维护较好但达到了强制报废船龄的船舶，假如此情况下报废则引发资源的浪费。而这种到龄强制报废的僵硬规定不利于鼓励船东对船舶进行日常的保养和维护。亚太地区港口国监督备忘录组织（T-MOU）发布的《2019年亚太地区港口国监督报告》指出：最常见的导致船舶滞留的10大缺陷中最多的就是维护保养方面的体系缺陷。

在船员聘用方面，香港特别行政区对于注册船舶聘用船员并没有国籍方面的限制，企业享有高度的用工自主权；内地则长期要求中国籍船舶必须全部使用中国籍船员，如聘用外籍船员需交通运输部审批。直到2014年《船舶登记条例》修订时才删除相关条款。① 不过，中国籍船舶上应持适任证书的外籍船员，仍然必须持有我国相应的适任证书。

（四）船检机构选择单一

在船检机构的选择方面，无论是法定检验还是入级检验，中国籍船舶只能选择中国的国内船检机构和中国船级社（CCS），特别是中国籍从事国际航行船舶的入级检验必须向中国船级社申请。中国船级社成为我国唯一办理船舶入级业务的国家船舶检验机构。② 这就决定了一方面国内船东缺乏选择检验机构的自主权和灵活性；另一方面，国内船东从国外购买的二手船移籍国内时，还将面临着必须转换船级社造成的巨大的船期损失。

当然，随着自由贸易试验区建设的推进，我国逐步放开在自由贸易试验区登记的中国籍国际航行船舶的入级检验和法定检验。2016年交通运输部《船舶检验管理规定》第六条允许外国验船公司经交通运输部海事局认可，对自由贸易试验区登记的中国籍国际航行船舶实施入级检验。2021年国务院印发《关于推进自由贸易试验区贸易投资便利化改革创新的若干措施》，要

---

① 1994年《船舶登记条例》第七条：中国籍船舶上的船员应当由中国公民担任；确需雇用外国籍船员的，应当报国务院交通主管部门批准。中国籍船舶上应持适任证书的船员，必须持有相应的中华人民共和国船员适任证书。

② 2019年《中华人民共和国船舶和海上设施检验条例》第七条：中国籍船舶的所有人或者经营人，必须向船舶检验机构申请下列检验：（一）建造或者改建船舶时，申请建造检验；（二）营运中的船舶，申请定期检验；（三）由外国籍船舶改为中国籍船舶的，申请初次检验。第十三条：下列中国籍船舶，必须向中国船级社申请入级检验：（一）从事国际航行的船舶；（二）在海上航行的乘客定额一百人以上的客船；（三）载重量一千吨以上的油船；（四）滚装船、液化气体运输船和散装化学品运输船；（五）船舶所有人或者经营人要求入级的其他船舶。

求开放国际登记船舶的法定检验，允许依法获批的外国船舶检验机构对自由贸易试验区国际登记船舶开展法定检验，但落实该措施的进度较慢。①

二、我国船舶国籍登记制度改革进程及其效果

在我国国内登记的船舶享有法律赋予的"沿海运输权"，原则上只有悬挂中国国旗的船舶才能经营中国港口之间的海上运输。② 正如本文前述，我国与船舶国籍登记相关的税费负担、限制条件、登记手续等方面严格、僵化的规定在全面深化改革开放、建设粤港澳大湾区和自由贸易试验区的新时代均有较大程度的改善。但是，由于相关政策改革开放的不全面性和不彻底性，相关制约因素并没有得到根本解决，中资船舶回籍国内虽然取得一定效果，但远未达到预期。下面对我国船舶国籍登记制度改革的进程进行全面系统的梳理和分析。

（一）特案免税登记政策

为扩大国轮船队的规模、鼓励中资外籍国际航运船舶转为中国国籍，根据国务院批准的中资国际航运船舶特案免税政策和财政部确定的有关实施方案，我国交通运输部于 2007 年 6 月发布《关于实施中资国际航运船舶特案免税登记政策的公告》（简称《公告》），该政策又分别在 2009 年、2011 年两次延长实施期限，直至 2015 年 12 月 31 日。2016 年，国务院再次批准调整完善中资"方便旗"船税收优惠政策，对 2012 年 12 月 31 日前已在境外办理船舶登记手续悬挂"方便旗"的中资船舶，在 2016 年 9 月 1 日至 2019 年 9 月 1 日期间报关进口的，继续免征关税和进口环节增值税。

根据特案免税登记政策，在规定的优惠期间内报关进口、办理船舶登

---

① 2019 年 6 月，中国海事局发布《关于放开自由贸易试验区国际登记船舶入级检验有关事项的公告》，相关政策落地。2020 年 6 月，中国海事局与法国海事部门签订对等开放协议，以试点方式推动国际登记船舶法定检验相关工作。

② 《中华人民共和国海商法》第四条："中华人民共和国港口之间的海上运输和拖航，由悬挂中华人民共和国国旗的船舶经营。但是，法律、行政法规另有规定的除外。非经国务院交通主管部门批准，外国籍船舶不得经营中华人民共和国港口之间的海上运输和拖航。"通过限制外国承运人和外籍船舶进入本国航运市场的方式来保障本国承运人利益，促进本国航运业发展，是美国、欧盟、加拿大、日本、韩国、印度等国家和地区的共同选择。2022 年我国完成水路营业性货运量 85.54 亿吨，其中内河货运量 44.02 亿吨，沿海运输货运量 32.33 亿吨，远洋货运量 9.18 亿吨，权重比为 51∶38∶11。

记的中资外籍船舶，符合《公告》规定的境外登记时间和船型船龄条件，[①]选择上海、大连、天津为船籍港（后扩大为"具有国际航行船舶登记权限的任一船籍港"），向当地海事局申请办理船舶登记手续，可以免征进口关税和进口环节增值税。特案免税登记船舶原则上应继续从事国际航运，经交通运输部批准方可从事国内航运。

尽管在该政策体系下船舶回籍能够享受免除进口关税和进口环节增值税的优惠，而且当地政府还会对航运企业给予不菲的财政补助，[②] 但是，不论从吸引外籍船舶的数量规模上，还是从对我国航运业的长远影响看，特案免税登记政策均未能达到期待的效果。[③] 一是特案免税登记政策的目的是吸引中方出资比例不低于50%的外籍国际航行船舶回归中国国籍，而且仅限于一定船型、船龄的船舶，其他类型的船舶被排除在外，适用面狭窄；二是申请材料要求多、不完全透明，审批办理流程慢，全部办妥通常需要6个月的时间，停航损失大；三是政策着力解决船舶登记中的进口税负问题，没有其他方面的配套改革，不足以抵消船舶回国登记后在运营、融资、投保等方面增加的成本。

（二）船舶保税登记政策

2011年12月，我国交通运输部海事局下发《关于同意上海海事局在洋山保税港区开展船舶登记工作的批复》，"中国洋山港"成为我国一个新的船籍港，对注册在洋山保税港区从事国际航运业务的企业开展退税或保税船舶登记业务。根据相关政策规定，可申请洋山港保税船舶登记的船舶，需要满足以下三个条件：一是由在港区内注册的企业所有或者由其从

[①] 《公告》规定的条件：（一）在2005年12月31日前已经在境外登记；（二）船龄范围：1. 船龄在4～12年的油船（包括沥青船）、散装化学品船等；2. 船龄在6～18年的散货船、矿砂船等；3. 船龄在9～20年的集装箱船、杂货船、多用途船、散装水泥船等。

[②] 2019年深圳市前海管理局《前海深港现代服务业合作区高端航运服务业专项扶持资金实施细则》规定，对登记为"中国深圳""中国前海"船籍港的国际船舶，给予最高70元/总吨的补贴，扶持金额不设上限。2023年《广州南沙新区（自贸片区）促进航运物流业高质量发展扶持办法》对登记为"广东南沙"船籍的奖励标准从原有的最高60元/总吨增加到80元/总吨，对使用液化天然气（LNG）、电力、甲醇、氨和氢能等清洁能源动力的船舶登记奖励额度提升到100元/总吨，每家企业年度最高奖励1500万元。

[③] 据统计，截至2011年第二阶段结束，共有59艘、共计195万载重吨船舶获准享受优惠政策。这些回归船舶的平均载重吨不足4万吨，且回归船舶的总载重吨不到中资方便旗船总载重吨的3%。

境外光租而来的船舶;二是船舶的运营作业范围局限于国际航运;三是船舶已在海关处申请或办理了一些保税、出口退税的手续。

相比较特案免税登记政策,船舶保税登记政策有如下四个特点:一是船籍港限定为"中国洋山港",船东限定为在洋山保税港区注册的企业;二是审批办理流程简化,入籍船舶作为"货物"进入保税港区,在办理完成进境备案手续后,取得海关免征进口关税和进口环节增值税的认可;三是扩大了船舶覆盖面,除没有将国内购置的非保税旧船纳入外,基本覆盖了航运企业取得的所有船舶;四是扩大了优惠范畴,特案免税登记只解决"方便旗"船舶回归的进口关税和增值税减免,而洋山港保税登记还接纳国内出口退税的新建造船舶,保税状态下的境外光船租赁入籍船舶。

保税登记是对我国原有登记制度的创新,在制度的制定上汲取了特案免税登记政策的经验教训。但是,由于政策的不稳定性、停航损失的巨大以及手续的繁杂,洋山港保税船舶登记的意义也并不凸显。

(三) 国际船舶登记制度

随后,我国又开始覆盖面更广、力度更大的国际船舶登记制度改革。目前学术界对国际船舶登记制度还未形成统一定义,一般认为,国际船舶登记是指一国在其传统登记制度之外建立、与传统登记制度并行的,登记船舶仅能从事国际航运,但在船东、船员、船龄、船检、保险等方面放开限制的船舶登记制度。

2013年5月,我国交通运输部批复同意《天津东疆保税港区国际船舶登记制度创新试点方案》(简称《天津方案》),天津东疆成为我国首个实施国际船舶登记的船籍港。该方案对船舶登记制度的改革集中在以下四个方面。一是与当时适用的1994年《船舶登记条例》相比,突破了中资控股的股权比例,中方投资人的出资额只需不低于50%。这改变了严格船舶登记制度下对于中外资比例的严格限制,有利于吸引外资,并且间接地为航运企业拓宽了融资渠道。二是放宽了对船龄的要求,这有利于降低航运企业的运营成本,改进管理维护方式并提高管理维护水平。① 三是突破了

---

① 《天津方案》第九条:按本方案登记的各类船舶船龄应符合如下范围:(1) 船龄在12年以下的高速客船、客滚船、客货船、客渡船、客货渡船(包括旅客列车轮渡)、旅游船、客船;(2) 船龄在14年以下的油船(包括沥青船)、散装化学品船、液化气船;(3) 船龄在20年以下的散货船、矿砂船;(4) 船龄在22年以下的货滚船、散装水泥船、冷藏船、杂货船、多用途船、集装箱船、木材船、拖轮、推轮、驳船等;(5) 船龄在22年以下的钻井平台、其他水上移动装置。

聘用外籍船员的限制。① 除了主要的岗位仍然要求是中籍船员外，其他岗位均允许比例在30%以内的外籍船员存在。但是，外籍船员应取得就业许可并持有所属国政府签发的身份证件。四是增加了船舶登记种类。将船舶融资租赁登记明确纳入登记种类，为船舶融资租赁产业的发展开辟了道路。② 但是，天津东疆保税港区与香港在税收、船级社以及融资环境等方面仍存在较大的差距。

2014年1月，我国交通运输部批复《中国（上海）自由贸易试验区国际船舶登记制度试点方案》，上海自由贸易试验区也开展国际船舶登记制度试点。2019年8月，国务院发布《关于印发中国（上海）自由贸易试验区临港新片区总体方案的通知》（简称《上海临港新片区方案》），明确对境内制造船舶在"中国洋山港"登记从事国际运输的，视同出口，给予出口退税（以下将关于上海自由贸易试验区国际船舶登记制度相关方案统称为"上海方案"）。"上海方案"与《天津方案》在监管理念、监管体制和登记流程的便利性方面都有很大的进步。

第一，在对国内登记国际航行船舶的定位上有重大创新，不再视其为国内船舶或者进口二手船，而是将其视为"出口船"来处理，这是自由贸易试验区理念深化带来的积极效果。过去中资国际航运外籍船舶回国登记可以免除进口关税和进口环节增值税，但这被视为一种"特别优惠待遇"，中资新建国际航行船舶在国内登记无法享受出口退税，这样就严重制约了航运企业在"国内造船、国内登记"的积极性，也极大地影响了中资船舶国内登记的政策效果。因此，《上海临港新片区方案》有利于解决已经在境外登记船舶即存量船舶的转籍问题，也有利于解决新造船舶即增量船舶的入籍问题。

第二，"上海方案"规定，国际船舶登记制度的应用范围限于已经办结海关完税、退税或者保税手续的船舶。不同于《天津方案》中限定船籍港的做法，"上海方案"分别针对不同情况设置了"中国洋山港"和"中国上海"两个国际船舶登记船籍港：如果船舶已经办结保税手续，则登记为前者；如果船舶已经办结完税手续，则登记为后者；二者均可享受国际

---

① 《天津方案》第十条：按照本方案登记并取得中国国籍的船舶，其船长、轮机长和主管机关要求由中国籍船员担任的岗位，应当由中国籍船员担任；确需聘用外国籍高级船员的，应当报天津海事局批准。但外国籍船员的比例不得超过30%。

② 参见王淑敏、杨欣、李瑞康《上海自由贸易区实施"国际船舶登记制度"的法律问题》，载《中国海商法研究》2015年第2期，第108页。

船舶登记制度的政策所带来的便利。

第三,"上海方案"允许在自由贸易试验区成立的外商投资企业运营进出国内港口的船舶运输业务,且适用于外资投资比例超过49%的中外合资、合作企业及其船舶。[1] 这使得国际船舶登记制度的适用对象范围进一步扩大,冲破了原有法规中关于外商在中外合资、合作企业中的出资比例不得超过49%的限制。

第四,"上海方案"没有采纳《天津方案》关于外籍船员比例的规定,放开了对船员的限制,并将监管方式由提前审批改为事后备案。以前外籍船员的聘用须经批准,如今只需要向上海海事局报备,在聘用船员领域赋予了登记船东更大的自由。

第五,"上海方案"中的登记程序更加便捷。相较于传统的登记制度中提供证书之后再给予相关执照的烦琐程序,目前国际船舶登记制度参照"先照后证"的原则,只要企业先提供规定所需的担保就可以先领到执照,相应证书可以事后再提供。在这种程序下,办证时间为1~2个工作日,大大节约了船舶登记的时间成本。[2]

(四)上海船舶登记现状

十多年来,我国不断探索改革传统的严格船舶登记制度,"上海方案"与原有严格登记制度相比有了很大的改变。上海是我国船舶国籍登记制度改革历史最长、力度最大和国际登记船舶数量最多的地方,但是由于综合税收、运营成本过高,航运金融和保险仍然不够发达,以及办理手续繁杂、时间不确定等限制因素仍没有得到有效的解决,其登记船舶效果也难以令人满意。

2016—2018年上海海事局在册登记船舶统计见表3。由表3数据可知,上海在册登记船舶的总数逐年减少,从2016年12月的2252艘减少到2018年6月的2201艘。2019—2023年上海辖区登记船舶数量进一步减少,从

---

[1] 2014年2月,交通运输部发布《关于中国(上海)自由贸易试验区试行扩大国际船舶运输和国际船舶管理业务外商投资比例实施办法的公告》(https://xxgk.mot.gov.cn/2020/jigou/syj/202006/t20200623_3314161.html)。

[2] 2021年,上海海事局《中国(上海)自由贸易试验区临港新片区国际船舶登记管理规定》第八条:登记机关应当自受理之日起两个工作日内办结船舶登记手续。

2019 年的 2181 艘减少到 2023 年的 1939 艘，整体也呈下降趋势。① 其中，国际航行登记船舶的数量维持在一个相对稳定的状态。可见，上海国际航行船舶登记数量并未出现显著增长，同时平均单船总吨位也呈现逐年下降的趋势。这一现象表明，我国对于国际航行船舶，尤其是大型船舶的吸引力仍有待提升。如果要达到扩大国轮船队的预期效果，则我国还需要更大的改革力度，这是粤港澳大湾区内自由贸易试验区船舶登记相关制度改革和配套规则衔接需要重视的问题。

表3 2016—2018 年上海海事局在册登记船舶统计

项目	船舶数量/艘			总吨			平均单船总吨		
	2016年12月31日	2017年12月31日	2018年6月30日	2016年12月31日	2017年12月31日	2018年6月30日	2016年12月31日	2017年12月31日	2018年6月30日
国际航行船舶	410	418	412	10776260	10919556	10730569	26283	26123	26045
国内航行海船	1124	1116	1125	6128905	6491055	6648647	5452	5816	5909
国内航行河船	718	689	664	1016794	967072	975708	1416	1403	1469
总计	2252	2223	2201	17921959	18377683	18354924	7958	8267	8339

---

① 参见上海海事局网（https://www.sh.msa.gov.cn/hstjsj/index.jhtml），2024 年 3 月 20 日访问。

三、粤港澳大湾区内自贸区国际船舶登记和配套制度规则衔接趋同的路径与相关思考

粤港澳大湾区协同发展和建立自由贸易试验区是党中央、国务院制定的重大国家战略，是新形势下全面深化改革、扩大开放和促进内地与港澳深度合作、融合发展的重大举措。粤港澳大湾区内香港、澳门是国际自由港，广东自由贸易试验区覆盖深圳前海蛇口、横琴粤澳深度合作区和广州南沙三个片区，三个片区拥有粤港澳大湾区和自由贸易试验区政策叠加的双重优势。在全球性特色鲜明的航运业，特别是船舶登记领域，粤港澳大湾区内的自由贸易试验区应当与香港自由港在规则衔接趋同方面走在全国前列。

（一）粤港澳大湾区规则衔接趋同的主要路径

在"一国两制"基本框架下，参考已有成功做法，借鉴国际经验，粤港澳大湾区内自由贸易试验区与香港自由港推动和实现规则衔接趋同主要有如下 8 条路径。

1. 单边接轨路径

单边接轨是操作性最强，也是最常见、最主要的一种规则衔接趋同的方式，是指内地、香港特别行政区、澳门特别行政区一方在制定内部适用的制度时参考借鉴另一方的可取做法，采用实质内容或者效果相同或类似的规则。单方主动接轨影响力最大的典型就是深圳率先借鉴香港特别行政区的土地批租制度建立了国有土地使用权的出让制度，后来得到法律支持在全国推广。又如，2019 年财政部、税务总局发布的《关于粤港澳大湾区个人所得税优惠政策的通知》规定对在粤港澳大湾区九市工作的境外高端人才和紧缺人才就内地与香港特别行政区个人所得税税负差额给予补贴。这属于单方主动接轨中的"外人港策"。地方上主动接轨的例子还有广州市南沙区法院 2018 年以来借鉴香港特别行政区的规则，先后出台《涉港商事案件属实申述规则适用规程》《民商事案件证据开示指引》《关于类似案例辩论程序的诉讼指引》等。

2. 诸边协议路径

诸边协议路径是指由内地、香港特别行政区、澳门特别行政区双边或三边相关方面签订协议、安排、备忘录等，以推动大湾区融合发展和规则

衔接趋同。诸边协议路径最典型的例子是自 2003 年开始，商务部和香港特别行政区政府财政司签署《内地与香港关于建立更紧密经贸关系的安排》（CEPA）及其系列补充协议。采取诸边协议路径的其他例子还有：2017 年国家发展和改革委员会、广东省人民政府、香港特别行政区政府、澳门特别行政区政府签署《深化粤港澳合作 推进大湾区建设框架协议》，2019 年广东省高级人民法院与香港特别行政区政府律政司签署《粤港澳大湾区法律交流与互鉴框架安排》，2020 年交通运输部海事局、香港海事处、澳门海事及水务局签署《粤港澳大湾区海事合作协议》等。内地、香港特别行政区、澳门特别行政区还可以就个人和企业破产等新兴、常用、急需领域的事务进行协商、达成协议安排。

3. 冲突法/国际私法路径

国际上解决拥有独立法律制度的不同国家或地区之间的法律冲突有两个基本途径：一个是统一实体法路径，另一个是冲突法/国际私法路径。诸边协议主要是实体法路径，而冲突法路径则是在内地与域外法律之间搭建桥梁，通过《中华人民共和国涉外民事关系法律适用法》等法律选择机制解决涉外法律关系的准据法问题。意思自治和最密切联系是国际私法上选择准据法的两项最重要的原则。国际私法上"涉外"既包括"涉及外国"，也包括"涉及港澳台"。冲突法路径是当前粤港澳大湾区规则衔接最基本的既有资源之一。在涉外关系的认定上，进一步扩大涉外民商事关系的范围，赋予当事人在民商事关系中选择准据法的更大权利和自由，也是更好发挥冲突法/国际私法在粤港澳大湾区规则衔接方面功能的重要进展。例如，2022 年《广东省高级人民法院关于粤港澳大湾区内地人民法院审理涉港澳商事纠纷司法规则衔接的指引（一）》明确规定港资、澳资在横琴、前海和南沙投资的国内企业与其他国内企业之间："在横琴粤澳深度合作区、前海深港现代服务业合作区、广州南沙新区（自贸片区）等注册的港资、澳资等投资企业协议选择域外法解决合同纠纷，在不违反国家法律基本原则的前提下，内地法院可予准许。"也就是说，这类企业可以协议选择香港法、澳门法，外国法，国际条约、国际惯例等法律法规作为合同纠纷的准据法。

4. 国际法路径

根据《中华人民共和国香港特别行政区基本法》（《简称《香港特别行政区基本法》）和《中华人民共和国澳门特别行政区基本法》（简称《澳门特别行政区基本法》）的规定，香港和澳门可以"中国香港""中国澳门"的名义参加有关国际组织、国际协定和国际会议。国际法路径即是指内地、香港特别行政区、澳门特别行政区共同加入一些国际组织和国际协定，共同认可一些国际惯例，或者按照共同参加或认可的国际条约、惯例，国际组织发布的手册、指南、示范法等来制定或修改本地的法律规则，以推动三地规则的实质趋同。内地、香港特别行政区、澳门特别行政区共同参加或认可的国际组织、条约和惯例包括世界贸易组织（WTO）、国际卫生组织（WHO）、国际海事组织（IMO）、海牙国际私法会议、国际商会，以及《区域全面经济伙伴关系协定》（RCEP）、《国际货物销售合同公约》、《国际海上人命安全公约》、《海员培训、发证和值班标准国际公约》（STCW）等。国际法路径是《基本法》框架下促进粤港澳大湾区规则趋同的重要方式。

5. 示范法路径

示范法路径是指在官方、半官方或民间专业组织向立法机关提供具有先进性但不具有法律效力的示范法的基础上，各立法机关采用相同或类似的实体法。示范法是国际社会和复合法制国家广泛应用的协调法律冲突、推动法律趋同的一种制度供给模式。示范法发轫于美国，美国统一州法全国委员会、美国法学会、美国律师协会等专业性组织向美国各州推荐了100多部示范性法律文本。其中，以1952年美国《统一商法典》影响最大，有的州稍加修改即全部采纳，有的州只采纳了部分章节。

借鉴国际通行的示范法模式，粤港澳大湾区相关法律团体和学术机构可以牵头成立若干个专家组，组织学术界和实务界的专家对粤、港、澳三地立法和司法进行系统深入的实证分析与前瞻研究，从易到难、从点到线，总结概括并编撰不同法律领域相关主题的示范法，久久为功，引领各自区域的立法和司法走向接近。

6. 行业自治路径

行业自治路径是指通过商会、行业协会等民间行业组织联手组建一体化平台，编纂行业惯例，制定示范合同，从实质上推动各地的规则衔接和趋同。例如，在纠纷解决领域，2011年12月，广州仲裁委员会与香港仲裁司学会和澳门世界贸易中心仲裁中心等共同设立南沙国际仲裁中心。南沙国际仲裁中心作为非营利性的国际商事仲裁平台，为粤、港、澳三地提供仲裁规则及《联合国国际贸易法委员会仲裁规则》供当事人自主选择适用，当事人还可自主选择适用的仲裁语言，香港、澳门的仲裁员，以及选择不同的开庭地点来处理仲裁事务。

7. 美国州际路径

《美利坚合众国宪法》第四条第一款规定有关于州际关系的"充分信任和尊重条款",要求每个州对其他各州的公共法律、案卷和司法程序应给予充分信任和尊重,承认其效力。① 粤港澳大湾区也可以"充分信任并且尊重"湾区内各方的法律规则,调解、仲裁、诉讼程序及其裁决结果,按照"先受理原则"推进管辖权协调,并在委托文书送达、证据调取、财产保全、法律查明、裁判结果的承认与执行等方面通力合作,鼓励互相参考或援引各自的判例,但违反本地法律基本原则和公序良俗的除外。②

8. 中央统一立法路径

在当前特别行政区基本法框架下,由全国人民代表大会常务委员会列入《香港特别行政区基本法》和《澳门特别行政区基本法》附件三的全国性法律可以适用于特别行政区。目前有《中华人民共和国国籍法》《中华人民共和国领海及毗连区法》《中华人民共和国外交特权与豁免条例》《中华人民共和国外国中央银行财产司法强制措施豁免法》《中华人民共和国香港特别行政区维护国家安全法》等法律可以适用于香港特别行政区和澳门特别行政区。

在"一国两制"基本国策下,随着时间的推移,中央可能会强化在特别行政区的全面管治权,指导特别行政区在语言文字、道路交通等一体化发展的必要领域自行制定或修改相关法律,或者增加列入《香港特别行政区基本法》和《澳门特别行政区基本法》附件三的全国性法律。

(二)粤港澳大湾区国际船舶登记和配套制度规则衔接趋同的相关思考

在上述规则衔接的8条路径中,单边接轨是最有效率、最成功的一条路径。如上撰述,香港特别行政区现行船舶登记的主要法律依据是《香港

---

① 不过《美利坚合众国宪法》中的这种充分信任是有条件的,即只能在他州的上述内容依照该州的法律合法成立并且有效时才可以;原来的州不承认的行为,不能要求他州承认;他州所承认的效力不能超过该行为所产生的州的法律所给予的效力。

② 2022年《广东省高级人民法院关于粤港澳大湾区内地人民法院审理涉港澳商事纠纷司法规则衔接的指引(一)》规定:香港、澳门政府机构和其他依法管理公共事务的组织或者其授权人员依职权制作的公文书证,内地法院可以依法认定其证明力;香港、澳门法院、仲裁机构及仲裁员生效裁判认定的基本事实,内地法院在审理同一事实中可予确认;当事人在香港法院、澳门法院诉讼中作出的陈述,内地法院经庭审质证可以将其作为认定案件事实的根据。

法例》第四百一十五章"商船（注册）条例",① 其所确立船舶登记制度及与船舶登记制度相关的船舶检验、运营、财税、金融、航运服务、法律服务等与中国内地法律相比差异原本很大。不过，在"四个全面"战略布局下，特别是经过自主的多年的船舶登记制度改革和自由贸易试验区建设，香港特别行政区与国内自由贸易试验区范围内的船舶登记制度已经较为接近。

2021年中共中央、国务院印发《全面深化前海深港现代服务业合作区改革开放方案》，将"探索研究推进国际船舶登记和配套制度改革"作为扩大航运业对外开放和推进现代服务业创新发展重大改革举措之一予以规定。2020年《交通运输部关于推进海事服务粤港澳大湾区发展的意见》也提出："以'香港''中国前海''广东南沙''广东横琴'国际登记船籍港为依托，研究探索大湾区国际船舶登记制度，优化船舶登记程序。"2023年4月，《交通运输部关于创新海事服务支持全面深化前海深港现代服务业合作区改革开放的意见》明确将协同协调海事规则衔接和机制对接。另外，2023年11月，深圳市充分借鉴香港等国际航运发达地区的有益经验，通过制定《深圳经济特区国际船舶条例》，对国际船舶登记、船舶检验、船员管理以及相关服务与保障等做出一系列创新安排，以吸引国际船舶登记，促进航运要素集聚和产业高质量发展。

因此，在目前阶段，研究推进"大湾区国际船舶登记和配套制度改革"与"大湾区海事规则衔接"具有十分重要的现实意义。站在船舶登记的角度，船舶检验、财税、金融等多个领域属于综合配套制度改革，但这些方面的改革往往牵一发而动全身，推进起来更加困难。下面，笔者就大湾区国际船舶登记和配套制度规则衔接问题提出若干建议，无论是单边接轨，还是诸边协议，都可以供有关部门参考。

1. 放宽船舶登记限制条件，完善登记强制注销制度

我国提出建立"宽进严管"的市场准入和监管制度，提高开放度和透明度。目前在自由贸易试验区内登记船舶国籍时在船东的股权比例要求上已经放开，主要是航运企业在聘用船员时在船员国籍、适任证书、培训考

---

① 香港船舶登记制度已有超过150年的历史，回归以后，香港特别行政区政府经中央政府授权继续进行船舶登记，具体由隶属于海事处的香港船舶注册处专门负责。香港船舶登记总署以"中国香港"的名义颁发相关证件。在香港特别行政区注册的船舶需要同时悬挂中华人民共和国国旗和香港特别行政区区旗。

核、就业许可等方面仍然存在较大的限制。

在船东的条件方面，如前所述，香港特别行政区较为宽松，船舶只要过半数权益由一名或以上的香港居民、香港法人或外地公司的香港分公司拥有就可在香港注册，不仅外地公司的香港分公司可以成为香港船舶过半数权益的大船东，而且作为香港船舶大船东的香港本地法人也无资金来源和股权比例上的限制。根据2016年交通运输部《船舶登记办法》的规定，在内地自由贸易试验区注册的企业法人所有或者光船租赁的船舶也可以进行国籍登记，对该企业法人的资金来源和股权比例也无限制，这样在前海深港现代服务业合作区、广州南沙新区（自贸片区）、横琴粤港澳深度合作区注册的外商独资企业也可以在"中国前海""广东南沙""广东横琴"国际船舶登记船籍港进行国籍登记。

在船员国籍方面，香港特别行政区无任何限制，航运企业拥有充分的经营自主权。《深圳经济特区国际船舶条例》在这方面基本做到了规则趋同，即无国际船舶外籍船员数量和比例的限制性规定，而且海事机构既可以签发外籍船员适任证书，也可以承认外国海事机构签发的适任证书。[①] 经国家海事管理机构同意后，取得船长适任证书承认签证的外籍船员可以在国际船舶上任职船长，免于参加海上交通安全、环境保护等方面的培训及考核。在国际船舶上任职的外籍船员还免于办理就业许可和就业证。该条例还规定用人单位应确保外籍船员享有符合相关国际公约或我国有关规定的社会保障。该条例通过后，深圳将在国际船舶船员聘用自主权方面与香港基本一致，其经验应当在广州南沙新区（自贸片区）、横琴粤澳深度合作区内推广。

完善国籍登记强制注销制度，明确国际船舶国籍登记强制注销的适用情形和有关程序。建议交通主管部门转变以船舶身份和船龄为基础的管理思路，强化以标准和规则为导向的船舶安全管理模式，取消船舶到龄强制报废的规定。尽管由于我国船舶强制报废年限较长，取消强制报废的实际意义可能不大，但从主管部门转变管理思路的角度看却非常重要。

2. 实现登记材料精减化、标准化、电子化

时间成本对于航运企业选择船舶登记地而言是一个非常重要的因素。国家推进行政审批标准化、信息化建设，这也是粤港澳大湾区船舶登记制

---

① 2022年，深圳海事局为豪华邮轮"招商伊敦"号签发了全国首单外国船员适任证书承认签证和国内首份外籍船员适任证书。

度改革的重要方向。

第一，明确登记所需材料，实现登记材料精减化、标准化。主管部门在航运企业申请船舶国籍登记时最重要的一点就是需要把"国籍登记"与"运营许可"分开，"国籍登记"只需要提供与国籍登记相关的资料，并且提前明确国籍登记所要求的文件目录，针对不同类型的船舶分别制定不同的所需材料一览表和样式要求，所需材料应当具有必要性和标准化，保证透明度和可预见性，以自信开放的心态和标准管理、过程管理的模式取消"其他有关文件"的兜底要求。

第二，船舶国籍登记全流程网络化办理及所需证书全部电子化。我国船舶登记实践中，船舶在登记期间不得不停航，船舶一天未完成登记，船东就要承担一天的停航损失。如果登记手续繁杂、衔接不畅，就会给船东带来巨大的时间成本和经济损失。实现船舶登记所需证书电子化是实现船舶"登记不停航"的最有效手段，我国已在全球率先实现100%国际航行船舶法定检验证书电子化，中国船级社也上线了船舶入级检验文件电子化系统，明确了中国籍国际航行船舶检验电子证书与纸质证书具有同等效力。另外，包括海员适任证书、海员培训合格证、海员外派机构资质证书、船员培训许可证等在内的海事电子证照实现了在线办理和发放。[1] 但在船舶国籍登记所需证书全部电子化及全流程网络化办理方面仍需要大力推动，建议广东自由贸易试验区借鉴吸收国际国内先进管理经验，[2] 通过

---

[1] 2020年10月，中国船级社上线船舶入级检验文件电子化系统，在总结应用电子证书的基础上，对CCS所签发的所有检验报告和记录全面实施电子化。

[2] 2013年召开的国际海事组织便利运输委员会（FAL）第39届会议通过了关于《电子证书使用导则》的FAL.5/Circ.39/Rev.1号通函，鼓励各成员国使用船舶电子证书，以避免船舶携带大量的法定证书、文件以及保存相关记录给船舶、船公司以及其他相关方面在船舶和船员管理、登记、记录等方面带来的沉重负担。2016年6月召开的国际海事组织便利运输委员会第40届会议又发布了新的通函（FAL.5/Circ.39/Rev.2），对《电子证书使用导则》进行更新，以减少因为依赖于传统证书等原因而对管理部门、港口国监督官员、船员和其他相关人员造成的行政负担，进一步促进电子证书的使用和认可。2021年3月，巴哈马海事管理局（Bahamas Maritime Authority, BMA）宣布其所有证书均可以电子方式提供。2020年底，BMA推出了其在线信息注册系统（BORIS）的一系列升级功能，此信息注册系统满足IMO FAL.5/Circ.39/Rev.2准则中关于电子证书的使用要求。巴拿马船舶登记局（Panama Ship Registry）也宣称将推出"电子船舶登记系统"（ESRS），该系统由巴拿马海事局的商船总局（船舶登记处）和公共财产总局登记处共同负责。登记所需材料包括船舶登记证书、注销证书、抵押登记证书、船舶和无线电执照、财产和抵押权证书和折扣、有关船舶名称保留和一般文件等。此外，ESRS将使用电子签名。该系统将有多种语言，具有多种功能，付款方式多样化，且用户可计算每项操作的成本。

证书电子化、电子政务、形式审查、临时登记等方式大幅缩短办证时限，实现船舶转籍"登记不停航"。

3. 推动中国船级社改制，加快开放船舶检验市场

第一，推动中国船级社改制，与交通运输部脱钩。1998年，交通运输部船舶检验局与中国船级社实行"局社分开，政事分开"的改革，中国船级社仍为交通运输部的直属机构，被定性为事业法人单位，实行企业化管理。因此，中国船级社同时具有社团法人和事业法人的性质，法律地位被界定为类行政组织。除了中国船级社以外，国际船级社协会（IACS）的其他船级社均属于民间机构。建议中国船级社进一步改制，与交通运输部脱钩，彻底实现"政事分开"，平等参与全球船舶检验市场竞争，不断提高船检服务水平。

第二，加快开放船舶入级检验和法定检验市场。目前，国际知名自由贸易港船舶登记实践中均放开船舶入级检验和法定检验市场。如前所述，我国在政策上已经逐步放开在自由贸易试验区登记的中国籍国际航行船舶的入级检验和法定检验。但在政策的落地，特别是放开法定检验市场上仍然行动迟缓，建议主管部门学习香港特别行政区的做法，加快步伐先行遴选一批技术先进、服务优质、世界著名的外国船级社，批准其在广东自由贸易试验区范围内对中国籍国际航行船舶实施入级检验，授权其对自由贸易试验区国际登记船舶开展法定检验，以"单边开放"对抗"脱钩断链"，以"单边开放"引领对等开放、全球开放，这必将进一步丰富我国船舶检验服务供给、提升船舶检验服务水平，增强自由贸易试验区国际船舶登记制度的吸引力，同时向国际社会展示全面改革开放的坚定决心。

4. 打造保障行业快速发展与维持有效监管之间平衡的船旗国监管系统

根据《国际海事组织履约规则（III Code）》[Resolution A.1070(28)]的要求，各船旗国应建立一个"适当和有效"的制度，对悬挂该国国旗的船舶实施监督。香港特别行政区政府在吸引海外船舶注册时不是单方面强调低税制度的优越性，而是突出香港优质的海事服务和船舶安全质量控制。"注册前质量管理"（PRQC）系统和"船旗国质量管理"（FSQC）系统

是香港海事处引以为傲的亮点。① 两个系统实现事前、事中、事后全链条监管，在保障行业快速发展与维持有效监管之间实现平衡，也是值得大湾区内自贸实验区创新船舶登记制度时加以借鉴的。

鉴于我国自1998年开始推行国际海事组织（IMO）《国际船舶安全营运和防止污染管理规则》（ISM规则），2001年开始实施《中华人民共和国船舶安全营运和防止污染管理规则》（NSM规则），粤港澳大湾区内自由贸易试验区可以从如下两个方面加以强化船旗国监管系统。

一是借鉴香港特别行政区的经验，加强对登记前船舶的品质管控，船舶登记中心在收到船舶转籍申请后对该船舶做出质量评估，评估时考虑船龄、船型、船员素质、港口国监管（PSC）滞留次数、港口国监管（PSC）缺陷数目、现有船旗、现有船级社、船舶检验记录和事故记录等因素，以决定是否需要登船进行评估检验。同时，明确船舶登记中心需要登船检验和不予登记的情形，从源头上杜绝高风险船舶登记。

二是加强对国际船舶登记后的事中监管，督促相关航运企业切实履行其应有的主体责任。粤港澳大湾区内自由贸易试验区海事主管机构可通过建立国际船舶、船检机构和航运公司三大关键主体质量控制制度、信用管理制度，对怀疑其有安全品质隐患的船舶进行质量管理审核，并向有关航运企业、船舶管理公司提出改善意见，以协助相关公司确保辖下船舶的质量。同时借鉴香港特别行政区的经验，对于国际登记船舶持续两年内未有在船旗国监管（FSC）和港口国监管（PSC）下滞留记录的，减免随后一年船舶吨税的一半。

5. 加大航运服务人才培养培训

香港、广州和深圳均为全球前列的航运枢纽城市，也是粤港澳大湾区建设的核心城市。粤港澳大湾区航运经济发达，航运人才需求量大，特别

---

① 所有拟在香港注册的船舶必须于注册前进行质量评估，"注册前质量管理"（PRQC）系统确保加入香港船舶注册的船舶有良好质量。海事处在收到船舶注册申请后会根据相关文件资料对该船舶作出质量评估，以决定是否需要登船检验。质量有疑问的船舶须由船东/船舶管理公司委托海事处认可的船级社登船进行PRQC评估检验。所有已在香港注册的船舶必须符合"船旗国质量管理"（FSQC）系统的要求。海事处于1999年推行船旗质量管理系统以监察和保持香港注册船舶的素质。海事处会对每艘船的维护管理作出故障风险评估，根据电脑数据库储藏资料的分析结果对品质存疑的船舶由认可的验船师对船舶进行质量管理审核，并会在审核后向有关船舶或其管理公司提出改善建议，以协助船公司确保辖下船舶的质量。关于香港注册船舶的质量保证，可参见香港海事处网（https://www.mardep.gov.hk/sc/aboutus/home.html），2023年11月20日访问。

是高素质航运人才存在较大缺口。当前粤港澳大湾区在航运人才培养方面仍然呈现"弱且分散"的状态。目前，香港船东不得不大量聘用缅甸、印度、菲律宾等外籍船员来满足需求，外籍船员占比高达65%。同时，香港于2014年设立"海运及空运人才培训基金"，以支持香港海运和航空业的长远发展。[①] 建议相关城市大力支持以广州航海学院为基础组建广州交通大学，推进"深圳海洋大学"的筹建，增设、完善航运与物流类、信息类、金融类、法律类等相关专业，加大培养高端航运人才的力度，以缓解人才供给滞后于高端航运服务业需求的困境，支持广东省航海学会、广东省法学会航运法学研究会、粤港澳大湾区供应链研究院等专业机构强化人才培训服务功能。

6. 融合发展，海运先行

在此基础上，进一步推动在粤港澳大湾区内自由贸易试验区和香港、澳门自由港登记的国际船舶可在粤港澳大湾区内从事沿海货物运输及捎带业务，促进自由贸易试验区内试行船员、引航员、验船师等专业技术人员的资质和证书互认，在海运领域率先实现香港、澳门与粤港澳大湾区其他城市的融合发展。

7. 进一步减税降费

香港作为"简单税制、低税率"的自由港对从事国际运营的注册船舶免除营业税、所得税、船舶进口关税和增值税。而我国内地税目多、税率高、进口征税、出口退税是中资航运企业愿意将船舶登记于境外的最主要动因。在关税方面，如果我国全球制造大国、出口大国的定位不改变，那么"实业重税""出口退税"的原则就很难改变。由于国家在政策上已经将自由贸易试验区视作"境内关外"，境内制造船舶登记到自由贸易试验区可以享受出口退税，从境外进口船舶到自由贸易试验区可以免征进口关税和进口环节增值税，这有利于中资航运企业将船舶登记于境内。尽管如此，在国际国内新局势和综合权衡利弊的基础上，我国在其他税费方面仍

---

① 香港特别行政区政府于2014年1月注资1亿元港币设立"海运及空运人才培训基金"，2019年和2023年再分别注资2亿元港币，基金总额达到5亿元港币。基金资助的具体项目包括：专业培训课程及考试费用发还计划，海运和航空业实习计划，本地船舶业训练奖励计划，本地船舶能力提升计划，航海训练奖励计划，船舶维修训练奖励计划，香港理工大学香港航运及物流奖学金计划、香港航海及海运奖学金计划，香港大学－大连海事大学/上海海事大学学术合作计划，海外交流学生资助计划，海事培训支援计划等。参见香港运输与物流局网站（https://www.tlb.gov.hk/tc/highlights/transport/20140401.html），2023年11月20日访问。

有进一步减税降费的空间。

  首先，可将航运业增值税税率调整为 6%。2011 年国家试点营业税改增值税，航运企业由原本征 3%～5% 的营业税改为征 11% 的增值税，但"营改增"政策在航运业的减税效果并不明显，甚至出现税负不减反增的情况。2017 年国务院将普通纳税人增值税税率由四档减至 17%、11% 和 6% 三档，取消了 13% 这一档税率，航运企业的增值税税率没有变动。2018 年原适用 17% 和 11% 税率的行业，税率分别调整为 16%、10%。2019 年国家进一步将制造业等行业 16% 的增值税税率降为 13%，将交通运输业等行业 10% 的税率降为 9%，[①] 金融业等服务业保持 6% 一档的税率不变。鉴于国际航运业的特殊性，特别是远洋船舶航行期间极少占用国内公共资源，因此，航运业或可适用 6% 的增值税税率。

  其次，企业所得税的标准税率可微调。过去 40 多年里，全球范围内公司所得税税率一直在下降，近两年才趋于平稳。从 1980 年至 2023 年，全球平均所得税税率由 40.18% 下降到 22.27%。2017 年年底，美国联邦企业所得税税率由 35% 调整到 21%，2023 年美国联邦和州法定税率合计为 25.77%。[②] 自 2008 年我国统一内外资企业所得税以来，我国企业所得税率一直保持为 25%，成为仅次于增值税的国内第二大税种。我国近年来经济增速放缓，企业经营成本上升，企业盈利能力下降，经济社会和国际形势面临前所未有的挑战。因此，顺应所得税减税的国际趋势、应对当前的经济形势，企业所得税税率有必要从 25% 下调至 23%，全国航运业可从这一普惠性减税政策中获益。当然，对于粤港澳大湾区内广州南沙自由贸易试验区而言，为贯彻落实国务院《广州南沙深化面向世界的粤港澳全面合作总体方案》，2022 年财政部、税务总局颁发《关于广州南沙企业所得税优惠政策的通知》，规定对设在南沙先行启动区符合条件的鼓励类产业企业，减按 15% 的税率征收企业所得税。水上运输、船代货代、船舶管理、船员培训、仓储物流、航运交易、海事纠纷解决等 13 项航运物流业属于广

---

  ① 增值税税率适用 13% 的行业有：制造业、销售或者进口货物，有形动产租赁服务、加工、修理修配劳务；适用 9% 税率的行业有：交通运输、邮政、基础电信、建筑、不动产租赁服务，销售不动产，转让土地使用权，销售或者进口 23 类货物；适用 6% 税率的行业有：金融服务，文化体育、教育医疗、旅游娱乐、餐饮住宿等生活服务，研发、信息技术、文化创意、物流辅助等现代服务业。

  ② 参见张文春《全球公司所得税税率的新特征和新趋势》，载中国社会科学网（https://www.cssn.cn/jjx/jjx_qqjjzl/202401/t20240105_5725854.shtml），2024 年 1 月 23 日访问。

州南沙鼓励类产业，可按15%的税率征收企业所得税，这与香港特别行政区和澳门特别行政区的公司所得税标准税率非常接近。不过，基于错位发展的需要，航运业在深圳前海和横琴粤澳深度合作区并未被纳入鼓励类产业目录。

最后，船员个人所得税方面可与香港特别行政区一致。目前粤港澳大湾区个人所得税规则衔接可以做到对在广州南沙、深圳前海工作的香港居民，其个人所得税税负超过香港税负的部分予以免征；对在广州南沙、横琴粤澳深度合作区工作的澳门居民，其个人所得税税负超过澳门税负的部分予以免征。① 就特殊的船员个人所得税而言，虽然我国目前对一个纳税年度内在船航行时间满183天的远洋船员实行工资薪金收入减半缴纳个人所得税的优惠，但这与中国香港和新加坡、菲律宾、挪威、英国等地区和国家"在国际航行船舶工作超过半年免征所得税"的做法相比仍然差距较大。由于航运业具有较少占有社会公共资源的特殊性和全球性，为了保持中国航运企业和船员的全球竞争力，粤港澳大湾区主要港口可与香港特别行政区的规则一致，在国际航行船舶工作超过半年的船员免征所得税，对在沿海、内河船舶工作超过半年的船员的所得税减半。

另外，我国对进出中国港口的国际航运船舶所征收的吨税标准过高，有必要向下调整并设立最高上限15万元。同时，船舶登记与船舶吨位大小也无比例关系，建议船舶所有权登记费也降低收费标准，并设立收费上限为1.5万元。

（三）建立粤港澳大湾区港航业监管磋商协调机制

参考《深化粤港澳合作　推进大湾区建设框架协议》四方机制，由交通运输部水运局、海事局，广东省交通运输厅、广东海事局，香港特别行政区运输及物流局、香港海事处，澳门特别行政区海事及水务局成立大湾区港航业监管磋商协调会议，实现工作机制对接。磋商机制每年定期召开一次会议，进一步提升粤港澳大湾区航运市场一体化水平，促进资金、人员、船舶、货物、技术等航运市场要素便捷流动，推进粤港澳之间港航与船舶相关资源共享、信息互通、标准协同、监管互认、执法互助。

---

① 参见《财政部　税务总局关于广州南沙个人所得税优惠政策的通知》《财政部　税务总局关于前海深港现代服务业合作区个人所得税优惠政策的通知》《财政部　税务总局关于横琴粤澳深度合作区个人所得税优惠政策的通知》。

我国国际船舶登记和配套制度改革是一个长期的系统工程，而且我国在市场规模、社会制度、价值观念和发展阶段上有自己的特殊性，不能也不应该在全国范围内经济领域完全向自由港看齐。但是，在粤港澳大湾区内自由贸易试验区这一多重政策叠加的独特区域，应在国际船舶登记和配套制度改革方面先行先试，无论是单边接轨还是诸边协调，对标自由港、促进一体化，打造开放型经济新体制先行区、高水平对外开放门户枢纽和粤港澳大湾区合作示范区都是非常必要且可行的。

专题四　航空法专论

亚轨道飞行多级监管：意大利案例

亚历山德罗·卡尔迪　弗朗西斯科·加斯帕里*

王冠丁**（译）　张超汉***（校）

摘要：空间，已成为一个孕育发展新经济的全球环境。空间新经济被认为有助于国家经济发展和竞争力提升，在改善社会福利、拉动经济增长和促进创新方面被寄予厚望。在此背景下，最初被设想为休闲活动和外空旅游形式之一的亚轨道飞行成为机构论坛以及学术著作的热议对象。然而，国际和区际法律尚未就亚轨道飞行进行规制，反而在国家层面存在着多种监管框架。本文对国际和区际（欧盟）监管框架进行分析，并重点介绍意大利在空间领域，尤其是在亚轨道飞行领域采取的举措及经验。

关键词：亚轨道飞行　空天运输　意大利监管　航天港条例

The Multilevel Regulation of Suborbital Flights: The Italian Case

Alessandro Cardi, Francesco Gaspari

Wang Guanding (translator), Zhang Chaohan (proofreader)

Abstract: Space represents a global environment, where new economies emerge and are developed, with the aim to attain objectives of social welfare, as well as economic growth and innovation, deemed as instrumental for the economic development and competitiveness of a country. Within such a scenario, suborbital flights have been gaining more interest in institutional fora and in academic works, while initially they were conceived as a leisure activity and a form of space

---

*　亚历山德罗·卡尔迪：意大利民用航空局（ENAC）原副局长。弗朗西斯科·加斯帕里：意大利古列尔莫·马可尼大学（罗马）行政法副教授、法律与经济及航运法教授、皇家航空学会会员（英国伦敦）。

**　王冠丁：西北政法大学涉外法治研究中心研究人员。

***　张超汉：西北政法大学"长安学者"特聘教授、涉外法治研究中心（国家级涉外法治研究基地）副主任，博士生导师。

tourism. However, suborbital flights have not yet been regulated either at international or regional levels. By contrast, various regulatory frameworks exist at national levels. After having analysed the international and regional regulatory frameworks (specifically, the European Union), this paper focuses on the Italian experience in the space domain (particularly suborbital flights), passing through the main initiatives undertaken recently in that country.

Key words: suborbital flights; aerospace transportation; Italian regulation; spaceport regulation

一、引 言

当下，外层空间不再是一个目的地，而代表着一种全球环境。各国为了实现社会福利提升、经济增长和创新等更广泛的目标，相继在外空开展活动，部署民用、商用、安全、防务等系统。这些活动被认为有助于提升其竞争力和促进经济发展。

按最初的设想，亚轨道飞行只是一种休闲活动，作为外空旅游的形式之一，为乘客提供短暂的外空飞行体验。[1] 然而，该飞行无论在国际，还是在区际层面上均未得到监管。相比之下，在国家层面倒是存在多种监管框架。[2] 最为完善的当属美国的实践，但最近不少国家也开始构建自己的方案，意大利便是其中之一。为了促进亚轨道飞行的可持续发展，意大利基础设施和交通部（Ministry of Infrastructure and Transport，MIT）于2017年公布了一项为期三年的综合监管措施，[3] 并授权意大利民用航空局

---

[1] See Michael P. Chatzipanagiotis, *Regulating Suborbital Flights in Europe: Selected Issues* (19 November 2012), online: SSRN (papers.ssrn.com/sol3papers.cfm?abstract_id=2177671).

[2] See Paul S. Dempsey, *The emergence of national space law* (18 November 2015), online: SSRN (papers.ssrn.com/sol3/papers.cfm?abstract_id=2692639).

[3] Ministry of Infrastructure and Transport, *Decree No. 354 of July* 2017 [*Decree* 10 *July* 2017, *No.* 354]. 意大利民航局在《航天港建设和运营条例》中回顾了该法令。See Ente Nazionale per l'Aviazione Civile (ENAC), "Regulation on Construction and Operations of Spaceports (Courtesy English Translation)", (21 October 2020), online (pdf): ENAC (www.enac.gov.it/sites/default/files/allegati/2020Ott/Regolamento_costruzione_e_esercizio_degli_spazioporti_30.10.20_Inglese.pdf). 另参见该法规的解释性备忘录: Ente Nazionale per l'Aviazione Civile (ENAC), *Relazione Illustrativa Regolamento Per La Costruzione El'Esercizio Degli Spazioporti*, (2020), online (pdf): ENAC (www.enac.gov.it/sites/default/files/allegati/2020-Mag/Relazione_illustrativa_Regolamento_spazioporti.pdf).

(Ente Nazionale per l'Aviazione Civile，ENAC) 在三年内制定出亚轨道飞行的监管框架。自 2014 年以来，意大利民航局一直致力于研究、分析和评估这一新兴领域，拟在现有的航空和空域体系下，为亚轨道飞行确立一个灵活有效的监管架构。① 例如，在 2018 年基础设施和交通部将格罗塔列机场确定为意大利亚轨道飞行可持续发展的航天港后，② 意大利民航局于近日发布了单行法规。③

二、亚轨道飞行监管的国际视角

（一）美国经验

亚轨道飞机或商业航天计划主要出现在美国。迄今为止，只有美国联邦航空管理局下属的商业航天运输办公室（FAA/AST）发布了亚轨道飞机的监管框架。

美国历史上第一个监管框架可追溯至 1984 年的《空间商业发射法案》（*Commercial Space Launch Act*），④ 此法案为商业航天在美国的许可及推广奠定了基础，同时也促成了商业航天运输办公室的建立（该办公室于 1995 年 11 月迁至美国联邦航空管理局）。2004 年，《空间商业发射法修正案》由国会通过，⑤ 并在当年的 12 月 23 日由美国总统签署。⑥

《空间商业发射法案》是美国联邦航空管理局对商业载人航天进行监

---

① See Giovanni Di Antonio et al. , *A Model for Setting a Regulatory Framework for the Development of suborbital operations in Italy*（2017）4 J Space Safety Engineering 138 at 138.

② Ministry of Infrastructure and Transport, *Act No. 250 of 9 May 2018*. 意大利民航局在《航天港建设和运营法规》的解释性备忘录中回顾了该文件。See Ente Nazionale per l'Aviazione Civile（ENAC），*Relazione Illustrativa Regola-mento Per La Costruzione El'Esercizio Degli Spazioporti*，（2020），online pdf：ENAC（www. enac. gov. it/sites/default/files/allegati/2020 – Mag/Relazione_illustrativa_Regolamento_spazioporti. pdf）.

③ 下文第四部分将深入分析意大利经验。

④ *Commercial Space Launch Act*, Pub L No. 98 – 575, 98 Stat 3055（1984）.

⑤ *Commercial Space Launch Act*, Pub L No. 98 – 575, 98 Stat 3055（1984）.

⑥ See Jean-Bruno Marciacq et al. , *Establishing a Regulatory Framework for the Development and Operations of Sub-Orbital & Orbital Aircraft（SoA）in the European Union*, in Ram Jakhu & Kuan-Wei Chen, eds *Regulation of Emerging Modes of Aerospace Transportation*（Montreal：Centre for Research in Air and Space Law, McGill University, 2014），261 at 272 – 273.

管的法律依据,意在保护地面第三人在航天器发射和再入阶段的安全。①
2006年12月,商业航天运输办公室公布了最终版的《载人航天飞行机组和空间飞行参与者行为准则》,这为空间发射许可确立了最低的标准和具体细则。②

此准则建立在机组人员和太空飞行参与者"知情同意"的基础上。③为获得许可证,亚轨道飞行运营商须告知付费乘客发射和再入阶段的风险以及飞行器的安全记录。之后,乘客须签署一份免责声明,由其本人承担所有风险。由此可见,乘客的安全尚不在法规的保障之列。④

在国际层面上,这种太空新经济⑤使得"商业航天和高空服务数量呈

---

① See Jean-Bruno Marciacq et al., *Establishing a Regulatory Framework for the Development and Operations of Sub-Orbital & Orbital Aircraft (SoA) in the European Union*, in Ram Jakhu & Kuan-Wei Chen, eds, *Regulation of Emerging Modes of Aerospace Transportation* (Montreal: Centre for Research in Air and Space Law, McGill University 2014) 261, at 273。

② See Jean-Bruno Marciacq et al., *Establishing a Regulatory Framework for the Development and Operations of Sub-Orbital & Orbital Aircraft (SoA) in the European Union*, in Ram Jakhu & Kuan-Wei Chen, eds, *Regulation of Emerging Modes of Aerospace Transportation* (Montreal: Centre for Research in Air and Space Law, McGill University 2014) 261, at 273。See also PJ Blount, *Informed consent v. ITAR: Regulatory Conflicts that could Constrain Commercial Human Space Flight* (2008) SSRN at 1 (papers.ssrn.com/sol3/papers.cfm?abstract_id=1364261)。

③ "太空飞行参与者"的定义是"参与太空飞行但并非机组成员或发射服务提供者的付费乘客"。See FAA, "Human Spaceflight", online: FAA (www.faa.gov/space/licenses/human_spaceflight/)。

④ EU, Commission, *EU Space Industrial Policy Releasing the Potential for Economic Growth in the Space Sector*, (Communication), COM (2013) 108 final (28 February 2013) at para 4.1.1 [COM (2013)]。

⑤ 新空间经济具有全球影响力,区域和国家一级的机构和学者纷纷参与其中。例如,意大利航天局申明,"空间部门可能成为国家经济增长的新引擎之一。只要围绕科学和技术优势进行发展设计,以可持续性为新关键,那么影响和利益将扩大到整个工业和生产系统"。See ASI, *New Space Economy*, online: ASI (www.asi.it/en/space-economy-innovation/new–space-economy/)。此外,经济合作与发展组织也承认,空间经济是经济增长最有效的动力之一,远超出严格意义上的空间部门边界。如2019年它所作的论述,由于世界各地政府空间计划的发展、价值链中商业行为体的倍增、持久的数字化趋势和新空间系统日渐成熟,空间经济正在扩大,并日益全球化。See OECD, *The Space Economy in Figures: How Space Contributes to the Global Economy* (5 July 2019), online: OECD (www.oecd-ilibrary.org/sites/c5996201-en/index.html?itemId=/content/publication/c5996201-en)。关于非传统新兴空间参与者的"新空间产业",参见 Francesco Gaspari & Alessandra Oliva, "The Consolidation of the Five UN Space Treaties into One Comprehensive and Modernized Law of Outer Space Convention: Towards a Global Space Organization", in George D Kyriakopoulos & Maria Manoli, eds, *The Space Treaties at Crossroads: Considerations de lege ferenda*, (Switzerland: Springer, 2019) 183, at 188。

现出爆炸式增长",① 以至于引起了国际社会对空间交通管制及其他监管问题的严重关切。②

上述许多方面被纳入国际民用航空组织（ICAO）的职权范围，特别是空中交通管制。而其他问题则可能涉及联合国（UN）体系下的组织或其他国际组织、机构，诸如国际电信联盟（ITU）、联合国和平利用外层空间委员会（UNCOPUOS）、联合国环境规划署（UNEP）、世界气象组织（WMO）、机构间空间碎片协调委员会（IADC）等。此外，还涉及一些国家机构，如美国联邦航空管理局下属的商业航天运输办公室（FAA/AST）、欧洲航空安全局（EASA）等。③

（二）新兴的空天运输方式与空气空间和外层空间的划界

影响空天运输监管的主要问题无疑是空气空间和外层空间的划界问题，其被称为"无休止的争端"。④

现有的航空法和空间法是两项不同且独立的制度，缺乏协调机制。⑤空天运输，即飞行器轨迹部分穿越空气空间，部分穿越外层空间的运输，凸显了这两种法律长期以来的对立：国家的领空主权与探索利用外层空间的自由（换言之，外空不涉及国家主权）。⑥ 航空法和空间法的基本原则

---

① See Joseph Pelton, "Regulatory Issues for New Global Aerospace Systems", in Ram Jakhu & Kuan-Wei Chen, eds, *Regulation of Emerging Modes of Aeros pace Transportation* (Montreal: Centre for Research in Air and Space Law, McGill University 2014) 77, at 80.

② 佩尔顿（Pelton）的论文记录了其中的许多问题。See Joseph Pelton, "Regulatory Issues for New Global Aerospace Systems", in Ram Jakhu & Kuan-Wei Chen, eds, *Regulation of Emerging Modes of Aeros pace Transportation* (Montreal: Centre for Research in Air and Space Law, McGill University 2014) 77, at 80.

③ See Joseph Pelton, "Regulatory Issues for New Global Aerospace Systems", in Ram Jakhu & Kuan-Wei Chen, eds, *Regulation of Emerging Modes of Aerospace Transportation* (Montreal: Centre for Research in Air and Space Law, McGill University 2014) 77, at 80.

④ See Robert F. A. Goedhart, "The Never Ending Dispute: Delimitation of Airspace And Outer Space", in Marietta Benko & William de Graaff, eds, *Forum for Air and Space Law*, Vol 4 (Paris: Éditions Frontières, 1996) at 122.

⑤ See Paul S Dempsey & Michael C Mineiro, *ICAO's Legal Authority to Regulate Aerospace Vehicles* (Paper delivered at the 3rd IAASS Conference-Rome, October 22, 2008) at 1.

⑥ See Peter Haanappel, "Regulation of Emerging Modes of Aerospace Transportation: Liability and Traffic Rights", in Ram Jakhu & Kuan-Wei Chen, eds, *Regulation of Emerging Modes of Aerospace Transportation* (Montreal: Centre for Research in Air and Space Law, McGill University 2014) 101, at 101.

截然不同：前者承认领土主权，后者否认领土主权；前者对承运人施加有限责任，后者对国家施加无限责任。①

遗憾的是，在现有的国际法律秩序中，航空法律制度与空间法律制度尚未实现统一或一体化。因此有学者指出，"首先，必须确定适用何种制度——航空法、空间法，抑或在某些情况下同时适用，然后再确定适用的具体规则。"②

一方面，国际公约、条约和软法规范构成了航空运输法律体系；另一方面，五项多边公约确立了外层空间法律体系。"空天飞行器"是否适用航空法，如果适用，那么当其进入外层空间后是否依旧遵循航空法，这些问题仍有待确定。③

事实上，由于空气空间和外层空间的划界问题长期以来悬而不决，学界发展出许多理论方法来界定该领域及活动，以空间论和功能论最为典型。④

过去15年来，这两种学说在多个国际论坛上被广泛讨论。2005年5月30日，国际民航组织秘书处准备了一份工作文件⑤并指出：一方面，从空间论看，"国际法中尚无空气空间和外层空间划界的明确规定，故而无

---

① See Ram Jakhu, Tommaso Sgobba & Paul S. Dempsey, *The Need for an Integrated Regulatory Regime for Aviation and Space: ICAO for Space?*, (New York: Springer, 2011) at 64.

② See Ram Jakhu, Tommaso Sgobba & Paul S. Dempsey, *The Need for an Integrated Regulatory Regime for Aviation and Space: ICAO for Space?*, (New York: Springer, 2011) at 49. See also Michael P Chatzipanagiotis, *Regulating Suborbital Flights in Europe: Selected Issues* (19 November 2012) SSRN (papers.ssrn.com/sol3papers.cfm?abstract_id=2177571).

③ See Ram Jakhu, Tommaso Sgobba & Paul S. Dempsey, *The Need for an Integrated Regulatory Regime for Aviation and Space: ICAO for Space?*, (New York: Springer, 2011) at 49; see Peter Haanappel, *Regulation of Emerging Modes of Aerospace Transportation: Liability and Traffic Rights*, in Ram Jakhu & Kuan-Wei Chen, eds, *Regulation of Emerging Modes of Aerospace Transportation* (Montreal: Centre for Research in Air and Space Law, McGill University 2014) 101, at 102.

④ See Peter Haanappel, "Regulation of Emerging Modes of Aerospace Transportation: Liability and Traffic Rights", in Ram Jakhu & Kuan-Wei Chen, eds, *Regulation of Emerging Modes of Aerospace Transportation* (Montreal: Centre for Research in Air and Space Law, McGill University 2014) 101, at 101; Paul S. Dempsey & Maria Manoli, *Suborbital Flights and the Delimitation of Air Space Vis-a-Vis outer Space: Functionalism, Spatialism and State Sovereignty* (2017) 42 Ann Air & Sp L 209. See also Francesca I Moretto & Gabriella Arrigo, "Chinese Space Station: A New Challenge for International Space Cooperation?", in Ram Jakhu, Kuan Wei Chen & Yaw Nyampong, eds, *Global Space Governance*, (Montreal: Centre for Research in Air and Space Law, McGill University, 2015) 135, at 154. 该书谈到了"基于合作的新空间时代"。

⑤ See ICAO, "Concept of Sub-Orbital Flights" (2005) Working Paper C-WP/12436 at s 1.2.

法得出亚轨道飞行适用航空法抑或空间法的结论";另一方面,从功能论看,"亚轨道飞行更宜适用航空法。因为在'地对地'运输过程中,飞行器的主要活动范围是空气空间而非外层空间,在外层空间飞行的时间很短暂"①。此外,该文件还指出:

> 如果亚轨道飞行器从事国际飞行时被视为航空器,那么《芝加哥公约》将对其产生约束力,主要体现在登记、适航认证、飞行员执照和操作要求等方面。②

然而,这两种学说并不尽如人意,国际法律界至今未选择支持或反对某种学说。③

根据一些学者的观点,当下的监管真空可通过加强国际合作④及拓展国际民用航空组织项下的法规适用范围来填补⑤。因此,应将临近空间和亚轨道飞行纳入国际民航组织的职权范围⑥,以此实现"从航空旅游到外

---

① See ICAO, "Concept of Sub-Orbital Flights" (2005) Working Paper C-WP/12436 at para 6.2.
② See ICAO, "Concept of Sub-Orbital Flights" (2005) Working Paper C-WP/12436 at para 2.3.
③ Peter Haanappel, "Regulation of Emerging Modes of Aerospace Transportation: Liability and Traffic Rights", in Ram Jakhu & Kuan-Wei Chen, eds, *Regulation of Emerging Modes of Aerospace Transportation* (Montreal: Centre for Research in Air and Space Law, McGill University 2014) 101, at 101.
④ 关于在空间领域开展更有效的国际和跨学科对话的必要性,参见 Ram Jakhu & Joseph N. Pelton, eds, *Global Space Governance: An International Study*, (Cham: Springer International Publishing AG, 2017) 3, at 3。
⑤ See Sanat Kaul, "To What Extent is the Current Regime Governing International Air Transport Relevant to Aerospace Transport?", in Ram Jakhu & Kuan-Wei Chen, eds, *Regulation of Emerging Modes of Aerospace Transportation* (Montreal: Centre for Research in Air and Space Law, McGill University 2014) 123, at 140. See also Francesco Gaspari, "Space Transportation and International Air Transportation: The Transition towards a Common Legal System", in Ram Jakhu & Kuan-Wei Chen, eds, *Regulation of Emerging Modes of Aerospace Transportation* (Montreal: Centre for Research in Air and Space Law, McGill University 2014) 141, at 155 ff.
⑥ 关于临近空间和亚轨道飞行的差异,参见 Peter Haanappel, "Regulation of Emerging Modes of Aerospace Transportation: Liability and Traffic Rights", in Ram Jakhu & Kuan-Wei Chen, eds, *Regulation of Emerging Modes of Aerospace Transportation* (Montreal: Centre for Research in Air and Space Law, McGill University 2014) 101, at 102–103。

空及亚轨道旅游"①的顺利过渡。

还有一些学者建议,可以采取折中、自愿的措施来完善国际协调机制,逐步标准化实践,以便在国际层面上达成全球协议,甚至是具有约束力的公约。②

国际民航组织最近也主动与其他组织和机构开展联合行动。正如国际民航组织秘书处在法律委员会第36届会议③上（关于"空间商业飞行"）所指出的,④国际民航组织理事会定期听取空间商业发展的简报。继2014年11月对亚轨道商业运输和空天一体化（成员国信函2014/41）进行调研后,为了更好地了解未来需求,国际民航组织与联合国外层空间事务厅（UNOSA）共同组织了一个研究小组。该小组由从事空间商业运输的人员组成,他们对会员国的监管材料进行了汇编。⑤ 2015年3月18日至20日,国际民航组织和联合国外层空间事务厅在蒙特利尔联合组织了一场关于航空航天的专题研讨会,主题之一就是"航空航天活动的监管实践",包含亚轨道飞行。后续在阿布扎比（2016年）和维也纳（2017年）举办的航空航天研讨会上,学者们又再次围绕亚轨道飞行进行了讨论。

---

① See Sanat Kaul, "To What Extent is the Current Regime Governing International Air Transport Relevant to Aerospace Transport?", in Ram Jakhu & Kuan-Wei Chen, eds, *Regulation of Emerging Modes of Aerospace Transportation* (Montreal: Centre for Research in Air and Space Law, McGill University 2014) 123, at 140. 关于国际民航组织在规制亚轨道商业旅行方面发挥的作用,另参见 Ruwantissa Abeyratne, *Regulation of Commercial Space Transport—The Astrocizing of ICAO*, (Cham: Springer, 2015) at 59ff.

② See Joseph Pelton, "Regulatory Issues for New Global Aerospace Systems", in Ram Jakhu & Kuan-Wei Chen, eds, *Regulation of Emerging Modes of Aerospace Transportation* (Montreal: Centre for Research in Air and Space Law, McGill University 2014) 77, at 80.

③ 该会议于2015年11月30日至12月3日在蒙特利尔举办。

④ ICAO, "Commercial Space Flights" (2015) Working Paper LC/36 – WP/3 – 2.

⑤ 这些材料可在国际民航组织官网获取。"Space Transportation", online: ICAO (www4.icao.int/space).

三、欧盟法律监管框架

（一）欧盟在空间领域行动的基础和当前的法律框架

早在20世纪80年代，欧盟就对空间事务表现出浓厚的兴趣，[1] 远早于2007年的《里斯本条约》。[2] 自20世纪90年代以来，欧盟不断增加对空间部门的投入。[3] 多年来，这种兴趣促使欧盟调整其内部事务，制定具体的空间目标。

2009年，《里斯本条约》生效。该条约与《欧洲联盟运作条约》（Treaty on the Functioning of the European Union，TFEU）的合并版两次提及"空间"：首先，第一编第一章对"欧盟的职权范围与领域"做出定义；其次，第三编第十九章规定"研究、技术开发与空间"。在第一章中，第3条规定了欧盟的专属权限，第4条列举了欧盟与成员国共享权限的领域。[4] 值得注意的是，应欧洲议会安全与防务委员会要求发起的一项研究强调，第4条第3款单独规定了一项共享权限领域，即研究、技术开发和空间政策。并且，欧盟在此领域行使权力时，不得妨碍成员国权力的行使。这意味着，"在成员国产业政策优先的领域，欧盟将与各国并行采取措施，强

---

[1] See e. g. EC, *Resolution of 17 September 1981 on European Spacy Policy*, [1981] OJ, C260 at 102.

[2] See EC, *Treaty of Lisbon amending the Treaty on European Union and the Treaty establishing the European Community*, signed at lisbon, 13 December, [2007] OJ, C306. 关于欧盟空间政策的产生与发展，参见 Emmanuel Sigalas, *Explaining the Rise of the European Union Space Policy: A Theoretical Introduction* (2015) 14: 3, The Aviation & Space J at 25. 关于欧盟委员会在欧洲空间政策制定中发挥的作用，参见 Lucia Marta & Paul Stephenson, "Role of the European Commission in Framing Space Policy", in Thomas Hörber & Paul Stephenson, eds, *The European Space Policy*, (London: Routledge Taylor & Francis Group, 2016) at 98 – 113。

[3] 甚至在《里斯本条约》之前，欧盟就已经成功开发了欧洲地球静止导航重叠服务（EGNOS）和伽利略系统。目前，这两个系统均在运行中，伽利略系统更是被视为欧盟的旗舰系统。

[4] 一般而言，共享权限确实阻止了欧盟成员国在欧盟已经采取行动的情况下采取立法行动。

化与各国及欧洲空间局的合作"①。关于第十九章,第 189 条赋予欧盟在空间政策方面的共享权限,以促进科技进步、产业竞争力以及推动政策实施。② 这为欧盟在该领域的行动奠定了基础。

由于成员国仍是欧洲空间活动的基本行为者,在欧盟法律秩序内增补一项关于空间的具体规定显得意蕴深刻,③ 一方面,它巩固了欧洲空间局(ESA)④ 和欧盟⑤在空间领域的合作;另一方面,也明确了欧盟"制定欧洲空间政策"的职责。⑥

鉴于此,欧洲议会和理事会应根据普通立法程序制定必要措施,该措施可采取欧洲空间计划的形式,但不得对成员国法律法规进行任何协调。⑦

《里斯本条约》通过后,欧盟出台了若干条例和决定,包括欧洲议会和理事会第 1285/2013 号条例(EU)⑧、欧洲议会和理事会第 377/2014 号

---

① European Parliament, Directorate-General for External Policies of the Union, *Space, Sovereign and European Security Building European Capabilities in an Advanced Institutional Framework* (2014) at 44, online (pdf): European Parliament [www.europarl.europa.eu/RegData/etudes/join/2014/433750/EXPO-SEDE_ET (2014) 433750_EN.pdf] (European Parliament Space Sovereignty). 该研究旨在全面分析天基能力在支持欧盟及成员国安全和防务政策方面的作用。

② EU Commission, *An Integrated Industrial Policy for the Globalisation Era Putting Competitiveness and Sustainability at Centre Stage*, (Communication), COM (2010) 614 final (28 October 2010) at 24 [COM (2010) 614]. See also EU, Council of the European Union, *Council Conclusions on "Space as an Enabler"*, 9713/19 (28 May 2019).

③ European Parliament Space Sovereignty, at 64.

④ 成立于 1975 年的欧空局是一个国际研究与发展组织,由 22 个成员国组成。See Sergio Marchisio, *Le clausole relative allo spazio nel Trattato sul funzionamento dell'Unione europea*, in *Studi in onore di Umberto Leanza*, vol 2 (Napoli: Editoriale scientifica, 2008) at para 1. 如欧盟议会所述,欧空局是欧洲政府间研发机构,根据成员国整体提出的具体利益,确定和实施科学、技术、空间应用开发计划:欧洲议会外空主权。See European Parliament, Directorate-General for External Policies of the Union, *Space, Sovereign and European Security Building European Capabilities in an Advanced Institutional Framework* (2014) at 56.

⑤ See EC, *Treaty on the Functioning of the European Union*, [2012], OJ, C 326/47 Art. 189 at para 3 [TFEU]; 欧盟委员会指出,欧盟越来越多地参与空间事务,"需要重新评估其与欧空局的关系,反过来,也需要欧空局逐步转变"。See COM (2010) 614, at 25.

⑥ See Sergio Marchisio, *Le clausole relative allo spazio nel Trattato sul funzionamento dell'Unione europea*, in *Studi in onore di Umberto Leanza*, vol.2 (Napoli: Editoriale scientifica, 2008) at para 5. 欧洲空间政策最初是一个纯粹的政府间事务,但随着欧洲议会的日益参与,它逐渐超越了国家层面。See Emmanuel Sigalas, *The Role of the European Parliament in the Development of a European Union Space Policy* (May 2012) 28: 2 Space Pol'y 110.

⑦ TFEU, Art.189 at para 2.

⑧ 关于欧洲卫星导航系统,伽利略和欧洲地球静止导航重叠服务的实施和开发。

条例（EU）①、欧洲议会和理事会第541/2014/EU号决定②、欧洲议会和理事会第912/2010号条例（EU）③、欧洲议会和理事会第1104/2011/EU号决定④、理事会第2014/496/CFSP号决定⑤。上述立法文件中的空间监管举措，值得进一步研究。

（二）"后里斯本时代"空间领域的监管举措

1. 欧盟空间产业政策及建立统一的空间法律框架之必要性

2007年《里斯本条约》签署后，欧盟委员会在《欧盟产业政策通报》（2010年10月通过）中强调，其将推行与欧洲空间局和成员国共同制定的空间产业政策。⑥

在2011年的一份通讯文件中，欧盟委员会进一步介绍了欧洲空间产业政策的潜质。⑦ 它特别强调，空间产业是欧盟的战略性产业，有助于欧洲2020战略的实施。为了落实欧盟的空间政策目标，委员会还确立了优先行动。⑧ 成员国在2011年5月和12月通过的理事会结论中支持了这一做法。⑨ 此外，这份文件还建立在欧盟委员会产业政策通讯文件《强大的欧盟工业有利于经济增长和复苏》的基础上。⑩

---

① 确立哥白尼计划。
② 建立空间跟踪与监视系统框架。
③ 设立欧洲全球导航卫星系统机构。
④ 关于公众使用伽利略系统提供的受管制服务的规则。
⑤ 关于伽利略系统的部署、运行和使用影响欧盟安全的方面。
⑥ COM（2010）614.
⑦ EU, Commission, *Towards a Space Strategy for the European Union that Benefits Its Citizens*, (Communication), COM（2011）152 final（4 April 2011）[COM（2011）].
⑧ 根据通讯文件COM（2011）（para 1 at 3）以及《欧洲联盟运作条约》第一百八十九条，欧盟的空间政策旨在实现以下目标：推动科学技术进步，促进产业革新及提升竞争力，使欧洲公民从空间应用中获得好处，提升欧洲在空间领域世界舞台上的形象。
⑨ EC, *Council Resolution of 6 December 2011—Orientations Concerning Added Value and Benefits of Space for the Security of European Citizens*, （2011/C377/01），[2011] OJ, C377/1. 根据结论，"空间产业政策应考虑到空间部门的特殊性及所有成员国对空间资产投资的兴趣，并以下列目标为共同目标：为欧洲设想、研发、发射、运营和空间系统开发能力提供支持；加强欧洲工业在国内和出口市场的竞争力；促进欧洲内部竞争、平衡发展以及能力投入"。同时，该文件也强调"有必要审查应在欧洲和国际层面采取适当措施，以保证空间活动的可持续性和经济发展，包括欧洲商业部门的活动"。
⑩ EU, Commission, *A Strong European Industry for Growth and Economic Recovery*, (Communication), COM（2012）582final,（10 October 2012）[COM（2012）].

具言之，委员会回顾了《欧洲联盟运作条约》第 189 条赋予欧盟与成员国在空间领域的共享权限，并指出，在此法律框架内，欧盟负有制定欧洲空间政策的职责，"为此，欧盟可推动达成联合倡议，支持研究和技术发展，并协调开发和利用外空所需的努力"。同时，"议会和理事会应出台必要措施，可采取欧洲空间计划的形式"①。在此背景下，欧盟的空间产业政策应围绕以下五个具体目标：

1）建立协调稳定的监管框架；
2）进一步发展欧洲具有竞争力、稳固、高效和平衡的工业基础，支持中小企业参与；
3）通过鼓励欧盟航天工业在价值链上更具成本效益，支持欧盟航天业的全球竞争力；
4）开发空间应用和服务市场；
5）确保技术自主和独立进入空间。②

为助力"欧盟 2020 战略"实施，欧盟委员会于 2013 年 2 月 28 日发布《欧盟空间产业政策》。③ 其中一个目标就是探讨商业航天活动应否被纳入法律框架。委员会认为，随着空间活动的扩展，现有监管框架的适当性亟待审查，以确保此类活动的安保、安全、可持续性及经济发展。④

监管框架的建立基于以下事实：随着空间活动的广泛开展，空间产品及服务市场规模的日趋扩大，一些法律问题逐渐暴露出来。这些问题在欧洲层面难以得到有效解决，通过成员国立法解决的也仅占少数。

有些成员国尚未制定空间法，已经完成立法的国家，其空间法的范围和目标也不尽相同，对外均产生了一定影响。仅靠国内立法难以保障监管框架的连贯性、全面性，同时也无法保障各国监管的一致性。这可能会对内部市场运作产生负面影响。⑤ 在这方面，委员会认为亚轨道飞行是一片蓝海，可用于：（i）科学实验，如微重力实验、宇航员训练、卫星有效载荷测试等；（ii）空间旅游；（iii）未来清洁、高空、高速、点对点的航空

---

① COM (2011), at 3.
② COM (2013), paras 1 & 3.
③ COM (2013).
④ COM (2013), para 4.1.
⑤ COM (2013), para 4.1.1.

运输。此外，亚轨道飞行器还可以为小型卫星等物体进入外层空间，提供更加经济高效的途径。①

这就是为什么委员会认为有必要结合现有立法，在欧盟层面建立统一的监管框架。② 由此，委员会将依据各部门的权限，探讨是否需要采取措施提高法律的连贯性，推动欧洲空间产品和服务市场的形成。③ 当然，在建立统一的监管框架前，欧盟应先发起一项研究，对亚轨道空间飞行的市场潜力进行评估，并明确是否制定欧洲的监管方案。④

此外，2013年的通讯文件聚焦航天产业面临的国际挑战。委员会特别指出，欧洲航天产业与其他国际竞争者的不同之处在于：预算较少、更依赖商业销售、军用开支份额小、民用和防务部门的协同机制远不完善。另外，与美国有所不同，欧洲的地球观测与导航服务下游市场才刚刚兴起。以上因素使欧洲产业正面临商业和创新的挑战。⑤

2.《欧洲空间战略》

最近，欧盟委员会强调了空间对欧盟的至关重要性，其在《欧洲空间战略》（*Space Strategy for Europe*，2016）中，⑥ 象征性地确认了"空间对欧洲的重要意义"，指出：

> 空间能力对民用、商业、防务、安全等目标具有重大战略意义。欧洲应确保在空间领域的行动自由和自主性；保证安全、自主地进入和利用空间；保障无线电频谱利用和不受干扰，实现无线电频谱资源效益最大化。⑦

---

① COM (2013), para 4.1.1.

② COM (2013), para 3.

③ COM (2013), para 3.

④ COM (2013), 附录第1.1.4段。See also Jean-Bruno Marciacq et al., "Establishing a Regulatory Framework for the Development and Operations of Sub-Orbital & Orbital Aircraft (SoA) in the European Union", in Ram Jakhu & Kuan-Wei Chen, eds, *Regulation of Emerging Modes of Aerospace Transportation* (Montreal: Centre for Research in Air and Space Law, McGill University 2014) 261, at 272.

⑤ COM (2013), para 2.1.

⑥ EU, Commission, *Space Strategy for Europe*, (Communication) COM (2016) 705 final (26 October 2016) at 2 [COM (2016)].

⑦ COM (2016), para 3.

欧盟委员会2018年的立法提案进一步阐明了制定此战略的理由。① 在提案的解释性备忘录中，它回顾了空间部门对欧盟的战略意义，并论述了欧洲空间部门适应国际形势变化的必要性。② 它还强调，空间发展与欧盟的多项政策和战略优先事项相契合。

欧盟委员会出台的《欧洲空间战略》专注于四个战略目标：实现空间对欧洲社会和经济的效益最大化；培育具有全球竞争力和创新力的欧洲空间部门；确保欧洲安全、自主地进入和利用空间；强化欧洲在全球空间活动中的地位，促进国际合作。只有通过国际合作，在世界舞台上发挥更大的作用，才能实现上述目标。③ 同时，委员会还聚焦太空新经济的主要问题，指出：

> 太空中的竞争和挑战不断加剧。随着卫星研制和发射成本的不断降低，世界各地正涌现出一大批新的竞争对手，包括国家和私人实体。同时，空中的威胁也与日俱增：从空间碎片到网络威胁，再到空间天气的影响。这些变化凸显出民用和防务活动协同的重要性。欧洲必须充分利用其资产，发挥其空间能力来满足欧盟和成员国对安全和安保的需求。④

欧盟委员会在2018年监管提案的解释性备忘录中也指出，欧盟面临诸多新挑战，如气候变化⑤、可持续发展、边境管制、海上监视、公民安全⑥等。而空间部门在有效应对上述挑战中发挥着关键作用。同时，理事会在

---

① EC, Commission, *Proposal for a Regulation of the European Parliament and of the Council Establishing the Space Programme of the Union and the European Union Agency for the Space Programme and Repealing Regulations (EU) No. 912/2010, (EU) No. 1285/2013, (EU) No. 377/2014 and Decision 541/2014/EU*, (Communication) COM (2018) 447 final (06 June 2018). On this proposal, see more widely *infra*, para 3.

② EC, Commission, *Proposal for a Regulation of the European Parliament and of the Council Establishing the Space Programme of the Union and the European Union Agency for the Space Programme and Repealing Regulations (EU) No. 912/2010, (EU) No. 1285/2013, (EU) No. 377/2014 and Decision 541/2014/EU*, (Communication) COM (2018) 447 final (06 June 2018), at Point 1 of such Proposal.

③ COM (2016), para 4. 欧盟委员会在其2010年的通讯文件中也强调了国际合作的重要性。See COM (2010), para 8.1. 国际合作被誉为"外空的钥匙"。

④ COM (2016), para 3–4.

⑤ 在这方面，正如强调的那样，全球环境与安全监测计划正是欧盟空间领域应对气候变化的主要贡献。COM (2010), para 8.1.

⑥ 关于空间应用对公民安全的重要性，参见COM (2010), para 8.1。

《空间促进可持续的欧洲》这一结论文件①（2020年6月4日通过）中也强调，空间部门通过提升经济和社会效益，为欧洲长期可持续发展提供了众多机遇。这有助于实现联合国可持续发展目标、《仙台框架》②、《巴黎协定》③；欧盟战略优先事项，如欧盟社会权利支柱计划；④ 以及各部门的知情决策和公共政策的完善。此外，理事会还强调，地球科学与欧洲空间数据、服务、技术将有助于落实《欧洲绿色协议》，使欧洲成为全球可持续发展的领导者，有效应对社会挑战，保护生态系统功能，造福子孙后代。⑤

2020年5月29日，各国负责空间事务的部长们讨论了空间数据、服务和技术对欧盟可持续发展的贡献，以及如何从新冠疫情中复苏的问题。同时，他们就如何提高空间应用的经济、环境和社会效益交换了意见。⑥

欧盟委员会《欧洲空间战略》通讯文件倡导的方法得到了欧洲理事会（2017年5月30日通过的结论文件）⑦ 和欧洲议会（2017年9月12日通过的决议）⑧ 的肯定。其中，理事会特别鼓励委员会和成员国根据实际情况，与欧洲空间局和各国空间机构加强技术合作。

3. 欧盟委员会2018年的立法提案

继欧盟委员会推出2016战略后，欧盟致力于研究"2021—2027空间

---

① Council Conclusions on "Space for a sustainable Europe", adopted on 4 June 2020, at Point 3 (Council Conclusions, 2020).

② United Nations Office for Disaster Risk Reduction, "Sendai Framework for Disaster Risk Reduction 2015-2030" (18 March 2015), online (pdf): UNISDR (www. unisdr. org/files/43291_sendaiframeworkfordrren. pdf).

③ Conference of the Parties, Report of the Conference of the Parties on its twenty-first session, held in Paris from 30 November to 13 December 2015, UNFCC, 21st Sess, FCCC/CP/2015/10/Add. 1.

④ 2017年10月20日，常驻代表委员会达成《欧洲社会权利支柱》机构间宣言，拟于2017年10月23日提交理事会（EPSCO）。See General Secretariat of the Council, "Doc – 13129/17 – Proposal for an Interinstitutional Proclamation on the European Pillar of Social Rights" (20 October 2017), online (pdf): Council of the European Union (data.consilium.europa.eu/doc/document/ST – 13129 – 2017 – INIT/en/pdf.).

⑤ Council Conclusions, 2020, at Point 3.

⑥ 会议成果获取：European Council, "Main Results-Video conference of ministers responsible for space, 29 May 2020", (29 May 2020), online: European Council (www.consilium.europa.eu/en/meetings/compet/2020/05/29/space/).

⑦ See EU, Council of the European Union, *Council Conclusions on "A Space Strategy for Europe"*, 9817/17 (30 May 2017).

⑧ See EU, European Parliament, *Space Strategy for Europe*, (Report), A8-0250/2017 (5 July 2017).

计划"①。委员会2018年的立法提案是《欧洲空间战略》的延续。② 正如提案的解释性备忘录中所阐述的：一项综合全面的空间计划将汇集欧盟所有的空间活动，为未来的投资提供一个连贯的框架，以提高预见性和灵活性。③

该提案以《欧洲联盟运作条约》第189条第二款为依据，拟梳理并整合迄今为止散落在单行法或决定中的规则，形成一个文本，从而实现欧盟空间法的精简化。④ 它规定了各部分普遍适用的规则，涵盖了伽利略、欧洲地球静止导航重叠服务（EGNOS）、哥白尼计划及空间跟踪与监视系统等，同时也针对各部分制定了特殊规则。

相反，提案不会修订第1104/2011/EU号决定。该决定将与立法案一起作为规制伽利略系统的一项特殊服务，即公众特许服务（PRS），并由特别法予以补充。此外，基于《欧洲联盟条约》第二十八条的第2014/496/CFSP号决定也将一如既往地适用。⑤ 欧盟推出的空间新政策彰显了其意欲在全球空间参与者中发挥关键作用的雄心。⑥

提案还为欧盟开展所设想的各种活动编制了预算，特别是在推进和完善伽利略系统、欧洲地球静止导航重叠服务、哥白尼计划、空间跟踪与监视系统以及启动政府卫星通讯倡议（Govsatcom）方面。⑦ 此外，提案还通过以下两种途径为新空间计划建章立制：一是厘清所涉各方的关系及职责（主要是成员国、欧盟委员会和欧盟空间机构），二是为计划的各组成部分建立统一的制度。该提案强化了前欧洲全球导航卫星系统机构的作用，将其安全认证管辖范围扩大至新计划的所有组成部分。该机构也将借机更

---

① 关于欧盟空间计划的更多信息，参见 Council of the European Union, "*EU space policy*", online: Council of the European Union (www.consilium.europa.eu/en/policies/eu-space-programmes/)。

② See COM (2018).

③ See COM (2018), at 2.

④ 具言之，该条例取代了 COM (2018) 中的条例和决定。正如2018年提案的解释性备忘录所阐明的，欧盟第912/2010号条例（EU）所需的修订如下：为了明确和简化，此文本应被废除，新机构（承接了欧洲全球导航卫星系统机构的职能）的规则纳入建立欧盟空间计划的条例中。See EC, Commission, *Proposal for a Regulation of the European Parliament and of the Council establishing the Space Programme of the Union and the European Union Agency for the Space Programme and Repealing Regulations (EU) No. 912/2010, (EU) No. 1285/2013, (EU) No. 377/2014 and Decision 541/2014/EU*, (Communication) COM (2018) 447 final (06 June 2018) Point 1 at 3–4.

⑤ COM (2018), Explanatory Memorandum, Point 1 at 4.

⑥ COM (2018), Explanatory Memorandum, Point 1 at 3.

⑦ COM (2018), Explanatory Memorandum, Point 1 at 3.

名,成为欧盟空间计划机构。①

提案最后详细规定了新空间计划的安全框架,特别是应遵守的原则、应遵循的程序和应采取的措施。鉴于行动的用途具有双重性质,安全显得尤为重要。②

2019年3月13日,欧盟理事会和欧洲议会就文本达成一致,尽管财政方面有待在下个"多年期财政框架"——欧盟长期预算中达成统一。③

(三)在自下而上和自上而下的方案间寻求新的多层次监管框架

首先,所有相关方都认同在欧盟层面建立空间监管框架的必要性④,这避免了"挑选法院"现象的出现⑤。其次,各方认同应加强区际和国际合作的必要性(包括政府部门和私营实体)。⑥ 此做法与欧盟委员会提出的措施如出一辙:

> 旨在促进欧盟委员会、欧盟成员国、欧洲空间局、欧洲全球导航卫星系统局(欧洲全球导航卫星系统机构)以及其他相关机构,如欧洲气象卫星应用组织、利益攸关方、空间产业、研究机构和用户群体之间的伙伴关系。⑦

---

① COM (2018), Explanatory Memorandum, Point 1 at 3.

② COM (2018), Explanatory Memorandum。

③ 2020年11月10日,在德国担任主席国期间,理事会与欧洲议会达成了一项政治协议。关于欧盟长期预算(2021—2027),参见 European Council, "Long-term EU Budget 2021 – 2027 and Recovery Package",(20 July 2021), online:European Council (www.consilium.europa.eu/en/policies/the-eu-budget/long-term-eu-budget-2021 – 2027/)。

④ See COM (2013), para 3 & 4.1.1.

⑤ 正如欧盟委员会所强调的 [COM (2013), para 4.1.1], 欧盟各国缺乏统一的规则可能会扭曲内部市场竞争,导致"挑选法院"现象出现。

⑥ Council Conclusions, 2020, at Point 21 着重强调了区域合作的重要性,尤其是空间教育和技能方面。此外,欧洲理事会呼吁地区和地方当局深度参与到技能发展和知识共享中来,以带动整个欧盟的就业创造、创新和创业。

⑦ COM (2016), para 5.

政府部门和私营实体间的伙伴关系反映了空间领域最新的发展趋势,[①]与以往不同的是,"空间越来越倾向于诉诸私法和商法"[②]。过去,调整空间活动的法律以国际、国内公法为主。此外,在所有空间国家中,空间部门的发展均高度依赖政府规划和补贴。[③]

原则上,欧洲的监管方案至少有两种选择。其一,一些行业利益相关者呼吁欧盟建立更严格的监管框架,并根据航空的最佳实践制定适当的认证规则,以更好地保障乘客安全。他们认为,监管框架的可预测性是私人投资者考虑的关键因素,因为其影响着空间技术的应用与开发活动。[④] 该方案被称为"自上而下"的方案,公权力在其中扮演着积极角色,职责包括但不限于提供财政资金。这是欧洲大陆(即欧洲和意大利)的传统方案,"自上而下"确定拟采取的措施意味着高效和创新。

其二,其他利益相关方则呼吁欧盟建立一个"创新友好型"的监管框架。[⑤] 这种方案源于美国的法律体系,以私营实体和行业发挥积极作用为

[①] 学者塞尔吉奥·马尔基西奥(Sergio Marchisio)将空间法定义为"所有旨在规范国家和其他主体(包括私人经营者)在外层空间活动的规则。"这些规则一方面分属不同的法律体系,即国际法抑或国内法秩序,另一方面属于公法或私法不同的分支。See Sergio Marchisio, "Space Law and Governance" (address delivered at the 10th United Nations Workshop on Space Law "Contribution of Space Law and Policy to Space Governance and Space Security in the 21th Century", Vienna, 5 – 8 September 2016) available online: UNOOSA (www. unoosa. org/pdf/SLW2016/Opening/2. _Marchisio_MARCHISIO_10th_United_Nations_Workshop_on_Space_Law. pdf) [Marchisio].

[②] See Sergio Marchisio, "Space Law and Governance" (address delivered at the 10th United Nations Workshop on Space Law "Contribution of Space Law and Policy to Space Governance and Space Security in the 21th Century", Vienna, 5 – 8 September 2016) at 2, available online: UNOOSA (www. unoosa. org/pdf/SLW2016/Opening/2. _Marchisio_MARCHISIO_10th_United_Nations_Workshop_on_Space_Law. pdf) [Marchisio].

[③] COM (2010), para 8. 1.

[④] COM (2010), para 4. 1. 1.

[⑤] COM (2010), para 4. 1. 1.

基础,① 蕴含"自下而上"的逻辑和助推理论。② 具言之,此方案植根于美国与众不同的创新理念,即创新是一个"自下而上"的过程,政府应简政放权,只负责构建一个有利于技术开发的监管框架;③ 同时此方案也建立在"能促型国家"理论和"共同管理"模式的基础上。

不可否认,空间私有化为私法介入该领域铺平了道路,空间合同法、空间合同责任法、空间知识产权法、空间保险法、空间活动融资法和空间项目贷款法等应运而生。然而,"现行空间法的根源在于国际(公)法"④,并且考虑到空间作为"全球公域"的法律地位,亚轨道飞行的立法

---

① 助推理论出现于 2020 年初,由芝加哥两位教授——经济学家泰勒(Thaler)和法学家桑斯坦(Sunstein)提出。该理论建立在人类只有理性行为的假设上,以对制度理论的不满为出发点。See Richard H. Thaler & Cass R. Sunstein, *Nudge*: *Improving Decisions about Health, Wealth, and Happiness* (New Haven: Yale University Press, 2008). 关于助推理论最新的研究成果,另参见 Cass R. Sunstein, *Nudges vs. Shoves* (2014) Harv L Rev 210; Cass R. Sunstein, *Do People Like Nudges*? (2015) Admin L Rev.1; Cass R. Sunstein, *The Ethics of Influence: Government in the Age of Behavioral Science* (Cambridge: Cambridge University Press, 2016); Cass R. Sunstein, *Regulation as Delegation* (2015) J Legal Analysis 1; Cass R. Sunstein, *Nudges That Fail* (2017) Notre Dame JL Ethics & Pub Pol'y 4; Cass R. Sunstein & Lucia A. Reisch, *The Economics of Nudge*, (New York: Routledge Taylor & Francis Group, 2017); Cass R. Sunstein, *Is Cost-Benefit Analysis a Foreign Language*? (2019) 72 Quarterly J Experimental Psychology 3. 泰勒和桑斯坦提出的方法在美国学者中引起了广泛激烈的争论,他们对"政府作为个人选择的设计师"这一理论进行了批判,认为政府代替了个人的自由选择。See R. Sudgen, *Do People Really Want to Be Nudged Towards Healthy Lifestyles*? (2017) Intl Rev. Economics 113. 助推理论蕴含一种监管模式,该模式并非通过法律义务起作用,表面上被认为是消除个人决策权的要素,而实则是"助推"。与大陆法系研究不同,在美国法律和政治研究中,软性或灵活的监管通常被认为是自由主义的家长制(即助推)。See Sara Valaguzza, *Nudging Pubblico vs. Pubblico: Nuovi Strumenti per una Regolazione Flessibile di ANAC* (2017) 1 Rivista della Regolazione dei Mercati 91 at 96.

② See COM (2012), at 7. 在该文件中,委员会旨在将"积极的产业政策方法"扩展到包括空间在内的不同关键领域。

③ See E. Ferrero, *Le Smart Cities Nell' Ordinamento Giuridico* (2015) Foro amministrativo 1267 at 1272. 作者回顾道,机制通常遵循所谓的启动机制,即建立企业并从一个想法开始研发直至投放市场,企业在此过程中通过风险投资的方式获得资金。

④ See Sergio Marchisio, *Space Law and Governance* (address delivered at the 10th United Nations Workshop on Space Law "Contribution of Space Law and Policy to Space Governance and Space Security in the 21th Century", Vienna, 5 – 8 September 2016) at 2, available online: UNOOSA (www. unoosa. org/pdf/SLW2016/Opening/2. _Marchisio_MARCHISIO_10th_United_Nations_Workshop_on_Space_Law. pdf) [Marchisio].

和监管框架只能是严格意义上的公法①。

因此,亟须在考虑所有利益和利益相关方的基础上,为空天部门和亚轨道飞行建立一个适当的法律框架,② 但无论如何,空间领域的主导权不能留给私营实体。

鉴于新空间经济政策的功能及空间物体的重要意义(安全与安保、研究与教育、创新、机动性等),笔者认为需要对其进行战略规划和政府干预。

塞尔吉奥·马尔基西奥(Sergio Marchisio)教授也明确阐述了上述方案的正当性。首先,外层空间活动对人类的生活至关重要。其次,空间活动(如亚轨道飞行)与经济的关联性越来越强。最后,符合空间法的目

---

① 公海上方的空气空间和外层空间被认为是人类共同的遗产,目前也被称为全球公域。See Sanat Kaul, "To What Extent is the Current Regime Governing International Air Transport Relevant to Aerospace Transport?", in Ram Jakhu & Kuan-Wei Chen, eds, *Regulation of Emerging Modes of Aerospace Transportation* (Montreal: Centre for Research in Air and Space Law, McGill University 2014) 123 at 140. On this point, see also Ram Jakhu, "We, the People of Planet Earth", (Introduction to the 2nd Manfred Lachs Conference on Global Space Governance), in Ram Jakhu, Kuan-Wei Chen & Yaw Nyampong, eds, *Global Space Governance*, (Montreal: Centre for Research in Air and Space Law, McGill University, 2015) at 14; Steven Freeland, "The Future Global Governance of Space Security: International Law and Armed Conflicts Involving Space Technology", in Ram Jakhu, Kuan-Wei Chen & Yaw Nyampong eds, *Global Space Governance*, (Centre for Research in Air and Space Law, McGill University, 2015) 163 at 173. 作者回顾到,联合国空间条约确认,外层空间应被视为"全球公域",外层空间的探索和利用应是出于"和平目的",尽管后者一直备受争议。然而,有学者指出,与其将外层空间描述为"全球公域",不如将其描述为"共有资源",这可能意味着空间是一种"公共物品",如同来自全球定位系统(GPS)卫星的信号一样。See Duncan P. Blake, "Star Laws: The Need for a Manual of International Law Applicable to Space Warfare", in Ram Jakhu, Kuan-Wei Chen & Yaw Nyampong, eds, *Global Space Governance*, (Montreal: Centre for Research in Air and Space Law, McGill University, 2015) 535 at 539. 关于外层空间作为全球公域地位的讨论,参见 Brian C. Weeden & Tiffany Chow, *Taking a Common-pool Resources Approach to Space Sustainability: A Framework and Potential Policies* (2012) 28 Space Pol'y 166;关于外层空间作为全球公域的其他内容,参见 Charlotte Hess, *Mapping the New Commons* (2008) at 13 and passim (therein other references), available online: papers. ssrn. com/sol3/papers. cfm? abstract_id = 1356835。

② 这也是学者乔瓦尼·迪·安东尼奥(Giovanni Di Antonio)的观点。See Giovanni Di Antonio, *The Development of a Regulatory Framework for Suborbital Flight Operations in Italy*, (address delivered at the 2nd International Symposium on Hypersonic Flight held in Rome on 30 June-1 July 2016) [unpublished]. See Jean-Bruno Marciacq et al., "Establishing a Regulatory Framework for the Development and Operations of Sub-Orbital & Orbital Aircraft (SoA) in the European Union", in Ram Jakhu & Kuan-Wei Chen, eds, *Regulation of Emerging Modes of Aerospace Transportation* (Montreal: Centre for Research in Air and Space Law, McGill University 2014) at 261 ff.

标，即确保以合理、负责任的方式探索和利用外层空间，造福人类。①

欧盟委员会认为有必要将空间活动监管视为重大全球挑战，由各国共同应对，任何一个成员国无法单独行动。在全面系统的空间法出台前，国家当局（如意大利民航局）应发挥战略作用，与欧洲航空安全局签署协议。②欧盟、欧盟成员国应与欧洲空间局一道，"作为全球利益相关者采取行动，促进和保护空间的可用性，造福子孙后代"③。

在欧盟层面，欧盟委员会进一步指出，它将与欧洲空间局、欧盟成员国和工业界合作，确保欧洲进入空间的自主性、可靠性和经济有效性。④欧盟委员会在2016年的通讯文件中指出：

> 欧盟和欧洲空间局的关系是成功的一大基石。欧洲空间局在技术、知识和能力方面具有核心优势，是值得欧盟委员会继续依赖的重要伙伴。⑤

四、意大利经验

（一）机构概况

1. 监管框架

国际和区际经验表明，空间部门在巩固经济和社会发展成果方面发挥着关键作用。意大利持有相同观点，并认为空间有助于经济发展和综合国力提升。

---

① See Sergio Marchisio, "Space Law and Governance", available online: UNOOSA（www.unoosa.org/pdf/SLW2016/Opening/2._Marchisio_MARCHISIO_10th_United_Nations_Workshop_on_Space_Law.pdf）[Marchisio].

② See Jean-Bruno Marciacq et al., "Establishing a Regulatory Framework for the Development and Operations of Sub-Orbital & Orbital Aircraft (SoA) in the European Union", in Ram Jakhu & Kuan-Wei Chen, eds, *Regulation of Emerging Modes of Aerospace Transportation*（Montreal: Centre for Research in Air and Space Law, McGill University 2014）at 288. 根据该文，如今，欧洲航空安全局和外层空间活动的责任国（通常是运营国）可以签署适当的协议，避免双重监管给产业带来负担。

③ COM (2016), para 5.

④ COM (2016), para 3.1.

⑤ COM (2016), para 5.

事实上，意大利政府认识到空间对其安全发展的战略价值，专门安排总理办公室协调空间及空天①计划涉及的所有政府部门，并在新空间经济的总体框架内推进空间产业措施落实。

意大利的空间政策分散于不同的监管法案中。首先，《政府对外空与航空航天的定位》（2019年3月25日发布）确定了国家战略事项，包括进入空间，亚轨道飞行和平流层平台等。② 其次，《空间国家安全战略》（2019年7月18日发布）指出，为了保障空间活动和服务在安全、安保方面的可持续性，国家应建设完善的空间基础设施。③ 具体而言，意大利空间政策确立了以下战略目标：

1) 支持研究和技术革新——以降低成本，提升产品和服务竞争力；
2) 推动天基服务部署，促进经济增长——将空间活动纳入全球经济形势；
3) 通讯、地球观测与导航——将卫星服务应用于日常生活；
4) 外层空间研究——支持开展国际合作科学研究；
5) 进入空间——充分利用本国"空间发射和再入"的专有技术，发挥产业价值链能力；
6) 亚轨道飞行和平流层平台——巩固发展国家空间产业技术能力，包括挖掘国家航天港潜力；
7) 在轨服务——巩固发展卫星服务产业能力，包括卫星脱轨服务；
8) 机器人空间探索——参与对月球、小行星与行星的科学探索；

---

① "空天"这一术语通常代指更高的空气空间，在那里航空或类似航天的飞行可能发生重叠。

② Presidenza del Consiglio dei Ministri, *Indirizzi del Governo in Materia Spaziale e Aerospaziale* (25 March 2019), online (pdf): Governo Italiano Presidenza del Consiglio dei Ministri (presidenza. governo. it/AmministrazioneTrasparente/Organizzazione/ArticolazioneUffici/UfficiDirettaPresidente/UfficiDiretta_CONTE/ COMINT/DEL_20190325_aero spazio. pdf).

③ See Presidenza del Consiglio dei Ministri, *Indirizzi del Governo in Materia Spaziale e Aerospaziale* (18 July 2019), online (pdf): Governo Italiano Presidenza del Consiglio dei Ministri (presidenza. governo. it/AmministrazioneTrasparente/Organizzazione/ArticolazioneUffici/UfficiDirettaPresidente/UfficiDiretta _ CO NTE/COMINT/Strategia_spazio_20190718. pdf).

9）人类空间探索——参与知识发展并利用科技进步。[1]

2013年3月，意大利出于国家战略利益考量，与美国签署了《和平探索利用外层空间的合作框架协议》，以谋求两国互惠互利发展。[2] 意大利民航局也在2014年3月与美国联邦航空管理局签署了一份谅解备忘录，并于2016年6月扩展至意大利航天局（ASI）。

意大利民航局认识到，明确空间部门向好发展的必备要素对监管体系的建立具有纲举目张的作用。基于此，它在2016年7月发布了一份题为《意大利未来空间运输认证和运营监管政策》的基本文件。该文件强调了意大利民航局作为监管者的角色，这为其制定亚轨道行业准入规则铺平了道路。[3] 同时，亚轨道行业的安全目标也初具雏形，涉及飞行资产、机组人员、操作风险、空域和航天港等。

该文件旨在为未来立法确立指导方针，并与相关方一起制定出系统的方案，识别所有利好条件。意大利民航局认识到监管是关键要素，因为运营监管规则明确了企业合法运营的要求。同时，要求的严格程度也决定了行业监管的成本。

在前期准备工作（2014—2016年）的基础上，基础设施和运输部长批准了一项关于亚轨道商业飞行可持续发展的政策（2017年7月10日颁布，

---

[1] See No.197, titled *Ratifica ed esecuzione dell'Accordo quadro tra il Governo della Repubblica italianae il Governo degli Stati Uniti d'America per la cooperazione nell'esplorazione ed utilizzazione dello spazio extra-atmosferico per scopi pacifici*, fatto a Washington il 19 marzo 2013，(OJ No.292 of 16 December 2015); see also Italian Civil Aviation Authority, *A Regulatory Policy for the Prospective Commercial Space Transportation Certification and Operations* (20 July 2016), online: ENAC (www. enac. gov. it/pubblicazioni/regulatory-policy-for-the-prospective-commercial-space-transportation-certification-and-operations). See Italian Civil Aviation Authority, *A Regulatory Policy for the Prospective Commercial Space Transportation Certification and Operations* (20 July 2016), online: ENAC (www. enac. gov. it/pubblicazioni/regulatory-policy-for-the-prospective-commercial-space-transportation-certification-and-operations).

[2] See No.197, titled *Ratifica ed esecuzione dell'Accordo quadro tra il Governo della Repubblica italianae il Governo degli Stati Uniti d' America per la cooperazione nell'esplorazione ed utilizzazione dello spazio extra-atmosferico per scopi pacifici*, fatto a Washington il 19 marzo 2013，(OJ No.292 of 16 December 2015); see also Italian Civil Aviation Authority, *A Regulatory Policy for the Prospective Commercial Space Transportation Certification and Operations* (20 July 2016), online: ENAC (www. enac. gov. it/pubblicazioni/regulatory-policy-for-the-prospective-commercial-space-transportation-certification-and-operations).

[3] See Italian Civil Aviation Authority, *A Regulatory Policy for the Prospective Commercial Space Transportation Certification and Operations* (20 July 2016), online: ENAC (www. enac. gov. it/pubblicazioni/regulatory-policy-for-the-prospective-commercial-space-transportation-certification-and-operations).

第 354 号法令）。① 意大利民航局作为项目负责方，致力于建立一个全面的监管框架，以规范运营安全、航天港、空域导航需求与使用等。该法令还根据既定标准，就航天港认证标准选择及选址事项提出了建议。

从法律视角看，该政策简要有效，并得到了完备的航空法律制度的支持，包括《航空法》和《1997 年 7 月 25 日第 250 号立法法令》（该法确立意大利民航局为唯一的航空监管当局）。② 政策的基本假设是，意大利民航局获得法律授权，对处于大气层中（至少在外层空间以下）的亚轨道飞行器进行监管。该假设建立在航空器定义的基础上。根据《航空法》第七百四十三条规定，意大利对航空器的定义采取"运输功能"标准，即航空器是指能够通过空气空间将人员或货物从 A 地运送至 B 地的飞行器。由此可见，航空器的定义明确包括亚轨道飞行器，其作为航空器落入意大利民航局的管辖范围。这一观点也得到了航空业多位专家、学者的支持。③

第 265/2004 号立法也证实了该假设。该法规定了国家空气空间，指定意大利民航局作为唯一的监管机构，赋予其监管职责（不受任何高度限制）。

---

① 参见 2017 年 6 月 10 日法令，第 354 号。See Ente Nazionale per l' Aviazione Civile（ENAC），*Regulation on Construction and Operation of Spaceports*（*Courtesy English Translation*），（21 October 2020），online（pdf）：ENAC（www. enac. gov. it/sites/default/files/allegati/2020Ott/Regolamento_costruzione_e_esercizio_degli_spazioporti_30. 10. 20_Inglese. pdf）.

② 1997 年 7 月 25 日，关于意大利民航局（ENAC）的第 250 号立法令（OJ No. 177 of 31 July 1997），根据 2004 年 11 月 9 日第 265 号法律整合，更名为 2004 年 9 月 8 日第 237 号法令的转化为法律及其修正案，这体现了对民航部门的紧急干预。*Delegation to the Government for the enactment of corrective and supplementary provisions to the Navigation Code*，（OJ No. 264 of 10 November 2004）.

③ See e. g. Gerardo Mastrandrea & Leopoldo Tullio, *La revisione della parte aeronautica del codice della navigazione*（2005）1 Diritto marittimo 1201 at 1218; Leopoldo Tullio, "Diritto della navigazione" in Massimo Deiana, ed, *Diritto della navigazione*,（Milano：Giuffré, 2010）1 at 1–2. 经 2005 年和 2006 年立法修订后的《意大利航行规则》第七百四十三条规定了航空器定义，关于该定义参见 Umberto La Torre, "Gli UAV：mezzi aerei senza pilota" in Rita Tranquilli-Leali & Elisabetta Rosafio, eds, *Sicurezza navigazione e trasporto*,（Milano：Giuffré, 2008）93 at 93; Michele M Comenale Pinto, "Assicurazioni e responsabilità extracontrattuale nella navigazione aerea"（2016）2 Rivista del diritto della navigazione 501 at 531–532; Elisabetta Rosafio, "Considerazioni sui mezzi aerei a pilotaggio remote e sul regolamento ENAC"（2014）2 Rivista del diritto della navigazione 787 at 787 ff. 关于该条款以前的版本，参见 Gabriele Pescatore, "Aeromobile（Diritto della navigazione）"（1988）Enciclopedia giuridica, vol I（Roma：Treccani）; Ludovico M Bentivoglio, "Problemi giuridici dei trasporti spaziali suborbitali" in XVII *Convegno internazionale delle comunicazioni. Genova 8–12–ottobre 1969*（Genova：IIC, 1969）, 3 at 7; Gustavo Romanelli and Gabriele Silingardi, "Trasporto"（1994）Enciclopedia giuridica, vol XXXI（Roma：Treccani）.

此外，第 250/1997 号立法令是意大利国内航空法的重要组成部分，根据该法令，机场所在地属于国家所有，意大利民航局有权批准基础设施发展总体规划。① 未来，航天港资产的处置方法也将参照机场执行。

2. 意大利民航局提出的监管举措

根据 2017 年 7 月 10 日第 354 号部长令，意大利民航局在交通部的支持下，实施了一项国家计划。该计划涉及所有利益相关方，从政府机构如意大利航天局（ASI）、宇航研究中心（CIRA）、空中导航服务提供商（ENAV）、意大利空军、意大利海军，到行业代表如莱昂纳多公司（Leonardo）②、空间通信公司（Telespazio）③、航空物流科技工程公司（ALTEC）④、维托塞特公司（Vitrociset）⑤、艾维欧公司（Avio）⑥ 等。参与其中的实体总数约 50 个，各方通过汲取不同经验，为整个计划提供高水平能力支撑。

工作方案以持续关注全球状况为目标，以一个详细明确的项目为基础，包含直观的工作分解结构，清晰的工作包。另外，监管规则的制定还遵循了一些基本准则。这些准则关乎安全和稳定性，由部长颁布，意在兼顾新兴部门的发展与商业航空运输的需求。具体而言，准则如下：

1）监管框架应具有灵活性，能够促进空间部门安全发展，维护

---

① See *Codice della navigazione*, Italy 1942, GU Serie Generale n 93, Article 702.

② 莱昂纳多（Leonardo）是一家国际航空航天、防务和安保公司。该公司可提供军用、民用双重性质的技术，其 30.2% 的股份由意大利经济和财政部持有。See Leonardo, "Profile", online: Leonardo（www.leonardocompany.com/en/about-us/profile）.

③ 空间通信公司（Telespazio）是莱昂纳多（Leonardo，持股 67%）与泰雷兹（Thales，持股 33%）的联营公司。它是欧洲领先的公司，也是全球卫星解决方案和服务领域的主要参与者之一。See Telespazio, "Profile", online: Telespazio（www.Telespazio.com/en/about-us/our-company/profile）.

④ 航空物流科技工程公司（ALTEC-Aerospace Logistics Technology Engineering Company），一家由泰雷兹阿莱尼亚公司（Thales Alenia，欧洲主要的航天公司）与意大利航天局共同持股的公私合营公司，它是意大利卓越的工程和后勤服务提供中心，旨在支持国际空间站的利用和运行，以及行星探测任务的开发和实施。其总部位于都灵，在美国航空航天局（NASA）和欧洲空间局（ESA）设有联络办公室。See Altec, "Welcome to Altec", online: Altec（www.altecspace.it/en/）.

⑤ 维托塞特公司（Vitrociset）是莱昂纳多的子公司。它通过整合信息通信技术、系统设计和模拟方面最先进的技术，为国防、安全和运输市场提供支持、培训和后勤服务。See Vitrociset, "Mission and Vision", online: Vitrociset（www.vitrociset.it/company/mission-and-vision）.

⑥ 艾维欧公司（Avio）拥有领先的航天助推器技术，总部位于意大利罗马附近的科莱费罗。该公司通过其织女星系列火箭为机构、政府或商业公司的载荷发射提供具有竞争力的解决方案。See Avio, "Who we are", online: Avio（www.avio.com/who-we-are）.

国家战略利益；

2）优先保障地面或海上第三方、空域用户和关键基础设施的安全；充分考虑亚轨道运营的特殊性和相关风险，保障乘客安全。对此，意大利民航局应发挥主要作用，因为系统和操作安全预期由航空当局根据最先进的水平设定，并不断更新；

3）亚轨道运营应尽可能在本国空域内开展，以减少对他方造成的影响，同时不得阻碍商业航空发展；

4）应重视安全和网络安全。①

根据上述准则，意大利民航局制定了以下监管架构和策略，并得到了所有合作伙伴的认同：

1）"基于绩效的监管"，也被称为"基于风险的监管"，旨在规范尚未被定义的运营模式（一种全新的商业模式），并追踪最先进的技术；

2）以运营为中心的监管，着重关注空间飞行器和运载器的适航性、操作，机组人员资格及心理-生理状况等。与传统方案只关注各环节的安全合规性不同，该方案充分考虑到亚轨道新技术尚不成熟这一事实，要求申请人和认证机构进行整体评估，即纵观亚轨道飞行/运载器、机组人员、程序、减缓措施、风险管理和环境等所有环节后，就各部分的贡献度进行评估。

3）三项主要条例，即航天港、飞行操作和空域航行条例，包含轨道跟踪和监视内容；

4）优先考虑航天港监管，以便运营商制定投资计划，设计符合要求的新基础设施，获得必要批准；同时能够预留充足的时间运行新系统，使获批的运营商开展运营。②

3. 航天港认证

亚轨道活动在专门工作组各部门的保障下有序开展，与此同时，意大

---

① See Decree 10 July 2017, No. 354, Point 5 at 4–5.
② See Giovanni Di Antonio et al., *A Model for Setting a Regulatory Framework for the Development of Suborbital Operations in Italy* (2017) 4 J Space Safety Engineering 138 at 138ff.

利民航局还成立了一个特别工作组，负责制定航天港的遴选标准。

遴选规则是国家计划的第一步，鉴于所涉亚轨道活动以水平方式起飞和着陆，其采取以下基本原则：

1）利用现有和运行中的高性能跑道，以避免消耗土地，环境效益明显；

2）利用商业机场运营商已获批的安全和风险管理方式（根据2014年第139号欧盟条例批准），受益于欧盟条例确立的高要求；

3）控制亚轨道运行对商业运输空域容量的影响。[1]

利用现有的机场跑道和基础设施改造航天港还具有其他优势。其一，改建花费的成本有限。其二，重建复杂的基础设施和系统耗费大量时间，而改建节省时间。其三，重建需要得到基建部门批准，从监管公共工程的环境部门到当地社区缺一不可，相比之下，改建节省了等待批准的时间。

遴选标准基于多维度，如航天港上方空域的拥堵程度、商业运营商对机场的利用水平、跑道性能（长度、宽度、相关滑行道和停机坪）、周边居住人口密度与城市化水平、是否存在可供起飞和着陆的不受限飞行走廊、全年的天气状况，以及是否有足够的空间来建造航天基础设施和系统。[2]

遴选文件包括遴选采用的程序，经交通运输部会同国防部商定，作为意大利民航局评估核实某机场是否符合遴选标准的依据。

所有获准用于商业运营的43个机场都按照既定标准进行了评估，最佳选择是塔兰托·格罗塔列机场。此结果与意大利航天局、空中导航服务提供商[3]和意大利空军共享，然后交由基础设施和交通部批准。

毋庸置疑，基于保护商业运营及其未来发展的标准，意大利北部和中部地区的所有机场被排除在外，因为这些地区的交通流量十分密集。此外，亚轨道飞行只能在目视气象条件下开展，这要求航天港全年保持良好

---

[1] See Ente Nazionale per l' Aviazione Civile (ENAC), *Criteri Di Individuazione Degli Spazioporti* [Ente Nazionale per l' Aviazione Civile (ENAC), Undated].

[2] See Ente Nazionale per l' Aviazione Civile (ENAC), *Criteri Di Individuazione Degli Spazioporti* [Ente Nazionale per l' Aviazione Civile (ENAC), Undated].

[3] 空中导航服务提供商（ENAV）旨在确保乘客在意大利空域飞行时的安全性和航班到达的准时性。

的天气状况,而南部地区具有得天独厚的优势。① 基础设施和交通部长对该结果表示认可,并于2018年5月9日签发第250号部长令,将塔兰托·格罗塔列机场指定为意大利首个航天港和国家战略基础设施,为政府空间政策实施如亚轨道飞行、空基发射、进入外空等活动提供支持。

根据第250号部长令,意大利民航局应批准相关干预措施,以确保航天港发挥功能和提供服务;监督工作执行情况是否符合安全要求和时间表;根据国家法规批准航天港和航天港运营商,并确保针对行业需求开展运营。

4. 意大利民航局 2020 年航天港条例

为航天港建设和运营提供清晰明确的标准是意大利民航局的目标之一,也是项目计划中的安排,为此,意大利民航局专门出台了一项条例。

对比可供水平起降的航天港与传统的商业机场可以发现,二者的基础设施和系统在技术与操作特征方面存在很多交集。因此,航天港条例以欧盟第139/2014号条例为法律基础顺理成章,② 同时还规定了针对航天港特定功能和服务的附加要求。某些功能和服务源于亚轨道运营商的需求,因此条例应保持适当的灵活性。

附加要求借鉴了美国联邦航空管理局多年来采用的规则和标准,吸收了美国实践的丰富经验。

要求旨在确定追求的目标或可实现的结果。至于研发特殊要求的技术,条例采取了绩效管理办法,使运营商能够以实际需求为导向设计和提供定制服务。此外,条例特别关注了航天港的内部风险,如防止推进剂燃烧、爆炸,以及航天港的外部风险,如飞行走廊的风险。

---

① 目视气象条件是2012年9月26日第923/2012号委员会实施条例中定义的目视飞行天气条件。根据该条例第一百四十二条第二款,目视气象条件指以能见度、距云的距离和云高等于或大于规定的目视最小数值的气象条件。参见欧盟委员会,委员会实施条例2012年9月26日第923号,该条例规定了有关航空服务和程序的通用航空规则和运营规定,并修订了第1035/2011号、第1265/2007号、第1794/2006号、第730/2006号、第1033/2006号和第255/2010号实施条例,[2012] OJ, L281/1。

② EU, *Commission Regulation (EU) No. 139/2014 of 12 February 2014 Laying down Requirements and Administrative Procedures Related to Aerodromes Pursuant to Regulation (EU) No. 216/2008 of the European Parliament and of the Council*, [2014] OJ, L44/1.

条例草案① 在工业危险材料和燃料处理方面，借鉴了国家消防队的广泛经验；在确定飞行走廊可接受的风险程度时，借鉴了国际经验和技术。同时，风险控制还离不开必要的缓解措施以及公众的认可。

航天港条例的发布点燃了业界和航空服务提供商的热情，在征求意见期间产生了约140条评论，这些评论普遍支持该文件和在开发阶段做出的选择。②

与往常一样，意大利民航局在充分吸收公众意见的基础上对文本进行了修改，形成了完善的最终版本，并于2020年10月21日提交管理委员会通过。该条例经正式通过后，在意大利民航局官网公布。③

5. 下一步：亚轨道商业运营条例

高效的亚轨道商业运营监管框架对培育新空间经济至关重要。此类监管应确保第三方和飞行器上人员的安全，将风险降至可接受水平。美国通过使用"知情同意"这一原则，减少了对飞行乘客的要求，④ 但欧洲普遍

---

① ENAC, "Bozza Regolamento per la costruzione e l'esercizio degli spazioporti." 条例草案是内部文件。2020年5月5日至6月30日，意大利民航局在其网站上公开此文件以征求公众意见。See ENAC, "Consultazione normativa-Bozza Regolamento per la costruzione e l'esercizio degli spazioporti", online：ENAC (www. enac. gov. it/news/consultazione-normativa-bozza-regolamento-per-la-costruzione-lesercizio-degli-spazioporti).

② ENAC, "Bozza Regolamento per la costruzione e l'esercizio degli spazioporti." 条例草案是内部文件。2020年5月5日至6月30日，意大利民航局在其网站上公开此文件以征求公众意见。See ENAC, "Consultazione normativa-Bozza Regolamento per la costruzione e l'esercizio degli spazioporti", online：ENAC (www. enac. gov. it/news/consultazione-normativa-bozza-regolamento-per-la-costruzione-lesercizio-degli-spazioporti).

③ See ENAC, "Regolamento per la costruzione e l'esercizio degli spazioporti" (21 October 2020), online：ENAC (www. enac. gov. it/la-normativa/normativa-enac/regolamenti/regolamenti-ad-hoc/regolamento-per-la-costruzione-lesercizio-degli-spazioporti).

④ 美国2004年《空间商业发射法案》针对伤亡免责，提出了"知情同意"这一概念。See Sanat Kaul, "To what extent is the Current Regime governing International Air Transport relevant to Aerospace Transport?" in Ram Jakhu & Kuan-Wei Chen, eds, *Regulation of Emerging Modes of Aerospace Transportation* (Montreal：Centre for Research in Air and Space Law, McGill University 2014) 123 at 137；See also EU, Commission, *EU Space Industrial Policy Releasing the Potential for Economic Growth in the Space Sector*, (Communication), COM (2013) 108 final (28 February 2013) at para 4.1.1 [COM (2013)]；See Michael PChatzipanagiotis, "Regulating Suborbital Flights in Europe：Selected Issues" (19 November 2012) at 56 - 58SSRN (papers. ssrn. com/sol3papers. cfm? abstract_id = 2177671). 该文认为"知情同意"是美国立法的核心。关于美国立法中合法的知情同意，另见Christopher M. Hearsey, "The Foreign Space Flight Participant Pro-blem：Can a Space Flight Operator Balance Satisfaction of FAA Informed Consent Information Requirem-ents with ITAR?" (2013) 6 Phoenix L Rev 303 at 310。

认为应提出强制性要求，将商业飞行乘员的风险控制在最低合理可行状态。

保障航空安全的传统方法是对安全链上的各部分进行认证，使每一部分都符合规定。国际民航组织在这方面发挥了主要作用，其成立于 1947 年 4 月 4 日，是联合国专门机构之一，① 负责颁布航空政策，如《芝加哥公约》19 个附件中的标准和建议做法（SARPs）。它通过制定必要的国际标准和规则，打造了安全可靠、高效、经济的航空运输体系，并为缔约国在民用航空各领域开展合作提供了平台。②

---

① See ICAO, *Manual on the Regulation of International Air Transport* 2nd ed, Doc 9626, 2004 para 3.4 - 1 [ICAO Manual]; Ruwantissa Abeyratne, "The legal effect of ICAO decisions and empowerment of ICAO by Contracting States" (2007) 32 Ann Air & Sp L 518; Ludwig Weber, *International Civil Aviation Organization: An Introduction* (Alphen aan den Rijn: Kluwer Law International, 2007) at 1, 11; Laurence E Gesell & Paul S Dempsey, *Air Transportation: Foundations for the 21st Century*, (Chandler: Coast Aire Publications, 2005) at 401, 649; Paul S Dempsey, *Law and Foreign Policy in International Aviation* (New York: Dobbs Ferry, 1987) at 12 - 13, 273 - 274; Adrianus D. Groenewege, *Compendium of International Civil Aviation*, 2nd ed, (Montreal: International Aviation Development Corp., 1998) at 19 - 20, 46; Michael Milde, "The Chicago Convention-After Forty Years" (1984) 9 Ann Air & Sp L 119; Stefano Zunarelli & Michele M Comenale Pinto, *Manuale di diritto della navigazione e dei trasporti*, (Assago: Kluwer, 2020) at 26; Antonio Lefebvre D'Ovidio, Gabriele Pescatore & Leopldo Tullo, *Manuale di diritto della navigazione*, (Milano: Giuffré, 2019) at 49; Conway W. Henderson, *Understanding International Law*, (Chichester: Wiley-Blackwell, 2010) at 124.

② See ICAO, *Manual on the Regulation of International Air Transport* 2nd ed, Doc 9626, 2004 para 3.4 - 1 [ICAO Manual]; see also L. Welch Pogue, "Personal recollections from the Chicago Conference: ICAO, then, now, and in the future" (1995) 20 Ann Air & Sp L 38; Laurence E. Gesell & Paul S. Dempsey, *Air Transportation: Foundations for the 21st Century*, (Chandler: Coast Aire Publications, 2005) at 401, 649 - 650; Ruwantissa Abeyratne, *Legal and Regulatory Issues in International Aviation*, (New York: Transnational Publishers, 1996) at 14 - 20; Elda Turco Bulgherini, *La disciplina giuridica degli accordi aerei bilaterali*, (Padova: Cedam, 1984) at 7, 10; Adrianus D. Groenewege, *Compendium of International Civil Aviation*, 2nd ed, (Montreal: International Aviation Development Corp., 1998) at 283; Isabelle Lelieur, *Law and Policy of Substantial Ownership and Effective Control of Airlines: Prospects for Change*, 1st ed (New York: Routledge Taylor & Francis Group, 2003) at 141. 关于国际民航组织的性质、意义和宗旨，参见 Ruwantissa Abeyratne, *Aviation and Diplomacy* (Montreal: ICAO, 2008) at 242 - 264; Ruwantissa Abeyratne, "*The legal effect of ICAO decisions and empowerment of ICAO by Contracting States*" (2007) 32 Ann Air & Sp L at 517ff; Ludwig Weber, *International Civil Aviation Organization: An Introduction* (Alphen aan den Rijn: Kluwer Law International, 2007) at 142。

在素有民航"宪章性文件"之称的《芝加哥公约》框架内,[1] 国际民航组织就空中航行技术享有广泛的立法权。[2] 具言之,根据《芝加哥公约》第四十四条：

> 本组织的宗旨和目的在于发展国际航行的原则和技术,并促进国际航空运输的规划和发展,以：
> a) 确保全世界国际民用航空安全有序发展。……

提升全球航空运输系统的安全性是国际民航组织的任务导向和最根本的战略目标。《国际民航组织安全年度报告》在此领域发挥着重要作用——向国际社会提供最新的安全指标,包括事故和相关风险因素。国际民航组织瞄准全球航空安全计划（GASP）中所列的目标,通过协调活动,持续提升全球航空安全。[3]

如今,"基于绩效的监管"方案为解决亚轨道监管问题提供了新思路。此外,无人机的批准经验表明,与运营相关的全球风险评估具有可行性。这种特殊的方案被称为"以运营为中心的监管"。在这种方案中,安全链的每个组成部分都具有其独特的贡献,如飞行器、飞行员、运营商、环境和运营措施等,它们被视为新技术风险控制的关键。通过严格运用上述概念,监管部门可以为新系统提供足够的安全性,以更好地彰显技术的先进性和成熟度。

意大利民航局认为亚轨道运营安全的两种监管模式——"基于绩效的监管"和"以运营为中心的监管"具有可行性。随即,它着手建立一套高层次的客观要求,涵盖设计、生产、维护、操作、乘组技能、培训、医疗等所有可能影响安全的方面。为确保这些客观要求得到遵守,民航局认为可以通过行业惯例推动或采取特定的风险评估方式。运营条例的主体部分

---

[1] See Assad Kotaite, *Legal Aspects of the International Regulation of Civil Aviation* (1995) 20 Ann Air & Sp L 9. 该书作者将《芝加哥公约》描述为"民用航空的宪法保护伞",因为"几乎所有国家都选择加入该公约,从而使其成为最普遍国际协定之一"。

[2] Ruwantissa Abeyratne, *Aviation and Diplomacy* (Montreal: ICAO, 2008) at 247; Ludwig Weber, *International Civil Aviation Organization: An Introduction* (Alphen aan den Rijn: Kluwer Law International, 2007) at 2, 5-8; Michael Milde, "The Chicago Convention: After Forty Years" (1984) 9 Ann Air & Sp L 119 at 122.

[3] See ICAO, "Safety Reports", online: ICAO (www. icao. int/safety/pages/safety-report. aspx).

已起草完成，包含空域运营商必须遵守的规定。只有遵守规定，运营商才能获准开展水平起降的亚轨道飞行（A–A 或点对点）、进入空间、离轨再入、空基发射等活动。

就安全性而言，意大利民航局在维持"基于绩效的监管"方案不变的前提下，又参考了美国联邦法规新修订的第 14 篇第 450 部分①，充分吸取了美国联邦航空管理局在批准亚轨道运营方面积累的宝贵经验。在乘员安全方面，它参考了美国联邦航空管理局的《载人航天飞行建议措施》（2014 年 8 月 27 日发布）②，以及欧洲航空安全局的《新一代通用航空适航标准》（EASA CS-23）③。

意大利监管机构的目标是在 2021 年底前出台新法规，确保风险控制在可接受的范围，以增强处于地面、海上、空中的普通民众、运营人员和航天器上人员的信心。

（二）产业视角

如上所述，意大利对空间业务，尤其是商业亚轨道运营的兴趣，是实施新空间经济战略方案的重要部分。产业政策声明基于以下认识，即国家系统及特定资产（制造业、学术机构、研究中心等）代表着空间产品生产和管理的独特价值链，空间产业各主体在参与欧洲空间项目过程中将获得

---

① 第 450 部分整合了多个监管部分，为所有类型的商业空间飞行发射和再入大气层操作创设了一个单一的许可制度，并以基于绩效的标准取代了规定性要求。See FAA, "Part 450: Streamlining of Launch and Reentry Licensing Requirements", online: Federal Aviation Administration (www.faa.gov/space/streamlined_licensing_process/).

② See Federal Aviation Administration, "Recommended Practices for Human Space Flight Occupant Safety-Version 1.0", (27 August 2014), online (pdf): Federal Aviation Administration (www.faa.gov/about/office_org/headquarters_offices/ast/media/recommended_practices_for_hsf_occupant_safety-version_1-tc14-0037.pdf).

③ See European Aviation Safety Agency, "Easy Access Rules for Normal, Utility, Aerobatic and Commuter Category Aeroplanes (CS-23) (Initial issue)", (June 2018), online (pdf): European Aviation Safety Agency (www.easa.europa.eu/sites/default/files/dfu/CS23%20Initial%20issue.pdf). 关于载人运输安全监管技术和方法以及亚轨道飞行乘员安全问题的深入研究，参见论文"A performance based approach for occupants safety in suborbital transportation"。See Giovanni Di Antonio & Marco Sandrucci, "A performance based approach for occupants safety in suborbital transportation" (paper delivered at the XXV International Congress of Italian Association of Aeronautics and Astronautics – AIDAA held in Rome on 9th to 12th September 2019).

能力提升。①

在亚轨道运营的特定领域，一些意大利企业，如阿尔泰克（ALTEC）和西泰尔（SITAEL，一家在卫星业务中非常活跃的私营公司）已经与维珍银河公司（Virgin Galactic）签署了备忘录，拟在意大利开展联合运营。②

就亚轨道运营而言，一项特别重要的安排似乎是 2016 年 11 月阿尔泰克与维珍银河签署的第一份谅解备忘录。二者拟在意大利开展亚轨道商业联营计划，初步定于 2020 年底实施，即美国商业运营一年后。双方正在讨论工业合作伙伴协议的内容，如该倡议的融资水平等，以确定具体条件和双方义务。

还值得一提的是，西泰尔也与维珍银河签署了一份备忘录。二者建立工业合作伙伴关系，由前者在意大利生产后者空间产品的组件。③ 建立工业合作伙伴关系必须遵守美国关于"商业航天工业出口管制"的规定，主要涉及技术和敏感数据的转让，包括管制军用产品与技术的《国际武器贸易管理条例》（ITAR）和管制军民两用产品与技术的《出口管理条例》（EAR）。④

鉴于规则的复杂性和投资回报的不确定性，所有的工业协议均应依据伙伴政策以及维珍银河为出口其商业模式所确立的产业布局进行仔细审查。维珍银河在美国部署"白骑士/太空船业务"时遇阻，这时常发生在创新产品和技术领域。因此，意大利的运营计划时间表也正在复审中。

意大利和美国政府之间的框架协议也将受此影响。双方应亟须调整协议以符合《国际武器贸易管理条例》和《出口管理条例》的规定，国家当局应与美国联邦航空管理局以及意大利民航局签署一项专门协议。

---

① See Ministerial Decree 10 July 2017, No 354, Point 1 at 2.

② See SITAEL, *Virgin Group and SITAEL Sign Agreements for Long-term Collaboration and Investment* (6 July 2018), online: SITAEL (www.sitael.com/virgin-group-sitael-sign-agreements-long-term-collaboration-investment).

③ See SITAEL, *Virgin Group and SITAEL Sign Agreements for Long-term Collaboration and Investment* (6 July 2018), online: SITAEL (www.sitael.com/virgin-group-sitael-sign-agreements-long-term-collaboration-investment).

④ 在此方面，参见 FAA, "Introduction to U.S. Export Controls for the Commercial Space Industry", online (pdf): FAA (www.faa.gov/about/office_org/headquarters_offices/ast/media/Intro%20to%20US%20Export%20Controls.pdf).

结　语

全球对航空航天领域（包括亚轨道飞行）政治、制度、立法抑或学术研究的浓厚兴趣表明，空间不再是美国的空间，空间研究也不再是以下格局：

以美国文化霸权为标志，倾向于使俄罗斯、中国、印度和欧洲的空间活动工作边缘化，使沙特阿拉伯、阿塞拜疆等目前参与空间活动的多个国家行为体边缘化。①

显然，只有通过多级立法和监管框架，才能推动空间商业的发展。②然而，国际社会尚未建立统一或综合的空天法律制度。相比之下，欧盟在《里斯本条约》通过后提出的政治和立法倡议表现出欧盟强烈的政治意愿，即将空间作为经济增长和复苏的战略部门以及构建欧盟空间政策的关键政策领域。

尽管欧盟正依据《欧洲联盟运作条约》第189条制定一项空间政策，但在更全面的区域性立法出台前，成员国仍是，至少目前是欧洲空间活动的基本行动者。

欧盟多国正探索建立先进的空天监管框架，意大利是发挥关键作用的成员国之一。它在亚轨道飞行领域出台的众多政治和监管举措以及2020年9月25日与美国签署的意向声明（美国航空航天局阿尔忒弥斯计划的一部分，表明了两国在月球探测活动方面的共同利益）均证明了这一点。③

---

① See Bastien Girard, *Le New Space en Europe：état des Lieux de la Littérature* （2019）Actualité des études européennes at 2.

② See Paul S. Dempsey, *The Emergence of National Space Law* （18 November 2015）at 3，online：SSRN（papers. ssrn. com/sol3/papers. cfm? abstract_id = 2692639）. 作者认为，如果发射或运营商的责任受到限制，并且标准能够得到明确、公平、有效实施，那么法律框架可以提高私营运营商融资和保险的能力。

③ See NASA, "NASA Administrator Signs Declaration of Intent with Italy on Artemis Cooperation" （25 September 2020），online：NASA（www. nasa. gov/feature/nasa-administrator-signs-declaration-of-intent-with-italy-on-artemis-cooperation）.

意大利位于格罗塔列的航天港已成为亚轨道飞行的战略枢纽。鉴于过去几年采取的政治和监管举措,意大利将成为未来空间计划和活动领域中闻名欧洲内外的关键国家。

专题五 研究生论坛

后疫情时代保障邮轮复航的法律问题与路径探索

罗 杰[*]

摘要：疫情防控常态化下为保障邮轮复航，理应对相关的法律问题予以厘清。港口国是否接受涉嫌受染邮轮停靠，应考虑邮轮船籍及能否达到授予"无疫通行"标准等因素。应针对新冠疫情传播特质制定相应港口应急处理规定，采取有效检疫措施。中国特色旅行社包船模式下旅行社与邮轮公司等经营者对受染旅客承担责任时，应以海上旅客运输的运送期间与提供服务内容为标准，进行适用法律与责任分担的划分。另外，还应考虑在邮轮复航期间探索新型邮轮旅游方式，解决相应法律滞碍，并尝试加入责任保险制度。

关键词：邮轮复航 国际法律义务 责任分担

Research on Legal Issues and Exploration to Ensure Cruise Reversion in the Post-epidemic Era

Luo Jie

Abstract: In order to ensure the reversion of cruises under the normalization of epidemic prevention and control, relevant legal issues should be clarified. Whether the port state accepts the docking of the suspected cruise should consider factors such as the cruise's nationality and whether it can meet the criteria for granting "free pratique". Corresponding port emergency handling regulations should be formulated according to the characteristics of the spread of the COVID-19 epidemic. Effective quarantine measures should be adopted. When operators such as travel agencies and cruise companies under the charter model of travel agencies with Chinese characteristics assume responsibility for the infected

---

[*] 罗杰：上海海事大学法学院法律硕士（法学）。

passengers, they should divide the applicable laws and the sharing of responsibilities based on the transportation period and service content of the carriage of passengers by sea. In addition, we should also consider exploring new ways of cruise travel during the reversion of cruises, with corresponding legal obstacles resolved, and try to join the liability insurance system.

Key words：reversion of cruises；international legal obligations；responsibility sharing

一、后疫情时代保障邮轮复航的法律问题梳理

（一）国际邮轮采"新航线"方案涉及沿海运输权的法律解释空缺

自2020年初新冠疫情暴发，至各国相继采取防控手段应对，现全球已进入疫情防控常态化的"后疫情时代"。中国邮轮旅游产业的发展历经萌芽、高速发展、疫情寒冬等时期，凭借市场韧性迎来新一轮复航转型期。[①] 在转型期内，除卫生防疫、政策支持、"新航线"市场开辟和推广宣传等问题外，法律问题为其基础性问题。

继"钻石公主"号事件后，各国对途经外域的人员皆有检疫限制，国际邮轮因航线涉外、须挂靠他国港口，而尤受打击。为避免出现域外行程信息而被限制，出现了邮轮旅游"无目的行"与"沿海行"等方案，但该方案被认为属于或包含中国港口之间的船舶运输业务，而受到市场准入等限制。主要的相关限制规定在于《中华人民共和国海商法》（简称《海商法》）第四条"中华人民共和国港口之间的海上运输和拖航，由悬挂中华人民共和国国旗的船舶经营"与《国际海运条例》第二十二条"外国国际船舶运输经营者不得经营中国港口之间的船舶运输业务"。

国际邮轮因市场准入限制无法实现"无目的行"与"沿海行"等新方案，危难中却为中资本土邮轮船队孕育了机遇，邮轮产业"内循环"得以加快运作。但我国邮轮产业此前发展的主力军仍是外资邮轮公司，中资本土邮轮产业尚不成熟，国际邮轮"外循环"仍不可偏废、亟待润滑重启运作。可借此次疫情危机，重新考虑对相关市场限制规定进行相应解释，先

---

① 参见周浩《中国邮轮产业发展2020年回顾与2021年展望》，载《中国港口》2021年第1期。

予明确不含中途挂靠港的"无目的行"模式海上游航线，其与包含中途挂靠港普通航线相较，实际皆为同一母港进出的闭环航线，并非"中国港口之间"的船舶运输，使得国际邮轮"无目的行"方案存在施行的可能。

(二) 国家接受外国邮轮停靠的国际义务探讨

此前，日本政府对待"钻石公主"号与"威士特丹"号迥乎不同之态度，引起大量对其未能正确履行国际义务的质疑。有观点认为，根据《国际卫生条例》（简称《条例》）第二十八条之规定，缔约国不应当以公共卫生为由阻止船舶在任何入境口岸停靠，除非不具备执行《条例》规定的卫生措施的能力，但日本横滨港经认证为"国际卫生港口"，且该邮轮由日本本土公司运营，以横滨港为母港，日本依《条例》不应当阻止外国邮轮停靠。[①] 与之相反的观点认为，外国邮轮因相对封闭特性，仅通过一国领海不会造成疫情扩散而享有无害通过权，但无害通过权不包括停靠他国港口的内容，沿海国并不当然负有接受外国邮轮停靠的义务；无疫通行制度虽主要涉及停靠、登岸内容，但此次疫情已于2020年1月30日由世界卫生组织宣布构成国际关注的突发公共卫生事件，符合无疫通行制度的例外情形，如船上已出现确诊病例，将不被授予无疫通行而遭拒绝停靠。另外，船籍国接收义务与沿海国管辖权等法律事项也有待明确。

中国在疫情暴发初始应对"歌诗达赛琳娜"号与"歌诗达威尼斯"号反应迅速、效果良好，主要源于中国政府非常手段之运用。如邮轮复航后出现"歌诗达赛琳娜"号未有的确诊病例或无症状感染者，是否应当接受停靠，接受停靠后如何依法采取应急措施，以及应急措施中造成损害将如何补偿，应从日本应对"钻石公主"号事件中获得启示，找寻船上人员与境内人员人身利益保护平衡点，尊重《条例》等国际软法，探索转化为切实可行的国内硬法，规范外国邮轮停靠处置措施。[②]

(三) 中国特色包船模式下各经营主体的归责冲突

受疫情影响，邮轮旅客的旅游意愿在一段时间内低迷，但仍保有对未

---

① 参见郭冉《对日本处置"钻石公主号"邮轮新冠肺炎疫情的国际法分析》，载《边界与海洋研究》2020年第5期。

② 参见徐峰《邮轮疫情事件中港口卫生应急法律制度研究》，载《武汉交通职业学院学报》2020年第1期。

来邮轮旅游的出行消费信心，邮轮旅游长期市场需求暗伏。因此，在邮轮复航转型期明晰旅客、船员、旅行社工作人员等的权益保障路径，解决与旅行社、邮轮公司等经营主体利益冲突，使得邮轮"开得出去，停得回来"，增强旅客的登船信心，为加快邮轮复航、顺应市场需求应有之义。

"钻石公主"号事件中，邮轮公司主动承诺向旅客全额退款，因在船上隔离产生的其他费用也予以免除，甚至为旅客提供未来航次的全额补偿；"歌诗达赛琳娜"号事件中，歌诗达公司同样提供退票服务，同时天津市政府将其中35位暂不可返乡的湖北籍旅客安置到政府招待所且提供免费食宿。上述举措虽可避免大部分旅客民事权益纠纷的发生，但邮轮复航期内苛重的赔偿义务将使原本受疫情影响亏损惨重的邮轮公司望而却步，也与鼓励邮轮复航政策精神相悖，应针对疫情重制船票内容，并以不可抗力为由与旅客共担合同风险，保护邮轮产业在疫情防控常态化下健康发展。另外，需考虑我国特色的旅行社包船模式对经营者责任分担的影响，该模式下海上运输要素显著、中国旅客岸上观光消费需求高，而与一般包价旅游以及传统邮轮旅游相区分，旅行社与邮轮公司为旅客面对的两大最直接经营主体，旅行社承担全程旅行的组织管理和日程安排工作，邮轮公司主要提供船上休闲娱乐及运输服务。疫情暴发初始，"歌诗达赛琳娜"号停驻锚地暂不进港，由邮轮公司工作人员配合国家卫生健康委员会等部门同志组织旅客进行健康筛查检测，以及指导个人卫生防控；排除疫情隐患靠港后，其中600余名旅客由旅行社安排离船返乡。[①] 在旅行社与邮轮公司执行疫情防控要求期间，导致旅客感染新冠病毒而遭受人身损害甚至死亡时，将涉及违约责任与侵权责任竞合及两大经营主体如何担责等法律问题，其核心在于我国邮轮旅游合同性质的明晰及不同法律适用矛盾的化解。

---

① 参见观界《"歌诗达赛琳娜号"的24小时：同样感染新冠，她命运比钻石公主好太多了》(https://mp.weixin.qq.com/s/AHypxfeaOzg3pS9FYpuhsg)，2021年10月10日访问。

二、中国保障邮轮复航视域下多元义务主体的责任分担

（一）中国政府对受染邮轮的应担义务与合理处置分析

1. 中国接受受染邮轮停靠的义务

论及中国是否负有接受受染邮轮停靠的义务，一是应遵循的逻辑是中国对该邮轮是否具有管辖权，二是哪些国家也负有接受受染邮轮停靠的义务，三是该义务的优先顺序或比例划分。

首先，有观点认为，外国船舶可视为一国的浮动领土，应仅由其船旗国管辖。但外国船舶毕竟仅是虚拟领土而不足取，即使认同该观点，也应仅限于公海上以及在外国领水内的军舰和其他公有船舶，商用邮轮不属此列，因而不应认定其为一国领土。根据国际法四大管辖原则，中国可根据属人管辖和属地管辖对进入领海的受染邮轮或船上有本国国民的受染邮轮进行管辖。

其次，根据《联合国海洋法公约》第九十四条第一款之规定，"每个国家应对悬挂该国旗帜的船舶有效地行使行政、技术及社会事项上的管辖和控制"。船旗国对于悬挂其旗帜的受染邮轮享有当然的管辖权，应承担相应疫情防控义务，便在一定程度上与沿海国属地管辖权、旅客国籍国属人管辖权产生冲突，但后两者并无必然的接受邮轮停靠及采取疫情防控等义务内容，所以船籍国仍是依法主要负有接受受染邮轮义务的国家，其义务最为优先、占比最大。

对于来港停靠涉嫌受染邮轮，应根据《条例》第四十三条规定，基于科学原则、现有的关于人类健康危险的科学证据、世界卫生组织的任何现有特定指导或建议等，针对病毒传播特质进行循证风险评估，基于评估结果对满足标准的应当授予"无疫通行"，允许其停靠。① 另外，实践中，邮轮航线远离船籍国或挂方便旗等情形较为常见，船籍国难以履行防疫管理义务，此时若各国均不理睬、放任受染邮轮成为"海上孤船"，未免过于冰冷。可根据《联合国海洋法公约》第九十八条第二款规定之精神，沿海国在必要时通过相互的区域性安排与邻国合作，对受染船舶进行"人道

---

① 参见孙思琪《国际邮轮突发公共卫生事件应急管理的法律检视》，载《大连海事大学学报（社会科学版）》2020 年第 5 期。

主义"救助、补给。而中国作为倡导"人类命运共同体"的有担当的大国，深知在国际公共卫生事件面前，任何国家都不可能独善其身，可在保障本国公共卫生安全的前提下，综合本国医疗卫生资源条件，对受染邮轮提供适当的帮助。

2. 中国港口公共卫生应急管理的规范

《中华人民共和国国境卫生检疫法》及实施细则基本是参照《条例》对国境卫生检疫作出的更为细致规定，《出入境邮轮检疫管理办法》（简称《邮轮检疫办法》）则更进一步针对出入境邮轮的检疫工作作出指引，但上述规范不足以完全支撑疫情防控常态化时期邮轮复航检疫管理工作，究其原因在于不能针对新冠疫情的传播特质制定更具操作性的规范。为应对疫情"长期化"的可能性，应当由海关总署与国家卫生健康委员会联合发布口岸疫情应急处理规定，由口岸地方出入境检验检疫局具体执行，充分利用中国政府的高执行力完成邮轮检疫工作，使得邮轮更高效地完成预定航行计划，减少各方利益损失及潜在诉讼争议。

根据《邮轮检疫办法》第十三条之规定，"海关根据入境邮轮申报信息及邮轮检疫风险等级确定检疫方式，及时通知邮轮负责人或者其代理人，检疫方式有：（一）靠泊检疫；（二）随船检疫；（三）锚地检疫；（四）电讯检疫"。该规定即为《条例》中缔约国应对国际关注的突发公共卫生事件而采取额外卫生措施的变通规定，"歌诗达赛琳娜"号即被认定为"邮轮上报告有疑似检疫传染病病例，且根据要求需对密切接触者采取集中隔离观察的"而依规定停驻检疫锚地暂不靠港，以最大限度控制疫情扩散的可能。《邮轮检疫办法》第十八条关于入境邮轮实施检疫查验内容的规定第三项中，仅对船员、旅客的健康监测情况采用"询问"的方式，该方式显然不能满足新冠病毒疫情的检疫标准。"歌诗达赛琳娜"号检疫过程中，工作人员首先对全体旅客和船员测量体温、统计户籍信息与14日内行程信息，对其中发热旅客、船员进行咽拭子采样后，由政府指派直升机送样检测，检验结果全为阴性后才允许邮轮靠港。以上检疫措施才符合《条例》规定采取额外卫生措施的标准，即基于科学原则与现有的关于人类健康危险的科学证据，因此，应及时更新、统一邮轮复航后检疫措施标准，采取更有效的检疫手段。

另外，《中华人民共和国国境卫生检疫法实施细则》（简称《实施细则》）第九十五条之规定，旅客请求在船上留验，经船长同意，并且船上有船医和医疗、消毒设备的，经卫生检疫机关同意，可以在船上留验。该规定与日本《检疫法》排除旅客申请船上隔离请求,仅由船长、检疫所长决定是否在船上采取扣留措施的规定不同,更加尊重船上旅客的利益保护。但是,该规定并未考虑到病毒疫情的传播特性,"钻石公主"号因仅依赖空调设备、未完善通风系统而长期闭塞,隔离检疫时间过长且没有实施有效隔离,才化为"毒皿"。① 因此应当对船上资源设备及管理提出更高要求,给予卫生检疫机关具体指引,满足必要条件时才可同意旅客在船上留验的申请。

(二) 两大经营主体在多重法律制度下的应担义务分析

1. 中国特色邮轮旅游合同的法律性质剖析

中国特色旅行社包船模式下邮轮旅游合同因涉及旅行社、邮轮公司、其他履行辅助人等多经营主体向旅客提供不同服务,各经营主体的法律定位有待明确,存在单一合同论和双重合同论等理论分歧,核心焦点在于旅客除与旅行社直接达成邮轮旅游合同外,是否与邮轮公司等其他履行辅助人分别存在合同关系。单一合同论认为,无论旅客与哪一方签订合同,该方即是其合同相对方,不存在在两类合同下分别认定主体的空间,在中国特色旅行社包船模式下邮轮船票已不能成为邮轮公司与旅客之间存在海上旅客运输合同的证明,不实际从事运输的旅行社的法律定位应为承运人;双重合同论认为,邮轮旅游涉及三个合同,即邮轮旅游合同、邮轮旅游辅助合同和邮轮船票所证明的海上旅客运输合同,邮轮旅游合同主要适用《中华人民共和国旅游法》(简称《旅游法》)与《中华人民共和国民法典》(简称《民法典》)合同编相关规定,不属于《海商法》第五章适用范围,而邮轮公司与旅客的法律关系则适用《海商法》第五章,邮轮公司具有承运人地位。②

本文认为,当邮轮公司直接与旅客达成邮轮旅游合同,在《海商法》第一百一十一条规定的海上旅客运输运送期间,邮轮公司具有承运人地位,受《海商法》约束;在运送期间外的岸上观光等服务期间适用《旅游法》和《民法典》等相关规定。因此,实际法律关系的确定主要依靠邮轮

---

① 参见陈海波《"救助""钻石公主"号邮轮旅客法律事项十五问》,载《珠江水运》2020年第4期。

② 参见陈琦《邮轮旅游经营者法律定位分歧的破解——以〈旅游法〉〈海商法〉的制度冲突为视角》,载《法学》2020年第6期。

旅游合同标的进行划分，并根据不同合同标的适用不同法律规范。邮轮旅游合同为一揽子包价旅游合同，明确旅行社及履行辅助人分别提供的相应旅游服务，也就是说，与旅客分别达成相应法律关系，通过邮轮公司提供海上运输服务即在海上运输领域仅由邮轮公司与旅客达成海上旅客运输关系，邮轮公司具有承运人的权利与义务。其他履行辅助人与旅客的法律关系同理。

2. 多层次法律关系间的冲突规制

邮轮公司向旅客提供船票所证明的海上旅客运输合同多公开发布于邮轮公司官网，其中对于管辖与适用法律的约定多为约定外国法院管辖及适用外国法律的格式条款，根据《民法典》第四百九十六条规定，提供格式条款一方未采取合理方式提示对方注意"与对方有重大利害关系的条款"，对方可以主张该条款不成为合同的内容。因此，在中国停靠的受染邮轮的旅客仍有机会要求中国法院管辖并适用中国法律。① 但是，在中国规范邮轮旅游的法律中，《旅游法》与《海商法》因立法目的与保护法益偏向不同，归责原则与责任承担的设置在实践运用中存在一定冲突。

《旅游法》较为偏向旅客权益保护，适用无过错归责原则，并设定惩罚性赔偿条款，出现违约、人身损害或财产损害情形时，可向任一有责任的经营方索赔，方便旅客进行维权；《海商法》则出于鼓励"海上冒险"、维护航运市场正常发展，较为偏向船方权益保护，适用过错与过错推定原则，并设定不负赔偿责任情形与责任限额条款，旅客对需证明承运人过失的情节负举证责任。当旅客在运送期间感染新冠病毒，则可能出现向不同主体索赔诉讼难度与诉讼策略大相径庭的情况。因此，不存在两法同时适用的空间，需明确特定情形下法律适用的优先等级。

3. 旅客受染产生的民事责任划分

《旅游法》第七十一条规定，"由于公共交通经营者的原因造成旅游者人身损害、财产损失的，由公共交通经营者依法承担赔偿责任，旅行社应当协助旅游者向公共交通经营者索赔"。本文认为，可根据该条规定尝试协调在不同期间两大经营者的责任分担冲突。邮轮公司作为公共交通经营者、旅行社履行辅助人，在海上旅客运输的运送期间出现旅客感染新冠病毒的情况时，应主要承担赔偿责任。旅行社应协助旅客向邮轮公司索赔。

---

① 参见薛兰心《新冠病毒感染旅客对邮轮承运人索赔相关法律问题》，载《珠江水运》2021年第10期。

此时，可回归到《海商法》责任负担制度，旅客需举证证明邮轮公司对于其受染存在过错。① 但在运送期间外的岸上观光、港口、申请离船前往医疗机构或其他检疫机关指定地点时受染，则应适用《旅游法》第七十条的规定，由旅行社承担因隔离、留验而未按约定行程安排离船或结束旅行的违约责任，退赔相应费用，以及承担相应期间旅客受染的人身损害、财产损失。

三、中国保障邮轮复航的法律问题疏解及新路径探索

（一）区分外国邮轮受染情形施与接受停靠或人道援助

中国基于属地管辖与属人管辖原则可对进入领海的邮轮或船上有本国国民的邮轮进行管辖，但对其是否接受停靠并不是"一刀切"的应对方案，而应区分邮轮是否受染及受染程度采取适宜的措施。船籍国依《联合国海洋法公约》负有的主动接受受染邮轮义务最为优先、占比最大，当外国受染邮轮有能力回归船籍国，或缺乏一定能力但有意愿回归船籍国，可对其予以劝返，或者给予适当物资补助和防疫指导后帮助其回归船籍国；当外国受染邮轮悬挂方便旗却不方便返回船籍国，且船籍国不具有相应执行卫生措施能力的，则应根据外国邮轮具体受染情形，实施不同程度的检疫手段。经循证风险评估风险较低的，根据《邮轮检疫办法》相关规定，采取靠泊检疫方式，授予无疫通行；经评估风险较高的，采取随船检疫或锚地检疫等接触距离受控的方式，考虑就近医疗资源能力，给予适当的医疗卫生及物资等方面的协助。

（二）完善卫生检疫制度及配套应急方案

基于疫情防控常态化的现状，应针对新冠疫情的传播特质与感染症状，由海关总署与国家卫生健康委员会联合出台入境口岸新冠疫情应急处理规定，保障邮轮产业复苏期的平稳发展。通过先行确立国内邮轮港口为疫情卫生检疫新规试点，将检疫手段提高至《条例》所要求的国际标准，围绕"核心能力要求"实施建设，并统一受染船舶人员隔离、留验时间，

---

① 参见黄晶、郑劼屹《论邮轮公司对旅客的民事法律责任》，载《武汉交通职业学院学报》2020年第4期。

以本土邮轮公司与以本土港口为母港的外国邮轮公司为主要规范对象，统一其内部卫生应急制度与船上通风系统等相关硬件标准以与港口卫生检疫措施相匹配。

（三）明确邮轮旅游两大经营主体的责任划分

中国特色旅行社包船模式下，旅行社与邮轮公司出现责任划分上的冲突局限于海上旅客运输的运送期间，运送期间外由旅行社承担责任，进行包价旅游费用和该期间发生人身损害费用的退赔，但有权以不可抗力为由，仅退赔未完成航程费用，在检疫人员有过错或旅客自身存在过错的情形下减轻赔偿责任。

运送期间内因旅客受染新冠病毒发生违约责任与侵权责任竞合，以及责任主体进行责任划分问题时，则应适用《旅游法》第七十一条的规定，选择由作为公共交通经营者的邮轮公司承担赔偿责任，旅行社协助旅客向其索赔。但该索赔将受限于《海商法》的规定，邮轮公司除丧失赔偿责任限制权利的例外情形下，依法享受赔偿责任限额，且旅客应举证证明邮轮公司存在过错，例如邮轮通风系统不符合规定，未按要求组织管理旅客船上活动，未严格区分感染区、密切接触区、疑似感染区，以及船员、船上医疗人员活动不规范等情节。

（四）探索新型邮轮经营方式与责任保险制度

当传统邮轮旅游方式有重大染疫风险且出入境不便时，可积极探索疫情防控常态化下新型邮轮旅游经营方式。如推行"无目的游"与"沿海游"等新航线，发展船上休闲娱乐项目，特别增添国际商品销售区，无需下船或无需出境即可满足部分本土旅客的购物需求，为邮轮复航注入稳定活力，并尝试通过司法解释等方式，限定《海商法》第四条"中华人民共和国港口之间的海上运输"范围不包括"同一母港进出、不含中途停靠港的海上旅客运输"，破除"无目的游"与"沿海游"等新航线的法律滞碍。

另外，为应对疫情对旅客造成损害的大规模侵权风险，可探索由旅行社与邮轮公司按一定比例分担投保费用，共同为旅客投保强制责任险，并参考包价邮轮旅游合同总价款与邮轮公司享受的海上旅客运输赔偿责任限额确定"风险"大小，使得保险人愿意承担、旅客能够快速得到赔付，更好地保障旅客权益。①

结　论

　　首先，中国对来港停靠的邮轮具有管辖权，船籍国、母港国、挂靠港国等皆负有接受受染邮轮停靠的义务，但船籍国是依《联合国海洋法公约》负有主动接受受染邮轮义务的国家，其义务最为优先、占比最大。中国应遵循《条例》采取额外卫生措施的规定，根据科学原则与现有的关于人类健康危险的科学证据等，对经过循证风险评估的船舶授予无疫通行，或可对受染邮轮进行人道主义救助、补给。

　　其次，应当由海关总署与国家卫生健康委员会针对新冠病毒的传播特质联合发布口岸疫情应急处理规定，使疫情防控常态化的邮轮复航管理有更具操作性的规范可依。

　　最后，中国特色旅行社包船模式下，旅行社与邮轮公司两大邮轮旅游经营主体在邮轮旅游中出现受染事件时，应以实质合同标的履行与运送期间的划分为标准，分别适用《旅游法》与《海商法》的规制，依法承担相应责任，明确旅客权益保障路径，并统一适用不可抗力抗辩情形的裁判标准，减轻邮轮旅游经营主体的责任与负担。

---

① 参见曾荣荣、张磊《新冠肺炎疫情防控背景下我国邮轮旅游责任保险制度的完善》，载《水运管理》2021年第3期。

互有过失碰撞非漏油船油污损害赔偿责任问题研究

李少璞[*]

摘要：随着国际航运业的不断发展，船舶碰撞已成为引发海洋油污损害的首要原因。当两船互有过失碰撞致单船漏油时，非漏油船的油污损害赔偿责任问题一直以来都是学术及实务界争论的焦点。本文首先梳理互有过失碰撞案件中非漏油船油污损害赔偿责任的不同观点，并结合最高人民法院"达飞佛罗里达"轮与"舟山"轮案分析当前实践中非漏油船油污损害赔偿责任争议产生的原因。在明确互有过失碰撞致单船漏油所涉法律关系以及非漏油船承担责任的必要性的基础上，本研究分别从国际、国内两个层面对当前争论最为激烈的《1992年油污公约》《2001年燃油公约》及国内《海商法》《民法典》等法规中非漏油船责任相关规定进行分析，提出应借《海商法》修改明确受害人可以同时或分别向漏油船与非漏油船索赔，仅向漏油船索赔时漏油船应承担全部赔偿责任，仅向非漏油船索赔时其在过失比例范围内承担责任。

关键词：互有过失碰撞 油污损害 赔偿责任 非漏油船

Research on the Compensation Liability for Oil Pollution Damage from Non-Spilling Vessel

Li Shaopu

Abstract: With the continuous development of the international shipping industry, ship collisions have become the primary cause of marine oil pollution damage. When two ships collide with each other due to negligence, resulting in a single ship leaking oil, the issue of compensation liability for oil pollution damage of the non-oil leaking ship has always been a focus of debate in academic and practical circles. This article first outlines the different perspectives on the liability

---

[*] 李少璞：华南师范大学2021级海商法硕士，大连海事大学2024级海商法博士研究生。

for compensation for oil pollution damage caused by non-oil spill vessels in cases of mutual negligence collision, and analyzes the reasons for the dispute over compensation liability for oil pollution damage caused by non-oil spill vessels in current practice, combined with the new approach of the Supreme Court. On the basis of clarifying the legal relationship involved in single ship oil leakage caused by mutual negligence collision and the necessity for non-oil leakage ships to bear responsibility, this paper analyzes the most controversial provisions on non-oil leakage ship responsibility in current regulations such as the *1992 Oil Pollution Convention*, *the 2001 Fuel Oil Convention*, and *the Maritime Code* and *Civil Code* from both international and domestic perspectives. It is proposed to amend the *Maritime Law* to clarify that victims can claim compensation from both oil leaking and non-oil leaking vessels simultaneously or separately. They should only claim compensation from oil leaking vessels and bear full compensation responsibility within the scope of fault proportion.

Key words: Mutually negligent collision; Oil pollution damage; Liability for compensation; Non-leaking vessel

引　言

船舶碰撞非漏油船的油污损害赔偿责任问题一直是学术界与实务界争论的焦点。包括《1992年国际油污损害民事责任公约》（简称《1992年油污公约》）和《2001年国际燃油污染损害民事责任公约》（简称《2001年燃油公约》）在内的国际公约中仅仅明确了漏油船船东的责任主体地位，然而关于两艘船舶在互有过失的情况下碰撞使一船漏油导致油污损害，过失的非漏油船方能否成为污染损害赔偿责任主体的问题缺乏明确规定。我国国内法对船舶碰撞油污损害赔偿案件中非漏油船的损害赔偿责任并无明确规定，司法实践中各个法院对相关法律的理解和适用亦有所不同，导致此类海事裁判案件中同案不同判的状况频发。研究互有过失碰撞中非漏油船油污损害赔偿责任对于明确不同情形下非漏油船的责任承担有着重要意义。分析责任主体是确定赔偿责任的前提，只有明确了具体的被告人，才能确保诉讼效率、减少诉讼案件堆积、节约司法资源。

一、互有过失碰撞非漏油船油污损害赔偿责任现存争议

两船互有过失碰撞致单船漏油中非漏油船的油污损害赔偿责任的问题作为海事界的哥德巴赫猜想，一直以来都是理论界和实务界的争论焦点。徒善不足以为政，徒法不足以自行。尽管国际公约与国内法均有涉及非漏油船油污损害赔偿责任的相关规定，但其规定较为模糊导致理论与实践上对该问题形成了几种不同的观点。2019年最高人民法院在"达飞佛罗里达"轮与"舟山"轮案判决中开创性地明确非漏油船可以直接对受害人承担过错比例范围内的责任引起了新的争议。梳理现存争议、分析争议的成因与最高人民法院的判决精神，有利于正确理解与适用国际公约及国内法有关规定，从而明晰非漏油船油污损害赔偿责任问题。

（一）关于非漏油船油污损害赔偿责任的不同观点

当前，我国尚未存在针对船舶油污损害赔偿的专门立法。尽管在国际公约及我国国内法层面均存在相关规定涉及碰撞船舶的油污赔偿责任，但规定不甚明确导致实践中对其含义产生了不同理解。当两船互有过失碰撞致单船漏油时，关于油污损害赔偿责任应该由漏油船承担还是由非漏油船承担出现了观点分歧，主要观点包括以下三种。

1. 非漏油船不承担油污损害赔偿责任

支持"非漏油船方无需承担油污损害赔偿责任"的学者认为，《1992年油污公约》和《2001年燃油公约》仅对漏油船方的油污损害责任作出规定。[①] 当发生两船互有过失碰撞而导致一船漏油的情况时，我国作为两公约的缔约国，应当依据公约仅由漏油船方承担油污损害赔偿责任，令非漏油船方担责于法无据。支持该观点的学者在因果关系上认为两船碰撞不必然导致油污损害，只有漏油船漏油才是导致油污损害的原因，因此非漏油船的碰撞与油污损害之间不存在因果关系，受害方不应享有对非漏油船方的索赔权。[②]

---

① 参见赵月林《船舶碰撞造成的非CLC油船油污损害赔偿责任主体的研究》，载《大连海事大学学报》2004年第2期，第12页。

② 参见吴莉婧《论船舶碰撞造成的油污损害赔偿》，载《中国海洋大学学报（社会科学版）》2003年第3期，第60页。

在司法实践层面，近年来我国多地法院均有相应判决体现此观点。在宁波海事法院一审、浙江省高级人民法院二审的"达飞佛罗里达"轮与"舟山"轮案中，宁波海事法院与浙江省高级人民法院在非漏油船油污损害赔偿责任这个争议焦点上均认为《1992年油污公约》和《2001年燃油公约》只规定了漏油船方的油污损害赔偿责任，非漏油船直接承担赔偿责任于法无据。① 同样，2012年由浙江省高级人民法院审理的"带什"轮与"闽龙渔2802"轮案，法院认定"闽龙渔2802"轮为漏油船应承担油污损害赔偿责任，"带什"轮并没有发生漏油，因此无需承担油污赔偿责任。②

该观点具有一定的优势。采用该观点在实际应用中无需判断两船的过错比例，使部分复杂的问题得以简化。但随着海事研究的不断发展，该观点也受到越来越多的质疑。在理论上的质疑源于对公约条文的理解。《1992年油污公约》和《2001年燃油公约》的确规定了漏油船方的责任，但是在两公约未提及非漏油船油污损害赔偿责任的情况下，能否简单认为两公约排除了非漏油船的油污损害赔偿责任有待商榷。而实务界的质疑则来自多方面，例如，现实情况下漏油船通常是两船碰撞中损伤较大的一方，且可能因漏油而进一步毁损、爆炸、沉没，此时漏油船方将无可执行财产。如果受害方仅能向漏油方请求赔偿，则不利于保护受害人权益。

2. 漏油船和非漏油船应按碰撞责任比例承担按份责任

支持"漏油船和非漏油船应按碰撞责任比例承担按份责任"的学者认为，两船在互有过失的前提下发生碰撞导致其中一方漏油，漏油船方与非漏油船方应该依照碰撞发生时双方过失比例承担油污损害赔偿责任。按份责任观点的法律依据为《中华人民共和国海商法》（简称《海商法》）第一百六十九条，其第二款规定互有过失碰撞时两船应在比例范围内对第三人财产损失承担赔偿责任。③ 在因果关系上，此种观点认为油污损害的结果由碰撞与漏油共同导致，两者均与油污损害结果密不可分。④

---

① 参见（2015）甬海法商初字第445号民事判决书、（2017）浙民终581号民事判决书。
② 参见（2012）浙海终字第19号民事判决书。
③ 《海商法》第一百六十九条第二款：互有过失的船舶，对碰撞造成的船舶以及船上货物和其他财产的损失，依照前款规定的比例负赔偿责任。碰撞造成第三人财产损失的，各船的赔偿责任均不超过其应当承担的比例。
④ 参见韩立新、刘红《油污损害赔偿中非漏油方的责任主体地位探析》，载《河北法学》2008年第9期，第152页。

在典型案例方面,"泰联达"轮与"宁连海606"轮案的判决体现了此种观点。"泰联达"轮在由宝山南锚地进入宝南航道航行过程中与"宁东湖680"轮发生了碰撞,随后"泰联达"轮向后方行驶又与"宁连海606"轮发生碰撞,"宁东湖680"轮与"宁连海606"轮当场沉没,并且事故发生地存在多个水库系重点保护水域,宝山海事局立刻指派作业船只展开油污防控和清除工作。该案中法院认为三艘船舶均存在过失从而导致碰撞漏油,最终法院根据《海商法》第一百六十九条判决由互有过失的船舶根据责任比例向受害人赔偿相应数额,明确不予采纳被告之一远顺达公司"非漏油船方不应承担涉案清防污费用"的抗辩主张。① 在广东省海洋与渔业局诉"通天顺"轮与"天神"轮油污损害赔偿纠纷案中,广州海事法院查明两船互有过失碰撞导致"通天顺"轮沉没,所载油类大量泄漏入海造成严重污染。最终,法院根据《海商法》第一百六十九条第二款判决非漏油船方与漏油船方按各自过错比例对受害人承担责任。② 2000年广东高级人民法院做出的"闵燃供2"轮二审判决也体现了该观点。③

该观点增加了受害人的获赔渠道,使受害方能够获得来自非漏油船方的油污损害赔偿,从而更好地保障受害方的利益。但是,该学说以《海商法》第一百六十九条为依据,条款中规定的"第三人财产损失"是否可以涵盖泄漏的油污对受害人造成的损失尚存在争议。海事理论界在非漏油船碰撞与油污损害间的因果关系问题上同样存在争议,不少学者认为造成油污损害的直接原因并不是非漏油船的过失碰撞,而是漏油船的漏油。因果关系层面使得非漏油船承担油污损害赔偿责任仍需要更多的理论支撑。因此,该学说的合理性仍有待商榷。

3. 非漏油船与漏油船应承担连带责任

支持"非漏油船与漏油船应承担连带责任"的学者认为,不论是漏油船还是非漏油船都与油污损害之间存在因果关系,两船对受害人构成共同侵权,非漏油船方与漏油船方承担连带责任。④ 支持此观点的底层逻辑为,在碰撞导致油污损害发生之前,漏油船方与非漏油船方都应有预见船舶可能发生漏油污染危险的可能。两船对危险的发生构成共同侵权行为,基于

---

① 参见(2014)沪海法商初字第931号民事判决书。
② 参见(2001)广海法初字第89号民事判决书。
③ 参见(2000)粤高法经二终字第328号民事判决书。
④ 参见谢明《船舶碰撞造成油污损害的连带责任及问题的解决》,见《海商法研究(第五辑)》法律出版社2001年版,第2页。

此，非漏油船方和漏油船方理应对受害人承担连带赔偿责任。① 《中华人民共和国民法典》（简称《民法典》）第一千一百六十八条以及《中华人民共和国海洋环境保护法》（简称《海洋环境保护法》）第八十九条常被用作该观点法律上的依据。②

在司法实践中，"潮河"轮与"VLACHERA BREEZE"轮案判决体现了此观点。1988 年"潮河"轮与"VLACHERA BREEZE"轮在粤东海域发生碰撞，受害人向广州海事法院起诉两船共同侵权。广州海事法院认为两船互有过失导致碰撞漏油，最终判决漏油船与非漏油船构成共同侵权，两船对受害人承担连带赔偿责任。③ 同样，"塔斯曼海"轮与"顺凯一号"轮案也体现了此观点。两船在天津东部海域发生碰撞，导致"塔斯曼海"轮 200 余吨原油泄漏，共有包括海洋局、渔政处、1500 名渔民及养殖户前后向法院起诉请求两被告承担赔偿责任共计 1.7 亿元人民币。法院认为两船互有过失碰撞应对油污损害承担连带责任，故一审判决两被告对原告损失承担连带赔偿责任。④

实践中采用此学说的案例较少。最高人民法院《第二次全国涉外商事海事审判工作会议纪要》第一百四十九条规定，"对于不受 1992 年油污公约调整的油污损害赔偿纠纷，因船舶碰撞造成油污损害的，由碰撞船舶所有人承担连带赔偿责任，但不影响油污损害赔偿责任人之间的追偿"⑤。尽管该条体现了此观点，但因该观点不符合民法共同侵权通说，反对该观点的学者较多。民法理论中，数个侵权人的连带责任承担需要有法律明确规定。在判断数个侵权人是否构成共同侵权时，通说即意思联络说要求数个侵权人之间必须具有事先的意思联络。⑥ 而互有过失碰撞的两船之间针对造成油污损害的结果并不存在事先的意思联络，很明显缺乏共同侵权构成

---

① 参见徐曾沧《互有过失碰撞引起油污损害赔偿法律适用》，载《海商法研究》2003 年第 1 期，第 234 页。
② 《民法典》第一千一百六十八条：二人以上共同实施侵权行为，造成他人损害的，应当承担连带责任。《海洋环境保护法》第八十九条：造成海洋环境污染损害的责任者，应当排除危害并承担损失。
③ 参见陈向勇、陈永灿《船舶碰撞油污损害赔偿非漏油方民事责任——兼评碰撞油污损害赔偿非漏油船船舶所有人民事责任》，载《中国海商法年刊》2010 年第 4 期，第 33 页。
④ 参见（2003）津海法事初字第 183 号民事判决书、（2003）津海法事初字第 184 号民事判决书、（2003）津海法事初字第 185 号民事判决书、（2003）津海法事初字第 186 号民事判决书。
⑤ 见《第二次全国涉外商事海事审判工作会议纪要》第一百四十九条第二款。
⑥ 参见邓大榜《共同侵权行为的民事责任初探》，载《法学季刊》1982 年第 3 期，第 41 页。

条件之一的"通谋"。因此，该观点也遭受到了较多质疑。

（二）最高人民法院开创性判决引发新争议

在两船互有过失发生碰撞导致单船漏油的案件中，我国各地法院判决中对非漏油船方油污损害赔偿责任并不一致。2013年，"达飞佛罗里达"轮与"舟山"轮在东海海域发生碰撞，"达飞佛罗里达"轮燃油舱内600余吨燃油泄漏，上海海事局立即安排上海打捞局等多家单位采取救助清污工作。在此之后，上海打捞局等11家单位向法院提起诉讼要求漏油船方与非漏油船方承担油污损害产生的清污费等相关费用。本案自2014年起先后经历了一审、二审，后洋山港海事局向最高人民法院申请再审。最终，最高人民法院于2019年作出再审判决，这也是最高人民法院首次对互有过失碰撞致单船漏油中的非漏油船油污损害赔偿责任问题表明态度。

1. 非漏油船责任承担类型突破固有模式

在"达飞佛罗里达"轮与"舟山"轮案判决中，最高人民法院判决认为：《2001年燃油公约》仅规定了漏油船的责任，没有涉及非漏油船责任。该公约第三条第一款以及第六款仅仅从正面表述漏油船应承担责任，不能反向推断非漏油船方不应当负责，也不代表油污损害索赔权利人不能直接请求除漏油船以外的其他责任人赔偿。① 两船在我国海域发生碰撞，且公约未排除非漏油船责任，根据法律选择规则本案应适用我国国内法进一步明确非漏油船的油污损害赔偿责任。由于2011年的《最高人民法院关于审理船舶油污损害赔偿纠纷案件若干问题的规定》（简称《油污损害司法解释》）第四条沿袭了《2001年燃油公约》第三条的规定，不涉及非漏油船责任承担问题。② 根据《中华人民共和国侵权责任法》（简称《侵权责任法》）第六十八条（现《民法典》第一千二百三十三条）以及《最高人民法院关于审理环境侵权责任纠纷案件适用法律若干问题的解释》（简称《环境侵权司法解释》）第五条确立的第三人侵权的规则，被侵权人向第三

---

① 《2001年燃油公约》第三条第一款：除第三款和四款所规定者外，事故发生时的船舶所有人应对由船上或源自船舶的任何燃油造成的污染损害负责，但如某一事故由具有同一起源的系列事件构成，则该责任应由此系列事件的首次事件发生时的船舶所有人承担；第六款：本公约中的任何规定均不应损害独立于本公约的船舶所有人的任何追索权。

② 《油污损害司法解释》第四条：船舶互有过失碰撞造成油污损害的，受害人可以请求漏油船所有人承担全部赔偿责任。

人索赔时法院应根据第三人的过错程度确定其相应赔偿责任。① 因此，最高人民法院认为一、二审法院判决非漏油船不承担油污损害赔偿责任在理解与适用法律上存在问题，最终判决漏油船所有人普罗旺斯公司、达飞公司对防污清污费承担全部赔偿责任，非漏油船所有人罗克韦尔公司按其过错程度对本案防污清污费用承担 50% 的责任，赔偿总额以全部防污清污费为限。②

从判决结果看，最高人民法院在非漏油船油污损害赔偿责任问题上开创了一种前所未有的新模式。首先，不同于仅漏油船承担油污损害赔偿责任，受害人可以分别或者同时起诉漏油船与非漏油船方；其次，按份责任受害人仅可向漏油船索赔比例范围内的赔偿，而新模式下受害人可以向漏油船索赔全部赔偿责任；最后，不同于连带责任，新模式下非漏油船方仅在其过错比例范围内承担油污损害赔偿责任。此种非漏油船责任承担新模式引起了部分学者的质疑，尤其是在公约是否排除非漏油船油污损害赔偿责任问题上。综上所述，如表 1 所示，若责任承担观点不同，则受害人的索赔权也各不相同。此外，最高人民法院在判决中认定公约没有排除非漏油船的油污损害赔偿责任进而适用国内《侵权责任法》确定非漏油船以其过错比例为限承担责任的新思路，引发了学界对国内法的进一步讨论。对于有学者认为最高人民法院适用《侵权责任法》而非《海商法》违背了法律规定不一致情况下特殊法优先于一般法原则，本案中最高人民法院特别注明适用《侵权责任法》而非《海商法》并不违反特别法优先于一般法原则。③ 一方面，尽管《海商法》为特殊法，但其第一百六十九条所在章节调整的法律关系为船舶碰撞而非船舶油污关系。《海商法》中调整船舶碰撞的条款当然不应适用于船舶油污关系。④ 另一方面，适用《侵权责任法》及司法解释令非漏油船在其过错比例范围内承担责任并没有与《海商法》中的归责原则发生冲突。

---

① 《侵权责任法》第六十八条：因第十三人的过错污染环境造成损害，被侵权人可以向污染者请求赔偿，也可以向第三人请求赔偿。污染者赔偿后，有权向第三人追偿。
② 参见（2018）最高法民再 368 号民事判决书。
③ 参见韩立新、刘红《油污损害赔偿中非漏油方的责任主体地位探析》，载《河北法学》2008 年第 9 期，第 153 页。
④ 参见余晓汉《船舶碰撞漏油事故中非漏油船舶的所有人过错归责相关问题辨析——"达飞佛罗里达"轮油污案再审判决内外的思考》，载《国际法研究》2023 年第 2 期，第 68 页。

表1 不同观点下受害人索赔权对照

责任承担观点	受害人索赔情况		
	仅向漏油船方索赔	仅向非漏油船方索赔	同时向漏油船方与非漏油船方索赔
仅应由漏油船方承担责任	受害人仅能向漏油船方索赔,漏油船方承担全部责任	受害人无权向其索赔	受害人无权向其索赔
漏油船方与非漏油船方承担比例责任	受害人能向漏油船方索赔过错比例责任	受害人能向非漏油船方索赔过错比例责任	漏油船方与非漏油船方各自在过错比例范围内担责
漏油船方与非漏油船方承担连带责任	受害人能向漏油船方索赔全部责任	受害人能向非漏油船方索赔全部责任	漏油船方或非漏油船方向受害人赔偿后,各自承担相应责任
非漏油船方承担补充责任	受害人仅能向漏油船方索赔,漏油船方赔偿后可以向非漏油船方追偿	受害人无权向其索赔	受害人无权向其索赔
最高人民法院新做法	受害人可向漏油船方主张承担全部赔偿责任,漏油船方赔偿后可向非漏油船方追偿	受害人可直接向非漏油船方主张过错比例责任	漏油船方与非漏油船方各自在其过错比例范围内承担责任,赔偿总额以全部责任为限

2. 非漏油船直接担责冲击现有赔偿机制

当前,国际上的船舶油污损害赔偿机制分为三层,分别为第一层船舶所有人(保险人)、第二层油污赔偿基金与第三层补充基金。在船舶碰撞致漏油事故发生后,船舶所有人(保险人)会成为第一层油污损害赔偿责任主体向油污受害人承担赔偿责任。为保障各方利益相对平衡,制度设计者在船舶油污损害制度中为船方赋予了责任限制机制。在船舶的油污损害保险制度方面，根据《防治船舶污染海洋环境管理条例》[①] 以及《中华人民共和国船舶油污损害民事责任保险实施办法》[②]（简称《船舶油污损害民事责任保险实施办法》）的规定，只要是在我国海域航行的1000总吨以上的船舶都要强制投污染责任保险或者取得财务保证，所以非漏油船满足上述情形也要投油污责任保险。但令非漏油船承担油污损害赔偿责任可能会对保险制度产生些许影响，主要表现在：船舶油污责任险的生效条件通常为被保险船舶即本船发生漏油损害，并不包括碰撞的对方船舶漏油。[③] 在船舶碰撞导致单船漏油事故中，如果认定非漏油船方也要直接对受害人承担油污责任，由于非漏油船方所承担的油污责任是由漏油船漏油而并非其本船漏油引起的，故非漏油船方承担的油污责任并不属于《船舶油污责任保险条款》第四条规定的承保条件中要求的本船"发生的燃油泄漏或排放油污事故"的情形。因此，如果最终非漏油船方亦需承担油污损害赔偿责任，则其保险人可能以油污并非出自非漏油船作为抗辩理由。如遇以上情况，非漏油船方的油污保险救济作用将大打折扣。

油污基金赔偿制度会在受害人因船舶所有人责任限制无法得到充分赔偿的情况下作为第二层赔偿主体进行补充赔偿。在《1992年油污公约》与《1992年设立国际油污损害赔偿基金国际公约》（简称《油污基金公约》）下形成的对受害人的双层赔偿模式目的是希望船方与货方共担油污损害风险，同时也能够为油污受害方提供尽可能公平合理的赔偿，保护受害人的合法权益。[④] 但国际上的双层赔偿机制仅限于《1992年油污公约》框架

[①] 《防治船舶污染海洋环境条例》第五十一条：在中华人民共和国管辖海域内航行的船舶，其所有人应当按照国务院交通运输主管部门的规定，投保船舶油污损害民事责任保险或者取得相应的财务担保。但是，1000总吨以下载运非油类物质的船舶除外。船舶所有人投保船舶油污损害民事责任保险或者取得的财务担保的额度应当不低于《中华人民共和国海商法》、中华人民共和国缔结或者参加的有关国际条约规定的油污赔偿限额。

[②] 《船舶油污损害民事责任保险实施办法》第二条：在中华人民共和国管辖海域内航行的载运油类物质的船舶和1000总吨以上载运非油类物质的船舶，其所有人应当按照本办法的规定投保船舶油污损害民事责任保险或者取得相应的财务担保。承担船舶油污损害民事责任保险的商业性保险机构和互助性保险机构，应当遵守本办法。

[③] 中国人民财产保险公司《船舶油污责任保险条款》第三条第一款：燃油从船上的溢出或排放引起的污染在该船之外所造成的灭失或损害，不论此种溢出或排放发生于何处；但是，对环境损害（不包括此种损害的利润损失）的赔偿，应限于已实际采取或将要采取的合理恢复措施的费用。

[④] 参见袁雪《国际船舶油污损害赔偿机制及我国的选择》，载《环境保护》2012年第1期，第101页。

下,《2001年燃油公约》下并未形成基金组织分散风险。我国大陆地区并未加入《油污基金公约》。随着我国海运事业的迅速发展,为分散风险、完善油污赔偿制度,交通运输部于2012年颁布实施《船舶油污损害赔偿基金征收使用管理办法》(简称《基金管理办法》),随着2015年基金管理委员会的成立,我国也形成了自己的油污基金赔偿制度。和《油污基金公约》只能与《1992年油污公约》下持久性货油引发的油污配套使用相比,我国确立的油污基金赔偿制度涵盖的油污种类更多,即我国的油污基金赔偿制度可以涵盖《2001年燃油公约》框架下的燃油油污种类,适用面更广。[①] 非漏油船方承担油污损害赔偿责任的新模式可能会带来基金赔偿限额、赔偿顺序等方面的一系列新问题。

从司法实践现状来看,对互有过失碰撞致单船漏油案件中非漏油船的油污损害赔偿责任问题依旧存在较大分歧。具体原因可概括为国际公约与国内法对非漏油船油污损害赔偿责任问题的规定较为模糊从而导致理解适用混乱。非漏油船油污损害赔偿责任的不同观点及其对应公约和国内法的适用情况见表2。

表2 非漏油船担责不同观点法律适用情况对照

观点	法律理解适用	
	国际法方面	国内法方面
仅漏油船方承担责任	根据《1992年油污公约》与《2001年燃油公约》规定仅应由漏油船方承担油污损害赔偿责任	无需适用
漏油船方与非漏油船方承担比例责任	根据《1992年油污公约》与《2001年燃油公约》规定漏油船方应承担油污损害赔偿责任,但未排除非漏油船方的油污损害赔偿责任	根据《海商法》第一百六十九条,漏油船方与非漏油船方承担比例责任

[①] 参见周舫震《中国船舶油污损害赔偿基金的运行模式》,载《中国海事》2015年第11期,第38页。

续表2

观点	法律理解适用	
	国际法方面	国内法方面
漏油船方与非漏油船方承担连带责任	根据《1992年油污公约》与《2001年燃油公约》规定漏油船方应承担油污损害赔偿责任,但未排除非漏油船方的油污损害赔偿责任	根据《民法典》第一千一百六十八条,漏油船方与非漏油船方承担连带责任
非漏油船方承担补充责任	根据《1992年油污公约》与《2001年燃油公约》规定仅应由漏油船方承担油污损害赔偿责任	引入补充责任原则,受害人必须先向漏油船方索赔,漏油船方赔偿后可以向非漏油船方追偿
最高人民法院新做法	根据《1992年油污公约》与《2001年燃油公约》规定漏油船方应承担油污损害赔偿责任,但未排除非漏油船方的油污损害赔偿责任	根据《民法典》第一千二百三十三条和《环境侵权司法解释》第五条,受害人选择只向漏油船方索赔,漏油船方应当承担全部责任;选择仅向非漏油船方索赔,非漏油船方承担过错比例范围内责任;同时向漏油船方与非漏油船方索赔,则各自承担过错比例责任

二、互有过失碰撞致油污损害因果的关系及非漏油船担责必要性

法律关系即以法律标准衡量人们日常社会生活关系从而得出人们相互之间的权利义务结果。[1] 如果想明确互有过失碰撞致单船漏油中非漏油船

---

[1] 参见韩光明《论民事法律关系的内容构建:一个基本概念的规范分析》,载《比较法研究》2009年第5期,第45页。

的油污损害赔偿责任，就必须剥开案件事实外壳，准确廓清法律关系，寻找其中的因果关系链条。

（一）互有过失碰撞与油污损害间的因果关系厘清

法院对碰撞与油污之间因果关系的判断将直接影响油污损害赔偿责任由谁承担的问题。互有过失碰撞引起的油污损害与单船过错导致的油污损害相比多了非漏油船主观过错这一情节，而正是这一情节为司法实践中合理划分各方责任增加了难度。

1. 船舶碰撞致油污损害的因果关系之争

基于对因果关系的理解不同，海事实务界对船舶碰撞与油污损害间的因果关系产生了完全不同的两种观点。第一种观点认为碰撞与油污损害之间具有因果关系，船舶碰撞是油污损害发生的原因。此观点的支持者认为，从表面上看，油污损害结果发生的原因似乎包括碰撞和漏油两个因素，但实际上碰撞与漏油之间相互关联而并非彼此割裂。① 碰撞并非必然导致油污损害，但是在互有过失碰撞中一旦导致油污损害发生，则客观上油污损害必然是由船舶的碰撞引起的。支持该观点的学者常运用相当因果关系理论论证碰撞与油污损害之间具有因果关系。② 他们认为如果排除了船舶碰撞这一因素就不会发生漏油，更不会导致油污损害的结果。另一种观点则认为，船舶碰撞与油污损害之间不具有因果关系，是漏油船的漏油而非船舶碰撞导致油污损害结果。此观点认为船舶碰撞从本质上看只能作为引发油污损害的条件，而不是油污损害的原因。船舶碰撞也并不必然导致漏油，而只有在船舶漏油时才会产生油污损害，因此船舶碰撞和油污损害之间不具有因果关系。③ 支持该观点的学者认为漏油作为一种介入因素插在原有的行为和损害结果之间，并且这一介因足够强大，从而替代了原来的碰撞行为成为油污损害的直接原因。原本的碰撞—油污的因果链条因

---

① 参见司玉琢《从因果关系要件解读船舶碰撞致油污损害的请求权竞合》，载《中国海商法年刊》（2008）第19卷，大连海事大学出版社2009年版，第10页。

② 参见陈向勇、陈永灿《船舶碰撞油污损害赔偿非漏油方民事责任——兼评油污损害赔偿司法解释草案的新发展》，载《中国海商法年刊》2010年第4期，第35页。

③ 参见吴莉婧《论船舶碰撞造成的油污损害赔偿》，载《中国海洋大学学报（社会科学版）》2003年第3期，第59页。

此发生中断，漏油自然而然成为了导致油污损害结果的原因。①

2. 相当因果关系理论更宜在船舶碰撞油污案件中运用

对于一起互有过失碰撞致单船漏油案件，如果运用"介因说"来判断碰撞与油污损害之间的因果关系，则认为碰撞与油污损害之间不具有因果关系。但若根据"相当因果关系"学说，则认为碰撞与油污损害间存在因果关系。下面将对当前争议较大的"介因说"与"相当因果关系说"进行比较研究。

（1）相当因果关系判断逻辑更具优势。反对相当因果关系的学者会认为，相当因果关系中的一般社会判断标准过于抽象，会影响因果关系的客观性。但笔者认为，利用相当因果关系理论来判断行为与结果之间的因果关系并不会否定客观性。首先，因果关系确实是客观的。只要发生了某一客观事实，那么因果关系链条就客观存在，且该链条不因行为人事后的主观意志而发生改变。但承认因果关系的客观性并不等同于否认人的意识对因果链条的影响。② 人类的一般经验正是在长期的客观实践过程中逐步积累的，社会一般经验正是对社会客观性的反映和总结。因此，根据人类一般经验来判断行为与结果之间的因果关系并不等同于否认因果关系的客观性，运用相当因果关系标准来判断行为与结果并不会与因果关系客观性产生冲突；相反，相当因果关系理论本身具有客观性强、在实践中易于判断的特点，并且克服了直接因果关系僵化的缺点。目前，我国包括杨立新、王利明、梁慧星在内的不少学者均主张在实践中采用相当因果关系说。③

相当因果关系理论经过了多年发展和实践检验，已成为多个国家尤其是大陆法系国家最重要的因果关系理论。实践中适用相当因果关系来判断行为与结果间的因果关系更为合理。相当因果关系在通过第一层"条件关系"确定事实上的因果关系之后，在第二层"相当性"判断中会赋予法官一定自由裁量权，以便对行为与结果间是否具有法律上的因果进行判断。适用相当因果关系理论判断因果关系是适应世界因果关系判断实践发展趋势的。不论是英美法系还是大陆法系，在因果关系的判断标准上都逐渐从

---

① 参见韩立新、初北平《船舶碰撞油污损害承担连带赔偿责任的法理分析——兼评最高人民法院2005年〈纪要〉第149条》，载《辽宁大学学报》2008年第4期，第137页。
② 参见王卫国《过错责任原则：第三次勃兴》，中国法制出版社2001年版，第69页。
③ 参见杨立新《侵权法判例与学说》，吉林人民出版社2003年版，第41页；王利明《侵权行为法研究》（上卷），中国人民大学出版社2004年版，第418页；梁慧星《民商法论丛》（第11卷），法律出版社1999年版，第546页。

绝对抽象的概括模式中剥脱，由必然性逐渐转变为采用社会一般经验标准下的可能性标准。同时，对可能性施加一定条件限制以避免在实践中判断因果关系时因果链条过长或因条件过于宽松而被滥用。① 而这种社会一般经验和认知水平可以理解为行为人以正常的一般理性判断（reasonable man test）能够对其行为的结果做出合理预见，而"相当因果关系"中的相当性恰恰符合这一趋势。②

（2）运用相当因果关系判断船舶碰撞与油污损害因果关系更为合理。对于船舶互有过失碰撞与油污损害的因果关系认定，适用相当因果关系确立碰撞与油污损害间的因果关系是合理判断各方责任的最佳选择，这也与我国著名海商法学家司玉琢教授的观点一致。③

有学者对"相当性"下的社会一般经验标准提出质疑。反对者主张应设定一个固定数值来明确社会一般标准，在行为导致结果的概率超过50%时可以认为符合社会一般经验，若低于50%则不符合社会一般经验。④ 据此，反对者认为一般船舶碰撞造成漏油污染的概率不会高于50%，因此碰撞与油污损害之间不满足"相当性"标准。在社会一般标准认定上，各个国家所采取的判断基准宽严程度并不相同，但各国一致认为因果关系判断不应是机械标准，而是保护人民权益的政策工具。⑤ 社会一般经验标准是该社会当前阶段合理性价值内涵的体现，而将"相当性"判断标准机械地确定为50%的概率与因果判断的价值内核相悖。如果在因果关系相当性判断中均采用50%标准，那么船舶碰撞造成人身伤亡的概率低于50%，但因概率低就否认碰撞与人身伤亡结果间客观的因果关系使侵权方逃避责任明显不合理。为"相当性"设定的固定概率在国外被称为"可能率"，其因数值过于僵化对因果关系判断有害无益同样遭到了外国学者的抵制。⑥ 且即便采用50%作为"相当性"的标准，根据最新研究船舶碰撞致油污损害事故发生的概率也超过了50%。1974年至2023年，我国50吨以上较大漏

---

① 参见杨立新《侵权法论》（第三版），人民法院出版社2005年版，第187-188页。
② 参见韩强《法律因果关系理论研究——以学说史为素材》，北京大学出版社2008年版，第110页。
③ 参见司玉琢《从因果关系要件解读船舶碰撞致油污损害的请求权竞合》，载《中国海商法年刊》（2008）第19卷，大连海事大学出版社2009年版，第9页。
④ 参见韩立新《船舶污染损害赔偿法律制度研究》，大连海事大学出版社2004年版，第76页。
⑤ 参见王泽鉴《侵权行为法》（第一册），中国政法大学出版社2001年版，第204页。
⑥ 参见曾世雄《损害赔偿法原理》，中国政法大学出版社2001年版，第104页。

油事故约 110 余次,可以发现因船舶碰撞导致漏油约 60 余次,由碰撞导致的漏油总量多达 159987 吨,占全部海洋溢油总量的 85%。① 如图 1 所示,船舶碰撞确实已成为导致油污损害事故发生的最主要原因。

因此,笼统地以 50% 概率替代"相当性"判断标准过于僵化和机械,一般社会经验标准能够淡化法学因果关系中的僵化数学概率。在实践中,应赋予法官一定的自由裁量权,使其根据案件不同情况在社会一般经验的限度内判断漏油与油污损害之间是否具有因果关系。

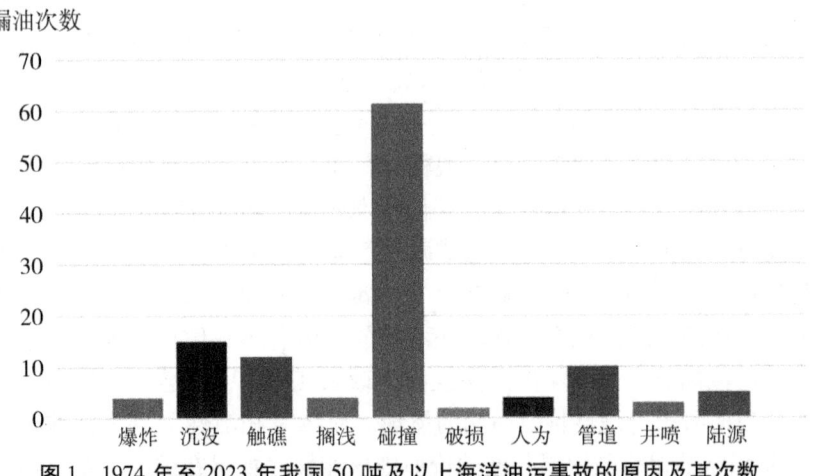

图 1　1974 年至 2023 年我国 50 吨及以上海洋油污事故的原因及其次数

此外,还有学者坚持采用"介因说",认为真正导致油污损害结果的是漏油因素的介入而非碰撞。② 但此观点也遭到了许多学者的反对。笔者同样认为,采用"介因说"否定碰撞与油污损害之间的因果关系值得商榷。"介因说"要求因果关系中插入的介入因素必须是完全独立于行为人实施侵权行为之外的因素,③ 并且该介入因素以一般人的标准看是行为人实施行为时无法预料到的。随着该介入因素的介入,原行为与结果之间的

---

① 参见陈勤思、胡松《中国近海沿岸海洋溢油事故研究》,载《海洋开发与管理》2022 年 12 期,第 51 页。

② 参见王小军、戴超《船舶油污损害赔偿民事责任主体探析》,载《中国海洋大学学报(社会科学版)》2014 年第 5 期,第 21 页。

③ 参见闫晓丽《侵权行为法上因果关系问题探讨——第三因素介入的因果关系认定》,载《当代法学》2002 年第 12 期,第 50 页。

自然逻辑被打破。① 如果某因素属于行为人实施行为的涵盖范畴，并且行为人在实施行为时可能预见到该因素，那么这一因素就没有中断原来的因果关系链条，介入因素也就无法替代原行为成为导致损害发生的直接原因。在互有过失碰撞导致的油污损害案件中，漏油因素明显涵盖在碰撞可能造成的危险范围内，并且船员对于碰撞导致漏油具有一定的预见性。在漏油因碰撞而发生的情况下，油污损害可以被合理地纳入船舶碰撞引发的自然延续结果中。因此，漏油不满足介入因素中断条件，不能取代船舶碰撞与油污损害之间产生因果关系。

（二）我国非漏油船承担油污损害赔偿责任的必要性

鉴于非漏油船过失碰撞与油污损害间存在因果关系，结合当前互有过失碰撞致单船漏油案件实际情况，令非漏油船承担油污损害赔偿责任有利于保护受害人的合法权益，同时符合我国海洋环境保护、建立绿色中国的发展目标。

1. 非漏油船承担油污损害赔偿责任利于解决赔偿少、赔偿慢的问题

首先，互有过失船舶碰撞导致的油污损害数额往往是巨大的，赔偿范围涵盖海洋自然资源损失、沿海渔业损失、清污单位工作费用等多个方面。在司法实践中，漏油船一方往往是互有过失碰撞中遭受损害较大的一方，船舶在碰撞导致漏油后往往也会产生燃烧、毁损、沉没等连锁反应。因此，漏油船方在事故发生后其赔偿能力可能大大减弱。假如漏油船未投保或发生保险公司倒闭，保险单有瑕疵、过期等情况，受害人仅向漏油方主张油污损害赔偿责任将无法得到合理赔付。与漏油船的不堪重负相比，倘若存在主观过错且与油污损害结果间存在因果关系的非漏油船方可以不承担油污损害赔偿责任，对漏油船方及受害人的利益而言无疑是一种不公。以"宝赛斯"轮与"德航298"轮为例，内河小船"德航"轮在碰撞后200余吨燃油发生泄漏，该轮漏油后随即沉没，船东宣布失去赔偿能力。此种情况漏油船方无法做到先赔偿受害人再向非漏油船追偿，而倘若剥夺受害人向非漏油船索赔的权利，受害方可能陷入独自承担污染损害的

---

① 参见马荣春《介入因素的类型及其因果论立场》，载《政法论丛》2022年第5期，第83页。

窘境。①

其次，事实上，漏油船方即便在碰撞后具备损害赔偿能力也很难独自对受害人全面赔偿，"达飞佛罗里达"轮与"舟山"轮一案单渔业资源受损索赔数额就高达 2 亿元人民币。仅靠漏油船方常常无法对受害方主张的损失进行合理赔偿。此外，非漏油船对受害人承担油污损害赔偿责任可以解决油污基金赔偿不足的问题。我国内地未加入《油污基金公约》，为加强对受害人权益保护，我国以《基金管理办法》和《船舶油污损害赔偿基金征收使用管理办法实施细则》（简称《基金实施细则》）建立起类似于基金公约的船舶油污损害赔偿基金制度。从当前基金赔偿的实际情况来看，其难以为受害人提供有力保障。《基金管理办法》中基金赔偿划定的最高限额只有 3000 万元人民币，较低的限额导致其无法满足多数案件中受害人高昂的油污损害赔偿费用需求。② 以 2018 年的"桑吉"轮与"长峰水晶"轮案为例，案件中债权人申报债权的登记总额已达 19 亿元人民币，而长宏集团有限公司作为"长峰水晶"轮的所有人为其船舶造成人身伤亡和非人身伤亡分别设立了 13342250 SDR 和 6477625 SDR 的赔偿责任限制。此时，油污基金仅 3000 万元人民币的最高限额面对受害方申报数额显得杯水车薪。③ 较低的基金赔偿限额无法弥补船舶重大污染对受害方造成的损害，对清污单位、海洋资源、沿海养殖居民的权益产生不利影响。因此，将非漏油船纳入油污损害赔偿责任承担者范围内有利于避免受害人因漏油船受损严重且油污损害赔偿基金限额较低得不到赔偿而陷入尴尬境地。

最后，中国船舶油污损害赔偿基金的补偿标准是补贴成本损失。基金赔偿审核程序严格且受害人获赔周期较长。根据我国《基金管理办法》受害人需要在发生油污损害后先起诉侵权方的船东（保险人），在法院作出判决船东已经承担赔偿责任但赔偿不足或船东缺乏赔偿能力的情况下，受害人才能向基金索赔赔偿不足的部分。此外，受害人还要经历基金赔偿冗

---

① 参见许光玉、李振海《海事案件若干法律问题探讨——兼评〈第二次全国涉外商事海事审判工作会议纪要〉相关规定》，载《中国律师 2006 年海事业务研讨会暨年会资料集》，第 103 页。

② 《基金管理办法》第十八条：船舶油污损害赔偿基金对任一船舶油污事故的赔偿或补偿金额不超过 3000 万元人民币。财政部可以依据船舶油污事故赔偿需求、累积的船舶油污损害赔偿基金规模等因素，会同交通运输部调整基金赔偿限额。

③ 参见（2018）沪 72 民特 10 号公告、（2018）沪 72 民特 11 号公告。

长的流程才能获得最终赔偿款。① 结合实践来看，因互有过失碰撞致油污损害涉及多方利益，案件情节复杂，受害人遭受油污损害后请求基金赔偿耗时普遍较长。"达飞佛罗里达"轮与"舟山"轮案从案发到最高人民法院再审判决经历了7年多的时间，再加上油污基金申请至获赔的流程耗时，受害人获赔会耗时更久。根据中国船舶油污损害赔偿事务中心公布的已获油污基金赔偿案件情况，受害人平均要经过2~3年时间才能取得基金赔偿。② 由于清污单位、渔民等受害者在获得赔偿前会选择先垫付相关费用，在经历多次垫付后一些小的清污单位若无法及时获赔将难以维系经济运转。实践中许多单位还未等到来自船东及基金的赔偿就已经宣告破产。③ 大法官休尼特曾言，"Justice delayed is justice denied"④。获赔时间过分延长对于本就遭受损害的受害人一方更加不利。况且过分依赖基金补偿，而作为肇事船之一的非漏油船却置身事外，明显不合理。

2. 非漏油船承担油污损害赔偿责任有利于环境保护

为进行更远的航行和节约成本，船舶在专业化、巨大化的同时其配置的燃油舱和货油舱也更大，相应的这些庞然巨物一旦发生事故将对海洋环境安全带来更大危害。由于航运市场竞争加剧，近年来，超龄服役的船舶数量不断增加。老旧船只抵御海上风险的能力通常更加薄弱，事故发生率也随之大大增加。根据最新研究，近十年发生的大型船舶溢油事故明显增加，2010年后，500吨以上船舶的漏油事故在漏油次数及总量上都要高于2000—2010年。⑤ 在此情形下，非漏油船承担油污损害赔偿责任相较于仅由漏油船承担油污损害赔偿责任有利于为清污单位等受害方带来更加充分、及时的赔偿。在越来越多的船舶碰撞油污损害案件中，作为受害方的清污单位仅向漏油船方索赔往往难以得到足额赔偿从而维系企业经营，长此以往将极不利于清污行业的持续发展，而非漏油船方作为侵权人之一向

---

① 参见周舫震、朱羿峥《关于〈船舶油污损害赔偿基金征收使用管理办法〉修改的若干建议》，载《浙江海洋大学学报（人文社科版）》2019年第1期，第2页。
② 参见中国船舶油污损害赔偿基金官网《理赔案例》（https://www.sh.msa.gov.cn/spal/index.jhtml）。
③ 参见潘浠《〈船舶油污损害赔偿基金征收使用管理办法〉修改的必要性和要点建议》，见上海海事大学海商法研究中心编《海大法律评论（2018—2019）》，上海浦江教育出版社2021年版，第226页。
④ 李叙明：《司法正义研究》（学位论文），湖南师范大学2013年，第115页。
⑤ 参见陈勤思、胡松《中国近海沿岸海洋溢油事故研究》，载《海洋开发与管理》2020年第12期，第52页。

受害方赔偿将能够很好地解决这一难题。例如,在巴拿马籍"现代促进"轮与"地中海伊伦娜"轮碰撞案和荷属安的列斯籍"密斯姆"轮燃油泄漏事故中,受害人索赔金额过亿元而漏油船无法承担巨额赔款。最终,法院判决非漏油船与漏油船向受害方赔偿油污损害费用,使参加清污工作的企业获得合理赔款以继续开展其他清污工作。① 实践中,互有过失船舶碰撞引起的油污损害案情往往比较复杂,案件审理时间也会更长,清污企业在事故发生后的清污工作中需先行垫付费用,许多清污企业可能在案件审理的过程中因缺乏资金周转而破产倒闭。即便清污企业尚能等到法院作出裁决,但最终如果仅由漏油船单方承担油污损害赔偿责任,极其有限的赔偿金额还需要在多个受害人间分配。在更为极端的案例中,漏油船方因碰撞而沉没且丧失赔偿能力后,清污单位将无法获得赔偿,久而久之将不利于清污行业的发展和海洋环境保护工作。

此外,非漏油船承担油污损害赔偿责任能够警醒船舶提高油污事故预防意识以尽量避免油污损害事件的发生。法律在本质上属于国家创制的行为规则,对人的行为产生指引、评价、预测、教育、强制的作用。法律是社会主体进行决策时的外部环境组成部分,能够影响人做出选择时的主观利弊判断。当法律规定某种行为将产生一定代价时,人们在做出选择时往往会希望避开不利代价或畏惧某种结果从而放弃采取某种行为以防减损自身利益。② 相较于仅由漏油船单方承担油污损害赔偿责任,将非漏油船纳入油污损害赔偿责任的范围内更能发挥法律的引导作用,标本兼治,防止油污损害事故的发生。一方面,互有过失碰撞后非漏油船承担油污损害赔偿能够对受害方利益进行更好的保护,有益于环境保护事业;另一方面,有利于非漏油船方加强船员培训,敦促其改进技术、定期检测船舶质量、更新维修雷达等设备、淘汰老旧船只从而降低船舶"脆皮"风险,最大限度地避免发生漏油事故。多么完善的法律都无法杜绝损害的发生,而以法律引导船舶采取实际行动以提高防范意识则能尽可能避免污染损害发生。

---

① 参见中国新闻网《国内最大海洋污染事故案宣判 两外籍船赔6800万》(https://www.chinanews.com/other/news/2006/08-16/774522.shtml)、中华人民共和国宁波海事法院《奥列格等外籍船员申请扣押"密斯姆"轮案》(http://www.nbhsfy.cn/art/2015/3/4/art_1229571842_2907.html)。

② 参见张文显《法理学》,法律出版社2007年版,第360页。

三、互有过失碰撞中非漏油船油污损害赔偿责任相关国际公约的理解与适用

奥本海曾言:"国际公约常因其本身条款晦涩、含义复杂造成缔结公约成员对公约条文理解、解释适用等方面存在冲突"①。船舶互有过失碰撞致单船漏油主要涉及《1992年油污公约》和《2001年燃油公约》。在调整的对象范围上两公约是互补而非对立关系。② 当前互有过失碰撞非漏油船油污损害赔偿责任的争议,在很大程度上源于对国际公约条款的不同理解。当今国际社会已普遍认可《维也纳条约法公约》,且我国作为该国际公约的缔约国,在解释国际公约条款时应严格遵守其规定。在"达飞佛罗里达"案中,最高人民法院也采用了《维也纳条约法公约》中的解释方法,但是并没有具体的论证过程。因此,有必要借助《维也纳条约法公约》对《1992年油污公约》和《2001年燃油公约》是否排除了非漏油船责任进行深入研究。

(一) 国际公约未排除非漏油船承担赔偿责任

鉴于对国际公约是否排除非漏油船的油污损害赔偿责任存在争议,下面利用《维也纳条约法公约》对《1992年油污公约》《2001年燃油公约》中非漏油船的油污损害赔偿责任进行全面、系统的解释。

1.《1992年油污公约》第三条未限定仅由漏油船承担责任

首先,依据文义解释可以得出《1992年油污公约》并没有限定仅仅由漏油船承担油污损害赔偿责任。"从文义出发对法律条文进行理解往往是解释的第一步。"③ 文义解释即一般情况下公约的含义仅限于公约条文的字面意思,不需要对其擅自扩张,与公约无关的信息不能因公约条文未涵盖

---

① 参见[德]奥本海《奥本海国际法》(上卷),岑德彰译,上海社会科学院出版社2017年版,第532页。
② 《1992年油污公约》第一条第五款:"油类"系指任何持久性烃类矿物油,如原油、燃料油、重柴油和润滑油,不论是在船上作为货物运输还是在此种船舶的燃料舱中。《2001年燃油公约》第一条第五款:"燃油"系指用于或拟用于船舶运行或推进的包括润滑油在内的任何烃类矿物油,以及此类油的任何残余物。
③ 张文显:《法理学》,高等教育出版社2018年版,第254页。

或不明确就认为公约涵盖。①

《1992年油污公约》第三条第一款被部分学者理解为排除了非漏油船方的油污损害赔偿责任。② 从公约原文来看，其表述为"the owner of a ship at the time of an incident…shall be liable for any pollution damage caused by the ship as a result of the incident."③ 直译为：在所有的事故中船舶所有人应该对因船舶泄漏造成的任何损失承担责任。据此，该条款确实明确了漏油船的油污损害赔偿责任，漏油船船舶所有人应承担油污损害赔偿责任。但本条含有的所有用词并没有包含非漏油船责任，仅根据公约该条款不能排除非漏油船的油污损害赔偿责任。根据文义解释规则，条款应从字面意思出发，对条款不包含的内容不能做超越词义的射程范围的推论。《1992年油污公约》第三条在文义上明显不涉及非漏油船，无法根据本条推断公约排除了非漏油船的油污损害赔偿责任。且英美法系的条款对于责任规定的惯常做法也可以体现出第三条并非排除非漏油船责任。在英美法系下限定责任仅能由某方承担的文字表述通常为"污染造成的损害应由漏油船船舶所有人承担"，而本条款的表述为"船舶所有人应当对其造成的油污损害负责"，两种表述具有明显区别。"这个表述并不能得出其他人（其他对事故发生有过错的第三人）不应当承担责任的含义。"④

《2001年燃油公约》的条约体系在很大程度上借鉴了《1992年油污公约》，但与《1992年油污公约》不同，其调整对象为作为船舶动力的燃油。《2001年燃油公约》第一条明确了公约所指船舶为任何海船及航行器，船舶所有人包括船舶登记所有人、光船承租人、经营人和管理人，相较于《1992年油污公约》，其关于船舶所有人的定义明显涵盖范围更广，其第三条船舶所有人归责条款与《1992年燃油公约》一样未将油污损害赔偿责任限定仅由漏油船方承担。且《2001年燃油公约》因扩大了船舶所有人的定义而将《1992年油污公约》第三条中的"除依据公约外不得向船舶所有人提出污染损害赔偿"和"以列举方式规定不得对哪些主体索赔"规定删

---

① See William Baude and Ryan D. Doerfler, *The (Not So) Plain Meaning Rule*, The University of Chicago Law Review, Vol. 84, Issue 2, 2017, p.539.
② 参见吴莉婧《论船舶碰撞造成的油污损害赔偿》，载《中国海洋大学学报（社会科学版）》2003年第3期，第60页。
③ 见《1992年油污公约》第三条。
④ 余晓汉：《船舶碰撞漏油事故中非漏油船舶的所有人过错归责相关问题辨析——"达飞佛罗里达"轮油污案再审判决内外的思考》，载《国际法研究》2023年第2期，第62页。

去以保证公约逻辑。① 在扩大责任主体范围的同时对船舶所有人苛以无过错责任，在一定程度上扩大了无过错责任的适用范围。② 这在责任分配方面明显要求船方承担较多的责任，更倾向于对于受害人权利的保护。《2001 年燃油公约》的设立，就是为了填补《1992 年油污公约》只调整货油的国际公约空白。③ 与《1992 年油污公约》相似，《2001 年燃油公约》第三条对于船舶所有人的规定仅限在漏油船舶方承担责任的人原则上为该船舶的所有人，但是并没有涉及非漏油船一方的任何规定。公约排除非漏油船油污损害赔偿责任的观点更是无从谈起。

2.《1992 年油污公约》无意于排除非漏油船油污损害赔偿责任

体系解释是指：将争议条款及其上下文作为一个整体来看待，从整个法律体系和条款间关系出发理解并系统解读条文的内涵。④ 从公约体系上看，公约无意于调整非漏油船的油污损害赔偿责任，更未刻意排除非漏油船的油污损害赔偿责任。首先，《1992 年油污公约》开门见山地在第一条明确了该公约调整的船舶仅限于油轮，包括专门或改装运输散装货物油的船舶，以及能够作为运输货物油且实际运输的船舶。⑤ 紧接着，公约第一条第三款阐明了其所指船舶所有人为登记船舶所有人。⑥ 综上所述，公约的调整对象相当明确，一开始就把其调整对象限定为油船的船舶所有人。根据该公约规定，倘若非漏油船并非油船，则其根本不在公约的规制范围内，更谈不上故意排除非漏油船的油污损害赔偿责任。《1992 年油污公约》之所以仅仅规定漏油船应对其漏油负责而未规定非漏油船，正是因为与公约各条文之间形成了相互匹配的合理化制度体系。脱离公约体系而主观认

---

① 参见付本超《船舶油污损害赔偿法律问题研究——基于司法的视角》，法律出版社 2017 年版，第 53 页。

② 参见陈为《论海上侵权责任中的无过错责任原则》，载《河北法学》2011 年第 11 期，第 155 页。

③ 参见张宏凯《船舶碰撞致油污损害中非漏油船责任承担之研判与构想》，载《河北法学》2018 年第 8 期，第 180 页。

④ 《维也纳条约法公约》第三十一条第一款：条约应依其用语按其上下文并参照条约之目的及宗旨所具有之通常意义，善意解释之。

⑤ 《1992 年油污公约》第一条第一款："船舶"系指为运输散装油类货物而建造或改建的任何类型的海船和海上航行器。

⑥ 《1992 年油污公约》第一条第三款："船舶所有人"系指登记为船舶所有人的人，如果没有这种登记则是指拥有该船的人。

定公约排除非漏油船责任的观点实为无源之水。①

该公约除第一条外，第三条第一款明确了除免责情形外船舶所有人应当对其船舶产生的漏油承担责任，即漏油船应当对其漏油承担赔偿责任。第三条第四款规定只有符合公约才能对船舶所有人提出污染损害赔偿。结合第一条，公约所指为油轮船舶所有人，可见本条意欲明确漏油船（油轮）船舶所有人的油污损害赔偿责任。并且第四款下设（a）（b）（c）……（f）多个小项，以列举的形式规定无论是否依据公约都不能对船舶所有人雇佣的船员、引航员、承租人、船舶经营人或管理人等提出油污损害赔偿请求。② 通过第三条，公约将漏油船方承担油污损害赔偿责任的主体限定为其船舶所有人，且公约6个下设条款以极其详尽的列举形式明确了不承担油污损害赔偿责任的主体，但非漏油船方并未出现在列。这从侧面体现出公约只是无意于在专门调整漏油船的公约中插入调整非漏油船相关规定，而非将油污损害赔偿责任限定由漏油船一方承担。

公约的免责条款也可以从侧面体现出公约无意于排除非漏油船的油污损害赔偿责任。公约第三条第二款主要规定了船舶所有人的免责情形，第二项和第三项明确了在损害完全由负责助航设备的政府或其他主管当局因疏忽或第三人故意引起时，船舶所有人可以对该损害免责。③ 由此可见，公约注意到了互有过失碰撞中漏油船外存在作为第三人的非漏油船主体，而并非因疏忽遗漏非漏油船责任相关规定。且公约在第三条中仅规定了完全由第三人造成的损害漏油船可以免责，并没有在此基础上进一步规定——应由第三人（非漏油船方）对此承担责任。换句话说，作为第三人的非漏油船完全过错时公约也仅仅明确了漏油船可以免责，而没有规定非漏油船方作为第三人应担责，这更可以证明公约明明注意到碰撞中可能存在一个有过错的第三方（非漏油船方），但依然没有形成一项涉及非漏油船责任的条款，而是选择不越过界限，仅仅规制漏油船的责任。

---

① 参见［德］魏德士《法理学》，丁晓春译，法律出版社2013年版，第321页。
② 《1992年油污公约》第三条第四款："以本条第五款为准，不得根据本公约或其他规定向下述人员提出污染损害赔偿请求：……"
③ 《1992年油污公约》第三条第二款：船舶所有人如证明损害属于以下情况，则不得由其承担油污损害责任。(a) 由于战争行为、敌对行为、内战、暴动，或特殊的、不可避免的和不可抗拒性质的自然现象所引起的损害，或 (b) 完全是由于第三方故意造成损害的行为或不作为所引起的损害，或 (c) 完全是由于负责维护灯标或其他助航设施管理的政府或其他主管当局在履行该职责时的疏忽或其他错误行为所造成的损害。

《2001年燃油公约》与《1992年油污公约》的条文设置大体相似，同理可知《2001年燃油公约》亦无意于排除非漏油船的油污损害赔偿责任。因《2001年燃油公约》并未形成同《1992年油污公约》相似的双层赔偿体制，为弥补空白，《2001年燃油公约》在石油运输业兴盛、海上溢油事故频发的背景下对于船舶所有人的定义更加宽泛可能为船方带来更多责任，因此，该公约在尚未出台时就遭受到来自船舶、石油业等多方压力。保险行业面对更高的责任风险同样提出抗议。作为多方利益博弈妥协的产物，公约最终做出让步而并没有建立起油污损害赔偿基金制度。由于没有形成油污基金赔偿制度，在船舶所有人适用《2001年燃油公约》条款向受害人承担责任后，即使船方赔偿不足，受害人也无法再得到来自油污基金的赔偿。受害人向油污基金求偿的道路被切断，结合实践中油污损害赔偿金额往往非常巨大的客观事实，在适用《2001年燃油公约》时受害人仅向漏油船方索赔更加难以得到充分赔偿。在此种情况下，互有过失碰撞后的油污损害人自然而然地会选择将非漏油船作为索赔的对象。①

3.《维也纳条约法公约》相关文件未否定非漏油船油污损害的赔偿责任

根据《维也纳条约法公约》第三十二条规定，可以通过分析公约相关补充资料以证实对公约所做解释。② 国际海事委员会（CMI）在官网发布的文件中包含了一份公约问世前代表国在东京会议上对公约草案的讨论记录。检索记录可知，公约成员代表在草案形成阶段对船舶所有人归责问题进行了深入探讨并最终明确了漏油船（油轮）的无过错责任。草案中的第二条和第三条与正式文本中的规定并无差别，均规定了发生油污损害时船舶所有人的责任并列举了船舶所有人的雇员等主体不承担责任。③ 结合草案第一条可以发现，草案中的船舶已经限定为油轮，船舶所有人也如正式公约一样限定为登记船舶所有人。公约下船舶所有人的责任就可以理解为在油船漏油时该油船的油污损害赔偿责任，而无过多涉及作为第三人的非

---

① 参见张春昌、帅月新《船舶碰撞溢油污染损害赔偿责任认定的法律问题》，载《中华海洋法评论》2020年第3期，第85页。

② 《维也纳条约法公约》第三十二条：解释之补充资料，为证实由适用第三十一条所得之意义起见，或遇依第三十一条作解释而意义仍属不明或难解或所获结果显属荒谬或不合理时，为确定其意义起见，得使用解释之补充资料，包括条约之准备工作及缔约之情况在内。

③ See CMI, Documentation 1970 I Tokyo, p. 48. https：//comitemaritime.org/publications-documents/cmi-yearbook/.

漏油船方。

　　会议发言记录也可以从侧面体现出公约未排除非漏油船的油污损害赔偿责任。比利时代表 Etienne GUTT 提到"删改条约文字时应特别小心，避免剥夺受害人在船舶双方都有过错情况下起诉另一艘船的权利，因为剥夺这样的权利不是我们的初衷"①。意大利方代表 Francesco Berlingieri 同样表示"决定不断地修改第三条正是为了允许受害人在漏油船和非漏油船都应对碰撞负责的情况下能够对非漏油船采取行动"②。从记录来看，对于两位成员代表提出的问题并无人提出反对意见，草案也并没有明确对非漏油船的油污损害赔偿责任予以排除。在 1992 年 10 月国际海事委员会召开的讨论和评估《1992 年油污公约》法律体系的研讨会上，Emond-Gouilloud 教授表示：《1969 年油污公约》将油污损害赔偿责任转移给油轮船东的任务只完成了一半，责任的转移并不代表限定责任，因为仍然可以直接或间接的方式要求他人进行赔偿。除了被明确排除的船舶所有人的雇员、代理人等，所有的其他人仍然可能对油污损害承担赔偿责任。③ 因此，从这些早前的记录来看，《1992 年油污公约》的责任疏导机制仅完成了一半，公约没有打算禁止受害人向漏油船船东以外的另一半——非漏油船方提出索赔。④ 这印证了本文前述结论：公约中的船舶所有人仅指作为油轮的漏油船一方，并未对互有过失碰撞中可能为非油轮的另一方的责任作出规定。

　　综上所述，公约调整的主要对象为互有过失碰撞中属于油船的漏油船，而漏油船以外的第三人（非漏油船）并非公约调整对象。一旦公约意图同时调整非漏油船油污损害赔偿责任，则要进一步考虑公约如何规定非漏油船的归责原则、非漏油船的赔偿责任限制等一系列细化规定，从而使公约庞杂化。同时，实际案件中互有过失碰撞的非漏油船一方很有可能为公约调整对象之外的非油轮类船舶，如公约意欲涉及非漏油船的油污损害

---

① See CMI Documentation 1969 V, p. 8. https://comitemaritime.org/publications-documents/cmi-yearbook/.

② See CMI Documentation 1969 V, p. 88. https://comitemaritime.org/publications-documents/cmi-yearbook/.

③ See EMOND-GOUILLOUD, "The Future of the Compensation System as Established by International Convention", in Colin de la Rue (eds.), *Liability for Damage to the Marine Environment*, Lloyd's of London Press, (1993), p. 95.

④ See Qin Tianbao, Peng Xianwei, "The Polluter Pays Principle and Liability of Non-spilling Vessel in Ship Collision: Comment of Chinese Supreme Court's Decision in the CMA CGM Florida Case", *Journal of International Maritime Law*, Vol. 27 (2021), p. 275.

赔偿责任，则公约体系中关于调整船舶为油轮的限定也要进行调整。公约作为油轮、石油运输行业和沿海国等多方利益博弈妥协的产物能够在漏油船油污责任问题上达成一致已属不易，而将公约故意不涉足的非漏油船责任错误理解为公约包含了该规定与公约目的相矛盾。已经相对完善的公约无意调整而并非排除了非漏油船的油污损害赔偿责任。

（二）"谁漏油，谁赔偿"是对公约条款的片面理解

"谁漏油，谁赔偿"一直以来被部分海事实务者奉为圭臬。他们认为该理论脱胎于公约，并据此认为只有漏油船才应承担责任，非漏油船承担油污损害赔偿责任于法无据。[①] 但笔者认为，"谁漏油，谁赔偿"并非国际原则，而只是海事界部分学者对非漏油船油污损害赔偿责任观点的总结。

1. "谁漏油，谁赔偿"无法反映公约原意

《1992年油污公约》和《2001年燃油公约》的第三条被认为是"谁漏油，谁赔偿"的法律依据。"谁漏油，谁赔偿"的观点反映了公约中漏油船的油污损害赔偿责任，但如果凭此认为非漏油船无须承担责任则难称合理。两公约中均没有任何条款明确排除非漏油船的油污损害赔偿责任，且如本文前述分析，公约仅欲调节漏油船而非非漏油船的赔偿纠纷，排除非漏油船油污损害赔偿责任更无从谈起。将公约原意简单理解为"谁漏油，谁赔偿"不算完全误解，但难称理解全面。着眼公约体系，其中还存在针对漏油船免责的条款，例如完全因第三人故意作为或不作为引起的损害漏油船，则船舶所有人可以免责。[②] 在实践中，因不同国家管理部门和船上工作人员专业水平参差，航行在茫茫大海上的船舶难免遇到完全因第三人过失造成船舶漏油的情形。对于这些情况如果过于笼统简单地认为"谁漏油，谁赔偿"，则恰恰与公约原意背道而驰。公约规定漏油船方并非只要漏油就应赔偿，也并非只有漏油船应该赔偿，"谁漏油，谁赔偿"的理解

[①] 参见帅月新、施依柠《船舶碰撞导致油污损害之民事赔偿责任分析研究》，载《中国海事》2017年第6期，第41页。

[②] 《1992年油污公约》第三条第二款：船舶所有人如证明损害系属于以下情况，则不得由其承担油污损害责任。（a）由于战争行为、敌对行为、内战、暴动或特殊的、不可避免的和不可抗拒性质的自然现象所引起的损害或（b）完全是由于第三方故意造成损害的行为或不作为所引起的损害或（c）完全是由于负责维护灯标或其他助航设施管理的政府或其他主管当局在履行该职责时的疏忽或其他错误行为所造成的损害。

较为片面。

简单根据"谁漏油，谁赔偿"就不分情况地让漏油船承担责任会歪曲公约的本意。国际油污赔偿基金前主席雅格布森先生曾表示："公约机制并未排除油污受害人在公约体制外向船舶所有人以外的人提出索赔。"① 实践中，在多数情况下，漏油船都应该对油污损害承担无过错责任，的确此种无过错责任为受害人的直接对其保险人或担保人提起诉讼从而获得合理赔偿提供了便利。也就是说，污染受害人能够通过较为便利的途径来获得赔偿，那如果以此获得的赔偿能够充分弥补受害人的损失，受害方也就没有必要通过复杂的途径向漏油船以外的船舶提出索赔。因此有学者认为，"谁漏油，谁赔偿"在实践中能够使受害方更加便利地及时获得赔偿。② 此观点的优势在于责任主体唯一，因此不会相互推诿，表面上看确实会给受害人带来便捷，但实际上此种便捷性是建立在牺牲赔偿充分性的代价之上的。打着方便受害人及时获得赔偿的旗号，实则错误理解与适用公约，且在实践中运用此观点，可能会面临受害方只能向漏油船单方追偿，而漏油船作为碰撞中受损较大的一方往往因毁损沉没等原因丧失赔偿能力，最终有可能使受害人实际上得不到有力救济，这也违背了该观点所谓的方便受害人获得赔偿的宗旨。

2. 对"谁漏油，谁赔偿"理解适用的纠正

如何对"谁漏油，谁赔偿"进行理解与适用才能更准确地反映公约原意？笔者认为，首先应坚持对公约中可能限制主权国家权利的条款做严格的解释。从主权国家的立场出发，其加入公约的实质目的即以承担相应义务换取一定权利。不同国家的情况、利益诉求各不相同，在达成一致的过程中必然会伴随国家间的相互博弈，最终国家缔结公约并相应对某些权益进行自我限制。因此，国际条约中的相应权利是缔约国家以承担条约规定的义务为代价换取的，对于国家没有明确表示让渡的权利不能理解为已经让渡。③ 那么，在国际条约没有明确规定国家需承担某项义务时，主权国家大可不必自行扩大对于条约文本的解释而自缚手脚。也就是说，在理解

---

① See Mans Jacobsson, "Compensation for Oil Pollution Damage Caused by Oil Spills from Ships and the International Oil Pollution Compensation Fund", *Marine Pollution Bulletin*, Vol. 29, No. 6–12, 1994, pp. 378–384.

② See Wu Chao, *Pollution from the Carriage of Oil by Sea: Liability and Compensation*, Kluwer International, 1996, p. 50.

③ 参见杨泽伟《国际法析论》（第3版），中国人民大学出版社2012年版，第87页。

公约条款时，对于条约争议规定中有可能限制缔约国权利的应对其做狭义解释。

从其他缔约国对公约的理解来看，"谁漏油，谁赔偿"同样是片面理解公约的结果。英国作为公约缔约国，缔结公约后不久便颁布了《英国商船管理法》(*The Merchant Shipping Act*, 1995)。① 英国坚持"内外有别"双轨制处理船舶油污事故，对符合国际公约适用条件的案件，油污损害责任主体即按照公约确定为船舶所有人；而当不符合公约适用条件时，则按照国内法相应规定。我国当前船舶油污损害赔偿案件的处理方式与之类似。因此，研究英国学者对公约的理解对于我国具有一定的借鉴意义。

经研究发现，英国大多数学者均认同公约未排除非漏油船油污损害赔偿责任。首先，英国学者科林极其详尽地研究并表述了公约含义："国际赔偿制度归责于泄漏油类或其他污染物质的船舶所有人，其本身没有可供向造成污染的非漏油船舶进行索赔的依据……但是，没有任何条款限制污染受损方依据其他责任基础向非漏油船舶索赔。尽管该赔偿制度包含在一定情况下适用的指引条款排除了漏油船舶以外某些主体的责任，但非漏油船不在排除行列。因此非漏油船舶的所有人可以独立于公约体系赔付污染损害，其责任基础通常是因过失导致碰撞而承担的侵权责任；尽管实践中通常是漏油船舶根据法定赔偿制度支付赔偿款后，再向非漏油船舶追偿而使其承担责任，但遭受污染损害的第三方在很多情况下仍可以直接向非漏油船舶提出索赔。"② 该学者也坚决反对主张漏油船应先对受害人承担责任，漏油船承担责任后可以代位向非漏油船方追偿的观点。从侵权法理论来看，代位权的基础是受损害人本身有权直接向非漏油船舶索赔。如果否定受害人向非漏油船的直接索赔权利，则漏油船赔偿后的代位权也不复存在。此外，英国学者对于两公约中的"该船"为漏油船基本达成一致，并

---

① 英国1995年《商船航运法》第一百三十一条规定：如果船舶在英国的海船可航水域排放油类或者油混合物，下列人为责任人：(a) 若排放来自船舶，则该船舶所有人、船长负有责任，除非他们能证明此排放是在下述 (b) 情况下发生；(b) 若排放来自船舶，但发生在向另外某一船舶或者陆上某地输油或者自该船或者陆地向本船输油的过程中，并且排放是因为另一船舶或者陆地上管理设备的人或者另一船舶所有人或者船长及陆地占有人的行为或者疏忽，则该船船长或者船舶所有人负有责任，并且，如有可能，陆地占有人亦负有责任。

② See Colin de la Rue, Charles B. Anderson, *Shipping and the Environment: Law and Practice*, Lloyd's of London Press, 2009, pp. 669 – 670.

且认为公约没有任何条款禁止受害者直接向碰撞的另一方船舶索赔。①

在公约缔约国的司法实践中,非漏油船亦对受害人承担油污损害赔偿责任。以 1999 年"Erika"轮漏油案为例,负责清污作业的石油公司和法国政府选择依据法国法诉请非漏油船等主体承担赔偿责任。在此情况下,法国法院认为国际公约并未排除非漏油船的油污赔偿责任,因此最终诉讼得到支持。② 2008 年在韩国海域发生"河北精神"轮重大溢油案的总赔偿额超过 23 亿美元,事故受害人在非漏油船的责任限制程序中提起索赔请求,韩国最高法院认定公约未排除非漏油船责任并根据其国内法《船舶所有人等责任限制程序法》第六条第一款和第二十三条第一款的规定来判断索赔资格。③

四、互有过失碰撞中非漏油船油污损害赔偿责任我国相关国内法的适用争议与解读

在具有涉外因素的船舶漏油污染纠纷中,有关公约与国内法的适用关系应当遵循公约优先的原则,国内法不能优先作为直接划定责任的依据。④ 以"达飞佛罗里达"轮与"舟山"轮案为例,因碰撞船舶为外籍船舶,最高人民法院认定该案具有涉外性,我国已加入相关国际公约,因此应优先适用国际公约规定。国际公约中并未排除非漏油船油污损害赔偿责任,又因为案件发生在我国海域,且经当事人一致选择适用中国法,因此案件应适用我国国内法。在国际公约未排除非漏油船油污损害赔偿责任时,因需要进一步确定非漏油船的油污损害赔偿责任,案件会面临应适用哪一国内法的问题。然而在国内层面,学者对于具体应适用哪些法律存在不小的争议。

---

① See Andrew Tettenborn, *Pollution at Sea*, Informa Lawfrom Routledge, 2013, p. 14; Baris Soyer, A. Tettenborn, *Pollution at Sea*, Informa Law from Routledge, 2013, p. 220; Andrew Tettenborn, John Kimbell, *Marsden and Gault on Collisions at Sea*, Sweet & Maxwell Ltd, 2021, p. 370.

② 参见徐国平《"Erika"轮溢油事故推动船舶油污法制进步之回顾》,载《水运管理》2019 年第 3 期,第 33 页。

③ See *Reappellant*1 *et al. v. Samsung Heavy Industries Inc.* (2012) 9 KORSCD 65.

④ 参见车丕照《〈民法典〉颁行后国际条约与惯例在我国的适用》,载《中国应用法学》2020 年第 6 期,第 7 页。

（一）《海商法》争议条款不应用来确定非漏油船油污赔偿责任

具有涉外因素的两船互有过失发生碰撞导致单船漏油，在根据法律选择规则应适用我国国内法的情况下，有学者认为应优先适用我国《海商法》第一百六十九条。根据第一百六十九条第二款的规定，两船按照过错比例对受害人承担油污损害赔偿责任。[①] 支持该观点的学者认为油污泄漏导致他人的损害属于《海商法》第一百六十九条规定的"第三人财产损失"。实践中采用该观点判决的案件不算少数，如 1999 年广东省高级人民法院负责二审的"闽燃供2"轮与"东海"轮案就依据《海商法》第一百六十九条最终判决漏油船与非漏油船依过错比例承担责任。[②] 在"金盛"轮与"金玫瑰"轮案中，青岛海事法院同样判决两船承担比例责任。[③] 漏油船与非漏油船承担比例责任观点与仅漏油船承担责任观点相比能够为受害方提供更为充分的赔偿，因此在实践中具有很强的实用性。但采用此观点的底层逻辑认为船舶碰撞导致的油污泄漏造成的损害属于《海商法》第一百六十九条的"第三人财产损失"，这一点也遭到了较多学者的质疑。笔者认为，漏油造成的他人财产损失并不属于《海商法》第一百六十九条的"第三人财产损失"，漏油船与非漏油船不应依据《海商法》第一百六十九条承担比例责任，原因如下。

一方面，从《海商法》第一百六十九条出台的背景来看，该条并不调整船舶碰撞而导致的油污损害关系。《海商法》第一百六十九条及船舶碰撞章节的蓝本为《1910 年统一船舶碰撞若干法律规定的国际公约》（简称《碰撞公约》）。《碰撞公约》明确规定 "the compensation due for damages caused to the vessels, or to any things or person on board thereof"[④]。由 "on" 可知其调整范围仅包括船舶或者船舶所承载的人身、财产的损失。公约将其调整损害的空间范围限定为船舶或船舶上的损害，而不包含由船舶碰撞所造成的船舶物理空间以外的他人的损害。以公约为蓝本的我国《海商

[①] 参见陈向勇、陈永灿《船舶碰撞油污损害赔偿非漏油方民事责任——兼评〈油污损害赔偿司法解释草案〉的新发展》，载《中国海商法年刊》2010 年第 4 期，第 34 页。

[②] 参见广东省高级人民法院（2000）粤法经二终字第 144 号民事判决书。

[③] 参见许光玉《关于船舶污染损害赔偿法律问题的建议》，见《航运法律与政策评论》第 1 辑，中山大学出版社 2022 年版，第 3 页。

[④] 见《碰撞公约》第一条。

法》船舶碰撞章节将公约用词翻译为"碰撞造成第三人财产损失的",于公约原文而言我国《海商法》的表述更为模糊,导致实践中产生"第三人财产损失"争议。《海商法》出台后,最高人民法院也觉察出本条表意存在模糊,最高人民法院交通运输审判庭专门出版《中华人民共和国海商法诠释》以澄清对第一百六十九条的错误理解。其中明确"两船发生碰撞造成油污泄漏而损害他人财产的,因损害并非由碰撞直接导致,因此不在本条财产赔偿的归责原则的调整范围内"①。在此之后出台的相关国内法规和司法解释也都保持了上述观点。因此,船舶互有过失发生碰撞从而引发对船舶以外油污受害人的损害并不属于《海商法》中规定的"第三人财产损失"。

另一方面,《海商法》第一百六十九条属于第八章船舶碰撞章节,其调整的为船舶碰撞法律关系中的权利义务纠纷。学术界与理论界就船舶碰撞法律关系与油污损害法律关系是两种不同的法律关系已基本达成共识。②从不同法律关系体系的相对独立角度看,船舶碰撞应适用《海商法》第八章的相关规定。而环境污染法律关系(第三人环境侵权)则应适用《民法典》第一千二百三十三条。我国最高人民法院发布的《环境侵权司法解释》也将船舶油污损害赔偿、海事污染损害赔偿纳入其中。由此可见,我国倾向将船舶碰撞造成的环境污染损害定性为环境污染而不是把它当作船舶碰撞关系适用《海商法》调整。同时,《油污损害司法解释》第四条明确规定受害人可以主张漏油船所有人承担全部损害赔偿责任,倘若认定《海商法》第一百六十九条同样可以适用,则受害人应主张漏油船方承担过错比例责任,从而引起法律冲突,破坏法律的统一性。而适用《海商法》第一百六十九条调整船舶油污关系等于变相将船舶碰撞关系与船舶油污关系混为同一关系,是不可取的。

(二)《民法典》争议条款中的非漏油船油污损害赔偿责任

在互有过失船舶碰撞致单船漏油事故中,实务界和理论界对于能否适用《民法典》及应适用哪一条款存在争议。基于理论和实践中的争议,下面着重研究《民法典》下非漏油船的油污损害赔偿责任。

---

① 傅旭梅:《中华人民共和国海商法诠释》,人民法院出版社1995年版,第282-283页。
② 参见白佳玉《我国海上溢油事故海洋环境损害赔偿法律问题研究——以船舶溢油事故为视角》,载《中国海商法年刊》2011年第4期,第72页。

1. 漏油船与非漏油船不构成《民法典》第一千一百六十八条的共同侵权

《民法典》尚未出台前，有关共同侵权应承担连带责任的规定由《中华人民共和国民法通则》（简称《民法通则》）第一百三十条予以明确。在对互有过失碰撞致单船漏油案已有判决中，也存在法院认为两船存在共同侵权从而判决两船承担连带责任的案例。在早先由广州海事法院负责一审的"VLACHRNABREEZE"轮与"潮河"轮碰撞案件中，法院将漏油船与非漏油船认定为共同侵权，从而判决双方对受害人造成的油污损害承担连带责任。①《民法典》出台后关于共同侵权的规定为第一千一百六十八条，其内容与先前并无明显区别。②

笔者认为，漏油船与非漏油船之间不构成《民法典》第一千一百六十八条的共同侵权，漏油船与非漏油船之间不应承担连带责任。首先，从我国共同侵权理论发展进程来看，《民法通则》出台后最高人民法院紧接着在《最高人民法院关于审理人身损害赔偿案件适用法律若干问题的解释》（简称《人身损害赔偿解释》）中对共同侵权进行了进一步说明，将共同侵权的认定标准分为主观层面的意思关联和客观层面的行为关联。③ 可见，最高人民法院对主观层面和客观层面的共同侵权说均予以了肯定，无论是主观上具有意思联络亦或者仅客观上行为结合导致了不可分割的唯一结果都可以被视为共同侵权。随着共同侵权理论的进一步发展，在《侵权责任法》乃至《民法典》中此较为宽松认定共同侵权的标准并未得以保留。近两年重新修改后的《人身损害赔偿解释》更将原本的第三条删去。法律更迭和条款变换体现的正是立法者意欲限缩原本对共同侵权的认定标准。④ 意思联络说得到了学术界和理论界的广泛认可，而共同行为说则受到了越来越多的质疑。杨立新先生表示："不存在意思联络的多人侵权行为不属于共同侵权行为，因为其缺乏共同侵权最本质的特征——共同故意。"⑤ 且

---

① 参见陈向勇、陈永灿《船舶碰撞油污损害赔偿非漏油方民事责任——兼评油污损害赔偿司法解释草案的新发展》，载《中国海商法年刊》2010年第4期，第33页。

② 《民法典》第一千一百六十八条：二人以上共同实施侵权行为，造成他人损害的应承担连带责任。

③ 《人身损害司法解释》第三条：二人以上共同故意或者共同过失致人损害，或者虽无共同故意、共同过失，但其侵害行为直接结合发生同一损害后果的，构成共同侵权，应当依照民法通则第一百三十条规定承担连带责任。

④ 参见最高人民法院侵权责任法研究小组《〈中华人民共和国侵权责任法条文理解与适用〉》，人民法院出版社2016年版，第67页。

⑤ 杨立新：《侵权责任法》，法律出版社2021年版，第223页。

从国内法与公约关系角度看，公约在明确对两船都发生漏油且油污无法区分时，漏油船与非漏油船承担连带责任。① 而互有过失碰撞导致单船漏油明显区别于两船同时漏油且油污损害无法区分的情况，使其承担连带责任并不合理。

互有过失碰撞导致单船漏油案件中漏油船与非漏油船在主观层面均是过失而非故意，更不存在碰撞前的意思联络而形成共同故意。因此，两船不能适用《民法典》第一千一百六十八条构成共同侵权，漏油船与非漏油船的船舶所有人不应对受害人承担连带赔偿责任。

2.《民法典》第一千二百三十三条可适用于确定非漏油船责任

《民法典》第一千二百三十三条明确因第三人过错对环境造成损害的，被侵权人可以向侵权人索赔，也可以向第三人索赔。② 学界对于本条能否适用于确定互有过失碰撞中非漏油船责任的争议主要存在于本条所指的"第三人"是否可以指代非漏油船。有学者认为"第三人"仅在油污事故的污染者范围内指代，即仅指漏油船方的船员、乘客等。但也有学者认为，"第三人"并非限定在污染者一方指代，而是可以涵盖漏油船与受害人之外的第三方，即非漏油船一方。笔者赞成后一种观点，理由如下：

首先，非漏油船方应属于我国环境侵权法领域规定的"第三人"。我国环境侵权立法中所指的"第三人"可以涵盖侵权人与被侵权人之外的第三方主体。《民法典》第一千二百三十三条来源于原《侵权责任法》第六十八条，在《侵权责任法》中明确使用了"污染者"一词，明确规定被侵权人有权向污染者和第三人索赔。③ 这样便精准地将侵权方的范围限定为造成污染的整体即互有过失碰撞中的漏油船方，与作为"第三人"的非漏油船一方区分开来。《环境侵权司法解释》同样规定了：受害人同时向污染者和第三人提起诉讼，法院应受理。④ 在此"污染者"与"第三

---

① 《1992 年油污公约》第四条：当发生涉及两艘或两艘以上船舶的事故并造成污染损害时，全部有关船舶的所有人，除按第三条免责外须对所有无法合理区分的此种损害负连带责任。《2001 年燃油公约》第五条：当发生涉及两艘或两艘以上船舶的事故并引起污染损害时，所有有关的船舶所有人，除按第三条规定被免责者外，须对所有无法合理分开的此类损害负连带责任。

② 《民法典》第一千二百三十三条：因第三人的过错污染环境、破坏生态的，被侵权人可以向侵权人请求赔偿，也可以向第三人请求赔偿。侵权人赔偿后有权向第三人追偿。

③ 《侵权责任法》第六十八条：因第三人的过错污染环境造成损害的，被侵权人可以向污染者请求赔偿，也可以向第三人请求赔偿。污染者赔偿后，有权向第三人追偿。

④ 《环境侵权司法解释》第五条：被侵权人根据侵权责任法第六十八条规定分别或者同时起诉污染者、第三人的，人民法院应予受理。

人"作为受害人可以起诉的对象并列出现,可见与"第三人"相对应的概念是作为整体概念的"污染者",而非微观的漏油船与漏油船上的工作人员等。紧接着该司法解释的第六条规定:被侵权人需要证明侵权人排放污染物的事实。① 这就更加明确表示了侵权人为油污排放者而不包含没有泄漏污染物的主体。我国立法在环境侵权部分中"侵权人"与"污染者"指代泄漏主体,"第三人"指的是受害人与侵权人之外的其他人而并不是污染者一方的成员。在互有过失碰撞致单船漏油案件中,漏油船方作为泄漏主体自然属于《民法典》定义的"侵权者"或"污染者";非漏油船一方即没有直接漏油但存在过错的"第三人"。

其次,全国人民代表大会常务委员会法制工作委员会(简称法工委) 2010 年出版的官方解释资料采用法条与案例相结合的方式对《侵权责任法》第六十八条第三人环境侵权部分的案例说明,法工委对应选取了互有过失碰撞致单船漏油案件对该法条适用进行解读。在明确非漏油船责任可以适用本条第三人环境侵权责任的同时,其强调在漏油船遭受碰撞漏油后,第三人(非漏油船方)的赔偿能力常常强于漏油船,为保护受害人的合法权益,应认定受害人享有索赔的选择权利。② 如前所述,直接向漏油船索赔不会产生责任在双方间的推诿,且在后续基金获赔更加便利,因此受害人为更快获得赔偿往往将漏油船方作为"优选"进行索赔。但在特殊情况下漏油船可能会丧失赔偿能力或赔偿能力减弱,此时为保护受害人的合法权益,没有理由剥夺受害人依据《民法典》第一千二百三十三条向非漏油船索赔的权利。

(三) 其他适用争议条款中的非漏油船油污损害赔偿责任

除《海商法》和《民法典》外,我国法院在互有过失碰撞致单船漏油案中较多适用的其他国内法包括《油污损害赔偿规定》和《环境侵权司法解释》。研究上述条款的适用条件有利于进一步明确国内法下非漏油船的油污损害赔偿责任。

---

① 《环境侵权司法解释》第六条:被侵权人根据侵权责任法第六十五条规定请求赔偿的,应当提供证明以下事实的证据材料:(一)污染者排放了污染物;(二)被侵权人的损害;(三)污染者排放的污染物或者其次生污染物与损害之间具有关联性。

② 参见王胜明《〈中华人民共和国侵权责任法〉条文解释与立法背景》,人民法院出版社 2010 年版,第 273 页。

1. 《油污损害赔偿规定》第四条未禁止受害方向非漏油船索赔

从《油污损害赔偿规定》的背景来看，2011年前我国已出台《中华人民共和国海洋环境保护法》和《防治船舶污染海洋环境管理条例》等一系列专门法律，同时《民法通则》和《侵权责任法》中也存在调整环境侵权关系的一般法律。当时，船舶漏油已成为海洋环境污染的重要原因，而对船舶漏油法律适用问题存在争议造成实践中同案不同判情况频发。[①] 如今，我国已成为《1992年油污公约》和《2001年燃油公约》的缔约国，迫切需要在妥善处理公约与国内法关系的同时于公约体制外制定一部我国自己的船舶油污法以填补相关法律领域的空白。基于此，2011年《油污损害赔偿规定》应运而生，该规定出于协调国际公约与国内法的目的在内容方面较多地参照了公约规定。

对于《油污损害赔偿规定》的争议主要存在于第四条，本条款明确了在两船互有过失碰撞致油污损害时受害人可以请求漏油船承担全部赔偿责任。否定非漏油船责任的学者以本条规定作为其法律依据，声称该条款体现了最高人民法院意在通过此条排除互有过失碰撞致单船漏油案件中非漏油船的油污赔偿责任。笔者并不认同此观点。首先，从文义解释出发，《油污损害赔偿规定》第四条在受害人向漏油船主张责任时采用了"可以"一词。"可以"与"应该"相比，其体现的强制等级更低，即最高人民法院从保护受害人角度出发，在实际上赋予受害人更多选择权利。受害人可以选择向漏油船一方主张全部赔偿责任，同时也未剥夺受害人向非漏油船一方索赔的权利。最高人民法院在"达飞佛罗里达"轮与"舟山"轮案中正是采用了这一观点，判决受害人可以向漏油船主张全部赔偿责任，同时也可以向非漏油船方索赔比例责任，最大限度地保护了受害人的利益。

其次，结合《油污损害赔偿规定》从起草到出台的全过程，其并没有排除非漏油船的油污损害赔偿责任。有关专家对《油污损害赔偿规定》第四条从初步拟定到最终确定经历了多次争论，最高人民法院发布的征求意见稿的第四条拟定了四种方案以供论证。第一种方案拟将更多的选择权给予受害人，受害人可以依据公约选择向漏油船方主张全部责任，也可以同时或分别向漏油船和非漏油船索赔；第二种方案拟将非漏油船责任确定为补充责任，受害人一般情况下只能直接向漏油船索赔，但是在漏油船无能

[①] 参见刘寿杰《〈关于审理船舶油污损害赔偿纠纷案件若干问题的规定〉的理解与适用》，载《人民司法（应用）》2011年第17期，第35页。

力承担赔偿责任时，非漏油船应在其过错比例范围内对受害人承担赔偿责任；第三种方案拟将漏油船与非漏油船对受害人的责任确定为比例责任，漏油船与非漏油船按照其过错比例承担责任；第四种方案拟由漏油船与非漏油船承担连带责任。经过协商讨论，2010年9月的《油污损害赔偿规定第三次征求意见稿》采用了受害人可以选择同时或分别向漏油船方与非漏油船方索赔，仅向漏油船索赔时漏油船承担全部损害赔偿责任，向非漏油船索赔时非漏油船在其过错比例范围内承担赔偿责任这一做法。① 由此可见，最高人民法院是倾向于赋予受害人更多选择权利的。

有学者借此提出，最高人民法院在《油污损害赔偿规定》最终版本中仅规定了漏油船责任而对非漏油船责任留白正是立法者不想让非漏油船承担油污损害赔偿责任的体现。但也有学者认为本法留有空白实际上是立法者无法在多种方案中做出选择，因此只做模糊性规定，留待日后总结实践经验后进一步完善。② 笔者认为，《油污损害赔偿规定》第四条并不是排除了非漏油船的油污损害赔偿责任。其在第三次征求意见稿面向社会征求意见时，专门征求相关部门书面意见且并未收到明确的反对意见。该规定以我国参加的《1992年油污公约》与《2001年燃油公约》为蓝本，在公约并未对非漏油船油污损害赔偿责任做出过多规定的前提下，国内学者的确对于非漏油船油污损害赔偿责任存在争议，立法者为确保各方主体的利益均衡回避了这一复杂问题，但绝对不是排除非漏油船的油污损害赔偿责任。因此，由公约而来的《油污损害赔偿规定》对非漏油船责任留白的做法被部分学者解读为排除非漏油船的油污损害赔偿责任的说法是缺乏事实依据的。尽管最终版本的《油污损害赔偿规定》并未保留第三次征求意见稿的做法，但同时也没有采用排除漏油船的油污损害赔偿责任的方案，而是选择使用公约中没有使用的"可以"一词，对问题做缓和处理的同时体现出其意欲赋予受害人更多选择权的倾向。不论

---

① 《油污损害司法解释（第三次征求意见稿）》第四条：船舶互有过失碰撞引起油类泄漏，造成财产污染损害的，受损害人可以请求泄漏油船舶的所有人承担赔偿责任。受损害人也可以另行请求非泄漏油船舶的碰撞责任人在碰撞过失程度比例范围内承担赔偿责任。泄漏油船舶的所有人实际赔偿金额超过其过失程度比例的，可以向非泄漏油船舶的碰撞责任人追偿。非泄漏油船舶的碰撞责任人依照《海商法》第十一章的规定对该追偿请求提出海事赔偿责任限制抗辩的，人民法院应予支持。

② 参见刘寿杰、余晓汉《关于审理船舶油污损害赔偿纠纷案件若干问题研究的理解与适用》，载《人民司法》2011年第11期，第40页。

是从文义还是法律出台过程来看,《油污损害赔偿规定》第四条均应理解为没有排除非漏油船的油污损害赔偿责任,这样才符合法律实际情况和侵权法发展方向。

2. 《环境侵权司法解释》第五条下的非漏油船责任

对于互有过失碰撞致单船漏油案件中非漏油船方的责任,有学者认为根据《民法典》其应该承担无过错责任,但也有部分学者主张非漏油船应当在其过错比例范围内对受害方承担责任。笔者赞同后者。根据2023年8月最高人民法院发布的《环境侵权司法解释》,其中第五条明确规定受害人根据原《侵权责任法》第六十八条同时或分别起诉污染者和第三人的,人民法院应当受理。第二款规定受害人请求第三人承担赔偿责任,法院应根据第三人过错程度确定其责任。第三款规定污染者以第三人过错为理由试图减轻责任或不承担责任,法院不予支持。① 该规定明确了互有过失碰撞中第三人的责任为过错责任,其应当按照实践中的过错比例对受害人承担相应程度的责任,这与漏油船对受害人承担无过错责任形成了明显区别。但从法律体系的协调性来看,在互有过失碰撞中适用该规定确定漏油船与非漏油船的油污损害赔偿责任并无不妥。漏油船作为污染损害产生的重要原因,对受害人承担无过错责任原则与环境保护法中的"污染者付费原则"相一致。在国际法层面,《环境侵权司法解释》明确了漏油船的无过错责任与《1992年油污公约》和《2001年燃油公约》保持一致;在国内法层面,《环境侵权司法解释》第五条第三人责任可以适用于非漏油船方与《民法典》体系第三人侵权中非漏油船的油污损害赔偿责任相协调。在互有过失碰撞致单船漏油案件中受害人享有选择权,一方面受害人可以选择向漏油船主张全部损害赔偿,漏油船承担全部赔偿后有权向非漏油船一方追偿;另一方面,受害人选择直接向非漏油船索赔,则非漏油船在其过错比例范围内承担赔偿责任,其承担赔偿责任后漏油船一方不得再向其追偿。

---

① 见《环境侵权司法解释》第五条。

五、我国互有过失碰撞非漏油船油污损害赔偿责任理顺

当前非漏油船油污损害赔偿责任争议主要是国际公约与国内法相关条款规定不明从而导致法律从业者的不同理解与混乱适用。因此，对各相关法规能否适用于互有过失碰撞致单船漏油以及不同情况下非漏油船的油污赔偿责任进行理顺意义重大。

（一）互有过失碰撞油污损害赔偿责任的法律适用指引

实践中，在审理互有过失碰撞致单船漏油案件时，法院需要对各当事方主观层面的过错比例程度和客观层面船舶质量、碰撞情形、毁损程度、漏油损害情况进行综合考量。在不考虑不可抗力原因的情况下，碰撞船舶主观过失情况及最终漏油结果的差异将会导致漏油船与非漏油船适用法律与承担责任的不同。

对于互有过失碰撞导致的双船漏油，根据《油污损害赔偿规定》第三条，如果两船漏油造成的损害可以合理区分，则两船分别对其损害承担责任。[①] 在大部分油污损害无法区分的情况下两船应根据《1992年油污公约》第四条或《2001年燃油公约》第五条对共同的油污损害承担连带责任。[②] 在案件为两船碰撞导致的单船漏油时，应先判断两船在主观层面的具体情形，倘若在主观层面上漏油船完全过错而非漏油船不存在过错，则漏油船应根据《民法典》第一千二百二十九条对油污受害人承担全部油污损害赔偿责任。[③] 同时，由于漏油船完全过失与非漏油船构成碰撞侵权关系，依据《海商法》第一百六十八条漏油船应对非漏油船承担碰撞损害赔偿责任。[④] 在非漏油船一方主观层面具有完全过错时，则依据《1992年油

[①]《油污损害赔偿规定》第三条：不能合理分开各自造成的损害，各泄漏油船舶所有人承担连带责任。但泄漏船舶所有人依法免于承担责任的除外。

[②]《1992年油污公约》第四条：当发生涉及两艘或两艘以上船舶的事故并造成污染损害时，全部有关船舶的所有人，除按第三条免责外须对所有无法合理区分的此种损害负连带责任。《2001年燃油公约》第五条：当发生涉及两艘或两艘以上船舶的事故并引起污染损害时，所有有关的船舶所有人，除按第三条规定被免责者外，须对所有无法合理分开的此类损害负连带责任。

[③]《民法典》第一千二百二十九条：因污染环境、破坏生态造成他人损害的，侵权人应当承担侵权责任。

[④]《海商法》第一百六十八条：船舶发生碰撞，是由于一船的过失造成的，由有过失的船舶负赔偿责任。

污公约》第三条第二款和《2001年燃油公约》第三条第三款由非漏油船方对受害人承担油污损害赔偿责任，同时根据《海商法》第一百六十八条非漏油船方应当对漏油船方承担碰撞侵权赔偿责任。①

如果是双船碰撞致单船漏油且漏油船与非漏油船主观上均存在过失，则应先适用《1992年油污公约》和《2001年燃油公约》明确漏油船对受害人应承担的油污损害赔偿责任。② 根据国际公约无法进一步明确非漏油船的责任，对于根据法律选择规则应适用我国国内法的案件，应根据《民法典》第一千二百三十三条和《环境侵权司法解释》第五条判决非漏油船应在其过错比例范围内对受害人承担油污损害赔偿责任。③

综上所述，不同情形下非漏油船油污损害赔偿责任及法律适用见表3。

表3 不同情形下非漏油船油污损害赔偿责任及法律适用

漏油船舶数量	主观过失情形	赔偿责任承担	法律依据
两船均漏油	无论过失或故意	损害能够区分，则分别承担责任；损害无法区分，则承担连带责任	《1992年油污公约》第五条或《2001年燃油公约》第五条；《油污损害赔偿规定》第三条

---

① 《1992年油污公约》第三条第二款：船舶所有人如证明损害系属于以下情况，则不得由其承担油污损害责任。(a) 由于战争行为、敌对行为、内战、暴动或特殊的、不可避免的和不可抗拒性质的自然现象所引起的损害或 (b) 完全是由于第三方故意造成损害的行为或不作为所引起的损害或 (c) 完全是由于负责维护灯标或其他助航设施管理的政府或其他主管当局在履行该职责时的疏忽或其他错误行为所造成的损害。

② 《1992年油污公约》第三条第一款：除本条第二款和第三款规定外，在事故发生时的船舶所有人，或者如果该事故系由一系列事件构成，则第一起此种事件发生时的船舶所有人须对船舶因事故而造成的任何污染损害负责。《2001年燃油公约》第三条第一款：除本条第三款和第四款另有规定外，在事故发生时船舶所有人须对船载燃油或源自船舶的任何燃油引起的污染事故负责，但是，如果事故包括一系列具有同一起源的事件，则此系列事件的首起事件发生时的船舶所有人须承担责任。

③ 《民法典》第一千二百三十三条：因第三人的过错污染环境、破坏生态的，被侵权人可以向侵权人请求赔偿，也可以向第三人请求赔偿。侵权人赔偿后有权向第三人追偿。《环境侵权司法解释》第五条：被侵权人根据侵权责任法第六十八条规定分别或者同时起诉污染者、第三人的，人民法院应予受理。

续表3

漏油船舶数量	主观过失情形	赔偿责任承担	法律依据
只有一船漏油	漏油船完全过失	漏油船方对油污受害方承担油污损害赔偿责任	《民法典》第一千二百二十九条及《海洋环境保护法》第八十九条
		漏油船方对非漏油船承担碰撞损害赔偿责任	《海商法》第一百六十八条
	非漏油船完全过失	非漏油船方对油污受害方承担油污损害赔偿责任	《1992年油污公约》第三条第二款，《2001年燃油公约》第三条第三款
		非漏油船方对漏油船方承担碰撞损害赔偿责任	《海商法》第一百六十八条
只有一船漏油	双方互有过错	漏油船方对油污受害人承担全部油污损害赔偿责任	《1992年油污公约》和《2001年燃油公约》
		非漏油船方在其过错比例范围内对油污损害方承担油污损害赔偿责任	《民法典》第一千二百三十三条和《环境侵权司法解释》第五条
		非漏油船方与漏油船方相互承担过失比例范围内的碰撞损害赔偿责任	《海商法》第一百六十九条

（二）互有过失碰撞致单船漏油案件赔偿路径选择与优化

对于互有过失碰撞致单船漏油案件，在海事实践中漏油船方常常是受害人索赔的首选。① 其原因为：第一，国际公约中仅规定漏油船责任对受害者形成引导，且在小规模碰撞中受害人仅向漏油船方索赔能够获得充分的赔偿；第二，根据《环境侵权司法解释》，受害人向漏油船索赔时，漏

---

① See Qin Tianbao, Peng Xianwei, "The Polluter Pays Principle and Liability of Non-spilling Vessel in Ship Collision: Comment of Chinese Supreme Court's Decision in the CMA CGM Florida Case", *Journal of International Maritime Law*, Vol. 27, 2021, p. 276.

油船一方不能以"非漏油船方存在过错"为理由主张减轻或免除自身责任；第三，公约对漏油船船舶所有人苛以无过错责任，因此受害人仅向漏油船索赔需要对漏油船的漏油事实及损害与漏油间的因果关系承担举证责任，而无须对漏油船方主观上存在过错承担举证责任。如果受害方仅向漏油船索赔，则漏油船在向受害人承担全部责任后可以向非漏油船追偿其过错比例部分。除仅向漏油船索赔外，受害方同时向漏油船方和非漏油船方双方索赔的案件也较多。① 此种情况下，法院应该结合双方主观过错情形和损害情况确定双方过失比例，非漏油船方仅需在其过错比例范围内承担油污损害赔偿责任。

由此可见，首先，对于漏油船具备充足赔偿能力的情况，受害人选择仅向漏油船索赔是最为方便快捷的。一方面，受害人承担的举证责任较轻，漏油船方也应对受害人承担全部赔偿责任，避免了漏油船与非漏油船相互推诿责任的情况；另一方面，与漏油船赔偿相配套的保险和基金赔偿也更为成熟，更加有利于受害人获得及时充分的赔偿。其次，对于漏油船方赔偿能力较弱的情况，此时从保护受害人合法权益角度出发，同时起诉漏油船与非漏油船能够在争取尽可能充分赔偿的情况下节约时间成本。依据《环境侵权司法解释》，法院对受害人同时向漏油船与非漏油船提起诉讼的情况应予以受理，漏油船方与非漏油船方应当按照各自的过错比例对受害人承担油污损害赔偿责任。非漏油船方根据过错比例向受害人赔偿油污损害后，漏油船方即丧失对非漏油船方的追偿权。受害人需对非漏油船方存在过错承担举证责任。最后，对于受害人仅向漏油船索赔后未得到合理赔偿的情况，此时受害人依然可以选择直接向非漏油船方索赔，法院应根据《民法典》第一千二百三十三条令非漏油船在其过错比例范围内对受害人承担油污损害赔偿责任，以免在特大油污事故或漏油船方船舶毁损、沉没等丧失赔偿能力的情况下，油污受害人因无法得到及时有效赔偿而陷入窘境。

---

① 参见廖兵兵《船舶碰撞溢油责任主体司法实践研究》，载《中国海事》2022年第1期，第61页。

结　语

对于互有过失碰撞致单船漏油中非漏油船油污损害赔偿责任这一海事热点问题，理论界和实务界对国际公约是否排除非漏油船油污损害赔偿责任以及国内法如何选取适用仍存在较大争议。对于在我国发生的具有涉外因素的船舶碰撞致单船漏油事故应先适用国际公约。通过对公约的文义、目的、补充资料进行深入研究可知，《1992年油污公约》《2001年燃油公约》并没有排除非漏油船的油污损害赔偿责任。对于根据法律选择规则应适用我国国内法的案件应具体适用哪一条国内法的争议，首先，应明确油污损害并不属于《海商法》第一百六十九条"第三人财产损失"，因此不能适用该条款令两船承担比例责任。其次，漏油船与非漏油船碰撞前并不存在共同故意，不属于共同侵权，因而不应适用《民法典》第一千一百六十八条而承担连带责任。非漏油船的行为符合第三人环境侵权构成要件，因此可以适用《民法典》第一千二百三十三条与《环境侵权司法解释》第五条。借助本次修改《海商法》的契机，应在其中明确互有过失碰撞致单船漏油情况下的非漏油船油污损害赔偿责任问题。结合随着我国经济发展，船舶污染损害赔偿数额不断增大的实际情况，并考虑国际赔偿标准，可以适度调高我国赔偿限额标准，以更好地保障受害人的合法权益。